British Social Attitudes

Attitudes
The 23rd
REPORT

The **National Centre for Social Research** (NatCen) is an independent, non-profit social research organisation. It has a large professional staff together with its own interviewing and coding resources. Some of NatCen's work – such as the survey reported in this book – is initiated by NatCen itself and grant-funded by research councils or charitable foundations. Other work is initiated by government departments or quasi-government organisations to provide information on aspects of social or economic policy. NatCen also works frequently with other institutes and academics. Founded in 1969 and now Britain's largest social research organisation, NatCen has a high reputation for the standard of its work in both qualitative and quantitative research. NatCen has a Survey Methods Unit and, with the Department of Sociology, University of Oxford, houses the Centre for Research into Elections and Social Trends (CREST).

The contributors

Alex Bryson
Principal Research Fellow at the Policy Studies Institute and the Manpower Fellow at the Centre for Economic Performance at the London School of Economics

Elizabeth Clery
Senior Researcher at NatCen and Co-Director of the *British Social Attitudes* survey series

Rosemary Crompton
Professor of Sociology at City University

John Curtice
Research Consultant at the *Scottish Centre for Social Research* and Professor of Politics at Strathclyde University

Gabriella Elgenius
Research Fellow in the Department of Sociology, University of Oxford

Helen Fawcett
Lecturer in Politics at Strathclyde University

Stephen Fisher
Lecturer in Political Sociology and Fellow of Trinity College, University of Oxford

Conor Gearty
Professor of Human Rights Law and Rausing Director of the Centre for the Study of Human Rights at the London School of Economics

Anthony Heath
Professor of Sociology at the University of Oxford

Mark Johnson
Senior Researcher at NatCen and Co-Director of the *British Social Attitudes* survey series

Mansur Lalljee
University Lecturer in Social Psychology and Fellow of Jesus College, University of Oxford

Laurence Lessard-Phillips
DPhil student in the Department of Sociology and Nuffield College, University of Oxford

Clare Lyonette
Research Officer at City University

Sheila McLean
Professor of Law and Ethics in Medicine at Glasgow University

Jean Martin
Senior Research Fellow in the Department of Sociology, University of Oxford

Pippa Norris
McGuire Lecturer in Comparative Politics at the John F Kennedy School of Government, Harvard University

Rachel Ormston
Senior Researcher at the *Scottish Centre for Social Research*, part of NatCen

Alison Park
Research Director at NatCen and Co-Director of the *British Social Attitudes* survey series

Miranda Phillips
Research Director at NatCen and Co-Director of the *British Social Attitudes* survey series

John Rigg
Research Officer at the *Centre for Analysis of Social Exclusion* (CASE), an ESRC Research Centre at the London School of Economics

Katarina Thomson
Research Director at NatCen and Co-Director of the *British Social Attitudes* survey series

Katrin Voltmer
Senior Lecturer in Political Communication at the Institute of Communications Studies, University of Leeds

British Social Attitudes

Attitudes

The 23rd
REPORT

Perspectives on a changing society

EDITORS
Alison Park
John Curtice
Katarina Thomson
Miranda Phillips
Mark Johnson

SAGE Publications
London • Thousand Oaks • New Delhi

NatCen
National Centre *for* Social Research

First published 2007

Apart from any fair dealing for the purposes of research or private
study, or criticism or review, as permitted under the Copyright,
Designs and Patents Act, 1988, this publication may be reproduced,
stored or transmitted in any form, or by any means, only with the
prior permission in writing of the publishers, or in the case of
reprographic reproduction, in accordance with the terms of licences
issued by the Copyright Licensing Agency. Enquiries concerning
reproduction outside those terms should be sent to the publishers.

 SAGE Publications Ltd
1 Oliver's Yard
55 City Road
London EC1Y 1SP

SAGE Publications Inc.
2455 Teller Road
Thousand Oaks, California 91320

SAGE Publications India Pvt Ltd
B-42, Panchsheel Enclave
Post Box 4109
New Delhi 110 017

British Library Cataloguing in Publication data

A catalogue record for this book is available from the British Library

ISBN 10 1-4129-3432-X   ISBN 13 978-1-4129-3432-9

Library of Congress Control Number: 2006932622

Printed in Great Britain by The Cromwell Press Ltd, Trowbridge, Wiltshire
Printed on paper from sustainable resources

Contents

List of tables and figures ... xi

Introduction ... xvii

A changing society ... xvii
Our thanks ... xix

1 Who do we think we are? The decline of traditional social identities
Anthony Heath, Jean Martin and Gabriella Elgenius ... 1

The declining incidence of traditional social identities ... 3
Class identity ... 3
Political identity ... 6
Religious identity ... 8
National identity ... 9
The social significance of traditional identities in 2005 ... 13
Identity, sense of community and implications for social attitudes ... 17
Conclusions ... 27
Notes ... 29
References ... 32
Acknowledgements ... 33
Appendix ... 34

2 Quickening death: the euthanasia debate
Elizabeth Clery, Sheila McLean and Miranda Phillips ... 35

Defining assisted dying ... 36
The debate about assisted dying ... 37
Attitudes to assisted dying ... 38
Voluntary euthanasia administered by a doctor ... 39
Physician–assisted suicide and voluntary euthanasia administered by a relative ... 40
When a patient cannot express his or her wishes ... 42
Who supports assisted dying and why? ... 44
How have attitudes to assisted dying changed? ... 48
Conclusions ... 50
Notes ... 51
References ... 52
Acknowledgements ... 52
Appendix ... 53

3   Are we all working too hard? Women, men, and changing attitudes to employment
Rosemary Crompton and Clare Lyonette   **55**

Women's and men's attitudes to work   57
Work-life imbalance?   61
Conclusions   65
Notes   67
References   67
Acknowledgements   69
Appendix   70

4   Who should pay for my care – when I'm 64?
Rachel Ormston, John Curtice and Helen Fawcett   **71**

Who should pay for care?   73
The role of individuals   75
Why are attitudes towards personal care different?   77
Class, income and attitudes to pensions and care   78
The threat of losing one's home   80
Is free personal care viewed as redistributive?   82
Ability to provide care   84
Conclusions   85
Notes   86
References   87
Acknowledgements   88
Appendix   89

5   Agree to disagree: respect for political opponents
Katrin Voltmer and Mansur Lalljee   **95**

Political respect: concept and measurement   96
What encourages political respect?   98
The role of the media – and talking about politics   101
The news media   102
Everyday conversations   105
The sources of political respect   109
Does political respect matter for democracy?   111
Conclusions   113
Notes   114
References   115
Acknowledgements   117
Appendix   118

6   Proportional representation and the disappearing voter
John Curtice, Stephen Fisher and Laurence Lessard-Phillips   **119**

Turnout	119
The motivation to vote in 2005	121
Perceptions of the parties	125
Who stayed at home	126
Why people stayed at home again in 2005	128
Attitudes to the electoral system	128
The impact of the electoral system on who votes	131
Conclusions	136
Notes	137
References	139
Acknowledgements	141

7   Civil liberties and the challenge of terrorism
Mark Johnson and Conor Gearty   **143**

What rights are important for democracy?	144
Changing attitudes to civil liberties?	145
Political freedoms	145
Presumption of innocence	147
Right to legal representation	148
Identity cards	149
Death penalty	150
Why have libertarian attitudes declined?	151
Changes in the age structure of the population	151
Political change	153
The terrorist threat	156
The trade-off between civil liberties and tackling terrorism	159
Fear, and experience, of terrorism	160
Social characteristics	162
Media consumption and political interest	164
Multivariate analysis	165
Human rights, international law and the threat of terrorism	166
Conclusions	168
Notes	169
References	172
Acknowledgements	173
Appendix	174

8   New Labour, New unions?
Alex Bryson   **183**

Union membership	185
Union effectiveness	189

Union effects on employment relations   195
Union effects on wages   197
The 'representation gap'   198
Conclusions   201
Notes   202
References   205
Acknowledgements   207
Appendix   208

9   Disabling attitudes? Public perspectives on disabled people
John Rigg   **213**

Perceptions of what constitutes being disabled   216
Views on the extent of prejudice against disabled people   219
Respondents' own attitudes towards disabled people   222
'Negative' feelings about disabled people   222
Inclusionary and exclusionary attitudes   225
Attitudes towards different impairment types   227
Views on the extent of prejudice against different impairment types   228
People's own attitudes towards different impairment types   230
Conclusions   234
Notes   235
References   237
Acknowledgements   237

10   Isolates or socialites? The social ties of internet users
John Curtice and Pippa Norris   **239**

Who uses the internet?   241
Meeting friends and family   243
Joining in   246
Social trust and social capital   248
Conclusions   254
Notes   255
References   256
Acknowledgements   257
Appendix   258

Appendix I: Technical details of the survey   **261**

Sample design   261
Selection of sectors   261
Selection of addresses   262
Selection of individuals   262

Weighting 262
Selection weights 263
Non-response model 263
Calibration weighting 265
Effective sample size 266
Questionnaire versions 267
Fieldwork 267
Advance letter 268
Analysis variables 268
Region 268
Standard Occupational Classification 268
National Statistics Socio-Economic Classification (NS-SEC) 269
Registrar General's Social Class 269
Socio-Economic Group 270
Goldthorpe schema 270
Industry 270
Party identification 271
Attitude scales 271
Other analysis variables 273
Sampling errors 273
Analysis techniques 277
Regression 277
Factor analysis 278
International Social Survey Programme 279
Notes 279
References 280

Appendix II: Notes on the tabulations in the chapters **281**

Appendix III: The questionnaires **283**

Subject Index **419**

List of tables and figures

Chapter 1

Table 1.1	Prompted and unprompted class identity, 1965–2005	4
Table 1.2	Strength of party identification, 1987–2005	7
Table 1.3	Religious belonging, 1964–2005	9
Table 1.4	Trends in British national identity, 1996–2005	10
Table 1.5	Trends in 'forced choice' national identity, 1974–2003	11
Table 1.6	Sense of class community	14
Table 1.7	Sense of community with other party supporters	15
Table 1.8	Religion and sense of community	15
Table 1.9	National identity and sense of community	16
Table 1.10	Class identity, sense of community, and class attitudes	18
Table 1.11	Class identity and class attitudes, 1987–2005	20
Table 1.12	Party identity, sense of community and political attitudes	22
Table 1.13	Religious identity, sense of community and moral values	24
Table 1.14	The changing relation between religious identity and moral values, 1984–2005	25
Table 1.15	British identity and British attitudes	27

Chapter 2

Table 2.1	Levels of support for voluntary euthanasia	39
Table 2.2	Levels of support for alternative forms of assisted dying	41
Table 2.3	Attitudes towards living wills and patient representatives	43
Table 2.4	Mean scores on euthanasia scale, by respondent characteristics and attitudes	46
Table 2.5	Attitudes to voluntary euthanasia, 1984–2005	48
Table 2.6	Attitudes towards assisted dying, 1995–2005	49

Chapter 3

Table 3.1	Non-financial employment commitment, by year and sex	58
Table 3.2	Importance of extrinsic and intrinsic rewards of work, by year and sex	59
Table 3.3	Important attributes in a job, by year and sex	60
Table 3.4	Attributes of respondent's own job, by year and sex	60
Table 3.5	Time allocation preferences, by year, sex, and employment status	62
Table 3.6	'Work-life balance', by sex and employment status	63
Table 3.7	Job to family conflict, by social class and sex	64

Chapter 4

Table 4.1	Who should pay for care for elderly people, by country	73
Table 4.2	Belief in universal state funding of care for the elderly, by age and class	74
Table 4.3	Views on individual responsibility to save for care/pensions	76
Table 4.4	Views on compelling individuals to save for care/pensions	77
Table 4.5	Belief in government responsibility for paying for care/income in old age, by country and socio-economic class	79
Table 4.6	Belief in individual responsibility for saving for care/pensions, by socio-economic class	80
Table 4.7	Attitudes to individual responsibility for paying for care, by attitudes to selling homes	81
Table 4.8	Responsibility for paying for care/income in old age, by political orientation	83
Table 4.9	Agree/strongly agree individual responsible for saving for care/pensions, by political orientation	83
Table 4.10	Attitudes to providing 10 hours a week of care for parent(s)	85

Chapter 5

Table 5.1	Respect for political opponents	98
Table 5.2	Socio-demographic characteristics and political respect	99
Table 5.3	Political orientations and political respect	100
Table 5.4	Newspaper endorsement in 2005 election and readers' opposed party	103
Table 5.5	Exposure to news media and political respect	104
Table 5.6	Frequency of political discussion with different kinds of people	106
Table 5.7	Proportion of discussants supporting the party respondent opposes, by type of conversation partner	107
Table 5.8	Effect of similarity and difference in discussant and respondents' views on political respect	109
Table 5.9	Regression model of political respect	110
Table 5.10	Mean level of political trust (out of four), by party opposed and political respect	113

Chapter 6

Table 6.1	Trends in civic duty, 1991–2005	122
Table 6.2	Trends in trust in governments to place the needs of the nation above political party interests, 1987–2005	123
Table 6.3	Trend in government and electoral participation, 1997–2005	124
Table 6.4	Trends in system efficacy, 1987–2005	124
Table 6.5	Perceived difference between Conservative and Labour parties, 1964–2005	125

Table 6.6   Perceptions of party difference and interest in politics, 1997, 2001, 2005   126

Table 6.7   Political interest and electoral participation, 1997–2005   127

Table 6.8   Turnout, by political interest and perceptions of the parties, 2005   127

Table 6.9   Attitudes towards proportional representation, 1992–2005   129

Table 6.10   Turnout by political knowledge and electoral system   133

Table 6.11   Average difference in score given to most and least liked party, by political knowledge and electoral system   135

Figure 6.1   Trends in per cent with "a great deal" or "quite a lot" of interest in politics, 1986–2005   122

Figure 6.2   Trends in attitudes towards changing the electoral system, 1983–2005   130

Chapter 7

Table 7.1   Proportions viewing different rights as important or not important to democracy   144

Table 7.2   Attitudes to the right to protest against the government, 1985–2005   146

Table 7.3   Attitudes to the rights of revolutionaries, 1985–2005   147

Table 7.4   Attitudes to presumptions of innocence, 1985–2005   148

Table 7.5   Attitudes to legal representation for suspects, 1990–2005   149

Table 7.6   Attitudes to identity cards, 1990–2005   149

Table 7.7   Attitudes to civil liberties, by age   151

Table 7.8   Per cent thinking people who wish to overthrow the government by revolution should definitely be allowed to hold public meetings, by age cohort   152

Table 7.9   Per cent thinking that public meetings to protest against the government should definitely be allowed, by party support, 1985–2005   153

Table 7.10   Per cent disagreeing that the police should be allowed to question suspects for up to a week without letting them see a solicitor, by party support, 1990–2005   154

Table 7.11   Per cent disagreeing that every adult should have to carry an identity card, by party, 1990–2005   155

Table 7.12   Views on civil liberties, by views on the risk of terror attack   157

Table 7.13   Per cent viewing anti-terrorist measures as unacceptable or a price worth paying   159

Table 7.14   Per cent thinking various measures are unacceptable, by views on whether people exaggerate the risk of terrorism   161

Table 7.15   Attitudes to trade-offs, by party identification   163

Table 7.16   Acceptability of trade-offs, by newspaper readership   164

Table 7.17   Factors significant in regression model for believing the trade-offs are definitely unacceptable   166

Table 7.18   Attitudes to international human rights law   167

Figure 7.1   Per cent agreeing the death penalty is the most appropriate sentence for some crimes, 1986–2005   150

Chapter 8

Table 8.1   Workforce composition and union membership, 1998–2005   187
Table 8.2   The difference a union makes to the workplace, 1998 and 2005   190
Table 8.3   Management attitudes to union membership, 1998 and 2005   192
Table 8.4   Employee perceptions of union power at the workplace, 1989, 1998
                and 2005   193
Table 8.5   Additive scale of employee perceptions of union effectiveness,
                1998 and 2005   194
Table 8.6   The climate of employment relations, 1998 and 2005   195
Table 8.7   Likelihood that employees in non-union workplaces would join a union
                if there was one, 1998 and 2005   199

Figure 8.1   Union membership density among employees, 1983–2005   186

Chapter 9

Table 9.1   Whether respondent has any pre-defined health condition or
                disability   215
Table 9.2   Proportions thinking a person with each impairment is disabled, by
                exposure to disability   217
Table 9.3   Proportions thinking a person with each impairment is disabled, by
                age and education   218
Table 9.4   Perceptions of prejudice against disabled people, 1998, 2000, 2005   219
Table 9.5   Views on extent of prejudice against disabled people, by exposure
                to disability   220
Table 9.6   Views on extent of prejudice against disabled people, by age and
                education   221
Table 9.7   Views on societal attitudes to disabled people and personal views
                on disabled people   223
Table 9.8   Societal and personal attitudes to disabled people, by exposure to
                disability   224
Table 9.9   Societal and personal attitudes to disabled people, by age and
                education   225
Table 9.10   Views on participation of disabled people, by exposure to disability   226
Table 9.11   Views on amount of prejudice against different impairment groups   228
Table 9.12   Proportion who think there is a lot of prejudice against different
                impairment groups, by exposure to disability   229
Table 9.13   Views on amount of prejudice against different impairment groups,
                by age and education   230
Table 9.14   Level of comfort by impairment group and situation   231
Table 9.15   Proportion who would not feel very comfortable if disabled person
                were to move in next door, by exposure to disability   232
Table 9.16   Proportion who would not feel comfortable if disabled person were
                to move in next door, by age and education   233

Figure 9.1   The relationship between inclusionary attitudes towards disability and
                scope of definition of disability   227

Chapter 10

Table 10.1	Growth of internet use, 2000–2005	241
Table 10.2	Social profile of internet users	242
Table 10.3	Time spent with family and friends, and length of internet use	244
Table 10.4	Trends in time spent with family and friends, by internet use, 2003–2005	245
Table 10.5	Membership of organisations, by length of internet use	247
Table 10.6	Membership of organisations, by internet use, 2003–2005	248
Table 10.7	Trends in social trust, 1997–2005	249
Table 10.8	Trends in indicators of social capital, 1998–2005	251
Table 10.9	Social trust and length of internet use	251
Table 10.10	Social trust by internet use, 2000–2005	252
Table 10.11	Indicators of social capital by length of internet use	253
Table 10.12	Indicators of social capital, by internet use, 2000–2005	254

Appendix I

Table A.1	The final non-response model	264
Table A.2	Weighted and unweighted sample distribution, by GOR, age and sex	265
Table A.3	Range of weights	266
Table A.4	Response rate on *British Social Attitudes*, 2005	267
Table A.5	Complex standard errors and confidence intervals of selected variables	275

Introduction

A changing society

The *British Social Attitudes* survey series began as long ago as 1983 and the country whose views and opinions the survey has charted and analysed regularly ever since is now very different from the one in which that first survey was conducted. Analysing what the consequences of some of those changes have been for public attitudes is, indeed, the *leitmotiv* of this, our 23rd annual Report, based primarily on the findings of the 2005 *British Social Attitudes* survey.

To begin with, women are far more likely to be in employment now than they were in the 1980s. Chapter 3 examines whether this growth in female employment has been accompanied by a change in the attitudes of women towards work. It considers, too, how women – and men – react to the pressures of maintaining a satisfactory balance between work and life, given the need to combine the demands of work with family responsibilities.

Meanwhile the internet has only come to be used widely within the last ten years. Yet it appears to be one of the biggest revolutions so far in the history of communications technology. It has certainly changed the way that many of us shop, bank, acquire information or undertake our work. But its impact on our social lives is less clear. Perhaps it means we spend more time alone with our computers and less time socialising with each other. Or perhaps the internet helps us keep in contact with friends and relatives and to get involved in local groups. Chapter 10 assesses whether or not users of the internet have become more socially isolated.

Britain's population is ageing and is expected to do so further. This creates new challenges for public policy. One is how we should fund the cost of the care that older people may come to need. This question has occasioned one of the most heavily popularised differences in policy between the UK government and the devolved Scottish Executive. The former has decided that the amount of help someone living in England gets to pay for the cost of 'personal care' should depend on their means; the latter has decided such care should be provided 'free' to all who need it. Which of these two approaches is the more popular, and why, is the subject of Chapter 4.

The ageing of Britain's population has also helped to sharpen the debate about a difficult moral dilemma. This is whether there are ever circumstances, such as a painful terminal illness, in which the law should allow someone to help another person to die. Chapter 2 examines our attitudes towards this dilemma and whether there is much support for changing the current position whereby giving such help is illegal.

Meanwhile the incidence of disabled people has increased. At the same time government policy and the law has placed increasing emphasis on the need to include disabled people in the everyday life of the community. Attitudes towards disabled people are examined in Chapter 9, which asks in particular how far the public does, in fact, accept that they should be fully included in the life of their communities.

Since 1997 Britain has had a Labour government, whereas the Conservatives were in power throughout the first fourteen years of the *British Social Attitudes* survey series. But it is a very different Labour government from its predecessors. For example, although it has enacted some legislation designed to strengthen the power of trade unions, it has been less inclined to meet the policy demands of the union movement. Chapter 8 considers how the trade union movement is viewed after a number of years of New Labour government and whether the advent of that government has helped to reverse the decline in membership and influence that the trade unions suffered during much of the 1980s and 1990s.

The political environment has changed in other respects too. Systems of proportional representation have been introduced for European and devolved elections. Meanwhile, people have been inclined to stay away from the polls at election time. Turnout in the 2005 general election was only marginally higher than the record low recorded in 2001. Chapter 6 examines why people stayed away from the polls again in 2005, and considers whether the continued use of the first-past-the-post electoral system in elections to the House of Commons discourages some kinds of voters in particular from voting. Meanwhile, Chapter 5 assesses whether an electoral system that arguably encourages parties to emphasise their differences from each other, serves to undermine our willingness to respect the views of supporters of political parties with which we disagree.

But perhaps the biggest change of all in the political environment in recent years has been the increased concern with terrorism following the use of hijacked planes to demolish the Twin Towers in New York on 11th September 2001, and the use of suicide bombs in London on 7th July 2005. This concern has resulted in the passage of laws, such as the extension of the time that the police can hold a person without charging them, that some have argued threaten 'fundamental' civil rights. Chapter 7 undertakes an in-depth examination of how the public views the potential trade-off between civil liberties on the one hand and measures argued to reduce the threat of terrorism on the other.

We begin our analysis, however, with an examination of what impact long-term social change may have had on our sense of identity. Over the last few decades, the development of competitive and ever-changing labour markets, together with the existence of the modern welfare state, is thought to have eroded our linkages with traditional social groups. Instead of inheriting a sense of identity with a particular class, religion, or political party from our parents we now make and choose our own identities – and these may have little to do with class, religion or party at all. Chapter 1 tests whether this argument really does ring true.

Our thanks

British Social Attitudes could not take place without its many generous funders. The Gatsby Charitable Foundation (one of the Sainsbury Family Charitable Trusts) has provided core funding on a continuous basis since the survey's inception, and in so doing has ensured the survey's security and independence. A number of government departments have regularly funded modules of interest to them, while respecting the independence of the study. In 2005 we gratefully acknowledge the support of the Departments for Education and Skills, Health, Transport, Trade and Industry, and Work and Pensions. We are also grateful to the Disability Rights Commission for supporting a module on attitudes to disability.

The Economic and Social Research Council (ESRC), the body primarily responsible for funding academic social science research in Britain, has regularly provided the funds needed to field modules on the survey. In 2005 it continued to support the participation of Britain in the *International Social Survey Programme*, a collaboration whereby surveys in over 40 countries field an identical module of questions in order to facilitate comparative research. In 2005 this module was about attitudes to work and the data collected in Britain forms the basis of Chapter 3. Meanwhile, in 2005, the ESRC also funded our participation in a second international collaboration, the *Comparative Study of Electoral Systems* project, together with modules on social identities, political respect, civil liberties and terrorism, and the impact of the internet.

The Nuffield Foundation, a charitable foundation that supports a wide range of social research, has also provided invaluable support to the series. In 2005 it funded a module on attitudes towards euthanasia together with one on attitudes towards funding the needs of old age that was included in our sister survey, the *Scottish Social Attitudes* survey. This latter module provides much of the evidence reported in Chapter 4. Further information about the *Scottish Social Attitudes* survey itself can be found in Bromley *et al.* (2006).

We would also like to thank Professor Richard Topf of London Metropolitan University for all his work in creating and maintaining access to an easy to use internet-based website that provides a fully searchable database of all the questions that have ever been carried on a *British Social Attitudes* survey, together with details of the pattern of responses to every question. This site provides an invaluable resource for those who want to know more than can be found in this report. It is located at www.britsocat.com.

The *British Social Attitudes* survey is a team effort. The research group that designs, directs and reports on the study is supported by complementary teams who implement the survey's sampling strategy and carry out data processing. Those teams in turn depend on fieldwork controllers, area managers and field interviewers who are responsible for all the interviewing, and without whose efforts the survey would not happen at all. The survey is heavily dependent too on administrative staff who compile, organise and distribute the survey's extensive documentation, for which we would pay particular thanks to Neil Barton and his colleagues in NatCen's administrative office in Brentwood. We are also grateful to Sandra Beeson in our computing department who expertly translates our questions into a computer assisted questionnaire, and to Roger Stafford who has the uneviable task of editing, checking and documenting the data. Meanwhile the raw data have to be transformed into a workable SPSS system file – a task that has for many years been performed with great care and efficiency by Ann Mair at the Social Statistics Laboratory at the University of Strathclyde. Many thanks are also due to David Mainwaring, Kate Gofton-Salmond and Emily Lawrence at our publishers, Sage.

Finally, however, we must praise the people who anonymously gave of their time to answer our 2005 survey. They are the cornerstone of this enterprise. We hope that some of them might come across this volume and read about themselves and their fellow citizens with interest.

The Editors

References

Bromley, C., Curtice, J., McCrone, D. and Park, A. (eds.) (2006), *Has Devolution Delivered?*, Edinburgh: Edinburgh University Press

1 Who do we think we are? The decline of traditional social identities

Anthony Heath, Jean Martin and Gabriella Elgenius[*]

This chapter examines whether there have been long-term changes in the incidence and nature of traditional social identities such as those based on religion, politics, class and Britishness. In so doing we will test claims derived from modernisation theory about the changing nature of social group membership in post-industrial society. As well as measuring how the incidence of different kinds of identities might have changed, we will pay particular attention to the implications of these changes for people's social values and attitudes. In other words we will ask whether the relationships between identity and the values that someone upholds have weakened, suggesting that traditional social identities have declined in influence.

Many writers have suggested that, as we move from an industrial to a post-industrial society, traditional social cleavages such as class will decline in social significance. This idea is particularly prominent in the work of writers such as Ulrich Beck who have talked of the individualisation of modern society. On this account individuals are no longer members of social communities that have distinctive 'life-worlds', that is, ways of living their lives, but are 'condemned to choose' their own life-worlds. As Beck puts it: "each of us is both expected and forced to *lead our own life* outside the bounds of any particular community or group" (Beck and Beck-Gernsheim, 2002: 46, emphasis in the original).

Beck's argument is that the nature of the modern labour market in conjunction with the character of the modern welfare state, a welfare state that has replaced the communal provision of welfare needs via families and neighbourhoods with individual, bureaucratically organised provision, have between them dissolved "the social foundations both of class society and of the nuclear family" (Beck, 1992: 153). In his well-known aphorism, "community is dissolved in the acid bath of competition" (Beck, 1992: 94).

---

[*] Anthony Heath is Professor of Sociology, Jean Martin is a Senior Research Fellow and Gabriella Elgenius is a Research Fellow – all in the Department of Sociology, University of Oxford.

In part individualisation entails:

> the disintegration of previously existing social forms – for example, the increasing fragility of such categories as class and social status, gender roles, family, neighbourhood etc. (Beck and Beck-Gernsheim, 2002: 2–3)

Beck emphasises, however, that individualisation should not be equated with isolation, loneliness, atomisation or disconnectedness. Rather, it is:

> first the dis-embedding and, second, the re-embedding of industrial society ways of life by new ones, in which the individuals must produce, stage and cobble together their biographies themselves. (Beck 1994: 13)

In other words, traditional ascribed or 'given' group-based sources of identity such as class and status are expected to be replaced by *individually chosen* sources of belonging and identity. Beck still believes that there is a search for belonging in post-industrial societies but his key point is that:

> individualization therefore means that the standard biography becomes a chosen biography, a 'do-it-yourself biography' … or, as Giddens says, a 'reflexive biography'. (1994: 15)

It is also important to recognise that Beck does not claim that class inequalities *per se* have disappeared – although he does argue that risks are now much more evenly spread across the different classes rather than being concentrated in the working class. Beck's argument is not about 'objective' inequalities but about classes as social formations that have a sense of group belonging and solidarity. Rather, the key claim in this account of individualisation is that individuals are no longer so firmly rooted in 'given' social identities that provide social bases for how individuals should act and behave.

Beck focuses in particular on the decline of social class and of the conventional family, but his argument could easily be extended to other social sources of identity, such as the established churches and political parties. In the case of political parties, the title of Rose and McAllister's book '*Voters Begin to Choose: From Closed-Class to Open Elections in Britain*' (1986) suggests a parallel claim. There is a huge literature on secularisation and the declining social significance of the major religious denominations (see, for example, Bruce, 2002). There is also growing concern about a decline of a sense of British identity and the possible implications this has for social cohesion (see, for example, Goodhart, 2006).

In this chapter we focus on the alleged decline of the traditional 'given' identities of class, party, religion and Britishness. We have three aims. The first is to establish whether there has been any decline in the proportion of the population that adheres to these four traditional social identities. The second is to examine the social significance of these identities and in particular whether people feel they have something in common with and thus a shared sense of community with those who adhere to the same traditional identity as themselves. The third is to analyse whether there has been any decline in the relationship between adherence to a social identity and the values and attitudes that individuals uphold.

The declining incidence of traditional social identities

We begin by charting the changing proportions over time of the adult population who subscribe to each of our four key social identities. In the 2005 *British Social Attitudes* survey we were able to replicate some questions on identities that had previously been asked in the British Election Studies (BES), which began in 1963, thus enabling us to measure change over a forty-year period. Other questions had previously been included in the *British Social Attitudes* series stretching back to the 1980s. We also have access to in-depth follow-up interviews with some of the respondents to the 2005 survey that enable us to illustrate in greater depth some of the points that emerge from our survey data. Further details about these interviews are given in the appendix to this chapter.

We begin with social class, a key concern of the early election studies and, as we have seen, the key social identity in Beck's account of individualisation.

Class identity

As we emphasised earlier, our concern is not with people's 'objective' class, which is typically defined on the basis of occupation and employment status, but, rather, with people's subjective sense of belonging to a social class – that is, with class as a social identity.[1] This distinction between what might be termed objective and subjective class is one of the classic ones in sociology and goes back to the work of the 'founding fathers' of the discipline, such as Karl Marx and Max Weber. Marx, of course, saw class communities formed on the basis of a shared class identity as the crucial actors on the political stage.

Social class was also one of the central concerns of the political scientists who designed the first British Election Studies (Butler and Stokes, 1974) and the 1964 BES included a number of questions on class identity. One version in particular has stood the test of time and has been repeated in many subsequent studies with no more than minor changes or wording.[2] Respondents were asked:

> *Do you ever think of yourself as belonging to any particular class?*
> *If "Yes": Which class is that?*
> *If "No"/"Don't know": Most people say they belong to either the middle class or to the working class. Do you ever think of yourself as being in one of these classes?*

We can think of the first, unprompted, question as tapping those respondents who have a clear, relatively strong identity. Respondents, were of course, free to volunteer the name of any class that they wished to in response to this question, but the great majority volunteered either "middle class" or "working class". The follow-up question that prompts people with those two labels is likely to tap a more superficial recognition of class differences. Therefore, in order to obtain a first indication of whether class is still a meaningful social identity, we begin by examining how many people name a class in response to the unprompted question as opposed to only doing so in response to the prompted one – if at all. What we expect to find, if Beck's account is correct, is that the percentage of people who volunteer a class without being prompted has fallen while the proportion who do so only after being prompted, or do not give any class identity at all, has increased.

Table 1.1 Prompted and unprompted class identity, 1965–2005[3]

	1964	1970	1974	1983	1992	2005
Class identity	%	%	%	%	%	%
Unprompted: middle class	14	16	17	20	16	20
Unprompted: working class	33	25	24	33	29	25
Total unprompted	47	41	41	53	45	45
Prompted: middle class	16	17	17	14	19	17
Prompted: working class	31	37	38	26	31	32
Total prompted	47	54	55	40	50	49
Does not identify with any class	6	4	4	6	6	6
Base	*892*	*746*	*2435*	*3897*	*3512*	*2102*

Sources: 1964–1992 British Election Studies; 1974 figure is from the October rather than the February study of that year

Table 1.1 shows that this expectation is clearly not fulfilled. Even in 1964 only a little under half (47 per cent) declared unprompted that they were either middle or working class. Our most recent reading, 45 per cent, is almost identical. This figure has bumped up and down a bit during the intervening years, rising in particular to a peak in 1983 when issues of social class came to the fore in the wake of the polarisation of party politics between a middle-class-oriented Conservative Party under Margaret Thatcher and a working-class-oriented Labour Party under Michael Foot. But there is clearly no underlying downward trend of the sort we had expected.

What has changed is the balance between those calling themselves middle class and those calling themselves working class. In 1964, for every person who called themselves middle class there were 2.1 who said they were working class. Now that ratio is just 1:1.5. In short, while the incidence of class identities overall has not declined, the proportion with a working-class identity has. But we clearly should not mistake the latter for the former. This decline in working-class identity almost certainly reflects the change over the last forty years in the shape of the 'objective' class structure, as defined by the proportion in manual and non-manual jobs. Even so, it is notable that, whereas sociologists typically claim that the proportion of manual jobs has now declined to much less than 50 per cent of the labour force, the proportion who (either prompted or unprompted) identify themselves as working class is still clearly in a large majority. There is evidently no straightforward one-to-one relationship between objective and subjective class.

Our qualitative interviews help explain why some people who are currently in middle-class occupations nevertheless consider themselves to be working class. For many people their class identity is still a 'given' identity that was formed when they were growing up; as a result, people who grew up in working-class families continue to think of themselves as working class even though, in objective terms, they themselves may have been upwardly mobile into the middle class. As expressed by an accountant and manager working in the city of London:

> I belong to working class. Yes, just purely from my background, because my family pretty much are sort of from that, you know, working-class um people. [female, 32]

In a similar vein a retired office worker stated:

> I'm working class, because basically my parents came, you know, my parents were that. [male, 50]

As did a teacher by stating:

> I suppose I'm still working class, I still see myself as working class. That's where I came from, erm and that's where I see myself. [female, 47]

Meanwhile, a university graduate from a 'working-class' background explained why it might be difficult to cast off a given identity and replace it with an individually chosen one that might appear to reflect more accurately their current circumstances:

> to a certain extent there's a, a slight feeling that you're something of a fake if you're not the way that you were exactly brought up to be, if, you try to create your own class identity, which is separate from the, the class identity that you were given when you were born. I do sometimes feel that I er, if I'm, like, with someone who's got a more classic middle-class background kind of that they're the real deal and, and I'm not. [male, 36]

There does not, then, appear to have been any long-term secular drop in the incidence of class identities. What has happened is that fewer people now identify with the working class while more do so with the middle class. Nevertheless, the influence of 'given' class identities formed in childhood is such that adherence to a working-class identity still outstrips the proportion of the population that objectively have a working-class occupation.

Political identity

While class identity has been one of the classic concerns of sociologists, party identity has performed a similar role among political scientists. Psychological attachments to a political party have often been seen as performing important functions, both for the individual voter and for the political system more generally. For the individual voter they may provide a source of cues about politics and a short-cut to political decision making. Voters who identify with a particular party will tend to adopt the political views and judgements of 'their' party. They will also tend to be more committed to supporting their party and thus empirical research has found a strong link between strength of party identification and turnout in elections. A decline in party identification may thus be one of the underlying causes of the recent decline in turnout. It may also be a source of greater volatility and instability in voters' decisions about whom to support if they do vote. Declining identification may thus have real consequences for the way in which our political system operates.

There are, to be sure, some important differences between theories of class identity and those of party identity: in particular, class identity is concerned with how members of a given class relate to each other, whereas party identity is concerned with how people relate to an external organisation. There are, nonetheless, important similarities, in particular the notion that people are socialised by their family into identifying with a political party in much the same way that they are socialised into a class identity. In this sense, then, both theories hold that these identities are largely 'given' by the family and remain rather constant throughout adult life.

The *British Social Attitudes* survey has asked questions about party identity from its inception. We ask respondents:

> *Generally speaking, do you think of yourself as a supporter of any one political party?*

If the respondent says "No" or "Don't know" they are then asked:

> *Do you think of yourself as a little closer to one political party than to the others?*

If the respondent says "Yes" to either of these two questions they are then asked:

Which one?

If the respondent continues to say "No" or "Don't know" they are asked:

If there were a general election tomorrow, which political party do you think you would be most likely to support?

Thereafter, all those who name a party in response to any of these three questions are asked:

Would you call yourself very strong [Conservative etc.], fairly strong or not very strong?

This follow-up question, which looks at strength of party identity, gives us a measure that is, perhaps, functionally equivalent to the distinction between responding to the prompted and the unprompted class questions. But whereas in the case of class identity we were able to find little decline over time, Table 1.2 shows there has been a significant decline in party identity since the question was first asked on the 1987 *British Social Attitudes* survey. In 1987 no less than 46 per cent identified "very" or "fairly" strongly with a party; now only 35 per cent do so. Meanwhile, the proportion who fail, despite our persistent questioning, to name a party at all has nearly doubled over the same period from seven per cent to 13 per cent.

Table 1.2 Strength of party identification, 1987–2005

Strength of party identification[4]	1987	1993	1996	1998	2000	2002	2005
	%	%	%	%	%	%	%
Very strong	11	9	9	7	6	5	7
Fairly strong	35	33	28	28	26	27	28
Not very strong	41	44	47	48	49	48	47
No party identification	7	10	10	11	13	13	13
Base	*2597*	*2823*	*3407*	*2994*	*3240*	*3221*	*4037*

In fact, evidence from the British Election Study not only confirms this decline but, indeed, indicates that it stretches back over a forty-year period (Crewe and Thomson, 1994; Clarke *et al.*, 2004). In 1964 it found that no less than 82 per cent identified "very" or "fairly" strongly with a party. By 1987 that figure had already fallen to 64 per cent and in the most recent study, conducted in 2005, only 51 per cent did so.[5] It seems that we can safely conclude that the proportion with a strong sense of party identification has declined substantially over the course of recent decades.

Religious identity

It has been clearly established that there has been a long-term decline in church membership in Western European countries such as Britain. To be sure, there has been considerable debate about the social significance of this decline. Davie (1994) has suggested that the state of faith in Britain nowadays can be characterised as 'believing without belonging'. People may not attend church in the numbers that they used to, but they may still think of themselves as religious and may continue, for example, to believe in God, the afterlife, and so on. In contrast the growing indifference to religion in many of today's culturally diverse and egalitarian societies has led Bruce (2002) to claim that 'God is dead'. Equally, Voas and Crockett challenge Davie's claim, arguing that religion in Britain is characterised by "neither believing nor belonging" and that religious "belief has in fact eroded in Britain at the same rate as two key aspects of belonging: religious affiliation and attendance" (2005:11).

At this stage, however, our interest is simply in how many people belong. Both the BES and *British Social Attitudes* surveys have regularly asked questions about membership, although the wording has varied over time. In the 1964 BES respondents were asked, "What is your religion?" This is a rather unfortunate way to ask the question as it implies that everyone has a religion. It was subsequently changed in later BES surveys to:

> *Do you regard yourself as belonging to any particular religion?*
> *If yes: Which?*

This is a much better question and is in a sense equivalent to our unprompted social class identity question. However, sociologists of religion have often noted that claimed membership of the Anglican Church in England tends to have a rather nominal character and does not necessarily indicate any real sense of group membership. It has, therefore, become standard practice to distinguish between those who attend church, if only on a key occasion such as Easter, from the more nominal members who never attend (apart from on special occasions such as weddings, funerals and baptisms). Use of a question on religious attendance also allows us to compensate for the unfortunate question wording of the 1964 BES question. If we combine those who say they do not belong with those who say they do belong but never attend we can get a reasonably accurate picture of the trend in religious adherence over time.

Table 1.3 confirms that there has indeed been a major decline over time in membership of a religion. In 1964 just over a quarter (26 per cent) either did not claim membership of a religion or said that they never attended a religious service. Now over two-thirds (69 per cent) do so. It is also noticeable that, amongst those who do actually claim to belong to a religion, the proportion who attend a service regularly has been falling. In 1964 around three-quarters of those who claimed membership of a religion attended services; now only half do so.

Table 1.3 Religious belonging, 1964–2005[6]

	1964	1970	1983	1992	2005
	%	%	%	%	%
Belongs to a religion, attends services	74	71	55	37	31
Belongs to a religion, never attends services	23	24	30	31	31
Does not belong	3	5	26	31	38
Base	1752	1816	3934	2815	4268

Source: 1964–1992 British Election Studies

These results, then, parallel fairly closely those for the decline of party identity where we saw that as well as more people not having a party identity at all, there has also been a shift from having a stronger to a weaker identity. Here we see that as well as there having been an increase in the proportion who do not claim a religious identity at all, there has also been a decline in the commitment of those who still claim a religious identity. Overall, however (albeit remembering the methodological caveats), the decline in religion appears to have been even more marked than the decline in party identity.

National identity

Our fourth 'traditional' identity is British national identity. Historically, British identity is a relatively recent construct and dates from, at the earliest, the 18th century. It was gradually superimposed on earlier national identities of 'English', 'Welsh' and 'Scottish' following the 1707 Act of Union with Scotland.[7] In this sense, then, we are talking about a tradition that is a mere couple of hundred years old. On the other hand it should be remembered that class and party identities are even more recent.

As in the case of class, party and religion, however, many writers have suggested that national identity and, more specifically, British identity is in decline. General processes of globalisation and international interdependence, most strikingly through the developing institutions of the European Union, have been argued to lead to a blurring of national identities and a growth of cosmopolitanism (Dogan, 1994; Savage *et al.,* 2005).

In addition there are particular reasons why British national identity might be in decline. Some of the features that helped construct British identity in the 18th and 19th centuries – the existence of Protestant religious traditions in each of the four parts of the United Kingdom (in opposition to the Catholicism of France), distinctive traditions of British democracy (in opposition to the authoritarian rule of France), and the shared economic and political project of the British Empire that united the interests of English, Welsh, Scots and Irish – either are no longer present to the same degree or, if present, are much less distinctive.

Any decline in British identity might also have important consequences for British society. National identity has often been described as an 'imagined community'; those that share the same national identity consider themselves to share common bonds of comradeship and responsibility for each other (Anderson, 1991). The strength of these bonds is, according to Anderson manifested in citizens' willingness to die for their communities. This sense of comradeship is also often claimed to provide other important social functions, such as leading people to feel obligations to their fellow citizens, for example those in need (Miller, 1995).

As we noted earlier, we cannot construct such a long time-series for national identity as we can for class or party identity. Identical questions were, however, asked in the 1996 and 2005 *British Social Attitudes* surveys, and so we can look at the trend over the last decade. We asked respondents:

> *Please say which, if any, of the words on this card describes the way* **you** *think of yourself. Please choose as many or as few as apply*
>
> *If more than one given: And if you had to choose, which one* **best** *describes the way you think of yourself?*
>
> *[Answer options: British, English, European, Irish, Northern Irish, Scottish, Ulster, Welsh, Other answer]*

In Table 1.4 we show what proportion of people across Britain as a whole said they were British, subdivided into those who said that British was either the only or the best way of describing themselves and those who while they acknowledged that they were British did not feel this was the best way of describing themselves.

Table 1.4 Trends in British national identity, 1996–2005

	1996	2005
	%	%
British best or only national identity	52	44
British but not best identity	15	23
Does not identify as British	34	33
Base	*1177*	*4268*

We would not expect to find any major change in just a single decade. Nevertheless, while there has not been any decline in the proportion who say that they are British, the proportion who say that British is the best or only way of describing how they think of themselves has fallen from just over half (52 per cent) to rather less than half (44 per cent). However, this may be in part because of a heightened awareness in Scotland and Wales of separate identities such as Scottish or Welsh in the wake of the introduction of devolution, rather than from a general decline in Britishness that affects England as well. Table 1.5 examines this possibility by looking separately in each of three territories of Great Britain at the proportion who say that British is the only way of describing themselves and the proportion who say (as appropriate) that English, Scottish or Welsh is. Looking at this 'forced choice' version of national identity also has the advantage that national identity was asked in this way earlier than 1996 and so we can chart trends in adherence to Britishness somewhat further back.

Table 1.5 Trends in 'forced choice' national identity, 1974–2003

	1974	1979	1992	1997	1999	2001	2003	2005
Lives in England	%	%	%	%	%	%	%	%
English identity	n/a	n/a	31	34	44	43	38	40
British identity	n/a	n/a	63	59	44	44	48	48
Base			*2442*	*3150*	*2718*	*2761*	*3709*	*3643*
Lives in Scotland	%	%	%	%	%	%	%	%
Scottish identity	65	56	72	72	77	77	72	79
British identity	31	38	25	20	17	16	20	14
Base	*588*	*658*	*957*	*882*	*1482*	*1605*	*1508*	*1549*
Lives in Wales	%	%	%	%	%	%	%	%
Welsh identity	n/a	57	n/a	63	57	57	60	n/a
British identity	n/a	33	n/a	26	31	31	27	n/a
Base		*858*		*649*	*1256*	*1085*	*988*	

n/a = not asked
Sources: British Election Studies 1992–1997; Scottish Election surveys 1974–1997; *Scottish Social Attitudes* surveys 1999–2005; Welsh Election survey 1979; Welsh Referendum Survey 1997; Welsh Assembly Election Survey 1999; Welsh Life and Times surveys 2001 and 2003

In fact, the results suggest that if anything the decline in adherence to Britishness over the last decade has been more marked in England than it has been in either Scotland or Wales. In neither Scotland nor Wales has there been a consistent drop since 1997. In contrast, in England the proportion who say they are British fell from 59 per cent in 1997 to just 44 per cent in 1999, and this figure has subsequently recovered to no more than 48 per cent. On the other hand we can see that in Scotland there was a marked decline in adherence to Britishness between the 1970s and the 1990s and so there at least the decline in Britishness, is in fact, a much longer historical trend. Moreover we should also note that Britishness has long been no more than a secondary identity both in Scotland and in Wales.

In our qualitative research one of our interviewees explained how it was possible to feel both Scottish and British, but why when forced to choose between them his Scottishness was the more important:

> I'm a Scot – being a Scot is what stirs my blood. [...] Britishness is definitely the next largest core of my identity, because of some of the other issues like the politics etc. If we're talking about race and blood, it's Scotland. If we're talking about politics and values, it's probably Britain. [male, 51]

In contrast, in England people are generally much less clear about the difference between an English and a British identity. Nevertheless, the evidence in Table 1.5 of an apparently growing wish in the wake of Scottish and Welsh devolution to assert an English rather than a British identity was affirmed by some of our interviewees, who would say without hesitation "I consider myself very definitely English" [male, 43]. Another interviewee explained as follows:

> The Scottish, the Welsh, and, and the Irish to an extent, seem to cling on to their identities much better than the English do. Erm, well I suppose some people would say that that's because the English were always seen as a little bit arrogant and not needing to have that identity, but, erm, I think the result of all that is, that the English have sort of lost, lost a little bit of that, and, and I think we need to get a bit back. Er, we have the Scottish Parliament and the Welsh Assembly, we don't have anything for, for England *per se*, so I think, I think there is a void. [male, 53]

Another expressed similar sentiments:

> I get quite cross. I'm not allowed on a form to be anything other than white British. If I was Jamaican, I would be allowed to be British Jamaican, British Indian, British African, and have a nationality. I am not British Welsh, British Scottish, or British Irish so I've lost my country, I've lost my nationality. [female, 64]

So alongside the decline in strength of adherence to a party or a religion, there has evidently also been at least something of a decline in people's strength of adherence to a British national identity as well. Already relatively weak in Scotland and Wales, Britishness appears now to have lost some ground in

England to a sense of feeling English instead. Strikingly, however, the one instance where the thesis of 'declining traditional identities' is not affirmed at all by our evidence is in respect of class identity, the identity which has been the primary focus of much of the work on individualisation.

Our next step is to explore the social significance of these identities, that is, how much those who say they have any particular identity feel a bond with those who also claim that same identity and thus regard themselves as part of the same community as those other people. It could, of course, be that, even though the incidence of class identity has declined little over time, people no longer feel they are part of a 'class community'. In contrast, while fewer people nowadays may feel that they belong to a religion, those that do might still regard their co-religionists as part of a close community.

The social significance of traditional identities in 2005

A common theme running through the sociological literature on social identities is that of a sense of community with one's fellow group members. Thus sociologists used to talk of 'class solidarity' whereby members of a class would be willing to support each other in collective action such as strikes or political protests. This characteristic was particularly attributed to the working class, which was generally regarded as having higher levels of solidarity than the middle class. It has also been suggested that class solidarity might be a source of apolitical 'good neighbourliness', with members of a class willing to help out their fellows. The language of comradeship has also often been used to describe community relations in, for example, local working-class communities such as a mining village.

However, we need to distinguish the kind of comradeship that arises in local communities, where people know each other personally, from the sense of solidarity in the 'imagined community' of the nation or of the class as a whole, where the majority of group members cannot know each other personally. It is this sense of imagined community that is perhaps most at issue. There is little doubt that, with industrial restructuring, mining and other traditional working-class communities have been in numerical decline. What is less clear is whether a wider sense of imagined community is also in decline.

After detailed qualitative work that explored how best to tackle this concept in a social survey, we eventually decided to ask respondents to our 2005 survey how much they felt they had in common with other members of their class, party, religious group or nation. In the case of class, for example, we asked respondents:

> *Some people feel they have a lot in common with other people of their own class, but others don't feel this way so much. How about you? Would you say you feel pretty close to other [middle-/working-] class people, or, that you don't feel much closer to them than you do to people in other classes?*

The answers to this question are shown in Table 1.6 broken down both by respondents' subjective class and by whether that class was offered in response to our prompted or our unprompted question.

Table 1.6 Sense of class community

% feeling "pretty close"	Subjective class identity					
Class identity	Middle class	Base	Working class	Base	All who identify with a class	Base
Unprompted	48	394	47	549	47	943
Prompted	30	349	33	674	32	1023
All who identify with a class	39	743	39	1223	39	1966

The results confirm the value of our previous distinction between the prompted and unprompted measures of class identity. Nearly half (47 per cent) of those who identify as middle or working class without being prompted say that they feel "pretty close" to other members of the same class as themselves, compared with just under a third (32 per cent) of those who had to be prompted for their class identity.

More surprisingly, however, we do not find any difference between adherents to the two classes. Contrary to our expectations, those with working-class identity are no more likely than those with a middle-class identity to say they feel pretty close to other members of the same class as themselves. Of course, it may be that our measure of closeness does not tap the exact sense of class solidarity claimed by previous sociological writers to be particularly characteristic of the working class. Or it may be that a particularly strong sense of class solidarity amongst the working class is a thing of the past. We return to this later. However, analysis of data from the 1963 BES suggests that this pattern is rather long-standing.

We also asked a similar question about the extent to which party identifiers felt part of an 'imagined community' along with fellow-supporters of their political party:

> *How much do you feel you have in common with [own party] supporters in general, compared with other people?*
>
> *A lot more in common with them than with other people*
>
> *A little more in common with them than with other people*
>
> *No more in common with them than with other people*

Table 1.7 Sense of community with other party supporters

% feeling they have "a lot" or "a little" more in common	Party with which respondent identifies				
Strength of party identification	Conserva-tive	Labour	Liberal Democrat	Other	All with party identity
Very or fairly strong	51	52	62	70	54
Not very strong	31	21	31	28	26
All with party identity	42	37	44	53	32

Bases for this table are given in end note 8

Table 1.7 shows the pattern of answers to this question broken down by the party with which respondents identify and the strength of their identification.[9] It proves to be remarkably similar to that for class identity. We find a clear difference between strong and weak party identifiers just as we did between the prompted and unprompted class identifiers. Over half (54 per cent) of those with a strong party identification feel they have at least "a little" more in common with others who identify with the same party than they do with other people. This is more than twice the equivalent proportion (26 per cent) amongst weak identifiers. However, we do find a tendency for those who identify strongly with the Liberal Democrats or a small 'other' party to be more likely to feel a sense of community with fellow-identifiers than do supporters of the two largest parties, the Conservatives and Labour. Indeed, those who weakly identify with the Labour Party, which at the time of our survey was the most popular party of all, are particularly unlikely to feel they have anything in common with other Labour identifiers. There are suggestions here of an inverse relationship between the size of a group and its feeling of community.

Table 1.8 Religion and sense of community

% feeling they have "a lot" or "a little" more in common	Religion				
Strength of religious belonging	Anglican	Roman Catholic	Other Christian	Non-Christian	All who belong to a religion
Belongs to a religion, attends services	31	59	60	84	52
Belongs to a religion, never attends services	14	17	19	54	18
All who belong to a religion	20	39	41	74	34

Bases for this table are given in end note 10

In Table 1.8, meanwhile, we show the responses obtained by our 2005 survey when we asked about sense of community with fellow-members of a religion. These were obtained by asking exactly the same question that we administered in respect of fellow party identifiers. The pattern is much the same too. Over half (52 per cent) of those who both belong to a religion and attend services feel they have at least "a little" in common with those who belong to the same religion as themselves, compared with less than one in five (18 per cent) of those who do not attend services. A sense of being part of a community is thus strongly associated with actual participation.

Strikingly, however, when we asked those who said they were British how much they felt they had in common with other British people, those who said that British was either their only identity or the one that described them best were no more likely to feel a sense of community than were those for whom British was not their best or only identity. This almost certainly reflects the weak and 'fuzzy' nature of British identity that has been demonstrated by a number of previous writers (e.g. Cohen, 1995). Indeed, as Table 1.9 also shows, there is not much evidence, either, of a particularly strong sense of community amongst those for whom English is their only or best national identity. In contrast, those for whom Scottish, Welsh or European is their only or best identity are clearly more likely than are those for whom these identities are secondary to feel a sense of community with other people who share the same identity. Once again it appears that we have evidence of a stronger sense of community amongst adherents to (what are across Britain as a whole at least) minority identities.

Table 1.9 National identity and sense of community

% feeling they have "a lot" or "a little" more in common	National identity				
Strength of national identity	British	English	Scottish	Welsh	European
Best or only national identity	45	49	65	51	58
National identity but not best	45	43	54	36	40
All	45	47	63	47	44

Bases for this table are given in end note 11

One possible reason why identity should have greater social significance for those who belong to relatively small social groups is that the larger the group, the harder it is to sustain a sense of imagined community. The larger the community, the less it is founded on face-to-face relationships. Alternatively, the smaller the group, the more distinctive its members are likely to feel from mainstream society, if not indeed the more beleaguered too. A strong sense of community may indeed be central to their ability to maintain their minority identity. In contrast, members of dominant mainstream groups, such as the larger political parties or the Church of England, may be more inclined to take their identity for granted.

Identity, sense of community and implications for social attitudes

Perhaps the key question is, does any of this matter? Do people who feel a sense of community with other members of their group also follow the norms of their group in their attitudes and behaviour? In the language of technical sociology, do these traditional groups still play the role that they once did of 'normative reference groups', that is, as a source upon which to rely in deciding what to believe or what action to take. This is at the heart of the theories of individualisation. The implication of these theories is that traditional forms of identity are no longer such powerful stimuli to collective or, indeed, to individual action and no longer constitute significant reference points for values and action.[12]

A useful way to explore whether class, party, churches and nations constitute normative reference groups is to investigate whether subjective group membership and identity are linked to the distinctive attitudes traditionally associated with these groups. More specifically, we expect to find that people who feel a sense of community with other group members will be more likely than do those who do not feel such a sense of community to accept the group as their normative reference group. They will, therefore, be more likely to adopt those attitudes and values that typically characterise the group as a whole.

We begin by looking at social class. Traditionally, writers have associated the working class with distinctive support for the redistribution of income and wealth and for collective action in support of such redistribution. In contrast, the middle class is typically seen as a more conservative force in society, resisting such redistribution and more inclined to seek advancement through individual rather than collective action (see, for example, Heath *et al.*, 1985).

Three questions included in our 2005 survey can be regarded as typical examples of these kinds of class attitudes. Respondents were asked to indicate whether they agreed or disagreed with the following statements:

> *Ordinary working people do not get their fair share of the nation's wealth*
> *Government should redistribute income from the better-off to those who are less well off*
> *Big business benefits owners at the expense of workers*

As will become apparent, it is also useful to look at perceptions of class conflict:

On the whole, do you think there is bound to be some conflict between different social classes, or do you think they can get along together without any conflict?

Table 1.10 Class identity, sense of community, and class attitudes

% agree ...	Working people do not get their fair share	Government should redistribute income	Business benefits owners at the expense of workers	% "bound to be conflict" between social classes	Base (cols. 1–3)	Base (col. 4)
Class & sense of community						
Middle class; close	45	30	48	57	295	250
Middle class; not close	44	30	47	44	448	383
Working class; not close	58	33	56	41	734	621
Working class; close	65	29	58	50	489	385

Table 1.10 shows how middle- and working-class identifiers answered these questions, showing in each case the responses of those who do feel closer to other members of their class and those who do not. The first three columns demonstrate that there are indeed some differences in attitudes between the classes. Working-class identifiers tend to be more likely to favour greater egalitarianism, while there is also some evidence that this is particularly true of those who feel a sense of community with other working-class people. Thus, for example, nearly two-thirds (65 per cent) of those who feel a sense of working-class community agree that ordinary people do not get their fair share of wealth, compared with 58 per cent of those working-class identifiers who do not feel a sense of community and less than half (44 per cent) of all middle-class identifiers. However, for the most part the differences between the classes are rather small and indeed are almost non-existent in the case of government action to redistribute income. Meanwhile, apart from the example we have just cited, there is no evidence that those who feel a sense of community with their class have particularly distinctive attitudes. Overall there is only scanty evidence here of class acting as a normative reference group.

However, perhaps our failure, in particular, to find any evidence at all that sense of community makes a difference to the attitudes of middle-class identifiers may have arisen because the three questions we have examined so far focus on working-class issues rather than on middle-class ones. Indeed, when we look at our fourth question on perceptions of class conflict, we find that people who feel close to the middle class do have different perceptions from those middle-class identifiers who do not feel close to their class. Amongst the former group, no less than 57 per cent agree that there is bound to be conflict between the classes, compared with just 44 per cent of the latter. Indeed, this 13-point difference between the two groups of middle-class identifiers is rather greater than the equivalent gap of nine points amongst working-class identifiers.

We returned to the question of whether society is perceived as divided by class in our interviews. Many interviewees answered without hesitation, along the lines of: "Yes it is. People either look up or down" [male, 47]. Likewise, 'class division' was at times defined in the traditional fashion: "I see it [class divisions] in those pure terms, as ... oppressor and oppressed" [male, 51]. A similar sentiment was also expressed in the quotation below highlighting the divide in terms of financial security:

> I think there is a complete divide between the people that have and the people that haven't [...] I think it's just a constant struggle so I think there is a divide. And I think the people with money still look at the people without as if they're scum. So, yeah that's harsh, but I think there is a divide. [female, 34]

Many interviewees, however, also pointed to the transformation of the class structure, and argued: "society ... is not in my view as divided as it was" [male, 48]. Class divisions were also described in terms of symbolic and cultural codes rather than economic differences, as below by a female identifying herself as 'middle class':

> my generation [class], trying to er, get rid of the, the old-fashioned dusty lifestyle of our parents, I think we would recognise [each other], relatively quickly, say, when we were sitting on a train, because we, we wear similar clothes. I think this kind of recognition to those symbols – culture capital, or something. [female, 52]

There is, then, some evidence of the pattern of responses we were expecting. However, it is far from strong or consistent. Even for those who feel close to their class, that class does not seem to act as a very powerful normative reference group. A key question, however, is whether this has, in fact, always been the case or whether, in line with Beck's theory of individualisation, class has become a less powerful normative reference group than it used to be.

Unfortunately, we cannot trace responses to these questions on class attitudes all the way back to the 1960s as we did earlier with our measures of the incidence of class identity. However, we can go back nearly twenty years to the 1987 British Election Study, which did include two of the questions we have been examining so far. The pattern of responses obtained by that survey are compared with those in our 2005 survey in Table 1.11. However, as our measure of sense of community was not included in the 1987 survey, we divide respondents instead, according to whether they declared a class identity with or without prompting.

Table 1.11 Class identity and class attitudes, 1987–2005

Class identity	% agree government should redistribute income		% agree business benefits owners at the expense of workers		Base 1987	Base 2005
	1987	2005	1987	2005		
Unprompted; middle class	37	29	38	50	537	318
Prompted; middle class	31	31	36	44	610	298
Prompted; working class	44	30	51	52	1042	576
Unprompted; working class	56	36	63	57	1009	441

The table tells a clear story. First, those with a strong (unprompted) working-class identity were more distinctive in their attitudes in 1987 than they are now. In 1987 there was a difference of 12 points between the 'prompted' and the 'unprompted' working class both in their support for redistribution, and in their attitudes towards whether business benefits owners rather than workers. Now this difference is no more than six and five points respectively. Second, the difference in attitudes between all middle-class identifiers and all working-class ones has shrunk to an even greater degree. In 1987 nearly half (49 per cent) of all working-class identifiers agreed that government should redistribute income, whereas only a third (34 per cent) of middle-class identifiers did so. Now that 15-point gap has fallen to one of just three points. Equally, a 19-point difference between the two classes in attitudes towards whom business benefits is now no more than an eight-point one. The clear implication of this is that, although as we saw earlier the incidence of class identity has not changed a great deal, the extent to which class acts as a normative reference group has apparently diminished quite markedly.

However, we should bear in mind that at one time at least, class was closely intertwined with party (Pulzer, 1967). Some of the class differences we observed in 1987 may have reflected differences between the stances taken by the parties and their consequent impact on attitudes. But with the re-branding of the Labour Party under Tony Blair as New Labour, the abandonment by the party of nationalisation as a goal, and a general move by the party to the centre of the left–right dimension, we might anticipate that nowadays, at least, there are, in fact, relatively few differences between the supporters of the various parties (Curtice and Fisher, 2003). We turn next, therefore, to consider whether political parties act as normative reference groups.

Traditionally, at least, British party politics has been organised around a left–right dimension. Those on the right of the political spectrum favour free-market policies while those on the left support state ownership and state intervention in the economy (Heath *et al.*, 1994). The Conservative Party tended towards the former viewpoint while Labour backed the latter. To see whether their supporters can still be distinguished in this way, we use our 2005 survey to examine attitudes towards nationalisation, towards taxes and towards spending on welfare benefits. The first of these questions is as follows:

> *Some people talk about nationalising industry. Which of the statements on this card comes **closest** to what you yourself feel should be done? If you don't have an opinion, just say so*
>
> *A lot more industries should be nationalised*
>
> *Only a few more industries should be nationalised*
>
> *No more industries should be nationalised, but industries that are now nationalised should stay nationalised*
>
> *Some of the industries that are now nationalised should become private companies*

In the case of the second question respondents were asked whether they agreed or disagreed that:

> *The government should spend more money on welfare benefits for the poor, even if it leads to higher taxes*

However, a second major dimension around which Conservative politics, at least, have particularly revolved in recent years is that of Europe (Heath *et al.*, 1999; Heath *et al.*, 2001). Given the considerable hostility towards Europe that emerged in the Conservative Party in the 1990s, we might well expect to find that people who feel close to the Conservatives are now distinctively anti-European. Our question on Europe reads as follows:

> *Do you think Britain's long-term policy should be ...*
>
> *... to leave the European Union,*
>
> *to stay in the EU and try to **reduce** the EU's powers,*
>
> *to leave things as they are,*
>
> *to stay in the EU and try to **increase** the EU's powers,*
>
> *or, to work for the formation of a single European government?*

Finally, we also have available to us a question that asks respondents how much difference they perceive between the parties:

> *Now considering everything the Conservative and Labour parties*
> *stand for, would you say that there is a great difference between them,*
> *some difference, or, not much difference?*

As with the question on perceptions of class conflict, we expect to find that people who feel close to one of these two parties will perceive greater differences than will those who do not feel so close or who indeed identify with other parties.

Table 1.12 Party identity, sense of community and political attitudes

Party identity and sense of community	% support more nationalisation	% agree government should spend more on welfare benefits	% support leaving EU/reduction in EU powers	% perceive "great" or "some" difference between Labour and Conservative
Conservative; close	21	31	85	73
Conservative; not close	19	31	69	56
Labour; close	36	50	45	69
Labour; not close	31	37	46	58
Liberal Democrat; close	38	37	43	51
Liberal Democrat; not close	27	43	54	49

Bases for this table are given in end note 13

Table 1.12 shows the answers given to these four questions broken down by those who identified with one of the three largest parties, showing separately the answers of those who say they feel closer to others who also support the same party and those who do not. It shows that, in fact, there are still some left–right differences between Conservative and Labour identifiers. Overall, a third (33 per cent) of Labour identifiers support more nationalisation compared with just one in five (20 per cent) Conservatives identifiers. Equally, Labour identifiers who feel a sense of community with other Labour identifiers clearly comprise the group that is most supportive of more government spending on welfare benefits. Even so, we should note that on nationalisation, at least, Labour identifiers are little different in their attitudes from Liberal Democrat identifiers (32 per cent of whom support more nationalisation) while the issue no longer particularly resonates with Labour identifiers who feel close to other Labour identifiers. While the left–right dimension may not be dead, the differences between party supporters on this dimension are certainly relatively weak.

However, much bigger differences emerge on attitudes towards the European Union (EU). Here, we see that Conservative identifiers stand out; a clear majority (75 per cent) believe either that Britain should leave the EU or that the EU's powers should be reduced, whereas less than half of both Labour (45 per cent) and Liberal Democrat (49 per cent) identifiers take this view. Scepticism about the EU is particularly high among those who feel close to fellow Conservatives. Of course, we must be careful in assuming that all of these differences arise because party identifiers are following the lead of their party; some people may have come to identify with the Conservative Party because they were already critical of the EU. But nevertheless, even if party identification no longer makes much difference to people's views on the left–right dimension, we evidently cannot assume that parties do not sometimes at least act as distinctive reference groups. Certainly, as we can see in the fourth column of Table 1.12, those who feel close to other Conservative and Labour identifiers are more likely than those who do not feel so close (let alone Liberal Democrat or other identifiers) to feel that there is at least some difference between the two parties.

Overall, then, the picture is not altogether dissimilar from that for social class. There are some differences in the direction predicted by the theory of normative reference groups, but they are not especially large. Even among those who do feel close to their class or party, these groups do not act as powerfully distinctive frames of reference – in part, at least, because the parties themselves are no longer very distinctive in the messages they promote (Bromley and Curtice, 2002). These rather weak results are certainly put sharply into perspective when we turn to religion.

Our focus in the case of religion is not on doctrinal beliefs, such as beliefs in God or the afterlife, but on moral attitudes. All religions and denominations have tended to support family values and the right to life. We can tap whether these are reflected in the attitudes of their adherents by looking at the answers they gave to the following questions about sexual relationships, abortion and suicide, included on the 2005 *British Social Attitudes* survey. The questions read as follows:

> *Now I would like to ask you some questions about sexual relationships. If a man and woman have sexual relations before marriage, what would your general opinion be?*
>
> *Always wrong*
>
> *Mostly wrong*
>
> *Sometimes wrong*
>
> *Rarely wrong*
>
> *Not wrong at all*

(In our analysis we contrast the first four of these responses against the fifth.)

Here are [a number of] circumstances in which a woman might consider an abortion. Please say whether or not you think the law should allow an abortion [if] the woman decides on her own she does not wish to have the child.

Finally, respondents were asked whether they agreed or disagreed that:

Suicide is never justified, no matter how bad things are

Table 1.13 shows the proportion of those with and without a religious identity who give the morally conservative attitude in each case, that is, who think sexual relations before marriage are at least "rarely wrong", who say that the woman should not be allowed an abortion, and who agree that suicide is never justified. In the case of those who do profess a religious identity we again distinguish between those who do feel at least a little closer to those of the same persuasion and those who do not.

Table 1.13 Religious identity, sense of community and moral values

Religious identity and sense of community	% think sexual relations before marriage are wrong	% think woman should <u>not</u> be allowed abortion if does not want child	% agree suicide is never justified
Has identity; close	60	50	59
Has identity; not close	31	33	44
No religious identity	20	27	36

Bases for this table are given in end note 14

The table shows some large differences. For example, no less than three in five of those who have a sense of community with people who profess the same religion as themselves say that sexual relations before marriage are at least "rarely wrong". In contrast, amongst those who do not have a sense of community with fellow-believers just half as many (31 per cent) take that view, while amongst those who do not have a religious identity only a third as many (20 per cent) do. The differences are not quite as large in the case of our other two questions, but they still clearly outstrip most of the differences in class and party attitudes. Moreover, it seems less likely that people join a religion because, for example, they oppose pre-marital sex than it is that they might come to support a party because of its position on Europe. It seems, therefore, that we can conclude that religious groups do act as distinctive normative reference groups in the way that classes and parties nowadays do not.

Moreover, in contrast to class, religion seems to influence people's attitudes just as much now as it ever did. Two of our moral questions were also asked on the 1984 *British Social Attitudes* survey, so we can see whether religious identifiers differ as much in their attitudes now as they did then. However, as our questions about sense of community were not included on the 1984 survey, we subdivide those with a religious identity by whether or not they attend services. Table 1.14 shows the results. In the case of sexual relations before marriage the gap in attitudes between those religious identifiers who attend services and those who do not identify with a religion at all is 36 points now, little different from the 31-point difference that existed in 1984. In the case of our question on attitudes towards abortion the equivalent figures are 15 and 23 points respectively, so if anything the gap has widened rather than narrowed.

Table 1.14 The changing relation between religious identity and moral values, 1984–2005

	% think sexual relations before marriage are wrong		% think woman should not be allowed abortion if does not want child	
Religious identity and attendance	1984	2005	1984	2005
Has identity; attends services	67	53	77	51
Has identity; does not attend services	53	31	67	32
Does not have identity	36	17	62	28

Bases for this table are given in end note 15

If religious groups appear to be our most powerful example of a traditional normative reference group, Britishness is our weakest example. One difficulty here is that it is less clear what are the particular attitudes and values with which we expect a British identity to be particularly associated. Traditional core British values are more difficult to define than core class or religious values. Our qualitative interviews underlined this point. Interviewees were asked whether or not they considered any values or behaviours or customs to be 'typically' British, and if so could they describe them? Most interviewees struggled. Those examples that were mentioned, such as "the stiff upper lip type thing", "politeness", "fair play", "manners", "a sense of ambition", "pomp and ceremony", "history", "roast dinners", "drinking tea" and "brilliance at devising codes [of conduct]", make little reference to attitudes or values.

However, it might be argued that Britishness is traditionally associated with notions of fair play, freedom of speech and equality before the law (although

Miller (1995) argues that Britain was much more distinctive historically in these respects than it is today when most liberal democracies espouse the same views). It would not, therefore, be entirely surprising if people who shared a sense of imagined community with other Britons were especially supportive of such ideas. We thus look at their answers to two questions that might tap aspects of these historical British values, one about freedom of speech and the other about trial by jury:

> *There are different views about people's rights in a democratic society. On a scale of 1 to 7, where 1 is not at all important and 7 is very important, how important to democracy is it that **every** adult living in Britain has ...*
>
> *... the right to a trial by jury if they are charged with a serious crime?*
> *... the right to say whatever they think in public?*

One of the most important symbols of Britishness is, of course, the monarchy. So even if it is difficult to identify a wider set of core values that are associated with Britishness, one might anticipate that on this particular issue, at least, those who feel strongly British would have distinctive views. We asked:

> *How important or unimportant do you think it is for Britain to continue to have a monarchy*
>
> *... very important,*
> *quite important,*
> *not very important,*
> *not at all important,*
> *or, do you think the monarchy should be abolished?*

Finally, it is sometimes also argued that national identity may help to engender support for the political system and to promote social cohesion by increasing people's willingness to trust each other. The 2005 *British Social Attitudes* survey asked two relevant questions:

> *Which of these statements best describes your opinion on the present system of governing Britain?*
>
> *Works extremely well and could not be improved*
> *Could be improved in small ways but mainly works well*
> *Could be improved quite a lot*
> *Needs a great deal of improvement*
>
> *Generally speaking, would you say that most people can be trusted, or that you can't be too careful in dealing with people?*

Table 1.15 British identity and British attitudes

British identity and sense of community	Free speech very important	Trial by jury very important	Monarchy very/quite important	Present system of governing Britain works well	Most people can be trusted	Base (cols. 1–4)	Base (col. 5)
			% who think				
British; close	31	71	71	47	51	342	315
British; not close	28	70	69	41	42	389	321
Not British	35	74	65	37	46	341	308
All	31	72	69	42	46	1072	944

None of the differences in Table 1.15, either between the British and the non-British or between those who feel close to the 'imagined community' and those who do not, are at all large. While this might not be surprising so far as attitudes towards civil liberties are concerned, the differences are also surprisingly small on the importance of the monarchy. Those who feel a sense of community with fellow Britons are only five points more likely to say that it is "very" or "quite" important to have a monarchy than are those who do not feel British at all. However, there are somewhat larger differences – and in the direction we anticipated – so far as attitudes towards the present system of governing Britain are concerned. Those for whom being British is part of an imagined community are 10 points more likely than those who do not feel British to feel that the country is governed well, if not extremely well, and six points more likely than those who say they are British but do not feel particularly close to other British people.

Conclusions

We embarked on this chapter with three main aims. First, we wanted to establish whether the incidence of traditional identities had declined. Second, we wished to examine whether adherence to these identities had a social significance, that is, whether the people felt a sense of community with those who shared the same identity. Finally, we aimed to identify whether adherence to these identities was associated with support for particular values and attitudes. If the theory of individualisation is correct, then the incidence of traditional identities should have declined, while these identities should neither have much social significance nor be associated with particular values or attitudes.

However, perhaps the most important finding to emerge from this chapter is that these three sets of expectations derived from individualisation theory do not necessarily occur together. Thus, of the four traditional identities that we have examined, religious identity is the one that has declined the most yet it is also the one that is most strongly associated with support for a distinctive set of values. The proportion who claim adherence to a religious identity, let alone those who actually attend services, has declined markedly over the last forty years. Yet those who still claim adherence, and in particular those who feel close to those of the same persuasion and who attend services, are as distinctively conservative now in their attitudes towards a range of family and moral issues as they were twenty years ago. While their members may have become ever fewer in number, religious organisations continue to act as powerful normative reference groups for those that remain.

Our findings about British national identity are almost the very opposite. The decline in British identity has not been nearly as great as that in religious identity. But at the same time, we have been able to find few subjects on which those who identify themselves as British have particularly distinctive views. A sense of belonging to the 'imagined community' of Britain does not seem to have any marked effect on social attitudes. It is not in that sense a powerful normative reference group in the way that religious organisations are.

One obvious explanation for the contrast between religious identity and national identity is that the former involves not only an imagined community but a real community. Those who attend services regularly participate in and interact with each other in collective activities. While we regularly interact with our fellow-citizens in our daily lives, there is very little which brings us together specifically as British citizens. Indeed, while Britain does commemorate the fallen on Remembrance Sunday, it is relatively unusual in not having any great public days of national celebration, such as Bastille Day in France, Independence Day in Greece, Constitution Day in Norway, Liberation Day in Bulgaria, or 4th July in the USA. Imagination cannot, it seems, entirely make up for the lack of any real community relations.

Class identity and party identity (which have historically been closely associated with each other albeit less so recently) fall somewhere in between. There has been little, if any, decline in class identity, but nowadays, at least, differences in class values are relatively small compared with differences in religious values – and appear to have declined quite considerably over the past two decades. While people may still think of themselves as belonging to a particular class, social classes do not seem to act as distinctive normative references groups in the way that they once did. In part this may well be because parties are no longer particularly effective at promoting distinctively left-wing or right-wing attitudes.

There is, then, some apparent support for Beck's individualisation thesis. However, our analysis demonstrates, in a way that Beck's writing does not, the need to distinguish between the incidence of an identity and the impact of an identity. The incidence of class identity has not declined a great deal, but it no longer appears to engender support for a distinctive set of values in the contemporary world. The incidence of religious identity has declined, but it nonetheless remains highly significant for the minority who continue to belong to a religious community. 'Community is dissolved in the acid bath of competition' may be a brilliant one-liner, but the reality is that some communities, at least, still matter.

Notes

1. For a detailed discussion of the distinction and further references see Marshall *et al.* (1988).
2. In particular, since the 1970 BES the last sentence of the follow-up question addressed to those who did not say "Yes" has been "If you **had** to make a choice, would you call yourself middle class or working class" and it is this version that was implemented on our 2005 survey.
3. Table 1.1 notes: 1992 weighted to correct for over-sample in Scotland, and 2005 weighted to account for differential refusal; "Don't know" and refused included with 'did not identify'; 1964 sample is of adults aged 21 plus, others of those aged 18 plus.
4. Table 1.2 notes: people who gave a party identification but answered "Don't know" when asked how strong are included with "not very strong".
5. Readers will note that although the BES figures show the same trend over time, the proportion of strong identifiers is much higher than in the case of our survey. We, in fact, also included in our 2005 survey the sequence of questions that is asked on the BES to ascertain the direction and strength of party identification (the former of which is different from but the latter of which is the same as on *British Social Attitudes*). Just 39 per cent said that they identified "very" or "fairly" strongly with a party. One possibility for the difference is that a survey such as the BES, which is entirely about politics, is relatively less successful than a general social attitudes survey such as *British Social Attitudes* at securing the cooperation of respondents who do not have a strong party identification, a characteristic that, after all, is often accompanied by little interest in politics. Other possibilities are (i) that the content of an election survey helps arouse respondents' sense of partisanship, and (ii) that conducted somewhat closer to the election, the BES more accurately captured a heightened sense of partisanship created by the election campaign (though we should note that even when the 2005 BES respondents were first interviewed before the election the percentage that said they had a strong party identification was still as high as 45 per cent).
6. Table 1.3 notes: question not asked in 1974, hence 1970 used instead, using 'old' question wording; 1992 weighted to correct for Scottish over-sample; in 2005 those who say their attendance "varies too much to say" are included as not belonging to a religion, as are the "Don't knows".
7. See Colley (1992) for the classic account of the forging of a British nation and the emergence of British identity.

8. Bases for Table 1.7 are as follows:

% feeling they have "a lot" or "a little" more in common	Party with which respondent identifies				
Strength of party identification	Conserva-tive	Labour	Liberal Democrat	Other	All with party identity
Very or fairly strong	259	407	94	51	811
Not very strong	225	387	130	42	784
All with party identity	474	794	224	93	1595

9. Note that in this table and in Table 1.12 direction of party identity is based on the BES version of the party identification question not the *British Social Attitudes* version (see note 5 above). Respondents were asked "Generally speaking, do you think of yourself as Conservative, Labour, Liberal Democrat or what?" Only those who named a party in response to this question are regarded as party identifiers. (Although included in our 2005 survey, we ignore responses to the follow-up BES question, "Do you think of yourself as a little closer to one political party than to the others?", which is asked of those who do not name a party in response to the first question.) Strength of party identification was ascertained using the same question wording as presented at Table 1.2, but using the responses given when the question was asked (again) after the BES party identification. None of our substantive conclusions are contingent on these choices.

10. Bases for Table 1.8 are as follows:

% feeling they have "a lot" or "a little" more in common	Religion				
Strength of religious belonging	Anglican	Roman Catholic	Other Christian	Non-Christian	All who belong to a religion
Belongs to a religion, attends services	226	105	207	48	586
Belongs to a religion, never attends services	405	91	201	29	726
All who belong to a religion	631	196	408	77	1312

11. Bases for Table 1.9 are as follows:

% feeling they have "a lot" or "a little" more in common	National identity				
Strength of national identity	**British**	**English**	**Scottish**	**Welsh**	**European**
Best or only national identity	947	713	180	63	48
National identity but not best	472	377	32	22	172
All	1419	1090	212	85	220

12. See Merton (1957) for the classic statement on normative reference groups.
13. Bases for Table 1.12 are as follows:

Party identity and sense of community	% support more nationalisation	% agree government should spend more on welfare benefits	% support leaving EU/reduction in EU powers	% perceive "great" or "some" difference between Labour and Conservative
Conservative; close	204	78	204	116
Conservative; not close	274	120	274	131
Labour; close	297	119	297	158
Labour; not close	484	201	484	243
Liberal Democrat; close	91	43	91	45
Liberal Democrat; not close	129	52	129	69

14. Bases for Table 1.13 are as follows:

Religious identity and sense of community	% think sexual relations before marriage are wrong	% think woman should not be allowed abortion if does not want child	% agree suicide is never justified
Has identity; close	415	331	176
Has identity; not close	887	722	359
No identity	775	604	313

15. Bases for Table 1.14 are as follows:

Religious identity and attendance	% think sexual relations before marriage are wrong		% think woman should not be allowed abortion if does not want child	
	1984	2005	1984	2005
Has identity; attends services	629	586	562	440
Has identity; does not attend services	470	722	412	545
Does not have identity	527	783	486	582

References

Anderson, B. (1991), *Imagined Communities: Reflections on the Origin and Spread of Nationalism,* 2nd revised. edition, London: Verso

Beck, U. (1992), *Risk Society: Towards a New Modernity*, London: Sage

Beck, U. (1994), 'The reinvention of politics: towards a theory of reflexive modernization', in Beck, U., Giddens, A. and Lash, S., *Reflexive Modernization: Politics, Tradition and Aesthetics in the Modern Social Order*, Cambridge: Polity Press

Beck, U. and Beck-Gernsheim, E. (2002), *Individualization: institutionalized individualism and its social and political consequences*, London: Sage

Bromley, C. and Curtice, J. (2002), 'Where have all the voters gone?', in Park A., Curtice, J., Thomson, K., Jarvis, L. and Bromley, C. (eds.), *British Social Attitudes: the 19th report*, London: Sage

Bruce, S. (2002), *God is Dead: secularization in the West*, Cambridge: Blackwell

Butler, D.E and Stokes, D. (1974), *Political change in Britain: the evolution of electoral choice*, London: Macmillan

Clarke, H.D., Sanders, D., Stewart, M.C. and Whiteley, P. (2004), *Political Choice in Britain*, Oxford: OUP

Cohen, R. (1995), 'Fuzzy frontiers of identity: the British case', *Social Identities*, **1**: 35–62

Colley, L. (1992), *Britons: Forging the Nation 1707–1837*, New Haven: Yale University Press

Crewe, I. and Thomson, K. (1994), 'Party Loyalties: Dealignment or Realignment', in Evans, G. and Norris, P. (eds.), *Critical Elections: British Parties and Voters in Long-Term Perspective*, London: Sage

Curtice, J. and Fisher, S. (2003), 'The power to persuade? A tale of two Prime Ministers', in Park, A., Curtice, J., Thomson, K., Jarvis, L. and Bromley, C. (eds.), *British Social Attitudes: the 20th report – Continuity and change over two decades*, London: Sage

Davie, G. (1994), *Religion in Britain Since 1945: Believing without belonging*, Cambridge: Blackwell

Dogan, M. (1994), 'The decline of nationalisms within Western Europe', *Comparative Politics,* **26**: 281–305

Goodhart, D. (2006), 'National anxieties', *Prospect,* **123** (June): 30–35

Heath, A.F., Evans, G.A. and Martin, J. (1994), 'The measurement of core beliefs and values: the development of balanced socialist/laissez faire and libertarian/authoritarian scales', *British Journal of Political Science,* **24**: 115–132

Heath, A.F., Jowell, R.M. and Curtice, J.K. (1985), *How Britain Votes*, Oxford: Pergamon Press

Heath, A.F., Jowell, R. M. and Curtice, J. K. (2001), *The Rise of New Labour: Party Policies and Voter Choices*, Oxford: Oxford University Press

Heath, A.F., Taylor, B., Brook, L. and Park, A. (1999), 'British national sentiment', *British Journal of Political Science,* **29**: 155–175

Marshall, G., Newby, H., Rose, D. and Vogler, C. (1988), *Social Class in Modern Britain*, London: Hutchinson

Merton, R.K. (1957), *Social Theory and Social Structure*, New York: The Free Press

Miller, D. (1995), *On Nationality,* Oxford: OUP

Pulzer, P. (1967), *Political Representation and Elections in Britain*, London: Allen and Unwin

Rose, R. and McAllister, I. (1986), *Voters Begin to Choose: From Closed-Class to Open Elections in Britain*, London: Sage

Savage, M., Bagnall, G. and Longhurst, B. (2005), *Globalization and Belonging*, London: Sage

Voas, D. and Crockett, A. (2005), 'Religion in Britain: Neither Believing nor Belonging', *Sociology,* **39(1)**: 11–28

Acknowledgements

This chapter is based on an ESRC-funded project 'Are traditional identities in decline?' (Grant RES 154 25 0006), which is part of the ESRC's Identities Programme. We are very grateful to the Identities Programme Director, Margie Wetherell, for her encouragement and support. We have also received valuable help and advice from John Curtice, Katarina Thomson, Sarinder Hunjan and from the BSA editors, for which we are very grateful.

Appendix

In-depth qualitative interviews were conducted with 42 people between January and May 2006. All of the interviewees had previously completed our 2005 survey. Interviewees were selected to ensure that they included both genders and a wide range of ages, political affiliations, social class backgrounds and geographical locations. In the interviews respondents were invited to discuss the meaning and social significance for them of traditional identities such as 'class', 'nationality', 'Britishness', 'religion', etc. as well as of newer identities not considered in this chapter.

2 Quickening death: the euthanasia debate

Elizabeth Clery, Sheila McLean and Miranda Phillips[*]

Whether it should ever be legal to help someone who has a serious or terminal illness to end their life has become one of the most controversial and hotly debated topics of our time. The provision of such help has recently been legalised in certain circumstances in the Netherlands, Belgium and the US state of Oregon. Meanwhile, in Switzerland, where assisting someone to die is not a criminal offence so long as it is done for honourable motives,[1] a number of voluntary clinics that help people to end their lives have been established. These are used not only by Swiss citizens, but also by a growing number of foreigners including those from the UK.

Attempts to change the law have helped to stimulate debate in the UK, where hitherto it has been illegal to help someone to die. On three occasions (in 2003, 2004 and 2005), Lord Joffe introduced into the House of Lords private members' legislation that, if it had been passed, would have changed the legal position significantly. Meanwhile, controversy was occasioned by the decision of Diane Pretty – terminally ill as a result of motor neurone disease – to pursue her case that the Director of Public Prosecutions should guarantee not to prosecute her husband should he assist her to die. This went as far as the European Court of Human Rights (though the case failed).[2]

Just how topical the subject has become is demonstrated by a search we have conducted of the Lexis-Nexis database of all UK newspapers. In 1990 only around 100 articles were published that referred to assisted dying, euthanasia or assisted suicide. In 2005, in contrast, over 2,600 did. Yet even though as a result of the debate, the public has now been exposed to many an argument and counter-argument about the merits or otherwise of changing the law, it has still been argued that the public remains relatively uninformed about the subject. For

[*] Elizabeth Clery is a Senior Researcher at the *National Centre for Social Research* and is Co-Director of the *British Social Attitudes* survey series. Sheila McLean is Professor of Law and Ethics in Medicine at Glasgow University. Miranda Phillips is a Research Director at the *National Centre for Social Research* and is Co-Director of the *British Social Attitudes* survey series.

example, when Lord MacKay of Clashfern presented to the House of Lords the report of the Select Committee that examined in detail the most recent attempt to change the law (House of Lords Select Committee on the Assisted Dying for the Terminally Ill Bill, 2005), he argued that "there is a need to look behind the results of opinion polls in order to ascertain the extent to which the views expressed are based on informed opinion" and that in his view at least there was "very little public understanding of the issues involved".[3]

In this chapter we assess just what is the state of public opinion nowadays on helping someone to die in the wake of the debate that has taken place in recent years. In so doing we aim to avoid the Select Committee's dismissal of much previous opinion poll research on the subject as "simplistic ... with little or no attempt to explore the subtleties of the subject".[4] First, by showing how the public reacts when presented with a wide range of different hypothetical scenarios where someone might be helped to die, we are able to demonstrate the degree to which attitudes towards helping someone to die depend on the conditions and circumstances under which it might be done. Secondly, by looking at who supports and who opposes helping someone to die we can uncover some of the influences and arguments that underpin and explain why people hold the views that they do. At the same time we are also able to give an indication of how much public opinion has changed in the wake of the debate of recent years.

We begin, however, with two important preliminaries. First, we outline some of the key terms we use in the chapter and some of the distinctions that need to be drawn between different ways in which people might be helped to die. Then, secondly, we outline the arguments that are put forward by those on either side of the debate. This latter exercise will provide us with an invaluable guide when later in the chapter we attempt to ascertain why people have the views that they do.

Defining assisted dying

Our primary interest in this chapter is in what is known as 'assisted dying'. By this we mean helping an individual *who wishes to die* to do so. But assisted dying comes in a number of different forms. One crucial distinction is between 'assisted suicide' and 'voluntary euthanasia'. In the case of 'assisted suicide' someone is helped to take for themselves a substance that will end their life. In the case of 'voluntary euthanasia', in contrast, someone else administers a substance to the person to enable them to die, for example a lethal injection. Meanwhile, a second distinction concerns who provides the help, that is whether it is provided by a medical practitioner or someone else, such as a close relative. Thus an assisted suicide might be a 'physician-assisted suicide' or a 'suicide assisted by a relative'. Equally, we could have 'voluntary euthanasia administered by a doctor' or 'voluntary euthanasia administered by a relative'.

Clearly we cannot assume that all of these forms of assisted dying are equally acceptable to the general public and in this chapter we will examine how far these distinctions make a difference to people's attitudes to assisted dying. These distinctions have certainly proved important legally. True, the reform introduced in the Netherlands in 2002 legalised both voluntary euthanasia and assisted suicide, albeit only when performed by a doctor. However, in Belgium only voluntary euthanasia has been legalised while in Oregon only physician-assisted suicide has been. Although Lord Joffe's proposed reform in the UK would originally have permitted both voluntary euthanasia administered by a doctor and physician-assisted suicide, the House of Lords Select Committee recommended that any eventual reform should consider the two separately. Incidentally, existing legislative practice also draws our attention to another important distinction – in Oregon the practice of assisted dying is only allowed if someone is terminally ill (as was also the case in Lord Joffe's third attempt at reform), whereas in the Netherlands this is not the case.

We also need to bear in mind that there are practices that hasten a patient's death that are not voluntary. '*Non-voluntary* euthanasia' occurs when the views of the patient cannot be elicited, for example because they are in a coma, and euthanasia is requested or authorised by a relative or doctor. '*Involuntary* euthanasia' means ending the life of a patient against their expressed wishes, perhaps on the authorisation of a doctor or relative. While the principal focus of this chapter is on assisted dying, we will also pay some attention to people's attitudes towards what should happen when a patient is not currently in a position to express their views.

The debate about assisted dying

Advocates of the legalisation of at least some forms of assisted dying rely primarily on two arguments. (For a full discussion see McLean and Britton, 1996). The first, and more important, argues that people should be granted the autonomy to decide for themselves what to do with their lives. After all, people generally have a right to make their own decisions about how they live their life, so they should be permitted to make choices about their death too. To this essentially human-rights-based argument, two further considerations are often appended. First, in the event that they have an incurable and perhaps degenerative illness people should be able to decide at what point the *quality* of their lives is too poor for them to want to continue living. Second, where someone might be facing the prospect of a protracted and painful death, it is argued that they should be able to choose to die with 'dignity', that is, dying at a time of their own choosing when they are still in control of their faculties and abilities.

Supporters of legalisation also argue that the law is inconsistent as it stands. They point out that people are legally permitted to reject life-sustaining treatment.[5] More importantly, perhaps, people in hopeless conditions, such as a permanent vegetative state, are sometimes denied food and water in the certain knowledge that this will result in their death,[6] while severely ill or disabled babies are sometimes denied treatment, again in the certain expectation that they will die.[7] Both of these latter steps, it is argued, are practices by which the death of a patient is hastened even though they are not capable of expressing their wishes. Why then, should an assisted death be denied to those who are competently able to request it?

Opponents of assisted dying meanwhile deploy four main arguments. The first holds that all human life – irrespective of its actual or perceived quality – is sacred. It is, therefore, impermissible to take a life in any circumstances. Those of a religious persuasion sometimes further argue that life is a gift from God and therefore only God can take it away. Those who hold such a position will, of course, find suicide objectionable too. Their view is clearly contrary to the position that individuals have the right autonomously to choose whether to live or die.

The second argument is more pragmatic. It can broadly be called the 'slippery slope' argument. Essentially it takes the form that if we once permit A (which may be seen as morally neutral, or at least not 'bad'), we will then inevitably be driven to accept B (which is less acceptable) and then finally C (which is always objectionable). So if we allow some carefully controlled assisted deaths, it will be all too easy to expand the categories and loosen the controls, so that eventually we will reach the point where people are in danger of being killed even when they have not asked to die.

The third argument points out the pressure under which older people might be placed if assisted dying were to become available. If an older person falls ill or needs care, they might feel themselves to be a burden on their family and feel compelled to seek assisted dying as a result. Fourthly, it is argued that it should never be a doctor's job to kill. His or her obligation is to cure, to palliate and to care, not to end a patient's life.

Attitudes to assisted dying

We now turn to our first principal task, which is to assess how the public reacts when presented with a wide range of circumstances in which someone might be helped to die. We aim first of all to establish under what circumstances, if any, it might be acceptable to help someone to die. Then we consider attitudes to the different forms that such help might take.

We presented respondents to our 2005 survey with descriptions of patients with different conditions, a number of which were incurable or terminal. In each case we then asked them whether the law should allow someone to help them end their lives should they so wish. For the moment, we will focus on the option that this help is provided by a doctor in the form of voluntary euthanasia. This approach enables us to focus on how ill someone has to be before it is regarded as acceptable to provide help with dying to those that request it.

Voluntary euthanasia administered by a doctor

The introductory text to each of these scenarios read as follows:

> *Now I would like to ask some questions about voluntary euthanasia –*
> *that is, when someone ends the life of another person **at their request**.*
> *I will read you some circumstances in which someone might ask a*
> ***doctor** to end their life. In each case please tell me whether you think*
> *a doctor should be allowed by law to do so*

Then, for example, the first scenario was described as follows:

> *First, a person with an incurable and painful illness, from which they*
> *will die – for example someone dying of cancer. Do you think that, if*
> *they ask for it, a doctor should ever be allowed by law to end their*
> *life, or not?*

Altogether five scenarios were presented in this way. The results are shown in
Table 2.1.

Table 2.1 Levels of support for voluntary euthanasia

% saying that, if the person asks for it, a doctor should "definitely" or "probably" be allowed by law to end their life		*Base*
A person …		
… with an incurable and painful illness, from which they will die – for example, someone dying of cancer	80	*2176*
… with an incurable illness, from which they will die, and who says their suffering is unbearable	74	*1101*
… with an incurable and painful illness, from which they will not die	45	*1101*
… who is not in much pain nor in danger of death, but becomes permanently and completely dependent on relatives for all their needs – for example, someone who cannot feed, wash or go to the toilet by themselves	43	*2176*
… with an incurable and painful illness, from which they will not die – for example, someone with severe arthritis	33	*1075*

The public acceptability of voluntary euthanasia clearly depends on how ill
someone is. In the case of the two scenarios where the patient was described as
being terminally ill, a large majority of around three-quarters or so say that the
law should "definitely" or "probably" allow voluntary euthanasia. Indeed we
should note that the wording of the second of these – someone who is both
terminally ill and says that their suffering is unbearable – closely mirrors the

wording used in Lord Joffe's second Bill, suggesting that in this respect at least the Bill came quite close to reflecting public opinion. In contrast, in the case of the three scenarios where the patient's illness might be incurable and painful but is not terminal, less than half support voluntary euthanasia. Intriguingly, support was particularly low when the scenario mentioned a specific condition – severe arthritis. Only one in three felt that having this condition would render voluntary euthanasia acceptable. Perhaps some people underestimate the pain that those with severe arthritis can suffer – or perhaps they think voluntary euthanasia should be reserved for 'exceptional' circumstances, and that arthritis is simply too common a condition to be regarded as sufficient grounds to permit euthanasia.

These findings suggest that the public does not regard voluntary euthanasia in the black and white terms in which it tends to be regarded by its advocates and opponents. On the one hand, the public does not accept that individuals necessarily have the right to choose for themselves whether to end their life – a majority reject the right of those with an incurable but not terminal condition to request euthanasia. On the other hand, life is evidently not regarded as so sacred that a majority are not willing to accept that an apparently inevitable death might be hastened at a patient's request. Evidently, as the House of Lords Select Committee argued, it is necessary to address the subtleties of this subject if the public's stance is to be properly understood.

Physician-assisted suicide and voluntary euthanasia administered by a relative

So far, however, we have only examined the public's views in respect of one form of assisted dying, voluntary euthanasia administered by a doctor. We cannot assume that they will take the same view of assisted suicide or situations where a relative rather than a doctor administers euthanasia. In order to establish the public's attitudes towards these forms of assisted dying we repeated the scenarios outlined in Table 2.1 but asked instead either whether the law should allow a physician-assisted suicide or whether it should allow a relative to administer euthanasia. A physician-assisted suicide was described as follows:

> *Do you think that, if this person asks for it, a doctor should ever be allowed by law to give them lethal medication that will allow the person to take their own life?*

Meanwhile, voluntary euthanasia administered by a relative was introduced by asking:

> *And if they [i.e. the patient] ask a close **relative** to end their life, should the law ever allow the close relative to do so, or not?*

Table 2.2 compares for each scenario the level of support for these forms of assisted dying compared with that for voluntary euthanasia administered by a doctor.

Table 2.2 Levels of support for alternative forms of assisted dying

% "definitely" or "probably" should be allowed for a person …	Voluntary euthan-asia by doctor	Physician-assisted suicide	Voluntary euthan-asia by relative	Base
… with an incurable and painful illness, from which they will die – for example, someone dying of cancer	80	60	44	2176
… with an incurable illness, from which they will die, and who says their suffering is unbearable	74	58	n/a	1101
… with an incurable and painful illness, from which they will not die	45	40	n/a	1101
… who is not in much pain nor in danger of death, but becomes permanently and completely dependent on relatives for all their needs – for example, someone who cannot feed, wash or go to the toilet by themselves	43	n/a	24	2176
… with an incurable and painful illness, from which they will not die – for example, someone with severe arthritis	33	32	n/a	1075

n/a = not asked

Neither physician-assisted suicide nor (especially) voluntary euthanasia administered by a relative are as acceptable to the public as is voluntary euthanasia administered by a doctor. For example, as we have already seen, no less than four in five feel that the law should allow a doctor to administer voluntary euthanasia to someone dying of cancer. But only three in five feel that a doctor should be allowed to help them commit suicide, while well under half, 44 per cent, believe that a relative should be allowed to administer euthanasia. These results mimic those found in an earlier study in which patients themselves expressed a preference for voluntary euthanasia over physician-assisted suicide by two to one, whereas doctors took the opposite view (McLean and Britton, 1996). Even so, there is still majority support for physician-assisted suicide when a patient is terminally ill. In contrast, the distinction between voluntary euthanasia and physician-assisted suicide seems to matter less for the minority who believe that assisted dying should be legalised for those who are not terminally ill – perhaps because this group is more likely to support the 'principle' of assisted dying whatever the circumstances.

So overall it appears that majority support for assisted dying is confined to situations where the patient is terminally ill, and is dependent on a doctor rather than a relative being involved. There are a number of reasons why people might feel that a medical professional should be involved rather than a relative. A doctor can be expected to be able to take a more detached, less emotional view of the situation. Relatives may not have the expertise to administer euthanasia effectively. And, of course, it might be feared that relatives could pressurise an elderly relative into apparently asking for an assisted death. Evidently, if any form of assisted dying is ever to be introduced in the UK, it is doctors who will be expected to take on the role of hastening their patient's death.

When the patient cannot express his or her wishes

So far we have examined attitudes towards providing an assisted death to someone who has expressed a wish to die. However, people with serious conditions may not be in a position to state their wishes. They may, for example, be in a coma or a permanent vegetative state, with no apparent prospect of recovery. Yet, perhaps, they would prefer not to be kept alive in that situation. Equally, questions may be raised about whether someone should be kept alive when all that stands between them and death is the working of a life support machine.

First of all we asked respondents to our survey to consider the following situation where non-voluntary euthanasia might be being contemplated:

> Now think about what should happen to someone who has an incurable illness which leaves them unable to make a decision about their **own** future. For instance, imagine a person in a coma on a **life support machine** who is never expected to regain consciousness

They were then asked whether a doctor should ever be allowed by law to turn the machine off if (i) their relatives agreed, and (ii) if they did not agree. No less than 79 per cent feel that doctors "definitely" or "probably" should be allowed to turn the machine off if the relatives *did* agree. But on the other hand, just 34 per cent felt that they should be allowed to do so if the relatives *did not* agree. Although, as we saw earlier, there are doubts about whether relatives should be directly involved in voluntary euthanasia, they are evidently regarded as having an important role when non-voluntary euthanasia is being considered. Presumably it is hoped relatives will have some understanding of and respect for the likely wishes of the patient in this situation.

Indeed relatives are also regarded as having an important role in the event that consideration is being given to not resuscitating someone if they stop breathing. Over three-quarters (77 per cent) state that a doctor should consult relatives before implementing a 'do not resuscitate' order, while nearly two-thirds (65 per cent) think that doctors should follow the relatives' wishes even if the doctors themselves disagree with their decision.

However, it is possible for someone who falls into a coma or stops breathing to give an indication in advance of what they themselves would want to happen to them. This is done by making an 'advance directive' or 'living will'. Indeed, such wills have recently been given legal status in England and Wales by the Mental Capacity Act 2005 (sections 24–26). We explained to our respondents that:

> *Some people make what is called a 'living will', saying what they would wish to happen if they have an incurable illness which left them unable to make a decision about their own future. This living will might include instructions about what medical treatment they would or would not want to be given in the future to keep them alive*

We then asked them a series of questions about whether or not doctors should be required by law to follow such instructions. In addition we asked what should happen if a patient had nominated someone, who we term a "patient representative", to take a decision on their behalf about what treatment they should receive. Table 2.3 shows the answers we received.

Table 2.3 Attitudes towards living wills and patient representatives

% who think ...		Base
... the law should require that doctors carry out the instructions of a living will	78	1101
... the law should allow doctors to carry out the instructions of a living will, even if close relatives do not agree	76	1101
... the law should require that doctors carry out the instructions of a living will if it states that the patient should always be given the food and nutrition needed to stay alive if they fall into a coma from which they would not recover	56	1101
... doctors should always make the final decision about what is right, even if goes against the living will	20	1773
... the law should require that doctors consult a person chosen by the patient who they would like doctors to consult about their medical treatment in case they should become unable to make these decisions themselves	86	2176
... the law should require that doctors should carry out the wishes of a person chosen by a patient in this way	77	2176

For the most part clear majorities believe that the instructions of a living will should be followed – even if relatives or doctors disagree. Thus no less than 78 per cent say that the law should require doctors to carry out the instructions of a living will, a figure that only falls by two points should close relatives disagree with those instructions. Meanwhile only one in five feel that doctors should always make the final decision, irrespective of the instructions of a living will.

Similar views are also expressed about following the instructions of a nominated patient's representative; 77 per cent say that doctors should be required to follow the representative's wishes, almost exactly the same proportion as said that the instructions of a living will should be followed.

However, there is some ambivalence about the proper status of living wills in certain circumstances. Only somewhat more than half (56 per cent) think that doctors should be required to follow a patient's instructions if they have stated that they "should always be given the food and nutrition needed to stay alive if they fall into a coma from which they would not recover". This issue was recently considered in the case of *Burke v GMC* where the court repeated the position that doctors cannot be forced to provide treatment that is futile.[8] Since assisted nutrition and hydration (as opposed to someone being able to eat and drink for themselves) are regarded as a form of medical treatment, this position means that they can be withdrawn.[9] It appears to be a subject on which the public is significantly divided.

In any event we should bear in mind that, as described in our survey at least, a living will is a means by which a patient who is unconscious can refuse further medical treatment. It therefore in effect gives them the same rights that a conscious patient already has and is not a mechanism by which a patient can request an assisted death. This perhaps helps to explain the strong support for such wills that we have uncovered in our survey.

Who supports assisted dying and why?

We now turn to the second main aim of this chapter, which is to try to identify what induces people to support or oppose assisted dying, bearing in mind the arguments that are commonly put forward in support and opposition. Those arguments, as outlined above, certainly lead us to expect some groups to be more in favour of the legalisation of assisted dying than others. In particular, given that most religions and religious denominations emphasise the sanctity of life, we would expect that those who attend a religious service regularly would be most likely to oppose any form of assisted dying while those who do not adhere to any religion at all would be least likely to object. On the other hand, some denominations, such as the Roman Catholic Church, argue to a greater degree than others that life is a gift from God that no human should take away. So we might find that opposition is more common amongst those of some religious persuasions than others. At the same time we should also bear in mind Donnison and Bryson's finding (1996), based on the 1995 *British Social Attitudes* survey, that people with a disability were more likely to be in favour of assisted dying, perhaps because they had greater empathy with those in pain.

However, as well as looking at whether those in certain social groups are more or less likely to support assisted dying, we can also examine whether those who appear to support the values that lie behind the arguments for and against assisted dying adopt the position we would expect. In particular, are those who in other respects demonstrate an apparent belief in the sanctity of life more likely to oppose assisted dying? And are those who appear to believe in the autonomy of the individual more likely to support the legalisation of assisted dying? If the answer to these two questions is affirmative, then it would appear that public attitudes are shaped by the principal arguments espoused by the supporters and opponents of legalisation – and thus they might be regarded as reasonably consistent and well informed.

We are able to measure support for the broad principle of 'sanctity of life' in our 2005 survey by examining our respondents' attitudes to three questions: whether a woman who does not want a baby should be allowed an abortion; whether the death penalty is appropriate for some crimes; and whether suicide is ever justified. Meanwhile, we can measure a tendency to favour individual autonomy by looking at where respondents stand on a libertarian–authoritarian scale about which further details can be found in Appendix I of this Report. This scale is useful for our purposes, as those on the libertarian end of this scale give answers to the scale's component items that suggest they incline to the view that individuals should determine their own morality rather than being required to follow a moral code imposed by society as a whole. However, we also have available to us two further possible indicators. These are: how much say a patient should have in the timing of a hospital outpatients' appointment, and how much say those who are dying should have in how they are treated.[10]

Meanwhile we should perhaps also bear in mind that people's attitudes towards assisted dying might be influenced by their attitudes towards the National Health Service (NHS). Given the important role that doctors are likely to play in any provision of assisted dying we might anticipate that those who have little trust in the NHS or are dissatisfied with its performance will be less likely to support assisted dying.

We wish, then, to see whether those who belong to particular social groups or who adopt certain viewpoints are more or less likely to support assisted dying. To obtain a general measure of support for assisted dying, a scale was developed, based on responses to five of the scenarios outlined earlier.[11] The first three of these scenarios concerned the respondent's attitude to voluntary euthanasia administered by a doctor, physician-assisted suicide and voluntary euthanasia administered by a relative when the patient has "an incurable and painful disease from which they will die". The other two scenarios concerned the respondent's attitude to both forms of voluntary euthanasia in the case of a patient "who is not in much pain or danger of death, but becomes permanently and completely dependent on relatives for all their needs". Each respondent's scale score is simply the total number of these scenarios where the respondent said that assisted dying should "definitely" or "probably" be allowed by law.[12] Thus the higher a respondent's score the greater the number of scenarios in which they said that assisted dying should be allowed.

We have to bear in mind that a number of the possible influences on attitudes towards assisted dying that we have identified could well be correlated with each other. For example, we expect those who attend religious services to be more likely to be opposed to abortion. Once we have taken into account the link between one of these factors and attitudes towards assisted dying, the other may not add anything further to our analysis. Therefore, to establish which of the possible influences appear to make an independent contribution to our ability to account for people's attitudes towards assisted dying, we have undertaken a multivariate analysis (specifically, linear regression, more details about which can be found in Appendix I of this Report) of each respondent's scale score. First, we examined what happened when we only included as variables in our models the kinds of social groups to which a respondent belongs. Then we undertook an analysis in which all of the various attitudinal measures we have outlined were included as well. The full results of these models are given in the appendix to this chapter (Table A.1). Here in Table 2.4 we show the average scores on our five-point scale for those variables that proved to be significantly and independently associated with attitudes towards assisted dying.

Table 2.4 Mean scores on euthanasia scale, by respondent characteristics and attitudes

Variable	Mean score	Base
Attendance at religious service		
Once a week or more	1.4	206
Never or practically never	2.8	1081
Religion		
No religion	2.9	825
Anglican/Church of England	2.7	568
Roman Catholic	2.4	198
Other Christian	2.3	380
Non-Christian	2.2	77
Patient near end of life should have say in medical treatment		
A great deal	2.8	1216
Quite a lot	2.4	666
A little	2.3	112
None at all	1.6	28
For some crimes, the death penalty is the most appropriate sentence		
Agree strongly	2.9	473
Agree	2.7	537
Neither	2.4	233
Disagree	2.3	263
Disagree strongly	2.3	265
Woman who does not want to have child should be allowed an abortion		
Law should allow	2.9	1034
Law should not allow	2.2	545
Suicide is never justified, no matter how bad things are		
Agree strongly	1.9	288
Agree	2.4	425
Neither agree/disagree	2.8	383
Disagree	3.2	340
Disagree strongly	3.3	148

Thus, for example, we can see that those who attend a religious service once a week or more say that assisted dying should be allowed in only 1.4 of our five scenarios. In contrast, those who never or practically never attend a religious service support assisted dying in twice as many scenarios: 2.8. Indeed, how often someone attends a religious service proves to be the single most important variable in our analysis. It may be that a high level of attendance reflects a prior commitment to a faith and acceptance of its approach to issues of life and death. But, equally, regular exposure to religious teachings might inform and reinforce attitudes to assisted dying. Certainly, religion is a key mechanism through which opposition to assisted dying is both generated and maintained.

In contrast, we find only small and mostly insignificant differences in attitudes between those who belong to different Christian denominations. However, those who belong to a non-Christian religion are significantly less likely to support assisted dying than are those who do not claim membership of any religion at all. But more importantly we can see that even though we have taken into account a respondent's religious background, a belief in the sanctity of life is still independently associated with attitudes to dying. Those who oppose suicide, capital punishment and abortion are all significantly more likely to oppose assisted dying. For example, opponents of abortion support assisted dying on 2.2 of our scenarios while the average number for supporters is 2.9. That all three of our measures make a difference suggests that public opposition towards assisted dying is indeed strongly grounded in a belief that all human life is sacred and that it is unacceptable for humans to play a role in deciding the time of their death.

At the same time, one of our measures of individual autonomy also makes an appearance in our table. The more say that a respondent feels a patient near the end of his or her life should have in their medical treatment, the more likely they are to support assisted dying. Other measures of individual autonomy, such as views on the timing of hospital outpatient appointments, were related, but not significantly so. So there is some evidence that the main argument used in support of assisted dying – belief in the autonomy of the individual – is reflected in public attitudes too.

Two of our expectations, however, are not fulfilled. First, there is no evidence that attitudes towards assisted dying reflect attitudes towards the NHS. Secondly, and perhaps more importantly, in contrast to the results of the 1995 survey, those with a disability are not more likely to support assisted dying. Indeed at 2.4 their average score on our scale is actually slightly below that of 2.6 amongst those without a disability. This may be because disability was measured slightly differently in the 1995 and 2005 surveys, resulting in a higher proportion of disabled respondents in 2005,[13] or because the scales constructed to summarise support for assisted dying were not identical. But it may be that the increased media coverage and debate about assisted dying has helped to change the views of a group that might be thought to be particularly vulnerable in the event of a change of policy.

Public opinion towards assisted dying appears, then, to reflect rather well the arguments that have been put forward in support of and opposition to assisted dying. Those of a religious disposition and those who believe in the sanctity of life are most likely to oppose the legalisation of assisted dying. Meanwhile we have some evidence that those who particularly emphasise the autonomy of the individual are especially likely to be in favour. Rather than being superficial or unstructured our evidence suggests that public attitudes towards assisted dying are quite firmly rooted in certain beliefs – and thus cannot easily be dismissed, as Lord MacKay was inclined to do, as demonstrating very little understanding of the issues involved.

How have attitudes to assisted dying changed?

If attitudes towards assisted dying are embedded in certain beliefs then we might anticipate that they do not change very easily. We thus look briefly in this final section of the chapter at whether the picture we have painted of attitudes in 2005 is much the same as it has been in the past.

One general question on attitudes towards voluntary euthanasia has been asked on a number of occasions on previous *British Social Attitudes* surveys. The question reads:

> *Suppose a person has a painful incurable disease. Do you think that doctors should be allowed by law to end the patient's life, if the patient requests it?*

Table 2.5 Attitudes to voluntary euthanasia, 1984–2005

Should law allow doctor to end life of patient with painful incurable disease?	1984	1989	1994	2005
	%	%	%	%
Yes	75	79	82	80
No	24	20	15	18
Base	1562	1274	1000	1786

Table 2.5 shows that, in fact, the answers to this question have indeed been rather stable since it was first asked in 1984. However, whereas in 1984 three-quarters said the law should allow voluntary euthanasia in these circumstances, by 1994 the figure had increased to 82 per cent. It appeared that there was a slow secular trend towards increasing support for voluntary euthanasia. But if such a trend did exist between 1984 and 1994 it certainly seems subsequently to have come to a halt – now the proportion responding affirmatively to our question has slipped slightly to 80 per cent.

We can look further at whether or not there has been any change in attitudes over the last decade in particular, by comparing the pattern of responses to four of the scenarios included in our 2005 survey with those obtained when these same scenarios were included in the 1995 *British Social Attitudes* survey.[14] This exercise is undertaken in Table 2.6. It suggests that there has not been a consistent change in attitudes in either direction. In two instances support for assisted dying has been constant or increased, while in the remaining two it has fallen.

Table 2.6 Attitudes towards assisted dying, 1995–2005

% saying should definitely or probably be allowed by law	1995	2005	Change
Voluntary euthanasia administered by a doctor when patient ...			
... has an incurable, painful, terminal illness, for example, cancer	80	80	0
... is not in much pain or danger of death but dependent on relatives for all needs	51	43	-8
... has an incurable, painful illness from which they will not die, for example, severe arthritis	41	33	-8
Voluntary euthanasia administered by a relative when patient ...			
... has an incurable, painful, terminal illness, for example, cancer	31	44	+13
Base	*1234*	*2176*	

Still, it might be a mistake to assume that nothing of note has changed over the last decade. After all, the two scenarios where support for assisted dying has fallen share the characteristic that they refer to a situation where the patient is not terminally ill. It may be that our finding earlier in this chapter that a majority of the public only support assisted dying when a patient is terminally ill is even more the case now than it was a decade ago. Meanwhile, we might note too that the one instance where support for assisted dying has actually increased is in the case of the scenario involving voluntary euthanasia administered by a relative. It may be that some of the media attention on this issue in recent years, such as that stimulated by the Diane Pretty case, may have had a particular impact on people's attitudes.

Nevertheless, if we look at the trends over the last ten years in what we have identified as some of the key characteristics associated with opposition to assisted dying, we can see that there is little reason why any major across the board change should have occurred. The proportion who attend a religious service once a week or more has only declined from 12 per cent in 1995 to 10 per cent now. Attitudes to abortion are little changed, while the proportion agreeing that suicide is never justified has only fallen by four points from 48 per cent to 44 per cent. Perhaps only in the case of the death penalty has there been any change of note; 59 per cent now say the death penalty is sometimes the most appropriate punishment compared with 66 per cent ten years ago. But on its own this is far from sufficient to bring about a substantial change in attitudes towards assisted dying.

We should, though, note one feature of public opinion that has changed somewhat and is not revealed by Table 2.6. On all four of our scenarios there has been an increase in the combined proportion saying either that the law "probably" should allow assisted dying to take place or that it "probably" should not (and a decrease in the proportions choosing the "definitely" options). The increase ranges from four points in the case of the patient who is dependent on their relatives to 14 points in the case of voluntary euthanasia involving a relative. The public has apparently become a little less certain of its stance about assisted dying, an indication perhaps of an increasing awareness of the nuances and subtleties of the debate surrounding the subject.

Conclusions

In certain respects, at least, the current law that prohibits assisted dying seems to be at odds with public opinion. Clear majorities accept that a doctor should be allowed to hasten the death of someone who is painfully and terminally ill. Support for this position appears to be particularly strong in the case of voluntary euthanasia administered by a doctor, somewhat less so for physician-assisted suicide. On the other hand, only a minority support assisted dying if someone is in pain or dependent, but not terminally ill.

One of our objectives was to assess how well-informed public views are on this issue. Our evidence suggests two reasons why this balance of public support for and opposition to assisted dying cannot be dismissed as uninformed or superficial. First, despite the explosion of debate and media commentary on the subject, what is most remarkable about public opinion now is how similar it is to ten years ago. The picture of public opinion we have painted seems largely to be a stable one. Secondly, we have demonstrated that public attitudes reflect the arguments that have been put forward by advocates and opponents of the legalisation of assisted dying in recent years. Those who demonstrate a concern for the sanctity of life are those who are most opposed to assisted dying, especially if they practise a religion. Those who are concerned about individual autonomy are inclined to the opposite view. Attitudes towards assisted dying appear to be consistently rooted in a wider set of values.

The disjuncture between the current law on assisted dying and majority public opinion thus seems unlikely simply to disappear. Pressure to mount further attempts to change the law in some ways at least looks set to continue. When an attempt is made, the arguments on both sides are likely to be both passionate and well informed. It remains to be seen how the debate will be resolved.

Notes

1. Swiss Penal Code (1942), Article 115.
2. *Pretty v United Kingdom* (application 2346/02) (2002) Family Law Reports 45.
3. Lords Hansard, 10 October 2005, col. 14, available at
   http://www.publications.parliament.uk/pa/ld199900/ldhansrd/pdvn/lds05/text/51010
   -04.htm
4. Lords Hansard, 10 October 2005, col. 14, available at
   http://www.publications.parliament.uk/pa/ld199900/ldhansrd/pdvn/lds05/text/51010
   -04.htm
5. *Ms B v NHS Hospital Trust* (2002) 65 Butterworths Medico-Legal Reports 149.
6. See, for example, *Airedale NHS Trust v Bland* (1993) 1 All England Law Reports
   821.
7. See, for example, *Re C (a minor) (medical treatment)* (1997) 40 Butterworths
   Medico-Legal Reports 31; *Re Wyatt (a child) (medical treatment: parents' consent)*
   (2004) Family Law 866.
8. *Burke v GMC* (2005) EWCA Civ 1003 (28 July 2005), available at
   http://www.bailii.org
9. *Airedale NHS Trust v Bland*; for discussion, see McLean (2006).
10. Respondents were asked how much say an individual should have about the timing
    of their outpatients' appointments, and how much say the dying should have in their
    medical treatment. The answer options provided were "a great deal", "quite a lot",
    "a little" or "none at all".
11. These scenarios were chosen because they were the only ones to be asked of all
    respondents to the module. The remainder were only asked of (different) halves of
    the sample.
12. We also constructed a second scale in which we simply added up the total number of
    scenarios where the respondent said assisted dying should "definitely" be allowed.
    This did not make any difference to our substantive findings.
13. The 1995 survey asked respondents whether they had a "long-standing health
    condition or disability", whereas the 2005 survey asked if they had a "long-standing
    physical or mental health problem or disability", defining "long-standing" as having
    lasted at least 12 months. In 1995, 23 per cent defined themselves as disabled and in
    2005, 33 per cent place themselves in this category.
14. We should note that in 2005 respondents were given the option of not answering any
    of our questions on euthanasia, perhaps because they found them too painful. In
    contrast, this option was not available in 1995. In the event just two per cent availed
    themselves of the option in 2005.

References

Donnison, D. and Bryson, C. (1996), 'Matters of Life and Death: Attitudes to Euthanasia', in Jowell, R., Curtice, J., Park A., Brook, L. and Thomson, K. (eds.), *British Social Attitudes: the 13th Report*, Aldershot: Dartmouth

House of Lords Select Committee on the Assisted Dying for the Terminally Ill Bill (2005), *Assisted Dying for the Terminally Ill Bill [HL] Volume I: Report*, Session 2004–2005, HL Paper 86–I, London: The Stationery Office

McLean, S. (2006), 'From Bland to Burke: The Law and Politics of Assisted Nutrition and Hydration', in McLean, S. (ed.), *First Do No Harm: Law, Ethics and Healthcare*, Aldershot, Ashgate

McLean, S. and Britton A. (1996), *Sometimes a Small Victory*, Glasgow: Institute of Law and Ethics in Medicine

Acknowledgements

The *National Centre for Social Research* is grateful to the Nuffield Foundation for their financial support which enabled us to ask the questions reported in this chapter from 2005, although the views expressed are those of the authors alone.

Appendix

Table A.1 Linear regression – socio-demographic and attitudinal characteristics

Characteristic (comparison group in brackets)	Model 1 Socio-demographic characteristics	Model 2 Socio-demographic characteristics and attitudinal characteristics
N	2051	2051
R2	.120	.230
Socio-demographic characteristics		
Age (for increase by one year)	-.001	-.004
Marital status (married)		
Cohabiting	-.153	.102
Divorced/separated	-.371*	-.021
Widowed	.191	-.032
Never married	-.148	-.139
Ethnicity (white)		
Non-white	.560**	.429
Highest educational qualification (no qualification)		
Degree	-.037	.252
Higher education below degree	-.141	.258
A level or equivalent	-.251	.073
O level/GCSE or equivalent	-.090	.273
CSE or equivalent	.073	.640**
Region (Scotland)		
England/Wales	-.118	-.044
Attendance at religious service (less than once a week)		
Once a week or more	1.136**	828**
Religion (no religion)		
Other Christian	.301	.036
Roman Catholic	.077	-.050
Anglican/Church of England	.084	.140
Non-Christian	.434**	.309*
Gender (female)		
Male	.009	-.023
Disability (have disability)		
Do not have disability	.041	-.022
Satisfaction with NHS		
Decrease in satisfaction by one unit (very satisfied, quite satisfied, neither satisfied nor dissatisfied, quite dissatisfied, very dissatisfied)		.030

table continued on next page

Trust in NHS (How much trust in doctors to put patient's interests over those of hospital?)
Decrease in frequency by one unit (always, most of the time, some of the time, just about never)   .108

Hospital outpatient should have say over timing of appointment
Decrease in amount of say by one unit (a great deal, quite a lot, a little, none at all)   -.089

Patient near end of life should have say in medical treatment
Decrease in amount of say by one unit (a great deal, quite a lot, a little, none at all)   -.182*

Libertarian–authoritarian scale
Decrease by one unit from libertarian towards authoritarian   -.136

For some crimes, the death penalty is the most appropriate sentence
Decrease in support by one unit (agree strongly, agree, neither agree nor disagree, disagree, disagree strongly)   -.216**

Woman who does not want to have child should be allowed abortion (Law should allow)
Law should not allow   -.445**

Suicide is never justified, no matter how bad things are
Decrease in support by one unit (agree strongly, agree, neither agree nor disagree, disagree, disagree strongly)   .306**

* = Significant at 5% level
** = Significant at 1% level

3 Are we all working too hard? Women, men, and changing attitudes to employment

*Rosemary Crompton and Clare Lyonette**

In Britain, the world of paid employment has undergone considerable change over the last twenty years. After the de-industrialisation of the 1980s, it was increasingly argued not only that economic growth (and thus high levels of employment) was unsustainable, but also that the nature of paid work had changed irrevocably (Handy, 1984). Jobs were increasingly characterised by apparent insecurities, deriving from managerial practices such as organisational 'delayering' (for example, removing supervisory and managerial positions) and 'outsourcing' (subcontracting catering, cleaning and other tasks once carried out 'in-house'). It was suggested that self-employment would rise to meet the needs of outsourcing, as would non-permanent forms of employment such as fixed term contracts. Even by the year 2000, Beck was still describing 'the Brazilianization of the West' – that is, a massive shift towards casual, insecure employment – as virtually inevitable. In some contrast, more optimistic predictions argued that in wealthier societies (such as Britain) we should anticipate a move towards 'post-materialist' values, that is, less of an emphasis on material rewards. For example, Inglehart (1997: 44) has argued that:

> there is ... a gradual shift in what motivates people to work: emphasis shifts from maximising one's income and job security toward a growing insistence on interesting and meaningful work.

This change, it is suggested, is associated with a greater focus on non-work activities such as family life and leisure.

Neither the pessimists nor the optimists seem to have been correct in their predictions. Recent research suggests that job tenure has not declined markedly in recent years, and a third of the UK workforce has been with the same employer for over ten years (Nolan, 2003). Thus in aggregate, jobs are not becoming more insecure, rates of self-employment are not rising, and most employees have permanent contracts of employment (Taylor, 2002). Moreover,

* Rosemary Crompton is Professor of Sociology; Clare Lyonette is a Research Officer – both at City University.

the evidence we are going to present in this chapter suggests that work motivations have not changed substantially since the end of the 1980s.

Nevertheless, other substantial changes *have* taken place. Women have continued to play an increasingly important role in the labour market in Britain. Leaving aside those who were retired, only just over half (55 per cent) of women interviewed by the 1989 *British Social Attitudes* survey were in paid employment. Now just over two-thirds (68 per cent) are. Over the same period the proportion of non-retired men in employment has if anything decreased, from 84 per cent to 81 per cent. Women are still less likely to be in employment than men, but the gap has closed significantly. The shift to the service economy – which includes an increase in jobs traditionally associated with 'women's work', such as retail and personal service employment – brings with it demands for new skills and individual attributes such as emotional labour and employee 'entrepreneurship', rather than the technical skills and physical effort associated with mainstream manufacturing during the 'Fordist' era (Hochschild, 1983; Rose, 1989). In parallel, the development of techniques such as 'high commitment' management have been associated with an increased intensification of employment (Burchell *et al.*, 2002; Taylor, 2002; Green 2003), and the 'Working in Britain' survey (Taylor, 2002) revealed declining job satisfaction – particularly with the number of hours worked. These increases in work intensity and demand are also likely to impact on life outside work.

These parallel changes raise a number of questions that will be explored in this chapter. In the not too distant past, it was assumed that women had different attitudes to paid employment as compared to men. Historically, research on women as employees implicitly incorporated the assumptions of the 'breadwinner' model, in that whereas men's social positioning and identity has been assumed to be primarily shaped by their breadwinning role, their careers, and the jobs they do, women's 'central life interest' has been seen as having more of a focus on family life (Feldberg and Glenn, 1979). In contemporary research, this rather simplistic approach has long been transcended. Nevertheless, the assumption still persists that women's 'orientations to work' are, in aggregate, different to those of men, and that the majority of women will give priority to their families when seeking employment (for example, Hakim, 1991). As women become an increasingly important element of the labour force, are these assumptions still correct? Are women also less committed to work and to employment in a more general sense? Moreover, the increasing involvement of women in the labour market has helped to put a new spotlight on the relationship between the world of work and the domestic world. There has been increasing concern about 'work-life balance', that is, in ensuring that the demands of work do not impact adversely on domestic and family life – and *vice versa* (Lewis and Lewis, 1996; Hochschild, 1997).

Despite continuing debate as to the prevalence of a long hours' working culture in Britain, there is some evidence that *individual* working hours have actually gone down in the UK, particularly for men (Green, 2001, 2003), although there is evidence, as mentioned earlier, that work itself has become more intense and demanding. However, as many authors have suggested, a focus on individual hours tends to miss the point – particularly as far as families are concerned (Clarkberg and Merola, 2003). The increase in the employment of women will have the effect of increasing the *total* number of hours worked within the household, even if individual working hours have not increased. Moreover, if women are no longer available to carry out (unpaid) domestic work and caring, then this is likely to put pressure on family time for men, as well as women. Certainly, other research has demonstrated that the number of hours worked is the single most important factor that contributes to excessive levels of work-life conflict (White *et al.*, 2003; Crompton and Lyonette, 2006).

In the first part of this chapter, we compare trends in men's and women's 'orientations to work' in the light of these developments. Are there still fundamental differences between women and men in their attitudes towards work, or have these differences eroded over time? In the second part, we examine how difficult it is for men and women in employment to achieve a satisfactory 'work-life balance'. We do so using data on attitudes to work collected on the 1989, 1997 and 2005 *British Social Attitudes* surveys as part of the *International Social Survey Programme* (Davis and Jowell, 1989; Jowell *et al.*, 1993, 1998).

Women's and men's attitudes to work

Gallie *et al.* (1998) noted a considerable change in women's employment commitment since the 1980s, a trend also described in previous *British Social Attitudes* analyses in *The 11ᵗʰ Report* (Hedges, 1994). The key measure used was a question asking people whether or not they would wish to work even if they had enough money to live comfortably for the rest of their lives. This question measures the importance that people attach to employment on intrinsic grounds, that is, whether or not their motivation to work rests on more than the monetary reward it receives. Using this question, Gallie *et al.* (1998: 188) found that whereas men's commitment levels had remained broadly stable from 1981 to 1992 (at around 68 per cent), women's commitment had increased from 60 per cent to 67 per cent.

By the 1990s, therefore, women's level of commitment to employment as such was similar to that of men, and our surveys enable us to establish whether or not there have been any changes in this respect. We use here the same measure of non-financial employment commitment used in Russell's analysis (1998) of the 1989 and 1997 *International Social Survey Programme* work data in *The 15ᵗʰ Report*. We asked respondents if they agreed or disagreed with two statements:

> *A job is just a way of earning money – no more*

> *I would enjoy having a paid job even if I did not need the money*

The answers to these two questions are combined to create a composite score. Those who "strongly *agree*" with the first item and "strongly *disagree*" with the

BRITISH SOCIAL ATTITUDES

second are deemed to have a low level of employment commitment and are
given a score of two. At the other end of the spectrum, those that "strongly
disagree" with the first item and "strongly agree" with the second have a high
level of employment commitment with a score of 10. Table 3.1 displays this
composite score for men and women in each of 1989, 1997 and 2005.

Table 3.1. Non-financial employment commitment, by year and sex

		Mean score	*Base*
1989	Male	6.58	*548*
	Female	6.87	*599*
	All	*6.73*	*1147*
1997	Male	6.30	*384*
	Female	6.55	*543*
	All	*6.44*	*927*
2005	Male	6.35	*333*
	Female	6.72	*431*
	All	*6.55*	*764*

Base: all respondents

We can see that on this measure at least, women's employment commitment
was already greater than that of men in 1989. Although the commitment of both
sexes declined thereafter – something that had also been identified by Bryson
and McKay in *The 14th Report* (1997) – that pattern now seems to have been
reversed somewhat. This is particularly true amongst women, and the gap
between them and men on our composite measure is now greater than it has
ever been.

We might, however, examine this topic further by looking more broadly at the
attributes that men and women consider to be important in a job. In particular,
we can draw a distinction between the 'extrinsic' and 'intrinsic' rewards of
work. By 'extrinsic' rewards we mean the material benefits of paid employment
such as income, job security and promotion opportunities. By 'intrinsic' rewards
we are referring to non-material benefits such as having interesting work and
being able to work autonomously. If women have become less likely to work
simply for the money, we should find that they have come to value the extrinsic
rewards of work less, and perhaps also the intrinsic rewards more.

This possibility is examined in Table 3.2 where we show the average score for
men and women on two composite scales that have been constructed in a
similar manner to our employment commitment scale. Those who think it is
"very important" for a job to have high income, job security and good
opportunities for advancement secure a maximum extrinsic rewards score of 12;
those who think all these attributes are "not important at all" receive a score of
just four. The same procedure has then also been used to derive an intrinsic
rewards score based on how important respondents think it is for a job to be

interesting, to allow someone to work independently, and to allow someone to decide for themselves when they work.

Table 3.2 Importance of extrinsic and intrinsic rewards of work, by year and sex

		Extrinsic rewards score	Base	Intrinsic rewards score	Base
1989	Male	9.58	575	6.23	574
	Female	9.66	653	6.30	660
	All	9.62	1228	6.29	1234
1997	Male	9.47	404	6.32	415
	Female	9.40	597	6.20	600
	All	9.42	1001	6.25	1015
2005	Male	9.47	355	6.34	362
	Female	9.17	478	6.33	482
	All	9.30	833	6.34	844

Base: all respondents

We can see that there has, in fact, been a decline in the emphasis that women place on extrinsic rewards. Their average score on this scale fell from 9.66 to 9.17 – small perhaps, but still statistically significant. On the other hand, there is no consistent evidence that women have come to place an increased emphasis on intrinsic rewards. Indeed there is no statistically significant increase amongst men on this score either. In respect of paid work, therefore, the expectations of the 'post-materialists' (Inglehart, 1997) – that is, that there would be a shift towards a greater emphasis on 'intrinsic' rewards from work – have not been confirmed.

It is clear, therefore, that women do not simply go out to work to earn money while men have a more enduring, non-financial commitment to work. Nevertheless, given that occupational segregation still persists (i.e. men and women are concentrated in different jobs and occupational sectors), women will be more likely to be employed in jobs that involve caring and nurturing, and, as previous research has demonstrated, women are more likely than men to express a preference for jobs in which they can 'help others' (Lowe and Krahn, 2000). For example, nearly three-quarters (73 per cent) of women but a little under two-thirds (63 per cent) of men think that it is "very important" or "important" that a job "allows someone to help other people". Equally, women are more likely than men (by seven percentage points) to say it is important that a job "is useful to society". Moreover, there is no sign that these differences have narrowed over time.

Equally, as Table 3.3 shows, women are still somewhat more likely to feel that their job actually is one that allows them to be helpful and useful. Even so, the gap between women and men is no more than six percentage points. It should not be forgotten either that around three-fifths of *men* also consider these characteristics to be important; they are thus far from being the exclusive preserve of women or exclusively of interest to them.

Table 3.3 Important attributes in a job, by year and sex

% say important in a job	1989		1997		2005	
	Men	**Women**	**Men**	**Women**	**Men**	**Women**
A job that allows someone to help other people	61	68	61	74	63	73
Base	*598*	*699*	*442*	*638*	*390*	*523*
A job that is useful to society	61	64	59	69	60	67
Base	*598*	*699*	*442*	*638*	*390*	*523*

Base: all respondents

Indeed, intriguingly, Table 3.4 also suggests that the proportion of both men *and* women who feel that their job has these characteristics has increased. For example, now nearly three-quarters of men (73 per cent) feel that they can help other people in their job, compared with just three-fifths (59 per cent) in 1989. Amongst women, the increase has been from 69 per cent to 79 per cent. One possibility is that this trend reflects the fact that the shift to the service economy has brought with it an increase in the total amount of 'people work'. It is also possible that contemporary strategies of management are tailored so as to encourage employees to think of their jobs as being helpful and useful (Rose, 1989).

Table 3.4 Attributes of respondent's own job, by year and sex

% agree	1989		1997		2005	
	Men	**Women**	**Men**	**Women**	**Men**	**Women**
In my job I can help other people	59	69	62	74	73	79
Base	*397*	*320*	*259*	*283*	*216*	*249*
My job is useful to society	54	54	52	60	58	64
Base	*397*	*320*	*259*	*283*	*216*	*249*

Base: all in paid work

Women's opinions as to the kind of job they would prefer, then, are slightly different from those of men. Nevertheless, they are at least as committed to paid work as men are, and increasing numbers of women, particularly mothers, are in employment. However, what impact is their increased role in the workplace having on family and domestic life? It is to this subject that we now turn.

Work-life imbalance?

We identified earlier two potential sources of pressure from the workplace on attaining a satisfactory balance between work and life outside work – the number of hours worked in total by all those in the household and the intensity with which those hours are worked. We begin our assessment by examining how significant those pressures appear to be.

Unfortunately, the *International Social Survey Programme* only collects data on the number of hours worked by respondents themselves, and only did so in 1997 and 2005. Still, the information we do have is consistent with other evidence (see Green, 2003) that working hours amongst men have fallen slightly – for example, 22 per cent of men in full-time employment reported working more than 50 hours a week in 1997, but only 16 per cent do so now. In contrast, although women on average still work fewer hours than men, average working hours amongst women appear to be increasing. For example, 29 per cent of full-time women worked over 40 hours a week in 1997 but now 33 per cent do so. However, it is women working part-time amongst whom working hours have increased most markedly; 64 per cent of this group worked for less than 20 hours a week in 1997, but only 51 per cent now fall into this category. Although there is no significant change in the proportion of women working part-time, it appears that the number of hours women work, either part-time or full-time, has increased. It is thus apparent that the fall in men's working hours is being offset by an increase in the time spent at work by women.

We do not have any evidence in our surveys on how intensely people feel they have to work, but we do have information on how much stress they feel at work. This suggests that stress at work has increased for all categories of employee since 1989. Amongst both men and women in full-time employment, the proportion reporting that they "hardly ever" or "never" find their work stressful has halved since 1989, and stands now at just eight per cent. And although women in part-time work report lower stress levels than full-time women, now less than a quarter of part-time women say they "hardly ever" or "never" find their work stressful, compared with 36 per cent in 1989.

Women, therefore, are working longer hours while both men and women are more likely to report stress at work. One indication that these pressures are being felt can be seen in the responses given by those currently in paid employment to the following question:

*Suppose you could change the way you spend your time, spending
more time on some things and less time on others. Which...would you
like to spend more time on, which would you like to spend less time on
and which would you like to spend the same amount of time on as
now?*

Amongst the options offered to respondents were time spent in paid work, with
family, and with friends.

As Table 3.5 shows, there has been a sustained increase in the proportions of
both men and women – particularly full-time employees – who would prefer to
spend more time with family and friends and less time at work. For example, 84
per cent of full-time women would now like to spend more time with their
family, compared with three-quarters (75 per cent) in 1989. Although the
demand for more time with family is lower amongst part-time women, the trend
since 1989 has been much the same; 68 per cent would like more time now,
compared with 59 per cent in 1989. Of course, it might be the case that people's
expectations have changed; for example, as Inglehart (1997) has argued, there
may have been a long-term shift towards 'post-materialist' values. But equally
our results are consistent with the argument that increasing pressures within the
world of work are leading to growing difficulties in combining paid
employment with family and social life.

Table 3.5 Time allocation preferences, by year, sex, and employment status[1]

	Work status	1989	Base	1997	Base	2005	Base
Paid work	Men FT	52	326	64	201	50	161
(% saying *less*	Women FT	60	182	60	166	65	134
time preferred)	Women PT	17	115	28	97	25	105
Family	Men FT	70	326	72	201	82	161
(% saying *more*	Women FT	75	182	78	166	84	134
time preferred)	Women PT	59	115	69	97	68	105
Friends	Men FT	49	326	65	201	67	161
(% saying *more*	Women FT	62	182	70	166	77	134
time preferred)	Women PT	44	115	56	97	55	105

Base: all employees

Further evidence of the linkages between stress at work and family pressures is
suggested by multivariate analysis. This form of analysis allows us to assess the
importance of a range of factors while taking account of their relationship with
each other (further details can be found in Appendix I of this Report). The

results of the regression are given in the chapter appendix; this demonstrates that stress at work is significantly associated with wanting to spend more time with the family. As we anticipated, it also shows that the amount of reported stress has increased significantly over the three surveys. Again, not surprisingly, working full-time is also associated with higher levels of work stress (unfortunately, data on actual working hours was not available over the three surveys). Neither sex, nor the presence or absence of children, were significant. One interesting feature is that professional and managerial employees emerge as considerably more stressed at work than other social groupings – a finding that we will return to later in the chapter.

More evidence on the extent to which work-life balance is becoming increasingly problematic is available to us in the 2005 survey alone. In particular we have direct evidence of the degree to which those in employment feel that the demands of their work interfere with their family life – and *vice versa* (shown in Table 3.6).

Table 3.6 'Work-life balance', by sex and employment status

	Full-time men	Full-time women	Part-time women	All
How often demands of your job interfere with your family life	%	%	%	%
Always/often	28	21	13	21
Sometimes	41	37	37	39
Hardly ever/never	29	37	49	37
Base	*160*	*132*	*103*	*406*
How often demands of your family life interfere with your job	%	%	%	%
Always/often	2	4	8	4
Sometimes	27	15	28	24
Hardly ever/never	67	74	60	67
Base	*160*	*132*	*103*	*406*

Base: all in employment, excluding self-employed

As other research has demonstrated, work is more often thought to interfere with family life than *vice versa* (Moen, 2003). Only just over a third of all employees (37 per cent) say that the demands of their job "hardly ever" or "never" interfere with their family life, while two-thirds (67 per cent) claim that the demands of family life "hardly ever" or "never" interfere with their job. Surprisingly, perhaps, full-time men are more likely than full-time women, let alone part-time women, to say that their work interferes with their family life, a reflection perhaps of the fact that men still work longer hours than women. On the other hand, on one particular indicator of the 'family-friendliness' of employers, full-time women are more likely than full-time men (or indeed part-time women) to say that it would be difficult to take an hour or two off work to take care of personal or family matters. As many as 37 per cent say it would be "somewhat" or "very" difficult compared with 24 per cent of full-time men and 23 per cent of part-time women.

Our regression analysis indicated that professional and managerial employees were more likely to find work stressful than people in intermediate and routine and manual occupations. In fact, those in the Registrar-General's former social classes I and II[2] both work longer hours themselves and are more likely to live in a household where both partners are working. As many as 59 per cent of men in these two classes work 40 or more hours a week, compared with just 26 per cent in classes IV and V. Meanwhile, 81 per cent of the partners of men in classes I and II are in paid work, compared with 59 per cent in classes IV and V – a difference that has only emerged since 1989. At the same time, both men and women in classes I and II are more likely to report stress at work. In 2005, 45 per cent of full-time women in classes I and II said that they always or often felt stressed at work, compared with 42 per cent of women in class III and 24 per cent of women in classes IV and V. For men, 45 per cent also reported that they always or often felt stressed at work, compared with 43 per cent of men in class III and 19 per cent of men in classes IV and V.

If hours worked by the household and the intensity of work adversely affect work-life balance then we should find that it is employees in classes I and II who are most likely to say that work interferes with their family life. This is precisely what we find in Table 3.7 – especially so amongst women.

Table 3.7 Job to family conflict, by social class and sex

% job interferes with family always/often/sometimes		Class		
	I and II	III	IV and V	All
Men	69	75	56	69
Base	*78*	*60*	*22*	*160*
Women	73	50	40	59
Base	*63*	*51*	*18*	*132*

Base: full-time employees, excluding self-employed

Although small sample sizes mean the figures should be treated with some care, nearly three-quarters (73 per cent) of full-time women in social classes I and II say that their job always, often or sometimes interferes with their family life, compared with half (50 per cent) of women in class III, and two in five (40 per cent) of those in classes IV and V. For full-time men, the differences were narrower and, in fact, given the small sample sizes at our disposal were not statistically significant, but again the evidence is broadly consistent with our expectations. Other evidence in support of this argument has been found in the 2002 *International Social Survey Programme* 'Family' module. A work-life conflict scale revealed that, in the case of Britain, managerial and professional men (7.75) reported significantly more work-life conflict than routine and manual men (7.24). Women report higher levels of work-life conflict than men, but the level of work-life conflict reported by managerial and professional women was particularly high (8.40), as compared to routine and manual women (7.47) (Crompton and Brockmann, 2006).

On the other hand, previous research in *The 20th Report* suggests that professional and managerial employees tend to have better employment conditions than intermediate or routine and manual employees so far as taking time off work is concerned (Crompton *et al.*, 2003). Indeed, in confirmation of this, we find that only 19 per cent of men in classes I and II say they would find it difficult to take time off, as compared with 25 per cent of men in class III and no less than 42 per cent in classes IV and V. However, the same is not true for women. A third of all women, both full- and part-time in classes I and II say that they would find it difficult, as do 31 per cent of those in class III. In contrast, only just over a quarter (26 per cent) of women in classes IV and V would find it difficult. Although this latter set of differences is not statistically significant (and again, we have small sample sizes), the pattern is clearly different than it is amongst men. It appears possible that the intensification of work may be having a particularly adverse impact on the 'family-friendliness' of work at least so far as professional and managerial women are concerned.

Conclusions

During the sixteen years covered by the three surveys we have analysed in this chapter, there has been a substantial reshaping both of employment, and of the nature of the labour force, in Britain. Although individual working hours are not rising for men, women's employment rates continue to rise, and women are working longer hours. This increase in women's employment means that longer hours are being worked by families overall. Such long hours are particularly common amongst those in social classes I and II. Men and women in these families work longer hours than those in other social classes, while men in social classes I and II are considerably more likely to have partners in paid employment. Meanwhile, although our evidence is rather limited, it does suggest, in line with other research, that work has become more intense in Britain. Stress at work is increasing across the board, and is now particularly common amongst managerial and professional employees.

What has been the impact of the increasing involvement of women in the labour market on their attitudes to work? Although women's non-financial commitment to work might once have been lower than that of men, women are now at least as 'committed' to employment as men are, if not more so. On the other hand, women are still rather more likely than men to express a preference for jobs that allow them to help people, and make a contribution to society. Full-time women are also more likely than full-time men to say that they would like to spend more time with their family (and indeed to say that they would prefer to spend less time at work). These gendered 'preferences' reflect the fact that women still retain the major responsibility for childcare and work in the home (Harkness, 2003; Crompton, 2006). Thus, although the 'male breadwinner' model may no longer be regarded as the norm, it nevertheless persists in a mutated version. As a result, material inequalities between men and women can be expected to persist for the foreseeable future.

And what has been the impact of the trends we have identified on work-life balance? Although direct evidence on the degree to which work interferes with family life is only available in our 2005 survey, the level in Britain would seem to be rather high – three in five of those in employment report that the demands of their job interfere with their family lives. Meanwhile, since 1989 there has been an increase in the proportion of both men and women who say that they would like to spend more time with friends and family and less time at work. At the same time, work appears to adversely affect family life more for those in social classes I and II, while, as previous research has shown, full-time professional and managerial women emerge as a particularly pressured group (Lyonette et al., 2007). Recent government policies have emphasised flexible working options as the principal means of helping to secure 'work-life balance' (Bell and Bryson, 2005). However, if work itself is becoming more stressful, flexible working will not, by itself, improve this 'balance'. After all, although part-time employees do undoubtedly report lower levels of stress at work, even amongst this group, stress is rising.

There is not then any sustained rejection of the world of work, or any massive change in attitudes to work. It does appear, however, that employees are feeling more stressed at work, and that they would like to spend more time with their families and friends. Thus, perhaps, 'work-life' policies should have a more conscious focus on reducing stress and pressures at work, rather than simply, as in the case of present government policy, by promoting 'flexibility' (e.g. Department of Trade and Industry/HM Treasury, 2003). In making this argument, we do not wish to construct an argument 'against' flexible working per se, nor should 'flexibility' and 'work intensity' be seen as alternative targets so far as work-life policies are concerned. Indeed, as the evidence of this chapter has demonstrated, part-time work for women is clearly associated with a lower level of work to family conflict, and fewer time pressures. However, part-time work (and other flexible options such as career breaks) has been conclusively demonstrated to be associated with lower levels of occupational success for women (Purcell et al., 1999). Moreover, as other research has shown (Rubery et al., 2005; Crompton, 2006), 'flexibility' can often, in fact, be one employer strategy whereby work intensification is achieved. Part-timers are not entitled to the same workplace breaks as full-time employees, and are often recruited to cope with known peaks in workplace demands. Such workers often work 'non-standard' hours, such as evenings and weekends, and thus may find 'family time' problematic. Nevertheless, given women's increasing level of employment, it may be argued that as well as increasing flexible working for women *and* men, a better work-life balance will more likely be achieved if there were also a reduction in work intensity for both sexes.

Notes

1. Our definition of work status is taken from the respondents' description of "current economic activity" so part-time is self-defined. Part-time men are not included here due to the very small sample size.
2. We use the Registrar General's former social class rather than the more recent ONS socio-economic classification because the latter is not available for our 1989 and 1997 surveys. Class I consists of those in professional occupations; II, intermediate; III skilled; IV, partly skilled; and V unskilled.

References

Beck, U. (2000), *The Brave new World of Work*, Cambridge: Polity

Bell, A. and Bryson, C. (2005), 'Work-life balance – still a "women's issue"', in Park, A., Thompson, K., Bromley, C., Phillips, M. and Johnson, M. (eds.), *British Social Attitudes: the 22nd Report – Two terms of New Labour: the public's reaction*, London: Sage

Bryson, A. and McKay, S. (1997), 'What about the workers?', in Jowell, R., Curtice, J., Park, A., Brook, L., Thomson, K. and Bryson, C. (eds.), *British Social Attitudes: the 14th report*, Aldershot: Ashgate

Burchell, B., Ladipo, D. and Wilkinson, F. (eds.) (2002), *Job insecurity and work intensification*, London: Routledge

Clarkberg, M. and Merola, S. (2003), 'Competing clocks: work and leisure', in Moen, P. (ed.), *It's about time*, Ithaca and London: Cornell University Press

Crompton, R. (2006), *Employment and the family*, Cambridge: Cambridge University Press

Crompton, R. and Brockmann, M. (2006), 'Class, gender and work-life articulation' in Perrons, D., Fagan, C., McDowell, L., Ray, K. and Ward, K. (eds.), *Gender Divisions And Working Time In The New Economy*, London: Edward Elgar

Crompton, R., Brockmann, M. and Wiggins, D. (2003), 'A woman's place ... employment and family life for men and women', in Park, A., Curtice, J., Thomson, K., Jarvis, L. and Bromley, C. (eds.), *British Social Attitudes: the 20th Report*, London: Sage

Crompton, R. and Lyonette, C. (2006, forthcoming), 'Work-life conflict in Europe', *Acta Sociologica*, December

Davis, J.A. and Jowell, R. (1989), 'Measuring National Differences', in Jowell, R., Witherspoon, S., and Brook, L. (eds.), *British Social Attitudes: Special International Report*, Aldershot: Gower

Department of Trade and Industry/HM Treasury (2003), *Balancing work and family life: enhancing choice and support for parents*, London: Stationery Office

Feldberg, R.L. and Glenn, E.N. (1979), 'Male and female: job versus gender models in the sociology of work', *Social Problems,* **26(5)**: 524–538

Gallie, D., White, M., Cheng, Y. and Tomlinson, M. (1998), *Restructuring the employment relationship*, Oxford: Oxford University Press

Green, F. (2001), 'It's been a hard day's night: the concentration and intensification of work in late twentieth-century Britain', *British Journal of Industrial Relations,* **39(1)**: 53–80

Green, F. (2003), 'The demands of work', in Dickens, R., Gregg, P., and Wadsworth, J. (eds.), *The Labour Market under New Labour*, Basingstoke: Palgrave Macmillan

Hakim, C. (1991), 'Grateful slaves and self-made women: fact and fantasy in women's work orientations', *European Sociological Review,* **7(2)**: 101–121

Handy, C.B. (1984), *The future of work*, Oxford: Blackwell

Harkness, S. (2003), 'The household division of labour: changes in families' allocation of paid and unpaid work, 1992–2002', in Dickens, R., Gregg, P. and Wadsworth, J. (eds.), *The Labour Market under New Labour*, Basingstoke: Palgrave Macmillan

Hedges, B. (1994), 'Work in a Changing Climate', in Jowell, R., Curtice, J., Brook, L. and Ahrendt, D. (eds.), *British Social Attitudes: the 11th Report*, Aldershot: Dartmouth

Hochschild, A. (1983), *The Managed Heart*, Los Angeles: University of California Press

Hochschild, A. (1997), *The Time Bind*, New York: Metropolitan Books

Inglehart, R. (1997), *Modernisation and Postmodernisation: Cultural, Economic and Political Change in 43 societies*, Princeton: Princeton University Press

Jowell, R., Brook, L. and Dowds, L. (1993), *International Social Attitudes*, Aldershot: Dartmouth

Jowell, R., Curtice, J., Park, A., Brook, L., Thomson, K. and Bryson, C. (eds.) (1998), *British – and European – Social Attitudes: the 15th Report – How Britain Differs*, Aldershot: Ashgate

Lewis, S. and Lewis, J. (eds.) (1996), *The work-family challenge*, London: Sage

Lowe, G.S. and Krahn, H. (2000), 'Work aspiration and attitude in an era of labour market restructuring', *Work, Employment and Society,* **14(1)**: 1–22

Lyonette, C., Crompton, R. and Wall, K. (2007, in press), 'Gender, Occupational Class and Work-Life Conflict: A Comparison of Britain and Portugal', *Community, Work and Family,* **10(4)**

Moen, P. (ed.) (2003), *It's About Time: Couples and Careers*, Ithaca and London: Cornell University Press

Nolan, P. (2003), 'Reconnecting with history', *Work, Employment and Society,* **17(3)**: 473–480

Purcell, K., Hogarth, T. and Simm, C. (1999), *Whose flexibility?,* York: Joseph Rowntree Foundation

Rose, N. (1989), *Governing the soul*, London: Routledge

Rubery, J., Ward, K., Grimshaw, D. and Beynon, H. (2005), 'Time and the new employment relationship', *Time and Society*, **14(1)**: 89–111

Russell, H. (1998), 'The rewards of work', in Jowell, R., Curtice, J., Park, A., Brook, L., Thomson, K. and Bryson, C. (eds.), *British – and European – Social Attitudes: the 15th Report – How Britain Differs*, Aldershot: Ashgate

Taylor, R. (2002), 'Britain's world of work: Myths and Realities', *ESRC Future of Work programme*, University of Leeds

White, M, Hill, S., McGovern, P., Mills, C. and Smeaton, D. (2003), 'High-Performance' management practices, working hours and work-life balance, *British Journal of Industrial Relations*, **41(2)**:175–195

Acknowledgements

The *National Centre for Social Research* is grateful to the Economic and Social Research Council (ESRC) for their financial support which enabled us to ask the questions reported in this chapter; the views expressed are those of the authors alone.

Appendix

We used a multinomial logistic regression, the results of which are given in the table below. The dependent variable was "do you find work stressful". The "sometimes" response is not presented here, but it did not show any marked differences.

Regression on "do you find work stressful" (men in FT employment, women in FT or PT employment only; no self-employed)

Always or often find work stressful	Predictor variables	Beta (standardized)
	Intercept	
	Male	0.86
	Female	-
	1989	**0.55****
	1997	0.66
	2005	-
	Working full-time	**4.73****
	Working part-time	-
	No child in household	0.89
	Child <16 in household	-
	Prefer more time with family	**2.07****
	Prefer same/less time with family	-
	Prefer more time with friends	1.15
	Prefer same/less time with friends	-
	Professional/managerial class	**7.60****
	Intermediate class	1.32
	Routine/manual class	-
	Nagelkerke R2 = 0.156	
	Base	*1347*

** = significant at 1% level
Reference category is rarely or never stressed at work
Data for the three surveys (1989, 1997 and 2005) have been pooled

4 Who should pay for my care – when I'm 64?

*Rachel Ormston, John Curtice and Helen Fawcett**

Who should pay for the cost of care in old age has become the subject of considerable debate in Britain. On the one hand it is argued that all older people who have the misfortune to require long-term care because of increased frailty and poor health should have their care paid for by the state – in much the same way that most of the National Health Service provides medical treatment without charge at the point of use for all those who need it. On the other hand it is claimed the state cannot afford to pay the cost of long-term care for all who need it – especially as older people are due to become an increasing proportion of Britain's population – and that the state should only pay the care costs of those who cannot afford to do so themselves.

Not long after it was elected in 1997 the Labour government responded to this debate by establishing a Royal Commission (Royal Commission on Long Term Care, 1999). In its majority report the Commission recommended that the cost of providing personal care, such as help with washing and eating, should be provided for all free of charge. Individuals should only be expected to pay – depending on their means – for their living and housing costs, including the 'hotel' costs that arise if they are living in a residential home. It also recommended that those living in a nursing home should not have to contribute towards the cost of their nursing care, so that they were not disadvantaged as compared with those receiving nursing care in hospital.

However, the UK Labour government rejected much of the advice put forward by the Commission (Department of Health, 2000). Although it accepted that the state should pay for the cost of nursing care provided in nursing homes, it rejected the recommendation that the state should pay for the cost of personal care for everyone aged 65 and over. Instead state support would continue to be means-tested. In contrast in Scotland both recommendations were implemented

* Rachel Ormston is a Senior Researcher at the *Scottish Centre for Social Research*, part of NatCen. John Curtice is Research Consultant at the *Scottish Centre for Social Research*, part of NatCen, Deputy Director of CREST, and Professor of Politics at Strathclyde University. Helen Fawcett is Lecturer in Politics at Strathclyde University.

(albeit with less generous provision for nursing care; see Bell and Bowes, 2006). As a result those in receipt of personal care at home have the full costs of their care (as determined by a needs assessment) paid by their local authority. Meanwhile those living in a nursing or residential home receive a payment of £145 per week for personal care.

This policy difference in respect of personal care has become one of the iconic public policy differences between post-devolution Scotland and England. This status has helped ensure that debate on what is the right approach continues unabated on both sides of the border. For example, in early 2006 a commission established by the influential Kings Fund noted that there is "widespread dissatisfaction with the current system" in England and proposed a partial move towards the Scottish policy – a 'partnership' model under which the state would pay a proportion (such as two-thirds) of everyone's personal care costs, but that thereafter the individual would have to pay half of the remaining cost (Wanless, 2006). Meanwhile in Scotland the cost of the policy has proven to be somewhat greater than initially budgeted (Bell and Bowes, 2006), thereby fuelling doubts about the financial sustainability of a policy that was criticised in *The Economist* as "a terrifying blank cheque in a country whose pensioners are expected to increase by 35 per cent (to 1.3m) in the next 25 years".[1]

This chapter looks at where the adult public across the whole of Great Britain stands on this debate. Hitherto much of the research into public attitudes on this subject has consisted of focus groups and/or has been confined to those who either are already in receipt of care or are in an older age group (see, for example, Scottish Executive Care Development Group, 2001; Croucher and Rhodes, 2006; for a review of such research see Bell *et al.*, 2006). While this may be an effective means of ascertaining the views of current and potential users of personal care, it tells us nothing about the willingness of the adult tax-paying public in general to fund the costs of such care. Meanwhile, such limited survey research of the general population that has been conducted has excluded Scotland (Parker and Clarke, 1997; Deeming and Justin, 2003), thereby making it impossible to ascertain whether or not the differences in policy that have emerged between England and Scotland are a reflection of differences in public attitudes.

In contrast in this chapter we are able to examine attitudes amongst the general public on both sides of the border. We ask what does the adult population as a whole consider to be the roles and responsibilities of the state and the individual in paying for care? Are these roles and responsibilities thought to be the same as they are for pensions – or is the issue regarded differently? And are attitudes really different in Scotland from those in England? In answering these three key questions we are able to cast considerable light not only on who supports free personal care but on why they do so.

Our data come from two sources. Some key questions on attitudes towards providing and paying for personal care were included on the 2005 *British Social Attitudes* survey. However, a more extensive module of such questions – including all those asked on the British survey – was included on the 2005 *Scottish Social Attitudes* survey. This means that we are able to compare attitudes in Scotland with those in England and Wales. It also means, however, that some of our more detailed analysis of who holds particular attitudes and why is based on data from the Scottish survey alone. Where this latter survey is the source of our evidence this has been made explicit in the tables and the text.

Who should pay for care?

We asked respondents to both the 2005 *British* and the *Scottish Social Attitudes* surveys the following question:

> *[Still] thinking about an elderly person who needs* **regular** *help with looking after themselves. Which of these statements comes closest to what you believe about who should* **pay** *for this help?*
>
> *The government should pay, no matter how much money the person has*
> *The person should pay, no matter how much money he/she has*
> *Who pays should depend on how much money the person has*

The first option is intended to refer to the principle of free personal care.[2] As one might anticipate given the intensity of the debate outlined above, opinion proves to be quite sharply divided about its merits. Across Britain as a whole slightly over half (54 per cent) believe that 'who pays should depend on how much money the person has', that is that state support for the costs of personal care should be means-tested; only 43 per cent back the principle of free personal care.

Table 4.1 Who should pay for care for elderly people, by country[3]

	England/Wales	Scotland*	Britain
	%	%	%
The government should pay, no matter how much money the person has	43	57	42
The person should pay, no matter how much money he/she has	3	1	2
Who pays should depend on how much money the person has	53	41	54
Base	2903	1549	3193

*Source: *Scottish Social Attitudes*

However, the balance of opinion is different in Scotland. As many as 57 per cent of people in Scotland believe the state should pay for everyone's care, regardless of income, while only 41 per cent favour means-testing. (In England and Wales the equivalent figures are 43 per cent and 53 per cent respectively.) So the differences in public policy in the two parts of Britain do appear to reflect a real difference in the balance of public opinion.

Opinion does vary to some degree between those in different age groups and those in different classes. As we might anticipate (see Table 4.2), older people are more likely to support free personal care than are younger people. Doubtless this is because the issue of how to pay for the care they might need is more immediately pressing for older people. Nevertheless the differences between those in different age groups are not strong enough to suggest that older and younger people are sharply at variance in their views. Meanwhile those in professional and managerial occupations are less supportive than those in routine and semi-routine jobs, something to which we will return later. These patterns are more or less equally evident in Scotland as they are in England and Wales. Yet at the same time those in any given age group or social class in Scotland are more likely to support the provision of personal care than are their counterparts in England. Evidently the distinctiveness of opinion in Scotland has little to do with its demographic structure.

Table 4.2 Belief in universal state funding of care for the elderly, by age and class

% say government should pay, no matter how much money the person has	England/ Wales	Base	Scotland*	Base
Age				
18–29	36	422	51	184
30–44	42	819	56	443
45–64	45	974	58	535
65+	47	686	61	386
Social class				
Managerial/professional	36	1039	50	515
Routine/semi-routine	47	818	61	446
All	43	2903	57	1549

Source: Scottish Social Attitudes

Of course, one possible explanation of this Scottish distinctiveness is that it is a consequence of the introduction of free personal care. The very introduction of the policy by the Scottish Executive might itself have helped persuade some people of its merits. Unfortunately, as our question about who should pay for care for the elderly has not been asked in a previous *British* or *Scottish Social Attitudes* survey, we cannot establish whether opinion has shifted in Scotland in the wake of the introduction of free personal care. However, there is one clue in the Scottish survey that initially, at least, suggests that attitudes in Scotland may have been influenced by the introduction of the policy. We asked respondents to the *Scottish Social Attitudes* survey how strongly they agreed or disagreed with the statement:

> *There is no need for people in Scotland to save for care in old age because the government will pay for it*

Among those who agree or strongly agree with this statement, around three-quarters (73 per cent) believe the government should pay for care for the elderly, regardless of how much money the person has. In contrast, among those who disagree or strongly disagree with the statement, only 52 per cent support free personal care. In other words, those who think the government *will* pay (as indeed in Scotland it will) are more likely to think that it *should* pay.

However, agreement with our statement is very much a minority view. Just 17 per cent agree or strongly agree that there is no need to save for care in old age, because the government will pay. Over two-thirds (69 per cent) disagree. Moreover, at 52 per cent, support for free personal care amongst those in Scotland who are doubtful that the government will pay is still much higher than it is in England and Wales. Between them these figures cast severe doubt on the notion that support for the principle of free personal care in Scotland is simply being driven by an expectation (presumably not shared in England) that it will in fact be available.

Free personal care is then, apparently, a controversial policy. There are substantial bodies of opinion both for and against. Younger and older people have somewhat different views. The balance of opinion is, apparently, opposed to the policy in England and Wales, in line with the position adopted by the UK government, but appears to be in favour in Scotland, in tune with the distinctive measures adopted by the Scottish Executive. And as far as we can tell, this latter difference does not seem simply to be the result of the fact that free personal care is now the *status quo* in Scotland. It is little wonder then that the policy is the subject of continuing debate.

The role of individuals

We have seen that there is not inconsiderable support for means-testing the state's contribution towards the cost of personal care. But if individuals can be expected to pay the cost of care if in the event they can afford to do so, do they have a further responsibility to try and ensure they do in fact have the means to do so if necessary? Certainly, so far as attitudes towards pensions are concerned, this seems to be the case according to the evidence of previous *British Social Attitudes* surveys. While 59 per cent support the principle of a universal state pension (Sefton, 2005), at the same time more or less the same proportion (61 per cent) think that those on low incomes should get more money. As many as 80 per cent agree that "the government should encourage people to save for retirement" and 72 per cent that a young person should start saving for retirement as soon as they can, even if they have to cut back on other things (Phillips and Hancock, 2005). In short, it appears that the public accept that state provision for pensions should at least be partially means-tested and that individuals have a responsibility to ensure they have enough to live on in old age.

The 2005 *Scottish Social Attitudes* survey included two questions designed to establish whether people believe that people have as much responsibility to save for care as they do for pensions:

> *It's people's own responsibility to save so that they have a decent pension*

> *It's people's own responsibility to save enough so that they can pay for any care they need when they are older*

As the next table shows, people in Scotland react very differently towards the two propositions. While half agree that individuals have some responsibility to save for a decent pension, just 16 per cent think there is any equivalent responsibility for people to save for care in old age. No less than two-thirds do not feel that people have a responsibility to save for their care.

Table 4.3 Views on individual responsibility to save for care/pensions

It's people's own responsibility to ...	... save for any care they need when older	... save so they have a decent pension
	%	%
Agree	16	50
Neither agree nor disagree	16	18
Disagree	67	32
Base	*1549*	*1549*

Source: *Scottish Social Attitudes*

However, a possible criticism of this question is that respondents may have taken it as a factual, rather than a normative question. People in Scotland might disagree that people have a responsibility to save for care because they know the cost of care is now being provided by the Scottish Executive anyway. But as discussed above, just 17 per cent of people in Scotland believe there is no need for people in Scotland to save for care in old age, because the government will pay for it. In any event the same difference in attitudes towards care and pensions emerged in response to a further pair of questions where this potential ambiguity does not arise.

We asked:

> *Everyone who works should be required by law to save for their own retirement instead of relying only on the state pension*

> *Everyone who works should be required by law to save for care they might need when older instead of relying only on the government.*

Table 4.4 Views on compelling individuals to save for care/pensions

Everyone who works should be required by law to save ...	... for care they might need when older	... for their own retirement, instead of relying only on the state pension
	%	%
Agree	16	24
Neither agree nor disagree	19	17
Disagree	58	53
Base	*1409*	*1409*

Source: *Scottish Social Attitudes*

There is in truth little support for either proposition (see Table 4.4). But whereas 24 per cent say people should be legally required to make some private pension provision, just 16 per cent say the same thing about making provision for the costs of care. It appears that individuals are indeed not thought to have the same responsibility to save for care as they have to save for their pension.

Of course, we have to bear in mind that the data we have just presented only comes from Scotland. It may be that this difference in attitudes towards care and pensions does not exist in the rest of Great Britain. However, we have already seen that while the overall level of support for free personal care is higher in Scotland than it is in England and Wales, the pattern of attitudes by age and social class is much the same. This suggests that the pattern of *differences* in attitudes at least may well be the same throughout Great Britain.

Why are attitudes towards personal care different?

There are perhaps some fairly obvious reasons why people should adopt a different attitude towards care as they do pensions. Everyone hopes to live long enough to enjoy their retirement. So while it may be felt that the state pension should provide a 'basic' level of income for everyone, thereafter people can reasonably be expected to make provision themselves if they want to have a 'decent' income during an old age that the vast majority will reach. In contrast, whether any particular individual will require personal care is highly uncertain. Sefton (2005) argues that one possible motive for supporting state intervention is altruism – because it is right to help others who are in need through no fault of their own. In the case of personal care, people may object to individuals being held liable for their own care precisely because (in contrast with pensions) they cannot be expected to anticipate this need. Moreover, when the need does arise it does so as a result of ill-health, for which care *is* largely provided free for all at the point of use by the National Health Service, while the dividing line between what constitutes nursing care and what counts as personal care appears to be difficult for the public to comprehend (Royal Commission on Long Term Care, 1999).

But there is another interesting possible explanation. It is often argued that the current policy on personal care in England and Wales 'penalises thrift'; those who have saved or bought their own homes are expected to use these to pay for their care in old age, while others who have not been so 'thrifty' receive care free of charge (see, for example, the discussion in Croucher and Rhodes, 2006). Indeed, the fact that requiring people to pay for care puts people's houses (and thus their children's inheritances) at risk is perhaps one of the most emotive arguments deployed against current policy in England and Wales. In contrast, those who save for a pension do not in any way put their right to the basic universal state pension at risk, while many can hope as a result to secure a higher level of income than the state would pay in any circumstances.

If these arguments have any force then we might perhaps expect them particularly to influence the attitudes of those in middle-class occupations and those on high incomes. Usually these are groups that we would expect to oppose higher public expenditure because they would be the ones most likely to have to pay the taxes to fund it. But in this instance perhaps their opposition might be tempered by the fact that they would appear to be the principal beneficiaries of the spending. If so, then we would expect the difference between the attitudes of middle-class people towards care and the attitudes of working-class people to be smaller than it is in respect of attitudes towards pensions. Equally, we would expect less difference between the attitudes of those on high incomes and those on low incomes.

Class, income and attitudes to pensions and care

We can test whether class[4] and income make less difference to attitudes to care than they do to attitudes to pensions, by comparing the pattern of attitudes to four key questions, all but the second of which are familiar to us already:

- Belief that the government should always pay for personal care for the elderly, no matter how much money a person has.
- Belief that the government should mainly be responsible for ensuring people have enough money to live on in retirement.[5]

- Agreement that it's people's own responsibility to save enough to pay for any care they need when they are older.
- Agreement that it's people's own responsibility to save so they have a decent pension.

The first two were included in both the 2005 *British* and the 2005 *Scottish Social Attitudes* survey, while the second two were included only in the *Scottish Social Attitudes* survey.

We have already seen that throughout Great Britain those in professional and managerial occupations are in fact less likely to support free personal care than are those in routine and semi-routine occupations. However, Table 4.5 shows that the gap between these two groups is smaller than the difference in their attitudes towards whether the government should mainly be responsible for ensuring that people have enough money to live on in retirement. Across Britain as a whole the former gap is 12 points while the latter difference is no less than 19. Equally in Scotland the equivalent figures are 11 and 20 points respectively.

Table 4.5 Belief in <u>government</u> responsibility for paying for care/income in old age, by country and socio-economic class

% say government should ...	... pay for care for elderly person	... be mainly responsible for income in retirement	Base
Britain			
Managers/professionals	35	47	1126
Routine/semi-routine occupations	47	66	920
Gap between classes	12	19	
All respondents	42	56	3193
Scotland*			
Managers/professionals	50	55	515
Routine/Semi-routine occupations	61	75	446
Gap between classes	11	20	
All respondents	57	65	1549

*Source: Scottish Social Attitudes

Much the same is true when we look at attitudes towards individual responsibility for care and pensions. There is almost no difference at all between the proportion of managers and professionals who agree that individuals should be saving for care and the proportion of people in routine and semi-routine occupations who do so – the proportion is very low in each case. In contrast, on pensions 57 per cent of managers and professionals believe individuals have a responsibility to save – 15 points higher than the 42 per cent of those in routine and semi-routine occupations who agree individuals have such a responsibility.

Table 4.6 Belief in <u>individual</u> responsibility for saving for care/pensions, by socio-economic class

% agree it's people's own responsibility to ...	... save for any care they need when older	... save so they have a decent pension	Base
Managers/professionals	19	57	*515*
Routine/semi-routine occupations	16	42	*446*
Gap between classes	*3*	*15*	

Source: *Scottish Social Attitudes*

A similar pattern is found when these four measures are analysed by respondent's income. For example, in the British data 48 per cent of those with a household income of under £10,000 think the government should always pay for care, compared with 37 per cent of those with a household income of £38,000 or more – an 11-point gap. However, there is a much larger difference between these two groups – 26 points – in the proportion who think the government should be mainly responsible for income in old age.

The trends in these findings are broadly confirmed by regression analysis (more details and the full results are in the appendix to this chapter: see regression models A to C). While class is a significant factor in explaining differences in attitudes towards personal care, the pattern of association with class or with income (which is itself strongly correlated with class) is stronger in relation to attitudes to pensions or income in old age than they are in respect of care. Of course, the fact that middle- and working-class views are more similar on care than on pensions does not in itself prove that this is driven solely by 'self-interested' middle-class concerns about protecting homes and inheritances. However, it is at least consistent with our theory that the attitudes of the better off are affected by the fact that means-testing care can be particularly disadvantageous for them. It certainly suggests that we should look more closely at the impact of the argument that means-testing free personal care exposes people (unfairly) to the threat of losing their homes.

The threat of losing one's home

We asked respondents to the 2005 *Scottish Social Attitudes* survey how strongly they agreed or disagreed that:

> *Nobody should have to sell or re-mortgage their home, however valuable it is, in order to pay for care they need when they are elderly*

This statement was deliberately strongly worded in order to try and assess the extent to which people view having to release equity to pay for care, even if they have a very expensive home, as unacceptable. Nevertheless, no less than 76 per cent agreed with the statement (41 per cent strongly) while just 13 per cent disagreed. These figures help underline why this is such an emotive issue in the debate about funding care.

Meanwhile, unsurprisingly, those in middle-class occupations are at least as concerned about people having to sell their homes in order to fund care as are those in working-class jobs. As many as 75 per cent of those in managerial or professional occupations agree with our statement compared with 72 per cent of those in routine or semi-routine occupations. The pattern by income group is similar – 76 per cent of those in households with an annual income of £38,000 or more agree that no one should have to sell or re-mortgage their home, compared with 69 per cent of those with incomes below £10,000.

At the same time – and as we would expect – there is a close association between the belief that no one should have to sell their home to pay for care and (a) rejection of individual responsibility for saving for care (see Table 4.7) and (b) belief the government should be mainly responsible for paying for care.

Table 4.7 Attitudes to individual responsibility for paying for care, by attitudes to selling homes

	Nobody should have to sell or re-mortgage their home, however valuable it is, in order to pay for care they need when they are elderly				
	Agree strongly	Agree	Neither	Disagree/ disagree strongly	All
It's people's own responsibility to save enough to pay for care	%	%	%	%	%
Agree	12	18	15	23	16
Neither agree nor disagree	9	18	38	20	16
Disagree	77	63	46	57	67
Base	*598*	*470*	*129*	*177*	*1549*

Source: *Scottish Social Attitudes*

For example, 77 per cent of those who agree strongly that no one should have to sell or re-mortgage their home disagree that it is people's own responsibility to save for care in old age. In contrast, just 57 per cent of those who disagree or disagree strongly that no one should have to sell their home reject the idea that individuals have such a responsibility. Similarly, 68 per cent of those who agree strongly that no one should have to sell their home think the government should pay for care in old age, no matter how much money a person has, compared with 47 per cent of those who disagree or disagree strongly. (The statistical significance of these findings is demonstrated in models A3 and B2 in the appendix.) Put more simply, people who are concerned that people might need to sell or re-mortgage their homes to pay for care are more inclined both to reject the claim that individuals have a responsibility to save for care and to support free personal care. While this does not rule out other, more obviously altruistic, motivations for supporting state intervention, such concern is clearly an important explanation of why some people support free personal care.

Is free personal care viewed as redistributive?

Our analysis so far raises another interesting question. On the one hand the provision of free personal care can be regarded as an expansion of the welfare state, something that might commonly be regarded as a 'left-wing' stance. On the other hand it is far from clear that it is a redistributive policy (that is, a policy that disproportionately benefits the less well off in society). Indeed, the perception that it is a policy that would primarily benefit the better off was one of the key criticisms made by those members of the Royal Commission who issued a minority report dissenting from the views of their colleagues (Joffe and Lipsey, 1999).

How, though, does this apparent tension play out amongst the attitudes of the general public? Are those who primarily favour a left-wing viewpoint more or less likely to support free personal care? Even if they are more likely to be in favour, is this true to the same extent as it is of attitudes towards pensions? In this section we address these questions by examining the degree to which attitudes towards care and pensions vary according to how generally left-wing or right-wing someone is.

Both the *British* and the *Scottish Social Attitudes* surveys include a suite of questions that aim to measure where people stand on an underlying left–right value dimension (see Appendix I of this Report for more details). Broadly speaking, left-wing responses to these questions indicate support for state intervention (including redistribution of income) to secure more equality in society, while right-wing responses denote opposition to such views. Thus 'left-wing' in this context refers to views traditionally associated with the political left. It does not encompass other social attitudes that might now be described as 'left-wing', such as rejection of the death penalty or opposition to censorship – these are the focus of a separate, 'libertarian–authoritarian' scale (again, see Appendix 1). Individuals are given an additive score based on their responses to the suite of questions as a whole. For the purpose of the analysis conducted in this chapter, respondents have been divided into three roughly equal-sized bands based on this additive score, thereby distinguishing those who are generally more left-wing than average and those who are more right-wing than average from the remainder of the population.

Table 4.8 suggests that those of a more left-wing viewpoint are in fact somewhat more likely to support free personal care. However, the difference in attitudes between those who are more left-wing and those who are more right-wing is, at seven points, much smaller than the 18-point difference in their attitudes towards whether the government should be mainly responsible for ensuring that people have enough to live on in retirement.

Table 4.8 Responsibility for paying for care/income in old age, by political orientation

% say government ...	... should pay for care for elderly person	... mainly responsible for income in retirement	*Base*
More left	46	63	*853*
More right	39	45	*912*
Gap between the two	*7*	*18*	

Equally, our Scottish survey indicates that while those of a more left-wing viewpoint are somewhat less likely to say that it is an individual's responsibility to save for care, at five points the gap is only a third of the equivalent gap in respect of whether individuals should save so they have a decent pension (see Table 4.9).

Table 4.9 Agree/strongly agree individual responsible for saving for care/pensions, by political orientation

% agree it's people's own responsibility to ...	... save for any care they need when older	... save so they have a decent pension	*Base*
More left	13	43	*434*
More right	18	58	*497*
Gap between the two	*5*	*15*	

Source: *Scottish Social Attitudes*

It appears then that the tension in the elite level debate about free personal care is also reflected in popular opinion. The provision of free personal care is not associated as strongly with a more left-wing viewpoint as is an inclination to emphasise the role of government in the provision of pensions. And as middle-class people are less likely to hold traditional left-wing views (26 per cent of managers and professionals are more 'left-wing' compared with 38 per cent of semi-routine and routine workers), this helps us further understand why differences of opinion about free personal care are less strongly associated with social class than they are in the case of pensions.

Ability to provide care

Having either individuals or government pay for the cost of personal care are, of course, not the only ways in which the need of older people for care can be met. Another important possibility is that family members themselves might provide this care. Indeed, the more that this occurs the less expensive any policy of free personal care will be. However, the ability of family members to provide care for their relatives may increasingly be constrained by social changes, such as the growth in the involvement of women in the labour market and a growing tendency for children to live at some distance from their parents, a pattern most evident in middle-class families. At the same time the degree to which people feel they owe a duty to provide care for their older relatives may be diminished if the cost of having others provide such care is in fact largely met by the state.

On the 2005 *Scottish Social Attitudes* survey, we asked all those who had a living parent with whom they still had some contact the following question:

> *Some people feel they ought to care for older family members themselves, while others disagree. Imagine that either now or at some time in the future your parent/one of your parents needed regular help and that providing this help would take about 10 hours a week. Which of the statements ... comes closest to how you would feel about providing this care?*

Just 20 per cent of respondents said either that they would not want to provide any care for their parents themselves or that their parents were already in a home (see Table 4.10). In contrast, twice as many (41 per cent) said they were already providing their parents' care, would provide their parents' care whatever the circumstances, or would at least prefer to provide most or all of the care. Meanwhile a third (36 per cent) said they could provide some care, but not be the person mainly responsible. It would appear that there is still a widespread willingness to meet the care needs of fellow family members, a willingness that continues to be higher amongst women than amongst men, albeit less so in the case of women in employment.

However, those who live at some distance from their parents do acknowledge that they are less likely to be in a position to provide their care. Overall, more than one in five (22 per cent) of those in Scotland with a living parent live 50 or more miles away from them. Indeed, this figure reaches 26 per cent amongst those in professional and managerial occupations. Only 34 per cent of those living this far away said they would be willing to provide all or most of their parents' care compared with 50 per cent of those living a mile or less from their parents.

Table 4.10 Attitudes to providing 10 hours a week of care for parent(s)

	All
	%
I could not provide this care under any circumstances	4
If I could afford it, I would pay for someone else to provide care for my parent(s)	14
I could provide some of the care for my parent(s), but I would not want to be mainly responsible	36
I would want to provide most or all of this care for my parent(s)	23
I would provide most or all of this care in any circumstances	16
I am already providing care for my parent(s)	2
My parents are in a home already	2
Base	*810*

Base: all with at least one parent alive and some contact with parent(s)
Source: *Scottish Social Attitudes*

But while distance might attenuate people's willingness and ability to provide care, it does not seem to influence people's attitudes towards whether the government should pay. In fact, people who live more than 50 miles from their parents are slightly less likely (49 per cent) to say the government should always pay for care than are those living with, or within a mile of their parents (57 per cent). Support for free personal care does not then appear to be driven by geographical mobility.

Conclusions

Public opinion is heavily divided about whether the state should meet the costs of personal care for all older people or only some. In England and Wales that balance is tilted in favour of the state only meeting the costs of those who cannot afford to pay, whereas in Scotland it inclines towards the state paying the costs of all those in need. The divergence of policy across Britain appears to reflect real differences in public opinion.

But even if many feel that individuals should pay for the cost of their care should they in the event have the means to do so, it appears that people are not necessarily expected to save in order to ensure that they can meet the costs of their care should they require it. In this, attitudes are rather different than they are in respect of pensions where, despite widespread support for the universal state pension, there appears to be a widespread belief that individuals should save for their retirement. Having the means to be able to 'enjoy' retirement is regarded as primarily the responsibility of the individual. Ensuring that one has the ability to meet the costs of care is not. Thus even if it does not actually fund everyone's care, and even though there still appears to be a willingness on the part of many people to provide personal care for fellow family members, the state certainly is expected to act as the safety net that ensures that everyone can receive personal care should they need it.

The debates about how pensions should be funded and how the costs of care should be paid are also different in other respects. Those who would appear to have most to lose if personal care is not provided for free are those middle-class families with good incomes and the prospect of being able to pass on a substantial inheritance – including the family home – to their children. It is, of course, possible that attitudes towards paying for care are also informed by other, more altruistic motives – feeling that the state ought to support elderly people who need care through no fault of their own, for example. However, our data suggest that these more 'self-interested' concerns provide at least part of the explanation why the middle classes are not as distinctive in their attitudes towards care as they are in respect of pensions. Typical middle-class wariness about increased government spending appears to be tempered to some degree by the possibility that they might in this case be a beneficiary of the spending. This also helps explain why both those on the left and those on the right are particularly divided in their attitudes towards free care.

To this tension and division is added another crucial ingredient – the emotive issue of people having to sell their homes in order to pay for care. This, it seems, is a step too far for the majority of the population. While the principle of means-testing may be capable of commanding majority support, its popularity would always appear to be under threat for so long as someone's home is considered to be one of the means that they have at their disposal.

Notes

1. 'Home truths about home rule', *The Economist,* 18th May 2006, http://www.economist.com/world/displaystory.cfm?story_id=6941798.
2. Note that 'help with looking after themselves' was defined earlier in the questionnaire as 'help with things like getting dressed, shopping, cooking and cleaning'. This is somewhat wider than the definition of personal care proposed by the Royal Commission, or that actually implemented in Scotland, neither of which include shopping and cleaning. Our aim, however, was not to mimic the exact definition used in the relevant legislation in Scotland but rather to provide one that made it clear to respondents that we were referring to the provision of non-medical services.
3. Figures for Britain as a whole include Scotland. Although we have included figures for England and Wales separately in this section, due to the relatively small number of *British Social Attitudes* survey interviews conducted in Scotland (*c.*400 in total,

and around 300 for the modules reported in this chapter), excluding Scotland from the *British Social Attitudes* figures makes little difference to the overall proportions.

4. Socio-economic class is measured using the National Statistics Socio-Economic Classification (NS-SEC). See Appendix 1 for further details of this measure and how respondents are classified.

5. Respondents were asked to choose from three options: "mainly the government", "mainly a person's employer" and "mainly a person themselves and their family".

References

Bell, D. and Bowes, A. (2006), *Financial care models in Scotland and the UK*, York: Joseph Rowntree Foundation

Bell, D., Bowes, A., Dawson, A. and Roberts, E. (2006), *Establishing the Evidence Base for an Evaluation of Free Personal Care in Scotland*, Edinburgh: Scottish Executive Social Research

Croucher, K. and Rhodes, P. (2006), *Testing consumer views on paying for long-term care*, York: Joseph Rowntree Foundation

Deeming, C. and Justin, K. (2003), 'A fair deal for care in older age? Public attitudes towards the funding of long-term care', *Policy and Politics*, **31**: 431–446

Department of Health (2000), *The NHS Plan: The Government's Response to the Royal Commission on Long-Term Care*, Cmnd 4818–II, London: The Stationery Office

Joffe, J. and Lipsey, D. (1999), 'A Note of Dissent', in Royal Commission on Long Term Care, *With Respect to Old Age: Long Term Care – Rights and Responsibilities*, Cm 4192–I, London: The Stationery Office

Parker, G. and Clarke, H. (1997), 'Will you still need me, will you still feed me? Paying for care in old age', *Social Policy and Administration,* **31**: 119–135

Phillips, M. and Hancock, R. (2005), 'Planning for retirement: realism or denial?', in Park, A., Curtice, J., Thomson, K., Bromley, C., Phillips, M. and Johnson, M. (eds.), *British Social Attitudes: the 22nd report – Two terms of New Labour: the public's reaction*, London: Sage

Royal Commission on Long Term Care (1999), *With Respect to Old Age: Long Term Care – Rights and Responsibilities*, Cm 4192–I, London: The Stationery Office

Scottish Executive Care Development Group (2001), *Fair Care for Older People*, Edinburgh: Scottish Executive

Sefton, T. (2005), 'Give and take: attitudes towards redistribution', in Park, A., Curtice, J., Thomson, K., Bromley, C., Phillips, M. and Johnson, M. (eds.), *British Social Attitudes: the 22nd report – Two terms of New Labour: the public's reaction*, London: Sage

Wanless, D. (chm.) (2006), *Securing Good Care for Older People: Taking a long-term view*, London: King's Fund

Acknowledgements

The *National Centre for Social Research* is grateful to the Nuffield Foundation, the Department of Health and the Department for Work and Pensions for their financial support which enabled us to ask the questions reported in this chapter. Responsibility for the analysis of these data and the views expressed lies solely with the author.

Appendix

The multivariate analysis technique used is logistic regression (forward stepwise, simple contrast method), where categories of independent variables are compared to a specified comparison category. The statistic given is the parameter estimate (B). Models A1 to A3 follow. Model A3 includes factors found significant in A2 (i.e. class), plus attitudes towards selling homes and belief there is no need to save as government will pay for care.

Regression models A1–3: Saying the government should pay for care for elderly person, no matter how much money the person has (BSA and SSA 2005)

	Model A1 England/ Wales (BSA)	Model A2 Scotland (SSA)	Model A3 Scotland (SSA)
Sex			
Men	0.24**	-	n.a.
Women (reference category)			
Age			
18–29	-0.48**	-	n.a.
30–44	-0.07	-	n.a.
45–64	-0.08	-	n.a.
65+ (reference category)			
Social class			
Managerial/professional	-0.56**	-0.49**	-0.36*
Intermediate occupations	-0.38**	-0.18	-0.18
Small employers/own account workers	-0.05	0.16	0.15
Lower supervisory/technical	-0.19	0.09	0.07
Routine/semi-routine (reference category)			
R or someone known in need of care?			
Yes, respondent only	0.54**	-	n.a.
Yes, someone else only	0.10	-	n.a.
Yes, both	0.04	-	n.a.
No (reference category)			
No need for people in Scotland to save for care in old age as government will pay			
Agree/strongly agree (reference category)			
Neither	n.a.	n.a.	-0.62**
Disagree	n.a.	n.a.	-0.80**
Strongly disagree	n.a.	n.a.	-0.95**

table continued on next page

Regression models A1–3 cont.

	Model A1 England/ Wales (BSA)	Model A2 Scotland (SSA)	Model A3 Scotland (SSA)
No one should have to sell/re-mortgage home to pay for care			
Strongly agree (reference category)			
Agree	n.a.	n.a.	-0.76**
Neither	n.a.	n.a.	-1.08**
Strongly disagree/disagree	n.a.	n.a.	-0.91**
Political party identification	-	-	n.a.
Economic activity	-	-	n.a.
Household income quartiles	-	-	n.a.
Position on political left–right scale	-	-	n.a.
Whether respondent has ever been a carer	-	-	n.a.
Constant	-0.21**	0.41**	0.24**
Base	*2300*	*1250*	*1325*

* = significant at 95% level
** = significant at 99% level
- = not significant in the regression model
n.a. = not included in the analysis

Models B1–3 follow. Model B2 includes factors found significant in B1 (i.e. class and age), plus attitudes towards selling homes and belief there is no need to save as government will pay for care.

Regression models B1–3: Beliefs about individual responsibility for saving for care/pensions (SSA 2005)

Agree that it's people's own responsibility to …	Model B1 … save for any care they need when older	Model B2 … save for any care they need when older, incl. attitude statements	Model B3 … save so they have a decent pension
Age			
18–29	-0.57*	-0.16	-
30–44	-0.51*	-0.46*	-
45–64	-0.91**	-0.90**	-
65+ *(reference category)*			
Social class			
Managerial/professional	0.39[†]	-	0.73**
Intermediate occupations	0.30	-	0.19
Small employers/own account workers	-0.11	-	0.24
Lower supervisory/technical	-0.53	-	0.37
Routine/semi-routine (reference category)			
No one should have to sell/re-mortgage their home to pay for care			
Strongly agree (reference category)			
Agree	n.a.	0.48**	n.a.
Neither	n.a.	0.17	n.a.
Disagree strongly/disagree	n.a.	0.68**	n.a.
No need for people in Scotland to save for care in old age as government will pay			
Agree/strongly agree (reference category)			
Neither	n.a.	0.09	n.a.
Disagree	n.a.	0.17	n.a.
Disagree strongly	n.a.	0.77**	n.a.
Political party identification			
Labour (reference category)			
None	-	n.a.	0.01
Conservative	-	n.a.	0.62**
Liberal Democrat	-	n.a.	0.25
SNP	-	n.a.	-0.12

table continued on next page

Regression models B1-3 cont.

Agree that it's people's own responsibility to ...	Model B1 ... save for any care they need when older	Model B2 ... save for any care they need when older, incl. attitude statements	Model B3 ... save so they have a decent pension
Sex		n.a	
Economic activity	-	n.a.	-
Household income quartiles	-	n.a.	-
Position on political left–right scale	-	n.a.	-
R or someone known in need of care?	-	n.a.	n.a.
Whether respondent has ever been a carer	-	n.a.	n.a.
Constant	-1.87**	-1.52**	0.006
Base	1237	1314	1241

* = significant at 5% level
** = significant at 1% level
- = not significant in the regression model
n.a. = not included in the analysis
† This was included in the model, but was only marginally significant (p = 0.055)

Regression models C1 and C2: Saying the government should be mainly responsible for ensuring people have enough to live on in retirement (BSA and SSA 2005)

	Model C1 Britain (BSA)	Model C2 Scotland (SSA)
Sex		
Male	-0.26**	-
Female (reference category)		
Household income quartiles		
Lowest (reference category)		
Second lowest	-0.22	0.33
Second highest	-0.26	-0.01
Highest	-0.65**	-0.50**
Social class		
Managerial/professional	-0.43**	-0.85**
Intermediate occupations	-0.30*	-0.74**
Small employers/own account workers	0.01	-0.69**
Lower supervisory/technical	-0.27*	-0.30
Routine/semi-routine (reference category)		
Position on political left–right scale		
More left (reference category)		
Middle	-0.27**	-0.35*
More right	-0.57**	-0.53**
Economic activity		
Paid work	-	0.70**
Unemployed	-	0.42
Permanently sick/disabled	-	0.63*
Retired	-	0.92**
Looking after the home/doing something else (reference category)		
Age	-	-
Political party identification	-	-
R or someone known in need of care?	-	-
Whether respondent has ever been a carer	-	-
Constant	0.25**	0.45**
Base	2544	1248

 * = significant at 5% level
** = significant at 1% level
- = not significant in the regression model

5 Agree to disagree: respect for political opponents

*Katrin Voltmer and Mansur Lalljee**

Conflict and competition are key forces in modern democratic life. Competition is particularly important during elections, when political parties fight for the support needed to retain or gain power. Liberal democratic theorists claim this competition for power is essential for a healthy democracy, as it forces political parties to identify those policy proposals that have public support (Downs, 1957).

However, political conflict and electoral competition also potentially threaten the foundations upon which democracy is built. This is especially so in a country like Britain, where the so-called 'first past the post' system of allocating seats in parliament usually provides one party with a clear majority. The political parties tend to overemphasise the differences that distinguish them from their competitors and to underplay their similarities and possible areas of collaboration (Bogdanor and Butler, 1983). This applies in particular to the two main parties, the Labour Party and the Conservative Party, who have alternated in office and provided all of the country's governments since 1945.

This tendency has arguably been further exacerbated by the ever-growing dominance of the mass media. Conflict, negativism and clear-cut divisions between friend and foe are the ingredients of a good news story, and journalists try to exploit and emphasise these news values as much as possible to maximise audience ratings. Fierce party competition together with an increasingly aggressive style of journalism has led to elections being reported as horse races or even battlefields rather than occasions for public deliberation and rational decision making (Patterson, 1993). Indeed the run-up to the general election on 5th May 2005, which took place only a couple of months before the 2005 *British Social Attitudes* survey was conducted, was characterised by attacks, insults and mudslinging, even though the outcome of the election was fairly predictable from the outset (King, 2006).

---

* Katrin Voltmer is Senior Lecturer in Political Communication at the Institute of Communications Studies, University of Leeds. Mansur Lalljee is University Lecturer in Social Psychology and Fellow of Jesus College, University of Oxford.

How do voters respond to the polarised image of politics to which they are exposed not only during election campaigns, but also during the normal course of politics? Do they adopt confrontational and even hostile attitudes towards the opposing political camp? Or are they capable of thinking across party divisions? In this chapter we propose a notion of 'political respect'. By this we mean whether an individual is willing to recognise those who support the party they themselves oppose as reasonable persons and to attribute at least some value to their political views. We aim to identify what fosters political respect. In particular we are interested whether exposure to opposing political views, either through the media or in everyday conversations with others, ensures that people are more likely to respect the views of political opponents.

Political respect: concept and measurement

The notion of political respect[1] is based on a general concept of respect that was developed by the 18th century philosopher Immanuel Kant. Contemporary social theorists have become increasingly interested in this concept because of its potential role in addressing problems of integration and cooperation in modern society (Benhabib, 1996; Narveson, 2002). Respect involves acknowledging someone's dignity and inherent value as a human being regardless of what he or she thinks or does. It does not necessarily involve agreement with or even liking of that person. Respect is therefore an essential prerequisite of social life, especially in situations where cultural, historical or social differences have caused deep divisions between different segments of society (Lalljee *et al.*, 2006).

In politics, adherence to different ideologies and opposing party camps can lead to antagonisms that prevent people from realising the shortcomings of their own side and incline them to dismiss everything said by the opposing side. Deep party divisions can erode the legitimacy of majority rule when the losing side refuses to accept the authority of a government that is formed by a party they fundamentally reject. Such divisions can also limit the scope for cooperation and compromise between the party in government and opposition parties, as each of them may fear losing the support of their respective supporters if they make concessions to the other side.

But if people respect their political opponents, this can help bridge the lines of party divisions and consequently contribute to the effective functioning of a modern democracy. Almond and Verba (1963) pursue a similar line of argument in their seminal study on the civic culture in modern democracies. While they emphasise the advantages to democracy if people identify strongly with a political party, they also point to the necessity of tolerating partisan differences and moderating one's own political viewpoints. In contrast, sharp partisan antagonisms and hostility between political camps are seen as an impediment to citizens accepting the rules of the game if their preferred party fails to win power (Almond and Verba, 1963: 85–104).

On the basis of these considerations we developed some survey questions designed to measure political respect for political opponents. In a first step we established to which of the Conservatives and Labour respondents were most opposed. We restricted the choice to the Conservatives and Labour because since 1945 only these two have formed the British government. Supporters of smaller parties, such as the Liberal Democrats or the Scottish Nationalist Party, were assumed to be able to express opposition to one of these two main parties, even though they do not support the other. The exact wording of the question was:

> *In modern Britain two parties have been in government, the Conservative Party and the Labour Party. Which of these two parties do you **oppose** more strongly?*

If respondents answered this question by saying "both equally", "neither" or "don't know", they were further asked:

> *If you **had** to choose, is there one you like **less** than the other? If yes, which one?*

No less than 83 per cent expressed opposition to one of the two major parties.

Having established which party respondents most opposed, we then asked them whether they agreed or disagreed with a set of propositions about that party. These propositions were as follows:[2]

> *People who support the Conservative/Labour Party deserve our contempt*
>
> *If I'm honest with myself, I have to say that I don't really respect supporters of the Conservative/Labour Party*
>
> *When the Conservative/Labour Party is in power, I'm turned off politics*
>
> *The Conservative/Labour Party doesn't have any valid point of view*
>
> *It is important to treat supporters of the Conservative/Labour Party with respect*
>
> *I usually take the opinions of the Conservative/Labour Party seriously, even if I don't agree with them*

Those who *disagree* with the first four of these items are reckoned to be expressing political respect, as are those who *agree* with the last two.

Table 5.1 suggests that there is a reasonably high level of respect for political opponents. This is particularly true of those propositions that refer to the supporters of a party, where in each case three-fifths or more express respect. People find it somewhat easier, however, to be dismissive of parties themselves; here somewhat less than half give the respectful response.

Table 5.1 Respect for political opponents

		Agree	Neither agree nor disagree	Disagree
Supporters of the Conservative/Labour Party deserve contempt	%	14	21	63
I don't respect supporters of the Conservative/Labour Party	%	20	19	60
When the Conservative/Labour Party is in power I'm turned off politics	%	21	21	56
The Conservative/Labour Party has no valid point of view	%	28	27	43
Important to treat supporters of Conservative/Labour Party with respect	%	67	22	11
I usually take the opinions of the Conservative/Labour Party seriously	%	48	24	26

Base: 888

In order to simplify the analyses that follow, the six items shown in Table 5.1 were combined into an overall scale of political respect in which the minimum value of 1 indicates the lowest level of respect, and the maximum value of 5 the highest. Further details are given in the appendix to this chapter.

What encourages political respect?

We would anticipate that people become socialised into respecting others, including political opponents, through a range of lifetime experiences. First, the accumulation of experience as someone gets older might lead them to hold a more nuanced view of the strengths and weaknesses of different parties. Second, women are often thought to be encouraged to adopt cooperative attitudes whereas men learn to be more competitive. Finally, through education, individuals are exposed to a large variety of divergent and complex ideas, and this may contribute to more openness towards political differences. Table 5.2 examines whether these expectations are upheld. As well as showing the proportion in each group that has a low, medium and high level of respect, the table also provides, in the form of a correlation coefficient, an overall measure of the degree to which each characteristic is associated with a respondent's score on our political respect index. The bigger the coefficient, the stronger the association.[3]

Education certainly seems to make a difference to the level of political respect. The more formal education someone has received, the higher their level of political respect. Thus, whereas only 15 per cent of those with no qualifications have a high score on our political respect scale, no less than 45 per cent of those with a degree do so.

Table 5.2 Socio-demographic characteristics and political respect

		Political respect			
		Low	**Medium**	**High**	*Base*
Age					
18–24	%	41	27	23	*70*
25–34	%	40	21	32	*105*
35–44	%	32	32	34	*195*
45–54	%	29	29	38	*144*
55–64	%	34	29	33	*171*
65+	%	41	31	25	*203*
Correlation: -0.006					
Gender					
Men	%	33	28	35	*404*
Women	%	38	30	27	*484*
Correlation: -0.073*					
Education					
No qualification	%	52	25	15	*220*
CSE–A level	%	37	29	32	*381*
HE no degree	%	29	32	39	*119*
Degree	%	21	32	45	*149*
Correlation: 0.305**					

Correlations are based on the original full scale of each variable, not the collapsed versions shown in the table; * = significant at 5% level, ** = significant at 1% level

Our other expectations, however, are not fulfilled. True, people gradually seem more likely to exhibit political respect up to the age of 55, but the level of political respect is then somewhat lower again amongst older age groups, and especially so amongst those aged 65 and over. We cannot tell from a single survey, however, whether this pattern means that people become less respectful once again in old age or whether the pattern reflects generational differences in experience, such as perhaps having grown up at a time when partisan differences were sharper than they were subsequently. Meanwhile, women prove not to be more respectful of political opponents at all. Rather, if anything, the opposite is true.

Meanwhile we might also expect the degree to which someone is involved in politics to have an impact on their level of political respect. In particular, it would seem plausible to anticipate that having a strong partisan loyalty to a particular party inhibits voters from considering the validity of contradictory views and hence results in lower levels of respect. However, as Table 5.3 shows this proves not to be the case. The level of political respect amongst those who identify very strongly with a particular political party is much the same as it is amongst those who only identify with a party "fairly" strongly or "not very" strongly. Moreover, all three groups are more respectful than are those who do not identify with a political party at all, nearly half of whom show only a low level of respect for supporters of the party they themselves oppose most.[4] It appears that it is not strong convictions, but detachment from politics that is more likely to result in dismissive attitudes towards fellow citizens with different political views.

Table 5.3 Political orientations and political respect

		Political respect			
		Low	Medium	High	Base
Strength of party identification					
None	%	49	19	25	56
Not very strong	%	34	30	33	458
Fairly strong	%	34	30	31	252
Very strong	%	36	26	28	81
Correlation: 0.013					
Political interest					
Not at all/not very much	%	50	27	17	250
Some	%	35	26	32	311
Quite a lot/a great deal	%	27	31	41	327
Correlation: 0.253**					
Party respondent opposes					
Conservatives	%	36	30	28	545
Labour	%	36	26	36	343
Correlation: 0.046					

Correlations are based on the original full scale of each variable, not the collapsed versions shown in the table; * = significant at 5% level, ** = significant at 1% level

This observation is corroborated when we examine the relationship between how much interest someone has in politics and respect towards political opponents. Reported interest in politics can be regarded as an indicator of general involvement in political matters and in particular of a motivation to acquire and consider information about political issues (Van Deth, 1990). Exactly half of those who reported to be interested in politics "not at all" or "not very much" have a low level of political respect. In contrast only just over a quarter (27 per cent) of those with "a great deal" or "quite a lot" of interest in politics have a low level of respect. Evidently political interest motivates individuals to follow the public debate on political issues, as a result of which they both learn why supporters of the opposite party hold the views that they do and come to accept that they have at least some valid points.

On the other hand one expectation that we might have had given the particular circumstances under which the 2005 *British Social Attitudes* survey was conducted is not upheld. We might have anticipated that in the summer of 2005, after the Labour Party won a third term in office, those opposed to this party would have felt especially frustrated. As a result those who oppose Labour might exhibit lower levels of respect than those who oppose the Conservatives. In fact the two groups are largely similar to each other in their levels of respect. This suggests that political respect is not undermined if one section of the electorate finds itself on the losing side for a substantial period of time.

The role of the media – and talking about politics

When forming their opinions on political matters people rely on information from various sources, not least of which are the mass media. In fact, the media have become a pervasive force in politics that is widely believed to shape people's general political views and beliefs (Zaller, 1992; Norris and Kalb, 1997). However, research has shown that the media are not as all-powerful as they might appear. In their pioneering study of the impact of communications on voting behaviour Lazarsfeld *et al.* (1944/1968) found that instead of having a direct impact on individuals' opinions, media messages are filtered through the conversations that people have in their everyday lives. The impact of the media cannot be understood in isolation. Rather, the media provide citizens with information about political events and ongoing controversies, information which is then evaluated and interpreted in face-to-face conversations (Huckfeldt and Sprague, 1993; Dalton *et al.*, 1998; Schmitt-Beck, 2003).

Both the media and everyday conversations can be expected to influence political respect too. If people are exposed through the media and in their everyday conversations to views contrary to their own, this should encourage them to consider the reasons that other people have for their beliefs, and on the basis of this knowledge develop understanding and esteem for them. In contrast, if people are just exposed to information from the media that is in accord with their own beliefs and if they only discuss politics with people with whom they agree, existing convictions are likely to be reinforced while prejudices against political opponents are perpetuated and perhaps even hardened (Gutman and Thompson, 1996; Huckfeldt *et al.*, 2004; Mutz, 2006).

However, it could be argued that the link between political respect and both people's use of the media and their exposure to contradictory views in everyday conversations is the other way round. Those who cherish the diversity of people and world views may be more inclined to expose themselves to media information that challenges their own beliefs and to mix with people who hold opinions unlike their own. This 'chicken-and-egg' problem is a recurrent issue in studies of political communications (Newton, 1991). Norris (2000) assumes a "virtuous circle" of mutual reinforcement whereby involvement in politics increases the appetite for information from the media, which in turn further promotes political interest and participation. Conversely, an equivalent vicious circle might be at work for those with little interest and involvement in politics.

Nevertheless, we would argue people do not necessarily choose which newspaper to read, which channel to watch, or to whom to talk on the basis of the political views they espouse. In the case of the media, the sports coverage, for example, or the book reviews may matter more. And only a few political addicts will choose their friends simply on the basis of their political views. Moreover, once someone has chosen which newspaper to read or come to regard someone as a friend, they may not find it easy to change their minds, either because of the force of habit and daily routines or, more importantly, because of the social bonds that have been established with a person. Thus, the communication environment within which someone lives becomes a 'social fact' that exerts an independent influence on people's political views. We thus consider it reasonable to assume that if we do uncover a link between the level of political respect and both the kinds of media people use and the everyday conversations they have, this will constitute evidence that people's communication environment has an impact on their level of political respect.

The news media

Journalistic norms of objectivity mean that the mass media disseminate a range of views much wider than people are likely to incur in their day-to-day conversations. Mutz and Martin (2001) therefore argue that the mass media are more effective than interpersonal communication in providing an open forum of public debate. However, in Britain this observation applies primarily to television and radio, which is obliged to observe balance and fairness in covering public affairs. In contrast, most British national newspapers, quality as well as tabloid, avowedly support a particular political party or a related ideology (Brynin and Newton, 2001). This support is not confined to the editorial pages but also influences a paper's news coverage. In the 2005 election campaign the majority of the printed press clearly supported the Labour Party (59 per cent of the overall circulation), putting the Conservative Party (34 per cent of circulation) at a severe disadvantage in their ability to convey their messages to voters (Bartle, 2006). However, readers do not necessarily agree with the editorial line of the newspaper that they read – or indeed believe it. Rather, a significant minority of citizens can be classified as "cross-readers" who choose a newspaper that promotes a political position dissimilar to their own (Newton, 1991).

In any event, apart from the persisting bias in the British printed press, journalists are nowadays adopting a more professional approach to political reporting. This approach emphasises the media's role as a provider of information and watchdog of political power rather than as a partisan participant in political conflicts (McNair, 1999). This development has been further fuelled by the excessive use by politicians of 'spin', which has significantly increased the tension between the current government and the media. Journalists are no longer inclined to take government information at face value. Instead, by default they treat information from official sources with suspicion and 'grill' politicians in order to get at the truth behind the façade (Blumler and Gurevitch, 1995). The consequence of this more confrontational relationship between the media and political officials might be that it has become difficult for citizens to develop respect for political opponents, or indeed any politicians at all. On the other hand perhaps the continued commitment of the broadcast media in particular to balance and fairness might mean that they still help to engender political respect.

Table 5.4 Newspaper endorsement in 2005 election and readers' opposed party

	Opposed party	
	Conservatives	Labour
Affiliation of newspaper read	%	%
Supported Conservative Party	14	42
Supported Labour Party	42	25
Supported Liberal Democrats	3	1
No affiliation/regional paper	10	8
Doesn't read newspaper	29	23
Base	*545*	*343*

The affiliation of newspapers is based on Bartle (2006: 145). Those newspapers supporting the Conservatives are the *Daily Express*, the *Daily Mail* and *The Daily Telegraph*. Those backing Labour are the *Daily Mirrror*, the *Daily Record*, *The Sun*, *The Financial Times*, *The Guardian* and *The Times*. *The Independent* favoured the Liberal Democrats

Table 5.4 shows how many people read a newspaper that in the 2005 general election backed the party to which they are opposed.[5] While clearly more people read a paper that is consonant with their views than *vice versa*, one in four of those opposed to Labour read a paper that supported Labour in 2005, while one in seven (14 per cent) of those opposed to the Conservatives read a paper that supported the Conservatives. Altogether, 18 per cent are "cross-readers" (Newton, 1991). Even though a minority, the proportion of people who receive their political information from a source that favours a party they oppose is surprisingly high.

However, it should also be borne in mind that over a quarter of people (27 per cent) do not regularly read a newspaper at all. In contrast, television news is nearly all pervasive.[6] Just six per cent do not watch any political news on television at all. Equally the provision of television news is dominated by just one player. No less than 65 per cent say that they watch television news most often on the BBC, while a little under a quarter (24 per cent) rely mainly on ITV.

Table 5.5 analyses whether exposure through the mass media to incongruent views, i.e. views with which an individual does not agree, has the expected effect of contributing to respect for political opponents. In one instance at least, it apparently does. Those who usually watch television news at least a few days a week, a behaviour almost bound to ensure that people are exposed to a diversity of views, are more likely to have a high level of respect than are those who do not watch television news as frequently. Amongst the former group 33 per cent have a high level of respect, compared with 17 per cent amongst the latter. There is little sign here that the allegedly more adversarial style of political reporting nowadays is undermining the degree of respect that people have for their political opponents.

In contrast, neither the kind of newspaper that someone reads nor the frequency with which they do so appears to make much difference to their level of respect. In particular, contrary to our expectations, whether somebody reads a newspaper that is biased against or in favour of the political party to which they are opposed does not make any difference to their levels of respect. Meanwhile, those who read a newspaper regularly, exhibit very similar levels of respect to those who do not do so at all. It may be that while the bias displayed by many newspapers inhibits respect, this is counteracted by the fact that reading even a biased newspaper exposes people to a greater diversity of views than does not reading one at all.

Table 5.5 Exposure to news media and political respect

		Political respect			
		Low	**Medium**	**High**	*Base*
Newspaper bias in relation to own preference					
Congruent	%	35	30	31	*404*
Incongruent	%	36	32	30	*164*
Others	%	29	28	40	*73*
Frequency of reading newspaper					
Doesn't read newspaper	%	41	23	28	*247*
Once a week/less often than that	%	30	30	38	*138*
A few days a week/most days	%	38	30	27	*148*
Almost every day/every day	%	34	31	31	*353*
Correlation : 0.012					
Frequency of watching TV news					
Doesn't watch	%	58	20	12	*51*
Once a week/less often than that	%	44	31	19	*25*
A few days a week/most days	%	26	26	36	*128*
Almost every day/every day	%	34	29	32	*682*
Correlation: 0.160**					

Correlations are based on the original full scale of each variable, not the collapsed versions shown in the table; * = significant at 5% level, ** = significant at 1% level

Everyday conversations

How much do people talk to others about politics, and what impact does it have on their level of political respect? Compared with the mass media, interpersonal communication is much more limited in its scope because people can, at least to some extent, choose what to talk about and with whom. Most people tend to prefer to talk to like-minded others in order to avoid conflict and disharmony in personal relationships. They therefore seek the company of people who share their own views. As a consequence, social groups are characterised by a high degree of homogeneity (Mutz, 2002). As Berelson *et al.*, (1954: 108) observed in a study they conducted over 50 years ago: "Most of the political talk involved the exchange of mutually agreeable points of view." Moreover, the coherence of any social group is frequently established and maintained by collectively dismissing ideas and behaviour that do not conform with the group's norms (Noelle-Neumann, 1993). In these circumstances it seems unlikely that everyday conversations encourage people to consider the value of opposing views.

However, thanks to the level of social and spatial mobility in modern societies, social groups are in fact often relatively heterogeneous nowadays and it is now quite likely that an individual will interact with people who come from different social and political backgrounds. Huckfeldt *et al.*, (2004) found, in their study of communication networks, widespread diversity in social interaction along with a high capacity of citizens to tolerate political disagreement. Meanwhile, other characteristics of everyday conversations suggest that they may in fact be more likely to engender political respect than is exposure to the mass media. While the media convey the statements of politicians in their formal roles, statements that are often perceived as lacking authenticity and credibility, everyday conversation involves both speaking and listening to others in a shared environment. This could mean that face-to-face communication may be more likely to facilitate an understanding of other people, their motives, experiences and interests and may more easily generate respect for this person even when there is disagreement on the issue under discussion.

In the 2005 *British Social Attitudes* survey we asked a detailed set of questions designed to establish how often people talk about politics and to what extent these discussions cut across party lines. Moreover, we also ascertained with whom those conversations are held. This enables us to distinguish between close relationships where we can expect a high degree of homogeneity of political views, and more distant relationships, such as with colleagues at the workplace, where an individual has little control over whom they meet and with whom they converse. The questions were as follows:

> *From time to time people discuss political matters or current affairs with other people. How often do you talk about politics with the following people:*
> *Your husband/wife/partner*

(Other) family members

Friends

Fellow workers

Neighbours

Anyone else, for example, casual acquaintances or strangers?

In each case respondents were invited to give one of six possible answers ranging from "every day" to "never". Then, unless a respondent said they never talked politics to that kind of person, for each type of political discussion partner they were asked:

> *Does/Do any of your (discussion partners)* **support** *the Conservative/ Labour Party, that is, the party you yourself feel more opposed to?*

In the case of someone's spouse or partner, respondents were simply asked to state "yes" or "no". So far as the other kinds of discussion partners are concerned they were asked to indicate what proportion of them supported the party they most opposed by using a four-point scale ranging from "all of them" to "a few of them".

Table 5.6 Frequency of political discussion with different kinds of people

Frequency of political discussions if have this type of partner	Spouse/ partner	Family	Friends	Fellow workers	Neigh-bours	Others
	%	%	%	%	%	%
At least once a week	38	15	19	25	3	2
No more than a couple of times a month	41	48	46	39	21	1
Never discusses politics	21	36	34	35	76	77
Base	*585*	*1052*	*1070*	*540*	*1062*	*1057*
% of all respondents who don't have this type of conversation partner	37	2	1	48	2	2

Base: 1075

Table 5.6 provides an overview of the frequency with which people engage in political discussions with different kinds of discussion partners during the course of everyday conversation. Unsurprisingly, people talk about politics most frequently with their spouse or partner if they have one. Only just over one in five (21 per cent) of those with a spouse or partner say they never discuss politics with them. Thereafter people talk about politics most frequently with fellow workers, family and friends. In each case only just over a third say they never discuss politics with such persons (though, whereas nearly everyone says they have family or friends to whom they talk, only just over half have fellow workers with whom they converse at all). In contrast, politics plays only a marginal role in conversations with neighbours and casual acquaintances; in both cases over three-quarters say they never discuss politics at all.

Table 5.7 Proportion of discussants supporting the party respondent opposes, by type of conversation partner

| | Conversation partner | | | | | |
Proportion of political discussants supporting party respondent opposes	Spouse/ partner	Family	Friends	Fellow workers	Neigh- bours	Others
	%	%	%	%	%	%
None of them	84	60	36	26	33	29
At least a few/yes	7	27	48	48	29	49
Don't know	6	11	13	22	34	18
Base	*408*	*582*	*606*	*317*	*227*	*225*

+ People who do not discuss politics with that kind of person are excluded

Politics features then in many an everyday conversation. Indeed, overall only 17 per cent say they never talk to anyone about political matters. But how commonly are these conversations with those who hold different political views? Table 5.7 suggests that the more distant the relationship the more likely it is that different views will be encountered. Not surprisingly, people are least likely to disagree politically with their spouses or partners. Only seven per cent of those living with a spouse or partner oppose the party their partner supports. Similarly, most people usually find themselves in agreement when they talk about politics to other members of their family; no less than three in five say that none of the other family members with whom they discuss politics support the party they themselves opposed.

In contrast, even though individuals can exert a high degree of choice in the selection of their friends, more people say they have at least a few friends who support the party they themselves oppose than say they do not. Evidently most people do not choose their friends on the basis of their political views, which in any event may only become apparent once the relationship has been formed. It appears that people are also relatively likely to meet opposing views if they talk politics with fellow workers or casual acquaintances. Political discussions at work might be low-key occasions, for example over lunch, but they evidently provide exposure to opposing views expressed by people one knows well from day-to-day interactions. On the other hand even the minority who do talk politics with their neighbours are often not sure which party they support, perhaps because such conversations are often more fleeting and polite encounters.

Taking all types of discussion partners, 39 per cent of people do encounter disagreement in their political conversations, whereas as many as 45 per cent of people talk about politics exclusively to people who do not support the party they themselves oppose. It is difficult to judge whether this means the glass is half full or half empty. However, given people's tendency to prefer to talk to people with whom they get along, the extent to which face-to-face communication does bridge the lines of partisan divisions is perhaps rather surprising.

In any event, our expectation is that those who do talk with others of different views are more likely to exhibit a high level of political respect. Table 5.8 compares for each kind of discussion partner the degree of respect held by people who talk only to those with whom they agree about political matters with the level of respect amongst those who do talk to those with a different party preference.

Without exception, those who talk about politics to people who support the party they themselves oppose exhibit a higher degree of respect than do those who do not (though, exceptionally, in the case of neighbours this difference is not statistically significant). This holds in particular in the case of disagreement with friends, fellow workers and casual acquaintances. For example, 44 per cent of those who discuss politics with at least a few friends who support the party they themselves oppose have a high level of political respect, compared with only 26 per cent of those who only discuss politics with friends who do not support that party. However, much as we found that those who did not watch television news or read a newspaper at all, so also sometimes it is those who do not talk politics at all who exhibit the lowest level of respect of all. This is certainly true of those who do not talk politics with their spouse or partner or with friends or family, perhaps because not talking about politics with those with whom one is relatively intimate is associated with low involvement in politics of any kind.

Table 5.8 Effect of similarity and difference in discussant and respondents' views on political respect

Political discussants		Low	Medium	High	Base
			Political respect		
Spouse/partner					
Does not support opposed party	%	34	30	34	*341*
Supports opposed party	%	17	29	49	*29*
Do not talk politics	%	55	21	12	*94*
Correlation: 0.18**					
Family					
Do not support opposed party	%	33	34	31	*341*
Support opposed party	%	23	30	44	*157*
Do not talk politics	%	46	24	23	*308*
Correlation: 0.13**					
Friends					
Do not support opposed party	%	40	33	26	*213*
Support opposed party	%	21	30	47	*288*
Do not talk politics	%	48	24	19	*300*
Correlation: 0.28**					
Fellow workers					
Do not support opposed party	%	41	34	22	*84*
Support opposed party	%	20	33	46	*144*
Do not talk politics	%	41	23	29	*165*
Correlation: 0.26**					
Neighbours					
Do not support opposed party	%	38	31	29	*75*
Support opposed party	%	33	29	37	*55*
Do not talk politics	%	37	29	29	*679*
Correlation:0.08					
Others					
Do not support opposed party	%	41	30	28	*68*
Support opposed party	%	17	32	50	*102*
Do not talk politics	%	39	28	28	*674*
Correlation: 0.28**					

Correlations are based on the original full political respect scale, not the collapsed version shown in the table; they exclude those who did not talk politics to someone in the relevant category; * = significant at 5% level, ** = significant at 1% level

The sources of political respect

So far we have discussed various factors that might foster, or suppress, respect for political opponents. However, since none of these possible influences work in isolation, looking at each of them separately without taking into account the possible impact of the others cannot provide us with a comprehensive story. We have thus undertaken a regression analysis that allows us to assess the relative strength of each factor we have considered so far simultaneously while holding all the others constant (for further details about regression analysis see the appendix at the end of this Report). The model includes gender, age, education, as well as interest in politics and the strength of party identification. In addition, exposure to political information through the mass media is measured both by the frequency with which an individual reads a newspaper and by how often they watch television news. The possible impact of reading a biased newspaper is assessed by including two variables, which compare those who read a newspaper that *supports* the party they themselves oppose with those who read a newspaper that *opposes* the party they oppose. Finally, we include two variables, the first of which measures the frequency with which someone talks politics with anyone, and the second, the degree to which an individual talks to people who hold different political views from themselves.[7]

Table 5.9 Regression model of political respect

	Standardised Beta coefficient
Gender (male = 1, female = 2)	-0.008
Age	0.054
Education	0.251**
Political interest	0.155**
Strength of party identification	-0.061
Frequency of newspaper exposure	0.001
Newspaper biased in favour of opposed party	-0.141**
Newspaper biased against opposed party	-0.177**
Frequency of television news exposure	0.129**
Frequency of talk about politics	-0.033
Diversity of interpersonal communication	0.231**
R^2 0.19	

Method: enter, pairwise deletion of missing values. Number of cases in model: 624; * = significant at 5% level, ** = significant at 1% level. All variables are scored so that high values denote high degree or high frequency

Table 5.9 shows the results of this model. In particular, it shows the standardised coefficient for each variable in the model. The bigger this statistic the more it accounts for the level of political respect. The results, in fact, largely confirm the findings of our analysis to date.

As has been documented in many other studies on political culture (Almond and Verba, 1963; Jennings *et al.*, 1989), education plays a major role in providing citizens with the competencies and experiences that enable them to respond positively to the conflicts and contradictions of party politics. Interest in politics is another factor that motivates citizens to consider the value of political views they themselves do not share. However, regardless of these individual predispositions the diversity of views that someone encounters also influences the level of respect for supporters of the opposite political camp. The more people talk about politics with others with whom they disagree on political matters the more they are able to acknowledge divergent standpoints. Watching television news has a similar, albeit markedly weaker, positive effect. In contrast, obtaining political information from the printed press seems to undermine respect for the other side. Since these findings have not been evident from the bivariate analyses presented in previous tables they should be treated with caution. Reading a newspaper that is congruent with one's own view is related to lack of respect for political opponents. This makes sense, as such newspapers simply reinforce one's own views and present opposing views in an unfavourable light. Surprisingly, however, it seems that reading newspapers that are not congruent with one's views is also related to lack of respect. Contrast this with the results for interpersonal communication where talking to people with opposing views is related to greater respect.

Our findings thus imply that people do not respond to opposing viewpoints that come from the media, and especially from a biased media source, in the same way they do when they hear such viewpoints in personal encounters that form part of their everyday lives. We can only speculate why this should be so. One possibility could be that the impersonal nature of the media makes it relatively easy to dismiss arguments one disagrees with. Another could be that people have different normative expectations about the media than they do about interpersonal exchanges. Research has shown that while audiences may be willing to trust media outlets that are objective and fair, they certainly mistrust any news that they suspect to be biased (McQuail, 1992). This is not true of interpersonal communication. Here, views that are expressed are regarded as authentic, and as a result people are more willing to listen to what a person has to say even when they disagree with him or her.

Does political respect matter for democracy?

Undoubtedly, respect for political opponents is of high value in civic life and the way in which citizens interact with each other. It helps bridge the divisions between citizens who do not share the same preferences. However, theorists of democracy base their claim that political respect is desirable not only on the benefit it might have for the quality of civic life, but also on the wider consequences it has for the functioning and stability of democracy. In the final section of this chapter we briefly consider whether political respect for political opponents translates into a positive attitude towards political institutions more generally.

Democracy depends on its ability to secure the support of all citizens, not just those who support the current government, but also – and even more crucially – those who do not (Easton, 1965). In particular, it has been argued that the degree of trust in political institutions and those who occupy those institutions is one of the key resources of a healthy democracy (Hetherington, 2004). Without popular trust that transcends party loyalties, parliaments and governments would lose their legitimacy to make decisions that in some instances are likely to contradict the interests and preferences of some citizens. Trust in political institutions and respect for political opponents share some common features, so we can anticipate that the latter is likely to foster the former. Both orientations are based on a recognition of others – be it fellow citizens or officials and politicians acting in political institutions – as reasonable persons that hold their opinions and make their decisions on well-considered grounds. Further, both trust and respect are attitudes that are supposed to be maintained even when someone disagrees with decisions that are being taken or views that are being espoused.

In 2005 at the time of the *British Social Attitudes* survey the willingness of those who opposed the Labour Party to trust political institutions might have been particularly likely to have been undermined. Labour had after all just won its third election in a row (and did so despite winning just 36 per cent of the vote). We thus might anticipate that those who oppose Labour might show lower levels of political trust even if they are respectful of the views of those who support Labour.

To measure their level of political trust, respondents were asked the following two questions:

> *How much do you trust British governments of any party to place the needs of the nation above the interests of their own political party?*

> *And how much do you trust politicians of any party in Britain to tell the truth when they are in a tight corner?*

For both questions there were four possible answers, ranging from "just about always" to "almost never". The questions tap into two aspects of political trust, namely trust in institutions and trust in the credibility of politicians as individuals. However, for the purposes of our analysis the two questions were combined into a single index such that its maximum value of 4 indicates the highest level of trust, and the minimum value of 1 the lowest. Table 5.10 shows respondents' average score on this index broken down by both the level of political respect a person has and the party to which they are opposed.

There is a moderately strong relationship between respect for political opponents on the one hand and trust in government and politicians on the other. The higher the level of respect, the more individuals express a degree of political trust. The average trust score of all those with a low level of respect is 1.78 whereas it is 1.97 for those with a high level of respect. However, this relationship is markedly stronger for opponents of the present government. Levels of trust are particularly low amongst those opponents of Labour who have little respect for the party and its supporters. Those with a low level of respect who oppose the Conservatives have their trust in political institutions fostered by the fact that the Conservatives are out of power. Opponents of Labour do not. For them their level of trust depends crucially on their level of respect for their political opponents.

Table 5.10 Mean level of political trust (out of four), by party opposed and political respect

	Opposed party		All
Respect	Conservatives	Labour	
Low	1.87	1.63	1.78
Medium	1.99	1.75	1.91
High	2.01	1.93	1.97
Correlation	0.13**	0.23**	0.16**
Base	*501*	*333*	*834*

Correlations are based on the original full political respect scale, not the collapsed version shown in the table; * = significant at 5% level, ** = significant at 1% level

Conclusions

In this chapter we introduced the concept of respect for political opponents. This denotes an individual's willingness to acknowledge the validity of opposing views and to esteem fellow citizens who support a party of the opposite political camp. Respect for political opponents is thought to help bridge political divisions and to enable cooperation and dialogue amongst citizens regardless of their political beliefs. However, while democratic theorists have repeatedly emphasised the significance of political respect, it has rarely been empirically studied. In this chapter we have tried to fill that gap.

The basis of political respect lies in the communications that individuals receive. So long as it presents people with a diversity of views, communication provides individuals with the opportunity to learn about the views and experiences of other people and to develop an understanding of and esteem for those with whom they disagree. We thus analysed the degree to which both exposure to the mass media and discussion about politics in everyday conversations appear to generate respect across party lines.

Our results reveal a rather mixed picture so far as the mass media are concerned. On the one hand we found that those who follow political news on television regularly show higher levels of respect than those who watch rarely or avoid political programmes altogether. On the other hand it appears that the printed press in Britain contributes very little to the development of political respect. Even those who read a newspaper that supports the party they themselves oppose are apparently no more likely to be respectful as a result. Apparently the manifest partisan bias of British newspapers helps ensure that whatever information it does convey is discounted if not indeed ignored.

In any event, despite the media's pervasive presence in modern politics and its indispensable role in providing political information, it is interpersonal communication that appears to be the more effective source of respect for political opponents. Of course it does so only if it involves people who have different political convictions; political conversations with like-minded folk simply perpetuate and may even increase negative attitudes towards supporters of a different party. However, less than half socialise exclusively with like-minded others. While political disagreement with spouses and partners or even other members of one's family is relatively rare, it is relatively commonplace in less intense relationships and in environments such as the workplace, where an individual cannot necessarily choose to whom they talk.

Still, even discussion with like-minded others may be better than no discussion at all. For those with the lowest level of respect are those who appear to be disengaged from the political process, i.e. those with little interest in politics, with no party identification, with low exposure to media information and who avoid discussing politics with anyone. Lack of any kind of engagement simply breeds dismissive attitudes towards people with different political beliefs.

However, political respect not only facilitates mutual understanding amongst and between fellow citizens but also helps promote trust in political institutions outside an individual's immediate social environment. This is particularly true for those who oppose the party currently in government. For them, respect for fellow citizens can serve as a vital mechanism that enables them to accept the government of the day, even though they disagree with many of its actual policies. Evidently there is a need for a balance between on the one hand the adversarial politics of liberal democracy, and on the other a political culture that is built on mutual recognition and openness to "hearing the other side" (Mutz, 2006).

Notes

1. It needs to be emphasised that the concept of respect presented here is not related to Tony Blair's respect agenda, which focuses on respectful behaviour towards authorities and adherence to law and order.

2. In the survey we originally included eight statements designed to measure respect for political opponents. However, a factor analysis of these produced two dimensions, with the first factor accounting for 36 per cent of the variance, the second factor for 16 per cent. Since the two items on the second factor showed only weak correlations with the variables relevant to this study, we omitted them from the analyses presented here.

3. Our correlation coefficient is Pearson's R.

4. This observation is, however, based on only 63 respondents so has to be treated with some caution.

5. Although *The Independent* backed the Liberal Democrats, in subsequent analyses we regard it as having been more favourable to Labour than to the Conservatives. Thus

those who read this newspaper and are opposed to Labour are classified as being exposed to political views with which they normally disagree.

6. Television news, regardless of which channel, is regarded as balanced without systematic endorsement of a particular political party. It is therefore not included in Table 5.5.

7. The index that measures the degree to which an individual talks to people who support the opposed party is based on the set of six variables of political disagreement with one's partner, family, friends, fellow workers, neighbours and others presented in Table 5.8. In each of these six variables talking to people who support the opposed party is indicated by 1, whereas talking to people who hold congruent political views is indicated by 0. Counting across all types of discussant results in a variable that can range between 0, indicating that none of a person's political discussants supports the opposed party, and 6, indicating political disagreement within each type of discussants. However, the highest empirically observed value is 5.

References

Almond, G.A. and Verba, S. (1963), *The Civic Culture: Political Attitudes and Democracy in Five Nations*, Princeton: Princeton University Press

Bartle, J. (2006), 'The Labour government and the media', in Bartle, J. and King, A. (eds.), *Britain at the Polls 2005*, Washington, DC: CQ Press

Benhabib, S. (ed.) (1996), *Democracy and Difference: Contesting the Boundaries of the Political*, Princeton: Princeton University Press

Berelson, B.R., Lazarsfeld, P.F. and McPhee, W.N. (1954), *Voting: A Study of Opinion Formation in a Presidential Campaign*, Chicago: University of Chicago Press

Blumler, J.G. and Gurevitch, M. (1995), *The Crisis of Public Communication*, London/New York: Routledge

Bogdanor, V. and Butler, D. (eds.) (1983), *Democracy and Elections: Electoral Systems and their Political Consequences,* Cambridge: Cambridge University Press

Brynin, M. and Newton, K. (2003), 'The national press and voting turnout: British general elections of 1992 and 1997', in *Political Communication*, **20**: 59–77

Dalton, R.J., Beck, P.A. and Huckfeldt, R. (1998), 'Partisan cues and the media: Information flows in the 1992 presidential election', *American Political Science Review*, **92**: 111–126

Downs, A. (1957), *An Economic Theory of Democracy*, New York: Harper & Row

Easton, D. (1965), *A Systems Analysis of Political Life*, Chicago: University of Chicago Press

Gutman, A. and Thompson, D. (1996), *Democracy and Disagreement*, Cambridge: Cambridge University Press

Hetherington, M.J. (2004), *Why Trust Matters: Declining Political Trust and the Demise of American Liberal Democracy*, Princeton: Princeton University Press

Huckfeldt, R., Johnson, P.E. and Sprague, J. (2004), *Political Disagreement: The Survival of Diverse Opinions within Communication Networks*, Cambridge: Cambridge University Press

Huckfeldt, R. and Sprague, J. (1993), 'Citizens, politics, and social communication', in Finifter, A.W. (ed.), *Political Science: The State of the Discipline II*, Washington DC: American Political Science Association

Jennings, M.K., Van Deth, J.W. *et al.* (1989), *Continuities in Political Action: A Longitudinal Study of Political Orientations in Three Western Democra*cies, Berlin/New York: De Gruyter

King, A. (2006), 'Why Labour won – yet again', in Bartle, J. and King, A. (eds.), *Britain at the Polls 2005*, Washington DC: CQ Press

Lalljee, M., Tam, T. and Lee, J. (2006, forthcoming), Unconditional respect for persons and its relationship with intergroup attitudes and action tendencies

Lazarsfeld, P.F., Berelson, B. and Gaudet, H. (1944/1968), *The People's Choice: How the Voter Makes up His Mind in a Presidential Campaign*, New York: Columbia University Press

McNair, B. (1999), *News and Journalism in the UK*, London/New York: Routledge

McQuail, D. (1992), *Media Performance: Mass Communication and the Public Interest*, London: Sage

Mutz, D.C. (2002), 'Cross-cutting social networks: Testing democratic theory in practice', *American Political Science Review*, **96**: 111–126

Mutz, D.C. (2006), *Hearing the Other Side: Deliberative versus Participatory Democracy*, Cambridge: Cambridge University Press

Mutz, D.C. and Martin, P.S. (2001), 'Facilitating communication across lines of political difference: The role of mass media', *American Political Science Review*, **95**: 97–114

Narveson, J. (2002), *Respecting Persons in Theory and Practice: Essays on Moral and Political Philosophy*, Lanham: Rowman & Littlefield

Newton, K. (1991), 'Do people read everything they believe in the papers? Newspapers and voters in the 1983 and 1987 elections', in Crewe, I. *et al.* (eds.), *British Elections and Parties Yearbook*, Hemel Hempstead: Simon & Schuster

Noelle-Neumann, E. (1993), *The Spiral of Silence: Public Opinion – Our Social Skin*, 2nd edition, Chicago: Chicago University Press

Norris, P. (2000), *A Virtuous Circle: Political Communications in Post-Industrial Democracies*, Cambridge: Cambridge University Press

Norris, P. and Kalb, M. (eds.) (1997), *Politics and the Press: The News Media and their Influences*, Boulder: Rienner

Patterson, T.E. (1993), *Out of Order*, New York: Knopf

Schmitt-Beck, R. (2003), 'Mass communication, personal communication and vote choice: The filter hypothesis of media influence in comparative perspective', *British Journal of Political Science*, **33**: 233–259

Van Deth, J.W. (1990), 'Interest in politics', in Jennings, M.K., Van Deth, J.W. *et al.*, *Continuities in Political Action: A Longitudinal Study of Political Orientations in Three Western Democracies*, Berlin/New York: De Gruyter

Zaller, J.R. (1992), *The Nature and Origins of Mass Opinion*, Cambridge: Cambridge University Press

Acknowledgements

The authors wish to thank the Economic and Social Research Council (ESRC) for providing funding that enabled us to include the questions on political respect, involvement in interpersonal communication and mass media use in the 2005 *British Social Attitudes* survey. The questions are part of a project on 'Conflict, Communication and Respect for Political Opponents', Ref No RES–000–22–1257.

Appendix

Construction of the variable 'Political Respect'

The initial set of questions designed to measure political respect consisted of eight items. A factor analysis produced two dimensions with the first factor accounting for 36 per cent of the variance and the second factor for 16 per cent. Because the second factor showed only weak correlations with the variables relevant for the present study, it was omitted from the analyses. The items in the second factor are:

> *The (Conservative/Labour) Party looks after the genuine needs and interests of some people in our society*
> *People should give careful consideration to suggestions made by the (Conservative/Labour) Party*

Thus, in the present analysis we are exclusively using the first factor that includes the six items described earlier. After reversing items with negative question wording we constructed an additive index across all six items. This index was then divided by the number of items to regain the original scale range, with 1 indicating the lowest level of political respect and 5 indicating the highest. Cronbach's alpha for the political respect scale is .77.

For presentation in cross-tables the index was divided into three percentiles indicating low, medium and high levels of political respect. 'Low' respect is scores between 1 and 3.17 on the scale, 'medium' is scores between 3.33 and 3.67, and 'high' is scores between 3.83 and 5.

6 Proportional representation and the disappearing voter

John Curtice, Stephen Fisher and Laurence Lessard-Phillips[*]

The outcome of the 2005 general election raised a number of important questions about the health of Britain's democracy. At 61 per cent, turnout was only two points higher than it had been in 2001, when the proportion that voted had been lower than at any time since 1918. Such an outcome appeared to confirm the widely espoused argument that the electorate is now 'disengaged' from politics. Meanwhile, although Labour was re-elected with a comfortable overall majority of 66 seats, it did so on the basis of just 36 per cent of the popular vote, the lowest share of the vote ever secured by a majority government in British electoral history.[1] For its critics, this feature of the result provided more than ample evidence that the first-past-the-post electoral system used in elections to the House of Commons is deeply flawed and 'unfair'.

This chapter looks beneath the rhetoric with which these features of the 2005 results were greeted. It addresses three questions. Why, once again, did so few people vote? Did the outcome generate disenchantment with the first-past-the-post electoral system amongst the wider public? And does the electoral system have an impact on who does or does not vote? By looking more closely at why, once again, so few people voted and how the public reacts to the first-past-the-post electoral system we aim to inform the debate about how to 'reform' and 'improve' our democracy.

Turnout

There are two broad classes of explanations as to why turnout has been so low in the last two general elections. The first focuses primarily on the motivations

---

[*] John Curtice is Research Consultant at the *Scottish Centre for Social Research*, part of NatCen, Deputy Director of CREST, and Professor of Politics at Strathclyde University. Stephen Fisher is Lecturer in Political Sociology and Fellow of Trinity College, University of Oxford. Laurence Lessard-Phillips is a DPhil student in the Department of Sociology and Nuffield College, University of Oxford.

of voters. It argues that voters have become increasingly 'disengaged' from politics, by which is usually meant that they are both less interested in and more cynical about conventional politics and politicians. A number of reasons have been offered as to why this might have happened. One is that society has become more 'individualistic' and as a result younger people in particular are less likely to feel they have a duty to engage in an activity from which they are unlikely to benefit (Clarke *et al.*, 2004). Another is that as society has become better educated so expectations of what government should do have increased while governments' capacity to deliver has if anything declined; the resulting gap makes people cynical about politics and less likely to get involved (Dalton, 2004). A third lays the blame on the media, either because its style of political reporting has allegedly become more critical and obsessed with personal scandal, thereby eroding trust (Blumler, 1997), or else simply because spending too much time watching television stops people from getting involved in collective social activities including getting involved in politics (Putnam, 2000).

The second class of explanations suggests that turnout has been low at recent general elections not because voters have changed but, rather, because the choice put before voters has (Heath and Taylor, 1999; Franklin, 2004). First, thanks primarily to the reinvention of the Labour Party as 'New Labour' in the 1990s, the differences between the parties' policy positions has been much narrower than before (Bara and Budge, 2001; Bara, 2006). Second, the Labour Party has enjoyed an unprecedented period of dominance in the opinion polls. By the time of the 2005 election Labour had been continuously in the lead in the polls for more than twelve years – ever since 'Black Wednesday' in September 1992 when the then Conservative government suffered the ignominy of being forced to withdraw the pound from the European Exchange Rate Mechanism. Although, at five points, the average Labour lead in the final polls of the 2005 campaign was lower than the double digit leads recorded in both 1997 and 2001, the polls (especially when converted into predicted outcomes in seats by the media) arguably, once again, sent the message in 2005 that a Labour victory was not in doubt (Curtice, 2005). In short, in 2005 as in 2001, voters were arguably given the message that it was clear that the incumbent government would be re-elected while who won would not make much difference to the policies that were pursued in government anyway, conditions that rational theorists of voting behaviour have long suggested are likely to depress turnout (Aldrich, 1993).

Analysis of data collected by the 2001 *British Social Attitudes* survey suggested that the second class of explanations appeared to provide the more convincing explanation of why turnout fell so heavily at that election (Bromley and Curtice, 2002). The narrowing of the policy differences between the parties was noticed by voters; fewer felt there was a big difference between the Conservatives and Labour than at any time since the 1960s. In contrast, while cynicism about politics had become more widespread, political cynics were *not* markedly less likely to vote. Meanwhile, people were just as likely as ever to evince an interest in politics or to say that they had a duty to vote. Rather, what did appear to have happened is that turnout fell particularly heavily amongst those who were *already* 'disengaged' from the political process – that is, amongst the group that *always* needs persuading that it is worth turning out to vote, and who are most likely to be dissuaded from doing so if the outcome looks like a foregone conclusion and there are few apparent differences between the parties.

Most of the questions that formed the basis of this analysis of what happened in 2001 were repeated in our 2005 survey. We can therefore establish whether the picture that we painted of what happened in 2001 was repeated in 2005. If our original picture was accurate, we should expect to find that few people continued to see much difference between the parties and that those with low levels of interest in politics should once again have been particularly likely to have stayed at home. At the same time we should be able to show that the proportion of people with an interest in politics or who feel they have a duty to vote should continue to exhibit little change.

The motivation to vote in 2005

We begin by considering what motivations to vote the public brought to the 2005 election. Perhaps the most obvious such motivation is how interested someone is in politics. This is measured in the *British Social Attitudes* survey by asking:

> *How much interest do you generally have in what is going on in politics…*
>
> *…a great deal,*
>
> *quite a lot,*
>
> *some,*
>
> *not very much,*
>
> *or, none at all?*

Figure 6.1 illustrates just how remarkably stable the pattern of answers to this question has been over the last twenty years. Never has the proportion that says it has a "great deal" or "quite a lot" of interest in politics been either less than 27 per cent or more than 33 per cent (the figure that was obtained in 2005). In other words, around three in ten adults in Britain have a high degree of interest in politics, and this is no more or no less than was the case twenty years ago. Politics is largely a minority interest, but that has always been true.

Figure 6.1 Trends in per cent with "a great deal" or "quite a lot" of interest in politics, 1986–2005[2]

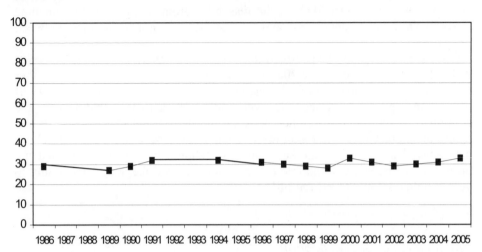

Much the same can be said about reported duty to vote. This was ascertained by asking respondents:

> *Which of these statements comes <u>closest</u> to your view about general elections?*
>
> *In a general election…*
>
> *It's not really worth voting*
>
> *People should vote only if they care who wins*
>
> *It's everyone's duty to vote*

Table 6.1 Trends in civic duty, 1991–2005

	'91	'94	'96	'98	'00	'01	'05	Net change '91–'05
% who say …								
It's not worth voting	8	9	8	8	11	11	12	+4
Should only vote if you care who wins	24	21	26	26	24	23	23	-1
Duty to vote	68	68	64	65	64	65	64	-4
Base	1224	970	989	1654	2008	2795	1732	

While, as Table 6.1 shows, the proportion who say it is everyone's duty to vote has been three or four points lower on every occasion on which this question has been asked since 1996 than it was prior to that date, there is no evidence of a continuous secular decline (or indeed of any decline at all) since the time of the 1997 election. Moreover, whatever decline may have occurred since the early 1990s has been far too small to account for the fact that turnout was nearly 20 points lower in 2001 and 2005 than it had been in 1992.

In contrast, the same could not be said about levels of political cynicism. As Table 6.2 shows, the proportion that trust "governments of any party to place the needs of the nation above the interests of their own political party" has fallen steadily and consistently over the last twenty years.[3] Only just over one in four now say that they trust governments "just about always" or "most of the time", whereas nearly half said that they did so at the time of the 1987 general election.

Table 6.2 Trends in trust in governments to place the needs of the nation above political party interests, 1987–2005

	1987	1997	2001	2005	Net change 1987–2005
	%	%	%	%	
Just about always/most of the time	47	33	29	26	-21
Only some of the time/ almost never	52	65	70	73	+21
Base	*3414*	*2906*	*1099*	*3167*	

Source: 1987 and 1997: British Election Study

Nevertheless, we should note that much of this decline in political trust occurred between 1987 and 1997, whereas most of the fall in turnout has occurred since 1997. (Turnout was only four points lower in 1997 than it was in 1987.) This raises some doubt about the degree to which the fall in turnout can simply be accounted for by the increase in cynicism. In any event, Table 6.3 confirms that the turnout gap between those with high and low political cynicism is not large enough for the decline in trust (documented in Table 6.2) to account for the fall in turnout. Those who say they trust governments "only some of the time" are only a little less likely to say they voted than are those who say they trust them "just about always" or "most of the time". Only amongst those who "almost never" trust governments, who even by 2005 constituted little more than a quarter of the public, is turnout clearly somewhat lower. In any event, if the decline in turnout were simply the result of the decline in trust, we should find that the level of turnout amongst those with any given level of trust should have been just the same in 2001 and 2005 as it was in 1997. In practice, even those with relatively high levels of trust were less likely to vote in 2001 and 2005 than they had been in 1997.

Table 6.3 Trust in government and electoral participation, 1997–2005[4]

Trust government to place needs of the nation above those of own party ...	% voted 1997	% voted 2001	% voted 2005	Change 1997– 2005	Change 2001– 2005
... just about always/most of the time	85	74	74	-11	0
... only some of the time	78	69	71	-7	+2
... almost never	67	51	61	-6	+10

Moreover, in one respect at least there appears to have been some recovery of public confidence in the political system in recent years. The degree of confidence that people have in the ability and willingness of the political system to respond to their demands, a characteristic known as 'system efficacy' (Almond and Verba, 1963), no longer appears to be in decline. Table 6.4 shows the proportion who, after the 1987 election, together with the three most recent elections, strongly agreed with three negative statements about the political process, thereby exhibiting a very low level of system efficacy. These proportions clearly increased between 1997 and 2001, but now appear to have fallen back again to little more than their previous level.

Table 6.4 Trends in system efficacy, 1987–2005

% strongly agree	1987	1997	2001	2005
Parties are only interested in people's votes, not in their opinions	16	16	27	17
Generally speaking, those we elect as MPs lose touch with people pretty quickly	n/a	n/a	25	16
It doesn't really matter which party is in power, in the end things go on much the same	7	8	18	12
Base	3826	2906	1099	3167

Source: 1987 and 1997: British Election Study
n/a = not asked

Still, we should acknowledge that in one respect at least the public do now appear to be more disconnected from politics than they once were. As demonstrated in Chapter 1 of this Report, there has been a long-term decline in the proportion who feel a strong sense of identity with a political party. Thus, whereas in 1987 nearly half felt a "very" or "fairly" strong sense of identity with a political party, now barely more than a third do. Someone who feels a strong sense of identity with a political party is likely to want to vote because in backing a particular party they are making a statement about who they are and what they believe. However, the decline in the proportion who feel a strong sense of identity long predates the fall in turnout in 2001 (see also Crewe and Thomson, 1999) and before then had not been accompanied by a marked fall in turnout. The decline in party identification cannot then, on its own at least, be a sufficient explanation of the much lower levels of turnout that occurred in 2001 and 2005.

Perceptions of the parties

What of the argument that turnout has been low at recent general elections because voters did not feel they had much of a choice? The first piece of evidence required to support such an argument is that voters feel that there are fewer differences these days between the policy positions of the parties. We can assess this by looking at how people have responded over the years to the following question:

> *Now considering everything the Conservative and Labour parties stand for, would you say that...*
>
> *... there is a great difference between them,*
>
> *some difference,*
>
> *or, not much difference?*

Table 6.5 Perceived difference between Conservative and Labour parties, 1964–2005

	'64	'66	'70	'74 F	'74 O	'79	'83	'87	'92	'97	'01	'05
Difference between parties ...	%	%	%	%	%	%	%	%	%	%	%	%
... great	48	44	33	34	40	48	88	85	56	33	17	13
... some	25	27	28	30	30	30	10	11	32	43	39	43
... not much	27	29	39	36	30	22	7	5	12	24	44	44
Base	*1699*	*1804*	*1780*	*2391*	*2332*	*1826*	*3893*	*3776*	*1794*	*2836*	*1076*	*1049*

Source: 1964–1997: British Election Study. Figures for 1964–1992 as quoted in Crewe *et al.* (1995). Respondents saying "don't know' or who refused to answer have been excluded. Between 1964 and October 1974 the question read, *"Considering everything the parties stand for would you say there is a good deal of difference between them, some difference or not much difference?"* There were two surveys in 1974: February (F) and October (O).

As indicated earlier, a sharp drop occurred between 1997 and 2001 in the proportion thinking that there is a great difference between the parties – from a third to a record low of 17 per cent (see Table 6.5). This drop was maintained in 2005.[5] Indeed, the proportion thinking that there is a great difference actually fell slightly further – to just 13 per cent. After the 2001 election Bromley and Curtice (2002) wrote, "Never before have the electorate felt that there was so little to choose between the two main parties." Their statement is equally valid after the 2005 election.

Moreover, the perception that there is not much difference between the parties grew most rapidly between 1997 and 2001 amongst those with least interest in politics, that is, the very group who have the lowest motivation to vote and who most needed to be stimulated into going to the polling station. The proportion who thought there was not much difference rose almost twice as much amongst those with not very much or no interest in politics as it did amongst those with a great deal or quite a lot of interest. Although the difference in the perceptions of these two groups appears to have narrowed somewhat between 2001 and 2005, nevertheless the increase since 1997 in the perception that there is little difference between the parties has still been greatest amongst the least interested.

Table 6.6 Perceptions of party difference and interest in politics, 1997, 2001, 2005

Interest in politics	% who say there is not much difference between the parties						Change 1997– 2001	Change 1997– 2005
	1997	Base	2001	Base	2005	Base		
A great deal/quite a lot	21	1296	36	326	41	361	+15	+20
Some	20	1472	38	376	37	356	+18	+17
Not very much/none	31	1320	58	374	55	332	+27	+24

Source: 1997: British Election Study

Who stayed at home?

Meanwhile, we indicated earlier that if indeed people stayed at home in 2001 and 2005 because they felt there was too little at stake, then it is amongst those with least motivation to vote that turnout should have dropped since 1997. Table 6.7 illustrates quite clearly that this indeed is what has happened. Turnout fell between 1997 and 2001 by no less than 28 points amongst those with no interest in politics at all and by 13 points amongst those with "not very much" interest.[6] In contrast, it fell by just six points amongst those with "a great deal" or "quite a lot" of interest. This pattern of turnout in 2001 was replicated almost exactly in 2005. While, as we saw in Figure 6.1, the electorate may not have been markedly more disengaged from politics in 2001 or in 2005 than it had been in 1997, those who were *already* disengaged were far more likely to stay at home.[7]

Table 6.7 Political interest and electoral participation, 1997–2005

Interest in politics	% voted 1997	Base	% voted 2001	Base	% voted 2005	Base	Change 1997– 2001	Change 2001– 2005
A great deal	87	278	81	294	81	442	-6	0
Quite a lot	87	662	81	715	82	980	-6	+1
Some	81	1066	72	1107	72	1484	-9	0
Not very much	74	712	61	806	61	949	-13	0
None at all	59	188	31	365	31	413	-28	0

Source: 1997: British Election Study

Meanwhile, we can see just how an election that appears to offer little choice should have most impact on the willingness to vote of those with little interest in politics, by looking in particular at the behaviour of those who both have little interest in politics *and* can see little difference between the parties. As Table 6.8 shows, whether or not someone feels there is much difference between the parties has a rather greater impact on their likelihood of voting if they themselves do not have much interest in politics. Amongst those with a great deal or quite a lot of interest in politics, turnout is eight points lower amongst those who do not see much difference between the parties than it is amongst those who think there is a great deal of difference. But amongst those with little or no interest in politics the equivalent gap is 14 points.

Table 6.8 Turnout, by political interest and perceptions of the parties, 2005

% who voted	Perceived difference between the parties					
Interest in politics	Great	Base	Some	Base	Not much	Base
A great deal/quite a lot	84	63	83	156	76	142
Some	74	46	83	174	70	136
Not very much/none at all	67	33	54	108	53	191

Why people stayed at home again in 2005

We have seen, then, that so far as the factors that might account for the level of turnout are concerned, the picture was remarkably similar in 2005 to what it had been in 2001. Voters remained as (un)interested in politics now as they ever were, while there is little sign of any significant erosion in perceived duty to vote. True, there has been a yet further decline in levels of political trust, but this was counterbalanced by a reversal of the decline in system efficacy. On the other hand we do need to bear in mind that there has been a long-term decline in the proportion who strongly identify with a party, and thus it is probably even more necessary nowadays to persuade the electorate that there is good reason to vote.

However, it appears that in 2005 just as in 2001 there was indeed too little incentive for people to vote. Even fewer people felt there was a great difference between Labour and the Conservatives than did so in 2001. We noted earlier that the opinion polls again pointed to a clear Labour victory. In these circumstances those with less motivation to vote, such as those with less interest in politics, were disproportionately likely to stay at home in exactly the same way as they did in 2001.

Attitudes to the electoral system

We now turn to the second feature of the outcome of the 2005 election that we highlighted at the beginning of this chapter – the fact that Labour won an overall majority of 66 seats even though it only won 36 per cent of the vote. Of course, there is nothing new about a party winning a majority of seats despite not securing a majority of the votes. No post-war British government has been elected on the basis of more than half the vote. Indeed, the ability of the first-past-the-post electoral system to produce a clear winner, even if no single party has secured a majority of the vote, has long been regarded by its advocates as one of its merits. This ability helps ensure that who forms the government is clearly determined by the electorate not by the outcome of some backroom coalition deal (Curtice, 1992).

However, it may be felt that there are limits to the circumstances in which this feature of first-past-the-post is considered desirable. While it might be thought reasonable for a party to secure an overall majority of seats on, say, 45 per cent of the vote, it might be thought to be stretching things too far for a party to be able to form a government on its own if it secures, say, less than 40 per cent of the vote. Certainly, on the four previous occasions in British electoral history when no party has secured more than 40 per cent, only once (in 1922) did any one party secure an overall majority. Labour's ability to do so in 2005 might thus be thought to have contradicted people's expectations of both what should and what would happen in such circumstances. And, certainly, opponents of the system, most prominently *The Independent* newspaper, used the alleged 'unfairness' of the result in 2005 to reinforce their argument that the electoral system should be changed.

We might then anticipate that the public will have become less supportive of the continued use of first-past-the-post in the wake of the outcome of the 2005 election. On the other hand previous research has suggested that relatively few people have firm and consistent attitudes towards electoral systems (Curtice, 1993; Curtice and Jowell, 1997; Curtice and Jowell, 1998; Independent Commission on Proportional Representation, 2003). For most it is a remote and arcane subject about which they have not thought a great deal. As a result, the answers obtained in survey research on the subject appear to be highly sensitive to the way in which the questions are worded. In these circumstances there is perhaps little reason to believe that the public will, in fact, have been much moved by the outcome of the 2005 election.

We included in our 2005 survey two different questions about attitudes towards the electoral system, both of which had been previously asked on a number of occasions. The first simply asks respondents how much they agreed or disagreed with the following statement:

> *Britain should introduce proportional representation, so that the number of MPs in the House of Commons each party gets, matches more closely the number of votes each party gets*

As Table 6.9 shows the answers to this question suggest that proportional representation is relatively popular. Around three times as many people agree with our proposition as disagree. But at the same time we should note that rather more than one in three either say that they "neither agree nor disagree" or else that they "don't know", an indication perhaps that this is a subject on which many do not have strong views one way or the other. In any event, we should note that on this reading support, for the introduction of proportional representation was no higher after the 2005 election than it had been on various occasions beforehand. It does not appear that the outcome of that election had much impact on public opinion.

Table 6.9 Attitudes towards proportional representation, 1992–2005

	'92	'94	'95	'96	'97	'99	'00	'01	'03	'05
Britain should have PR	%	%	%	%	%	%	%	%	%	%
Agree	48	52	49	45	48	50	48	48	44	46
Disagree	27	16	18	16	16	16	16	16	15	17
Base	*2855*	*870*	*1058*	*1002*	*2906*	*804*	*2008*	*912*	*972*	*870*

Source: 1992 and 1997: British Election Study

This last conclusion is confirmed by the answers to our second, very differently worded, question which asks:

> *Some people say we should change the voting system for general elections to the UK House of Commons to allow smaller political parties to get a fairer share of MPs. Others say that we should keep the voting system for the House of Commons as it is to produce effective government. Which view comes **closer** to your own…*
> *… that we should change the voting system for the House of Commons,*
> *or, keep it as it is?*

Support for changing the electoral system when the issue was posed in this way was also no higher in 2005 than it had been on the many previous occasions on which this question was asked (see Figure 6.2). At the same time, at around one in three, the level of support for electoral reform is much lower than the level of support for proportional representation registered by our previous question. Indeed, with around three in five saying that they want to keep the electoral system as it is, one might conclude from the evidence of this question that electoral reform is unpopular. Evidently, when people are simply asked whether the proportion of seats a party gets should match the number of votes it gets, there is an inclination to agree with an apparently reasonable proposition. But when the emphasis is placed on the fact that smaller parties might be the principal beneficiaries of proportional representation and that its introduction might be at the expense of 'effective government', opinion is easily swayed in a different direction. The outcome of the 2005 election not only has failed to change public opinion in one direction or another, but also has, apparently, failed to do anything to resolve this tension in public attitudes.

Figure 6.2 Trends in attitudes towards changing the electoral system, 1983–2005[8]

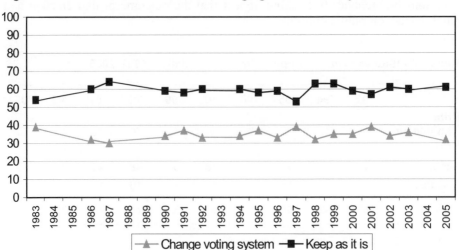

The impact of the electoral system on who votes

Still, the fact that people do not necessarily have consistent views about the electoral system does not mean that it does not have an impact on their behaviour and, in particular, on whether they vote or not. Indeed, it has commonly been argued that, other things being equal, fewer people are likely to vote when the first-past-the-post electoral system is used than when a proportional system is in operation (Powell, 1986; Jackman, 1987; Blais and Carty, 1990; Jackman and Miller, 1995; Franklin, 1996; Katz, 1997; Blais and Dobrzynska, 1998; Blais and Aarts, 2006). A variety of different arguments have been put forward as to why this might be the case.

First of all, under first-past-the-post, voters might be less likely to think that their vote will make a difference to the outcome, especially if they live in a constituency which one party always wins (Carey and Shugart, 1995). Large overall majorities are rarely secured under proportional representation, while increased votes for a party are likely to translate into increased seats even if the party does not come first either locally or nationally. Perhaps, too, parties have a strong incentive to concentrate their efforts to persuade people to turn out and vote in those marginal constituencies where the outcome appears to be in doubt, leaving voters in the rest of the country to their own devices. The perception that their vote may not make much difference together with a lack of contact with the parties in much of the country may also incline voters living in first-past-the-post systems to feel that the political system does not respond to their needs and wishes (that is, that they have a low level of system efficacy) and thus be disinclined to vote for that reason.

Finally, it is commonly argued that first-past-the-post encourages parties to cluster in the 'centre ground' of politics. First, the system discourages voters from voting for anyone other than the two largest parties, as otherwise their vote is likely to be 'wasted' on a party that has no chance of winning (Duverger, 1954). Then, in order to maximise their chances of winning, those two parties have a strong incentive to promote 'moderate' policies, as they compete for voters in the middle ground, relatively safe in the knowledge that those in their heartlands will have no other party worth voting for (Downs, 1957). However, because this means those two parties are then likely to be promulgating similar policies to each other, voters are less likely to think it is worth voting at all because there are so few differences between them.

Interestingly, some of these arguments in some ways echo those we have considered already to explain why so few people voted in 2001 and 2005. The outcome of those elections appeared to be yet another foregone conclusion, while the policies of the two main protagonists were widely thought to be similar to each other. Here it is being suggested that voters are more likely to feel this way in first-past-the-post elections in general. But, of course, we also argued above that feeling that way is most likely to have an impact on the behaviour of those who are least motivated to vote. So perhaps it is the case, too, that those who have the least motivation to vote are particularly likely to stay at home under first-past-the-post. Such a finding would add an important new ingredient to the debate about the merits of different electoral systems, as it would suggest that not only is turnout lower under first-past-the-post but inequalities in turnout are also greater.

We cannot, however, test this argument using data from Britain alone. Everyone who voted in Britain in 2005 did so under first-past-the-post, while for our purposes we need to be able to compare how voters behave under first-past-the-post with how they behave under proportional representation. To do that we have to compare how people in Britain voted, together with those living in other countries that use the same electoral system, with how people behaved in countries with more proportional systems. Fortunately we are able to do this because the 2005 *British Social Attitudes* survey included a module of questions that was also asked in surveys conducted in 25 other countries immediately after one of their recent national legislative elections, in a collaboration known as the Comparative Study of Electoral Systems (CSES) project (Comparative Study of Electoral Systems, no date).[9] In the remainder of this chapter we use these data alongside our British data.[10]

Unfortunately for our purposes this module did not contain a question on how interested someone was in politics, a key indicator of someone's motivation to vote in our analysis so far. However, we do have access to a different measure that arguably serves equally well. Each survey in the CSES project asked its respondents whether each of three statements was true or false. The aim was to acquire an indication of how knowledgeable someone is about politics. In the 2005 *British Social Attitudes* survey the three statements that were included were as follows:

The longest time allowed between general elections is four years

Britain's electoral system is based on proportional representation

MPs from different parties are on parliamentary committees

As many as 56 per cent correctly identified the last of these statements as true, 52 per cent recognised the second as false, but only 25 per cent appreciated that the first is also false. They thus would appear to have served quite well in distinguishing those who are less knowledgeable about politics from those who are more so.

Moreover, we can demonstrate that how accurately someone answered these questions is in fact quite closely linked to their level of political interest. Amongst those in our survey who identified the truth or otherwise of all three of our questions correctly, no less than 59 per cent said they had a great deal or quite a lot of interest in politics. Amongst those who provided two correct answers, 49 per cent had a similar level of interest. But amongst those who only had one correct answer the equivalent figure was just 28 per cent, while amongst those who did not answer any of our knowledge questions correctly this figure falls to just 20 per cent. So, in part at least, our measure of knowledge can be regarded as a surrogate for interest in politics (see also Smith, 1989; MacDonald *et al.*, 1995; Bartle, 2000) – although, of course, having a high level of knowledge about politics may incline people in its own right to turn out and vote because they feel they have the confidence and ability to make an informed decision at the ballot box.

Of course, CSES surveys in other countries provided their respondents with different statements from those asked in our survey. Ours, after all, were specifically about British politics. True, each survey aimed to distinguish the more from the less knowledgeable within each country by providing their respondents with three statements of a similar character to ours. However, this still means that we cannot assume that a person who identifies the status of, say, two questions correctly within one country is necessarily equally as knowledgeable as someone in another country that does the same. The questions may have been harder (or easier) in the former than in the latter. To deal with this we have to convert each person's score on their country's knowledge questions into a 'standardised' score which measures how far away they are from the average score for their country (taking into account also the amount of variation around that score).[11] This gives us a measure of how knowledgeable someone is relative to their fellow countrymen and women, whose relationship with turnout can then legitimately be compared across countries.

Thus equipped, we can now see whether how knowledgeable someone is makes more difference to their chances of voting in those countries that use the first-past-the-post system than it does elsewhere. Table 6.10 indicates that it does.

Table 6.10 Turnout by political knowledge and electoral system

% who voted		**Electoral system**		
Standardised knowledge score	**First-past-the-post**	*Base*	**Other**	*Base*
Very low	38	*1867*	55	*11067*
Low	54	*3862*	67	*16422*
High	68	*4927*	72	*18313*
Very high	78	*3724*	81	*13098*
All	60	*14380*	68	*58900*

Standardised knowledge score: Very low: less than -1; low: between -1 and 0; high: between 0 and 1; very high: more than 1. Source: Comparative Study of Electoral Systems (no date), Modules 1 and 2

Turnout is almost as high amongst those with a 'high' or 'very high' knowledge score in elections held under first-past-the-post as it is in elections held under a more proportional system. On the other hand amongst those with a 'low' or a 'very low' score turnout is markedly lower in elections held under first-past-the-post. In other words the difference in turnout between those with low and high knowledge is larger under first-past-the-post than it is amongst more proportional systems.[12] It would appear that, just as we expected, the use of first-past-the-post does indeed increase the inequality in turnout between the more and the less knowledgeable.

Why, however, is this the case? One of the possible explanations we outlined earlier – that parties are less likely to make contact with voters during an election campaign under first-past-the-post – can certainly be dismissed. In fact, the opposite appears to be true. On average, in those elections held under first-past-the-post no less than 39 per cent said that a candidate or someone from a party had been in contact with them during the campaign (as did 33 per cent in Britain). In contrast, just 21 per cent said this in elections held under other electoral systems.[13] Moreover, there does not appear to be any evidence that failure to receive any contact from a party or candidate has a particularly adverse impact on the level of turnout amongst those with low levels of knowledge.

On the other hand there is some evidence to support other of our expectations. First, voters living in countries where first-past-the-post is used do appear to be less likely to regard political parties as very different from each other. In the CSES module respondents were asked to indicate on a ten-point scale how much they liked or disliked each of the main parties in their country. If voters feel that some of the parties in their country are very different from each other, then we would expect the difference between the score they give to the party they most like and the party they most dislike to be relatively large. In contrast, if they can see few differences between the parties this score should be relatively low.

In those countries where first-past-the-post is in use the average difference between the score given by respondents to the party they like most and that which they like least is just 4.8, including just 4.5 in our 2005 survey in Britain. In contrast, elsewhere this difference is no less than 6.1. Moreover, not only are less knowledgeable voters generally less likely to feel that there is much difference between the parties (as we would expect from our earlier analysis at Table 6.6), but also this is particularly true of less knowledgeable voters in countries that use first-past-the-post. Thus, as Table 6.11 shows, in countries that use first-past-the-post those with a very high level of knowledge on average put their most and least liked parties as much as 5.5 points apart, where as those with a very low level put them only 4.2 points apart – a gap between the two groups of 1.3. In contrast, in countries that use a different electoral system the equivalent gap is just 0.6.

However, this pattern is seemingly no more than part – and perhaps no more than a small part – of the explanation as to why knowledge makes more difference to the chances that someone will vote if first-past-the-post is used. For this pattern is still evident even when we take into account how far apart people put their most and least liked party. For example, amongst those who put their liked and disliked parties less than four points apart and live in a country using first-past-the-post, those with very high levels of knowledge were 41 points more likely to vote than were those with very low levels of knowledge, whereas the equivalent figure for those living elsewhere is just 29 points.

Table 6.11 Average difference in score given to most and least liked party, by political knowledge and electoral system

Mean difference in score given to most and least liked party	Electoral system					
	First-past-the-post	*Base*	**Other**	*Base*	**All**	*Base*
Standardised knowledge score						
Very low	4.2	*1622*	5.8	*9635*	5.6	*11257*
Low	4.8	*3625*	6.0	*15571*	5.8	*19196*
High	4.9	*4769*	6.3	*17695*	6.0	*22464*
Very high	5.5	*3674*	6.4	*12803*	6.3	*16477*

Source: Comparative Study of Electoral Systems (no date)

Equally there is some evidence that those living in countries with first-past-the-post elections are less likely to feel efficacious about their political system. Certainly, at elections conducted in countries using first-past-the-post just 28 per cent strongly agree that "who people vote for can make a difference to what happens". On the other hand at elections where a different system has been used, as many as 38 per cent do so. However, while in general voters with low levels of knowledge are less likely to feel efficacious this is not any more true of less knowledgeable voters living in countries using first-past-the-post than it is of those residing elsewhere. Thus while lower levels of efficacy might help explain why overall levels of turnout tend to be lower in countries using first-past-the-post, they cannot explain why turnout is particularly low amongst those in such countries with low levels of knowledge.

More difficult to determine is whether voters in countries using first-past-the-post are simply more inclined to believe that there is little point in voting because the outcome is a foregone conclusion. Certainly, further analyses that we have conducted do not suggest that the behaviour of those who live in first-past-the-post constituencies that objectively at least might be regarded as 'safe' can account for the particular failure of those with low knowledge to vote where first-past-the-post is used. Indeed, to the very limited extent to which there is a difference in the level of turnout between people in safe and marginal constituencies, in Britain, at least, it is actually slightly bigger amongst those with most political knowledge. Whether those with low knowledge are simply more likely to be discouraged from voting by the fact that their vote is less likely to make a difference to the outcome nationally is, however, more difficult to unravel.

Conclusions

One key message emerges from this chapter. How many people vote in an election does not simply depend on the motivations that they bring to the ballot box. It depends, too, on the circumstances in which they are asked to vote. In particular, those whose motivation to vote is relatively weak are particularly sensitive to these circumstances. If an election appears to be a foregone conclusion or if there appear to be few differences between the parties, those with less interest in politics are more likely to stay at home. And while obviously circumstances vary from one election to another, it appears too that those with little interest in or knowledge of politics may generally be discouraged from voting by the circumstances created by first-past-the-post – albeit precisely why that is the case is not wholly clear.

This has important implications for the debate about the health of Britain's democracy. First, it suggests that claims that there is a need to 're-engage' the public with the political process – perhaps by in some way appealing to them in different ways – are rather wide of the mark. With the singular exception of the decline in party identification, voters seem no more 'disengaged' with politics now than they have ever been. Rather, turnout is only likely to increase significantly once more if elections once again offer voters what they feel is a real choice. Whether this will happen is uncertain. While at the time of writing Labour now no longer has a lead in the opinion polls, the rebranding of the Conservative Party under its new leader, David Cameron, could well persuade voters that Labour and the Conservatives have simply drawn even closer together.

But even if circumstances do change and turnout increases once more in Britain, our analysis still leaves a longer-term question. For it appears that as long as the first-past-the-post electoral system is used in elections to the House of Commons there will always be a greater likelihood that the less interested and knowledgeable will stay at home. If it is felt to be important to the health of Britain's democracy that inequalities in turnout are minimised, then there is reason to question the continued use of first-past-the-post.

Nevertheless, however important such an observation may be to the advocates of electoral reform, whether it is one that would be shared by the wider public is open to doubt. Evidently the apparent 'unfairness' of the outcome of the 2005 election failed to sway public opinion, which now appears neither more supportive of reform nor more consistent in its attitudes towards the subject than it has been previously. The debate about Britain's electoral system may be an important one, but seems set to remain largely one that is confined to politicians themselves.

Notes

1. All figures in this chapter referring to shares of the vote and turnout in general elections are those for Great Britain only and exclude Northern Ireland.
2. Data for Figure 6.1 are as follows (bases in brackets): 1986: 29 (1548); 1989: 27 (1516); 1990: 29 (1397); 1991: 32 (1445); 1994: 32 (2302); 1996: 31 (3620); 1997: 30 (1355); 1998: 29 (3146); 1999: 28 (3143); 2000: 33 (2293); 2001: 31 (3287); 2002: 29 (2286); 2003: 30 (4432); 2004: 31 (3198); 2005: 33 (4268).
3. In order to show this trend clearly, we only show in the table those readings that have been taken immediately after an election; such readings are consistently higher than those taken at other points in the electoral cycle. See Bromley and Curtice (2002).
4. Bases for Table 6.4 are as follows:

Trust government to place needs of the nation above those of party ...	% voted 1997	% voted 2001	% voted 2005
... just about always/most of the time	961	304	770
... only some of the time	1518	552	1509
... almost never	356	220	826

5. This question was also asked on the 2001 and 2005 British Election Studies (BES). This found a higher proportion, 28 per cent in 2001 and 22 per cent in 2005, saying that there was a great difference, but much the same trend. The question was administered by the BES in 2001 and 2005 on a self-completion questionnaire rather than face-to face as it had been on previous surveys (and was on the *British Social Attitudes* survey) and it may be that this switch of mode had an impact on the results obtained by the 2001 and 2005 BES.
6. Readers will note that the overall level of turnout in each of the surveys reported in Table 6.8 is higher than that recorded in the official results. As many as 79 per cent said that they voted in the 1997 survey, 68 per cent in 2001 and 69 per cent in 2005. Surveys usually report a higher level of turnout than do the actual results. While this may, in part, reflect a tendency for voters to say they have voted when in fact they have not, the gap also occurs both because surveys are more likely to secure the participation of those who vote and because the official turnout underestimates the 'true' level of turnout (both because the electoral register still contains the names of those who have died and because some people are registered at more than one address) (Swaddle and Heath, 1989). What should be noted here is that the 11 point drop in reported turnout between the 1997 and 2001 surveys closely matches the 13 point drop in the official turnout between those two elections. Equally, the one point increase in reported turnout between 2001 and 2005 is close to the two point increase in the results themselves. Thus there is every reason to believe that our survey data should be capable of capturing the patterns that underlie the *change* in turnout across the 1997, 2001 and 2005 elections.

7. Much the same pattern is found if we repeat the analysis in Table 6.8 by some of the other motivations to vote considered earlier in this chapter. Thus, as compared with 1997, turnout fell most heavily amongst those with no party identification and amongst those with a low level of system efficacy. Meanwhile, the pattern of change in turnout in Table 6.8 is also replicated by British Election Survey data (Curtice, 2006).

8. Data for Figure 6.2 are as follows: 1983 Change: 39, Keep: 54 (3955); 1986 Change: 32, Keep: 60 (1548); 1987: Change: 30, Keep: 64 (1410); 1990 Change: 34, Keep: 59 (1397); 1991 Change: 37, Keep: 58 (1445); 1992 Change: 33, Keep: 60 (2855); 1994 Change: 34; Keep: 60 (1137); 1995 Change: 37, Keep: 58 (1227); 1996 Change: 33, Keep: 59 (1196); 1997 Change: 39, Keep: 53 (1355); 1998 Change: 32, Keep: 63 (1035); 1999 Change: 35, Keep: 63 (1060); 2000 Change: 35, Keep: 59 (2293); 2001 Change: 39, Keep: 57 (1099); 2002 Change: 34, Keep: 61 (2287); 2003 Change: 36, Keep: 60 (1160); 2005 Change: 32; Keep: 61 (1075).

9. A more extensive version of the analysis presented here is to be found in Fisher *et al.* (2006).

10. Altogether the data we require are available for 44 legislative elections in 25 countries. The first-past-the-post elections are the Philippines (2004); Great Britain (1997 and 2005, the latter including both our survey and an internet survey conducted by the British Election Study); Canada (1997 and 2004); USA (1996 and 2004). The non-plurality (and mostly proportional) elections are Spain (1996, 2000 and 2004); Taiwan (1996 and 2001); Israel (1996 and 2003); Mexico (2000 and 2003); Japan (1996 and 2004); Brazil (2002); New Zealand (1996 and 2002); Netherlands (1998 and 2002); Portugal (2002 and 2005); South Korea (2004); Iceland (2003); Ireland (2002); Czech Republic (1996 and 2002); Norway (1997 and 2001); Finland (2003); Sweden (1998 and 2002); Germany (1998 and 2002 – two surveys); Poland (1997 and 2001); Romania (1996); Hungary (1998 and 2002); Switzerland (1999 and 2003). Note that Australia and Belgium are excluded because they have an effective system of compulsory voting, while those countries which are considered less than fully democratic (that is, had a Freedom House score of less than two) were also excluded. It should also be noted that in each case the data used in our comparative analyses have been weighted so that the overall reported level of turnout in each survey matches that recorded by the official election results.

11. In other words, each standardised score is their score minus the average score for their country, all divided by the standard deviation of the knowledge score for that country.

12. This proves to be true also of all the individual first-past-the-post elections for which we have data (including Britain) except for the Philippines in 2004 when turnout amongst those with relatively low knowledge of politics may have been stimulated by a contemporaneous relatively polarised presidential election.

13. The figures in this paragraph are based only on those CSES surveys conducted since 2001. The relevant question was not included in earlier surveys.

References

Aldrich, J. (1993), 'Rational Choice and Turnout', *American Journal of Political Science*, **37**: 246–278

Almond, G. and Verba, S. (1963), *The Civic Culture: Political Attitudes and Democracy in Five Nations*, Princeton, NJ: Princeton University Press

Bara, J. (2006), 'The 2005 Manifestos: A Sense of *Déja Vu*?', *Journal of Elections, Public Opinion and Parties*, **16**: 265–281

Bara, J. and Budge, I. (2001), 'Party Policy and Ideology: Still New Labour?', in Norris, P. (ed.), *Britain Votes 2001*, Oxford: Oxford University Press

Bartle, J. (2000), 'Political awareness, opinion constraint and the stability of ideological positions', *Political Studies*, **48**: 467–484

Blais, A. and Aarts, K. (2006), 'Electoral Systems and Turnout', *Acta Politica*, **41**: 180–196

Blais, A. and Carty, R. (1990), 'Does proportional representation foster voter turnout?', *European Journal of Political Research*, **18**: 167–181

Blais, A. and Dobrzynska, A. (1998), 'Turnout in electoral democracies', *European Journal of Political Research*, **33**: 239–261

Blumler, J. (1997), 'Origins of the crisis of communication for citizenship', *Political Communication*, **14**: 395–404

Bromley, C. and Curtice, J. (2002), 'Where have all the voters gone?', in Park A., Curtice, J., Thomson, K., Jarvis, L. and Bromley, C. (eds.), *British Social Attitudes: the 19th Report,* London: Sage

Carey, J. and Shugart, M. (1995), 'Incentives to cultivate a personal vote: a rank ordering of electoral formulas', *Electoral Studies*, **14**: 417–439

Clarke, H., Sanders, D., Stewart, M. and Whiteley, P. (2004), *Political Choice in Britain*, Oxford: Oxford University Press

Comparative Study of Electoral Systems (no date), http://www.cses.org/

Crewe, I., Fox, A. and Day, N. (1995), *The British Electorate 1963–1992*, Cambridge: Cambridge University Press

Crewe, I. and Thomson, K. (1999), 'Party Loyalties: Dealignment or Realignment?', in Evans, G. and Norris, P. (eds.), *Critical Elections: British Parties and Elections in Long-Term Perspective*, London: Sage

Curtice, J. (1992), 'The British Electoral System: Fixture without Foundation', in Kavanagh, D. (ed.), *Electoral Politics*, Oxford: Oxford University Press

Curtice, J. (1993), 'Popular support for electoral reform: the lessons of the 1992 election', *Scottish Affairs*, **4**: 23–32

Curtice, J. (2005), 'Turnout-electors stay at home again', in Norris, P. and Wlezien, C. (eds), *Britain Votes 2005*, Oxford: Oxford University Press

Curtice, J. (2006), 'Losing the voting habit? The 2056 electorate', in Gough, R. (ed.), *2056: What Future for Maggie's Children?*, London: Policy Exchange

Curtice, J. and Jowell, R. (1997), 'Trust in the Political System', in Jowell, R., Curtice, J., Park, A., Brook, L., Thomson, K. and Bryson, C. (eds.), *British Social Attitudes: the 14th Report - The end of Conservative values?*, Aldershot; Ashgate

Curtice, J. and Jowell, R. (1998), 'Is there really a demand for constitutional change?', *Scottish Affairs – Special Issue on Constitutional Change*, 61–93

Dalton, R. (2004), *Democratic Challenges, Democratic Choices*, Oxford: Oxford University Press

Downs, A. (1957), *An Economic Theory of Democracy*, New York: Harper Row

Duverger, M. (1954), *Political Parties*, London: Methuen

Fisher, S., Lessard-Phillips, L., Hobolt, S. and Curtice, J. (2006), 'How the effect of political knowledge on turnout differs in plurality electoral systems'. Paper presented at the Annual Meeting of the American Political Science Association, Philadelphia, Pa.

Franklin, M. (1996), 'Electoral Participation', in LeDuc, L., Niemi, R. and Norris, P. (eds.), *Comparing Democracies: Elections and Voting in Global Perspectives*, Thousand Oaks, Calif.: Sage

Franklin, M. (2004), *Voter Turnout and the Dynamics of Electoral Competition in Established Democracies since 1945*, Cambridge: Cambridge University Press

Heath, A., and Taylor, B. (1999), 'New Sources of Abstention?', in Evans, G. and Norris, P. (eds.), *Critical Elections: British Parties and Elections in Long-Term Perspective*, London: Sage

Independent Commission on Proportional Representation (2003), *Changed Voting, Changed Politics: Lessons of Britain's Experience of PR since 1997*, London: Constitution Unit

Jackman, R. (1987), 'Political institutions and voter turnout in the industrial democracies', *American Political Science Review*, **81**: 405–423

Jackman, R. and Miller, R. (1995), 'Voter turnout in the industrial democracies during the 1980s', *Comparative Political Studies*, **27**: 467–492

Katz, R. (1997), *Democracy and Elections*, Oxford: Oxford University Press

MacDonald, S., Rabinowitz, G. and Listhaug, O. (1995), 'Political sophistication and models of issue voting', *British Journal of Political Science*, **25**: 453–483

Powell, G. (1986), 'American voter turnout in comparative perspective', *American Political Science Review*, **80**: 17–43

Putnam, R. (2000), *Bowling Alone: The Collapse and Revival of American Community*, New York: Simon and Schuster

Smith, E. (1989), *The Unchanging American Voter*, Berkeley, Calif.: University of California Press

Swaddle, K. and Heath, A. (1989), 'Official and Reported Turnout in the British General Election of 1987', *British Journal of Political Science*, **19**: 537–570

Acknowledgements

The *National Centre for Social Research* and the authors are grateful to the Economic and Social Research Council for its funding of Britain's participation in the Comparative Study of Electoral Systems (grant number RES–000–22–1352), some of which is reported on in this chapter.

7 Civil liberties and the challenge of terrorism

*Mark Johnson and Conor Gearty**

Since at least 11th September 2001 the threat of terrorism has been a major concern in Britain and across the world. Political leaders have spoken frequently and at length about the severity and reality of the threat, and what it entails for the way of life for the people within their countries. The Labour government, like other Western governments, has passed various pieces of anti-terror legislation, and argued vehemently for further powers that were subsequently either rejected or severely truncated by Parliament.[1]

Simultaneously, from many quarters there have been serious concerns about the rhetoric being used to describe the threat and the means being used to tackle it. In particular, it has been strongly argued that many of the proposals, and indeed actual legislation, erode the civil liberties fundamental to, and defining of, our society.[2]

In this discussion there has been one very obvious dimension lacking: the views of the public. Here we present the most comprehensive survey to date of public attitudes to the issues surrounding the debate. Our analysis focuses on three main areas. First we look at changes in general attitudes to civil liberties that have occurred over the past twenty years. We then examine how those views are affected by the specific mention of the threat of terrorism, and show to what extent the public are willing to 'trade-off' various civil liberties to tackle that threat. Finally, we look at attitudes to human rights and international law, two areas that have been the subject of much debate, again examining whether fear of terrorism influences attitudes to these inherently progressive ideas.

---

[*] Mark Johnson is a Senior Researcher at the *National Centre for Social Research* and Co-Director of the *British Social Attitudes* survey. Conor Gearty is Professor of Human Rights Law at the London School of Economics, and Rausing Director of the Centre for the Study of Human Rights at the London School of Economics.

What rights are important for democracy?

Before we embark on our analysis of changes in attitudes to civil liberties, however, we begin by looking at what people believe is important for democracy. Understanding this provides a context to some of the issues we shall subsequently discuss, as many of these rights are exactly those that may be under threat from 'anti-terrorism' legislation. The question we posed was:

> *There are different views about people's rights in a democratic society. On a scale of 1 to 7, where 1 is not at all important and 7 is very important, how important to democracy is it that **every** adult living in Britain has...*
>
> *... the right to protest against government decisions they disagree with?*
>
> *... the right **not** to be detained by the police for more than a week or so without being charged with a crime?*
>
> *... the right to keep their life private from government?*
>
> *... the right **not** to be exposed to offensive views in public?*
>
> *... the right to a trial by jury if they are charged with a serious crime?*
>
> *... the right to say whatever they think in public?*

Large proportions of people deemed each of them to be important. Indeed, for all but one, a majority placed it at six or seven on the scale. However, the right of every adult to say whatever they think in public, which we assume people to have seen as the right to free speech by another name, received lower levels of support. In fact, fewer people placed this at six or seven on the scale than the right *not* to be exposed to offensive opinions.

Table 7.1 Proportions viewing different rights as important or not important to democracy

		Not important	Important
Trial by jury if charged with serious crime	%	1	88
Protest against government decisions	%	3	73
Keep life private from government	%	5	67
Not to be exposed to offensive views in public	%	8	64
Not to be detained by police for more than a week or so without being charged with a crime	%	10	56
Say whatever they think in public	%	10	47

Base: 1075

In this table 'not important' includes those who answered 1 or 2 on the scale, 'important' those who answered 6 or 7 on the scale

There was also, comparatively, low significance attached to the right not to be detained by the police without charge – something that has been the subject of sustained debate in recent years and particularly in the first months of 2005 – just before the interviews for the survey took place.

That apart, the results in Table 7.1 show no real pattern. It is not the case, for example, that the political freedoms are seen as more important to democracy than, say, criminal justice protections. But what is clear, is that there is a strong commitment among the public to each of these rights, with much larger proportions thinking they are important than not. In the next section we shall look at attitudes to civil liberties in more specific situations, and also examine change over time.

Changing attitudes to civil liberties?

Public attitudes to civil liberties is something of an understudied area. In particular, very little is known about *changes* in these public attitudes. This is despite the fact that *British Social Attitudes* has been asking the public about a number of civil liberties since its inception in 1983. A notable exception can be found in the twelfth *British Social Attitudes* report. Back then, Brooke and Cape (1995) found that attitudes were becoming less libertarian over time.

In this section we examine to what extent that trend has continued across a range of issues – political freedoms, protections in the field of the criminal justice system, identity cards and the death penalty – and delve into the underlying reasons why attitudes are changing. Understanding the reasons for past change is important if we are to predict what might happen in the future.

Political freedoms

One of the key political freedoms in a properly functioning democracy is the right to protest. *British Social Attitudes* has asked the following questions on a number of occasions since 1985:

> *There are many ways people or organisations can protest against a government action they strongly oppose. Please show which you think should be allowed and which should not be allowed [...]*
>
> *Organising public meetings to protest against the government*
>
> *Organising protest marches and demonstrations*

Respondents were invited to say whether these actions should definitely be allowed, probably be allowed, probably not be allowed or definitely not be allowed. In 2005, an overwhelming majority (84 per cent) thought public protest meetings should definitely or probably be allowed – and almost as many (73 per cent) took this view for marches and demonstrations. But, as shown in

Table 7.2, the proportions saying that they should *definitely* be allowed were substantially lower, at 51 and 39 per cent respectively. Whether or not this represents a move away from libertarianism depends very much on our point of reference. Compared to 1985, views on public meetings have become less libertarian, but compared to 1994 they are no different – the big change in attitudes seems to have happened in the early 1990s. Views on protest marches are similar now to what they were in 1985, but *more* libertarian than they were in 1994. So again, we see a hardening of views in the early 1990s, but this time with a reversal by 2005.[3]

Table 7.2 Attitudes to the right to protest against the government, 1985–2005

	1985	1990	1994	1996	2005
% saying "definitely should be allowed"					
Public protest meetings	59	62	48	54	51
Protest marches and demonstrations	36	39	30	31	39
Base	*1530*	*1197*	*970*	*989*	*860*

An alternative, and perhaps better, test of support for civil libertarian beliefs is the tolerance that people are prepared to extend to the rights of extremists. If people truly value these freedoms, then they should also support them for people with views different to their own (see Evans, 2002). Assuming most people do not themselves want to overthrow the government by revolution, the following question measures this tolerance:

> *There are some people whose views are considered extreme by the majority. Consider people who want to overthrow the government by revolution. Do you think such people should be allowed to...*
>
> *... hold public meetings to express their views?*
>
> *... publish books expressing their views?*

Perhaps, unsurprisingly, there is much less commitment to rights for revolutionaries. On holding meetings, the majority (52 per cent) believe they should (probably or definitely) *not* be allowed; on publishing books, 44 per cent believe this should *not* be allowed. Indeed, a mere 16 and 15 per cent respectively felt they should definitely be allowed. As Table 7.3 shows, this is the lowest we have ever seen in *British Social Attitudes* surveys – tolerance of the rights of extremists, as measured in this way, has virtually halved since 1985. Moreover, these differences over time are not accounted for by an increase in the proportion thinking that they *probably* should be allowed. The combined proportion of people thinking they should definitely and probably be allowed has fallen from 52 per cent in 1985 to 42 per cent now on holding public meetings and from 64 per cent in 1985 to 47 per cent now on publishing books.

Table 7.3 Attitudes to the rights of revolutionaries, 1985–2005

	1985	1990	1996	2005
% saying "definitely should be allowed"				
Hold public meetings	27	21	18	16
Publish books	27	21	21	15
Base	*1530*	*1197*	*989*	*860*

Interestingly, as with the more general questions, the change in attitudes to public meetings organised by revolutionaries occurred between the mid-1980s and the mid-1990s, but there has been no change since. When it comes to the publishing of revolutionary material, similar declines occurred both before and after the mid-1990s.

Presumption of innocence

The idea of people being innocent until proven guilty is one of the cornerstones of the British legal system and, by extension, of the British conception of democracy. As Brooke and Cape (1995: 193) stated:

> The committed civil libertarian, while recognising that this might inevitably lead to the acquital of some guilty defendants, would nonetheless regard it as an acceptable and necessary risk.

But to what extent do the public accept this? To address this we asked:

> *All systems of justice make mistakes, but which do you think is worse...*
>
> *... to convict an innocent person,*
>
> *or to let a guilty person go free?*

A bare majority of the public (52 per cent) believe it worse to convict an innocent person, whilst a substantial minority (23 per cent) take the view that it is worse to let a guilty person go free. Notably, the exact same proportion are unable to decide between the two – hardly overwhelming commitment to the fundamental premise of the British legal system. Has this always been the case? As Table 7.4 shows, back in 1985 a large majority of the public supported the notion of innocent until proven guilty – 67 per cent. In 1986, however, this had fallen to 58 per cent, a remarkable decline in a single year. There it remained steady until the mid-1990s. Interestingly, perhaps disturbingly, we did not find any revival in the figures committed to protecting the innocent during the high-profile miscarriage of justice cases that were such a feature of the 1990s.

Table 7.4 Attitudes to presumption of innocence, 1985–2005

	1985	1986	1990	1994	1996	2005
	%	%	%	%	%	%
Worse to convict innocent person	67	58	62	58	56	52
Worse to let guilty person go free	20	26	19	24	27	23
Can't choose	12	16	19	18	16	23
Base	1530	1321	1197	970	989	860

What is of particular note is that the proportion of people opting for "can't choose" has effectively doubled since 1985. Although the public are now less committed to the principle of innocent until proven guilty, the reason is not that more people now think it worse to let a guilty person go free, but rather that more people find it too hard to decide.

Right to legal representation

What of the right to legal representation? Given the complexities of the law we would expect the general public to regard such a right as pretty essential if ordinary people are to get a fair deal from the police. We asked respondents whether they agreed or disagreed that:

The police should be allowed to question suspects for up to a week without letting them see a solicitor

As expected, there is strong support for the right to legal representation: nearly two in three disagree with the statement, but a substantial minority of one in four agree. Moreover, as Table 7.5 shows, this represents a substantial weakening in support for this civil liberty: during the early 1990s eight in ten disagreed with the statement. It is also of note that there has been a sharp fall of seven percentage points between 2004 and now. To describe this trend another way, the proportion agreeing that the police *should* be allowed to question suspects without a solicitor present has almost trebled since 1990 and the majority of this move away from the civil libertarian position has occurred since the mid-1990s.

Table 7.5 Attitudes to legal representation for suspects, 1990–2005

	1990	1994	1996	2004	2005
Police should be allowed to question suspects for up to a week without seeing a solicitor	%	%	%	%	%
Agree	9	8	13	17	25
Disagree	80	83	73	65	58
Base	*1197*	*970*	*2047*	*853*	*860*

Identity cards

The issue of identity cards has received increasing prominence in recent years for many different reasons, and the picture painted by the media is often of a divided public. Is this actually the case? We asked people whether they agreed or disagreed with the following statement:

> *Every adult in Britain should have to carry an identity card*

Despite the strong wording of the statement – suggesting compulsion – we find that the public is actually in favour with 54 per cent agreeing, including 21 per cent agreeing strongly. Compared to 1990, the proportion disagreeing has roughly halved from 40 per cent to 22 per cent. Table 7.6 shows a complicated shift in attitudes: substantial and sustained growth in support for identity cards during the period from 1990 to a high point in 2004, and then a decline in support in 2005. The likely cause of this recent decline is the current public debate concerning, firstly, the efficacy and, secondly, the cost of identity cards. We return to the issue of identity cards later, in the specific context of tackling terrorism.

Table 7.6 Attitudes to identity cards, 1990–2005

	1990	1994	1996	2004	2005
Every adult in Britain should have to carry an identity card	%	%	%	%	%
Agree	37	53	57	65	54
Disagree	40	26	20	13	22
Base	*1197*	*970*	*2047*	*853*	*860*

Death penalty

The final area we consider in this section is the death penalty. This was abolished for murder in Britain in 1969, but was technically still in force for treason and piracy until 1999, when it was formally abolished by the signing of the Sixth Protocol of the European Convention of Human Rights. *British Social Attitudes* has long asked respondents to agree or disagree with the following statement:

> *For some crimes, the death penalty is the most appropriate sentence*

The majority of the public support the death penalty, with 28 per cent agreeing strongly with the statement and a further 30 per cent just agreeing. However, as shown by Figure 7.1, this actually represents a weakening of support. In contrast with most of the other civil liberties we examine, the trend is thus in the direction of more liberal views.

Figure 7.1 Per cent agreeing the death penalty is the most appropriate sentence for some crimes, 1986–2005

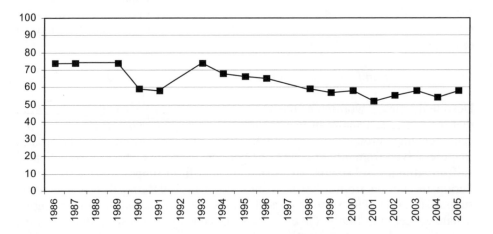

To summarise this section, we find that, across a range of civil libertarian issues, the public as a whole is committed to many of them, notably to the right to protest, protecting the innocent, and legal representation. They are less committed to the rights of expression for revolutionaries and tend to favour compulsory identity cards and the death penalty for some crimes (although for what crimes we do not know). However, in assessing whether there has been any *change* in public attitudes on these issues, our conclusions are dependent upon when we choose as our reference point. If we opt for the mid-1980s, then attitudes to six of the eight have become less libertarian, whilst one has stayed at about the same level, and one has become more libertarian. If we opt for the mid-1990s, then attitudes to three have become less libertarian, three of them have stayed at about the same level, and two have become more libertarian. In other words, most of the decline in libertarian views happened not in response to recent events, but mainly in the early 1990s. In the next section we focus on the longer-term changes since the mid-1980s and try to uncover the reasons for the observed shifts.

Why have libertarian attitudes declined?

Clearly something must be driving the decline in people's commitment to civil liberties[4] since the mid-1980s. In this section we attempt to uncover the likely causes, first discussing changes in the age profile of the population, then considering political change as the underlying cause and finally looking at the role that fear of terrorism may have played.

Changes in the age structure of the population

One of the most obvious candidates for the apparent shift in attitudes is that groups which tend to be less civil libertarian in their outlook have become proportionately larger within the population. One characteristic presents itself as particularly relevant: age.[5] Across a range of moral issues it is known that older generations tend to be more conservative than younger ones (Park, 2000). Normally, we would expect this to lead to a gradual liberalisation of views as younger generations replace older, more traditional ones (a 'generational effect'). However, the population is also known to be ageing. Therefore, the larger proportion of older people within the general public could be a reason for the observed changes in attitudes to civil liberties.

Table 7.7 Attitudes to civil liberties, by age

		Age		
		18–27	68+	Difference
Revolutionaries hold public meetings definitely should be allowed	%	31	12	-19
Revolutionaries publish books definitely should be allowed	%	26	12	-14
Public meetings definitely should be allowed	%	46	43	-4
Disagree police hold suspects for up to a week without solicitor	%	54	50	-4
Worse to convict innocent	%	49	50	1
Disagree every adult should have identity card	%	20	25	5
Base		*83*	*158*	

For this to be the case, though, we must first show that there are differences in views across age groups. The table above shows mixed evidence on this point. Only in the case of rights for revolutionaries do we, in fact, find that the oldest age groups hold less libertarian views than the youngest age group. However, on these two questions, the differences are quite large.

We cannot within the data from *British Social Attitudes* compare the views of particular individuals over time, but we can follow age cohorts over a period of 20 years. Table 7.8 presents the results for the right of revolutionaries to hold public meetings.[6]

Table 7.8 Per cent thinking people who wish to overthrow the government by revolution should definitely be allowed to hold public meetings, by age cohort[7]

Cohort	Age 1985	Age 2005	1985	2005	Difference
All			27	16	-11
1978–87		18–27		31	
1968–77		28–37		18	
1958–67	18–27	38–47	34	13	-21
1948–57	28–37	48–57	34	13	-21
1938–47	38–47	58–67	27	9	-18
1928–37	48–57	68+	24	12	-12
1918–27	58–67		20		
Pre-1917	68+		14		

As expected from Table 7.7, we see that older people are less libertarian than younger people. However, this pattern was much clearer in 1985 than in 2005. The table, in fact, shows two quite strong changes. First, each age group is now less libertarian than people of that age were in 1985. For example, in 1985, 27 per cent of 38–47 year olds said they supported the rights of revolutionaries to hold public meetings. This compares with 13 per cent of 38–47 year olds now. This change is particularly noticeable among the middle age groups, leading to a reduction in the overall difference in attitudes by age. Even stronger is the second effect: individuals of all ages seem to have become less libertarian. So, for example, among the age group who were aged 28–37 in 1985, 34 per cent said they supported the rights of revolutionaries to hold public meetings. This had fallen to 13 per cent among that same age cohort (now aged 48–57) in 2005. This is suggestive of a 'period effect', by which we mean that some kind of normative shift has occurred within society. It does not therefore look as if the ageing of the population is the primary reason for the overall change in public attitudes.

Political change

If we are seeing a 'period effect' where attitudes across the population are changing, then we need to look elsewhere for an explanation of this change. A strong contender is the lead given by political parties in the way they have discussed the issue. The Liberal Democrats and Labour were traditionally the parties most committed to civil liberties, whereas the Conservatives have been more comfortable presenting themselves as the party of law and order. However, Labour policies and rhetoric have undergone a shift since the early 1990s, linked to their reconception as New Labour – neatly exemplified by Tony Blair's oft-quoted speech about "tough on crime, tough on the causes of crime".[8] Since this coincided with the period when we saw the greatest change in attitudes to civil liberties, it is worth investigating the role of the political parties.

To do this, we look at the people who identify with each of the major parties. If the more robust position of the Labour Party has had an effect, we would expect Labour supporters to have become less libertarian.[9] Table 7.9 shows how the views of party supporters have changed on the right to hold public protest meetings.

Table 7.9 Per cent thinking that public meetings to protest against the government should definitely be allowed, by party support, 1985–2005[10]

% who think public protest meetings definitely should be allowed	1985	1990	1996	2005	Difference 1985–2005
All	59	62	54	51	-8
Conservative supporters	50	50	48	59	+9
Labour supporters	67	72	60	45	-22
Liberal Democrat supporters	71	73	55	59	-12
Not party supporter	36	55	41	42	+8

The change among Labour supporters is indeed startling, with the proportion thinking that such meetings should definitely be allowed declining from 67 per cent in 1985 to 45 per cent now. Indeed, there has been a 15 percentage point decline since 1996, the year before Labour was elected to government. In contrast, and most surprisingly, Conservative supporters have become *more* inclined to express support for the civil libertarian position, rising from one in two in 1985 to just under three in five now. Part of the explanation for this probably lies in the fact that the Conservative Party has now been out of power for nearly ten years. We can conjecture that party supporters are more likely to support civil liberties when it is the 'other side' who are in a position to lead on their erosion: in such circumstances there is no conflict between party and principle in maintaining one's support for traditional civil liberties.

Whether this is the case or not, these changes mean that the difference in view between supporters of the two main parties on public protest meetings has completely reversed – in 1985 Labour supporters were 17 points more likely than Conservatives to hold the libertarian view, whereas now, Conservative supporters are 14 points more likely than Labour supporters to do so. The table also shows that Liberal Democrat supporters have become less likely over the twenty years to support public meetings and are now level pegging with Conservatives.

The overall message is similar if we look at the questions about the rights of expression for revolutionaries. Here, the proportions who defend such rights have declined among the supporters of all the main parties. However, among Labour supporters the pro-civil liberties position has fallen by roughly twice as much as it has among Conservative supporters. In 1985, 34 per cent of Labour supporters held the view that revolutionaries should definitely be allowed to hold meetings and 33 per cent that they should definitely be allowed to publish material. These proportions are now 17 and 21 per cent. The proportion of Conservative supporters with such views in 1985 was 19 and 21 per cent respectively; now it is 12 and 14. Liberal Democrat supporters stand out as being the most in favour of these rights with 21 and 22 per cent thinking they should definitely be allowed.

We now move on to an area of civil libertarian concern that has received great political attention in recent years: the detention of suspects. Our precise question asked people how much they agreed or disagreed with the following:

The police should be allowed to question suspects for up to a week without letting them see a solicitor

Table 7.10 shows how the views of the supporters of the different parties have changed since 1990.

Table 7.10 Per cent disagreeing that the police should be allowed to question suspects for up to a week without letting them see a solicitor, by party support, 1990–2005[11]

% disagree police should be allowed to hold suspects without solicitor	1990	1994	1996	2004	2005	Difference 1990–2005
All	80	83	73	65	58	-22
Conservative supporters	81	86	71	63	60	-21
Labour supporters	79	79	73	66	55	-24
Liberal Democrat supporters	87	91	77	66	65	-22
Not party supporter	81	73	70	68	50	-31

Here the pattern is different: there were no great differences between supporters of the main parties in 1990, and changes in the anti-civil libertarian direction have been fairly uniform across the political spectrum over the period as a whole. Given that the right to legal representation, as set out in our question, has not been the subject of party political debate, this gives further support to the role of the parties. However, there is a subtle difference: three quarters of the change in view among Labour supporters (i.e. 18 of the 24 points) have occurred since 1996, which is approximately the period since their party has been in government and has taken a tougher line on such issues. On the contrary, civil libertarian attitudes among supporters of the other parties fell by a roughly similar amount pre- and post-1996.

Another area that has received considerable political attention is the issue of identity cards. The proportions of supporters of all parties objecting to making identity cards mandatory have declined since 1990, as shown in Table 7.11, but some changes have been particularly dramatic. In 1990, 45 per cent of Labour supporters objected to mandatory identity cards, compared with 38 per cent of Conservative supporters. Now, twice as many Conservative supporters object than do Labour supporters; indeed a mere 15 per cent of Labour supporters take this view.

It is also noteworthy that there was a sudden decline in the appetite for identity cards between 2004 and 2005. The proportion of Conservative supporters objecting to mandatory identity cards, for instance, almost trebled in just one year, whilst the proportion among Liberal Democrats rose by half. The most obvious explanation for this is that during this time a huge debate about their cost and effectiveness was taking place, leading people to question whether they were worth it. And, indeed, during this time the Conservatives changed their position from 'in principle' support to opposition to the specific Bill being proposed by the government. Interestingly, though, the views of Labour supporters remained comparatively stable, probably because it was their government that was pushing for the introduction of identity cards.

Table 7.11 Per cent disagreeing that every adult should have to carry an identity card, by party, 1990–2005[12]

% agree that every adult should carry identity card	1990	1994	1996	2004	2005	Difference 1990–2005
All	40	26	20	13	22	-18
Conservative supporters	38	19	11	11	30	-8
Labour supporters	45	31	25	11	15	-30
Liberal Democrat supporters	32	25	22	17	25	-7
Not party supporter	31	21	16	13	23	-8

So, it seems that there may be some mileage in the idea that political parties play a pivotal role in the development of public attitudes towards civil libertarian issues. Where the Labour Party has shifted its position, its supporters appear to have followed, contributing to the 'period effect' we saw in the previous section. Of course, there is an issue of cause and effect here. It might be argued that, actually, the public mood shifted first and the parties then changed their positions accordingly to increase their appeal. We cannot test this with *British Social Attitudes* data, as we do not have readings for the same people from different periods of time. However, it seems unlikely that this issue is salient enough in voting terms for the parties to implement major changes in policy in response to changes in public attitudes, particularly given the dominance of left–right politics in Britain.[13]

The terrorist threat

Important though the policies of the political parties are, this is not sufficient to explain the changes in public attitudes in full. This leads us to look at the external influence of the increased risk of terrorism, and the belief that the threat can be countered by more draconian legislation. Unfortunately we cannot track this over time, as we did not ask about fears of terrorism before the 2005 survey. We can do two things, though. First, we can observe the relationship between fears of terrorism and views on civil liberties. Secondly, we can compare the views of those interviewed before the violent events in London on 7th July 2005 and those interviewed after.

Before we do this, though, we need to enter a word of caution. Terrorism is not a new issue. It should be remembered that throughout the 1980s and early 1990s, Britain faced a constant terrorist threat in the form of an Irish-based republican extremism (principally in the form of the IRA) that struck far more frequently than has been seen so far with the relatively new threat from politicised versions of Islam. People may, of course, argue that the current threat is of a different nature: it is international and therefore more dangerous, not only in respect of the number of people who can be drawn in, but also in respect of the increased potential for the acquisition of biological, chemical or nuclear weapons. Further, it might be argued that the threat is more to a whole way of life than was that posed by the IRA, so that finding solutions is harder and as a result the threat can exist for longer. The symbolism and imagery associated with the 9/11 attacks may also have left a bigger scar in the public consciousness than anything that occurred before.

If this new fear was responsible for the observed changes in views on civil liberties, we would expect big changes in attitudes to have occurred between the late 1990s and early 21st century when the threat struck most dramatically and memorably. Recalling what we found in our earlier section, this is not in fact the case. Instead, most of the major changes in attitudes occurred in the early part of the 1990s, and the changes since have been comparatively small. So, at best, it seems that this heightened anxiety about terrorism may only explain part of the general trend away from commitment to civil liberties.

Nonetheless, we can observe a relationship between attitudes to many of these civil liberties and people's views on the threat of terrorism. We asked respondents to say how much they agreed or disagreed with the following statement:

People exaggerate the risks of there being a major terrorist attack in Britain

Overall, 22 per cent of people thought the risk was exaggerated and 43 per cent did not. Of these, about half (20 per cent) disagree strongly with the statement. As Table 7.12 illustrates, on each of our questions about civil liberties, those who thought that the risks of a terrorist attack were exaggerated were more likely to take the civil libertarian line. So, for example, nearly two-thirds of those who think the terrorist threat is exaggerated oppose the police being allowed to question suspects for about a week without letting them see a solicitor, compared to 55 per cent of those who do not think the terrorist threat is exaggerated. All of these differences were statistically significant except for two – holding public meetings to protest against the government, and whether it is worse to convict an innocent person than let a guilty person go free.

The question about the risk of a terrorist attack being exaggerated was new in 2005, but if we make the assumption that these fears have increased over time, we can deduce that this may have contributed to the decreasing commitment to civil liberties among the British public. However, note that even among those who do not think that the threat is exaggerated, majorities still support public protest meetings, believe that it is worse to convict an innocent person than let a guilty one go free, and oppose police questioning suspects for up to a week without legal representation.

Table 7.12 Views on civil liberties, by views on the risk of terror attack

	The risk of a terrorist attack is exaggerated	The risk of a terrorist attack is not exaggerated
% disagree police should be allowed to question suspects for up to a week without solicitor	64	55
% worse to convict innocent	56	50
% definitely allow public meetings to protest against government	54	51
% definitely allow protest marches	45	36
% disagree every adult should have to carry an identity card	28	19
% definitely allow revolutionaries to hold public meetings	23	13
% definitely allow revolutionaries to publish books	22	12
Base	*192*	*555*

What about the role of the 7th July 2005 attacks in London? Did the shock of these attacks cause a knee-jerk rejection of civil liberties? As it happens, fieldwork for our survey was in progress on 7th July and we can compare the answers given by those interviewed before the suicide bombings to those interviewed after.

At first glance, there were significant differences in attitudes before and after. This is true in respect of all of our questions on civil liberties except the two about the right to organise public meetings and the right to organise protest marches against the government. For all of the others, people interviewed after 7th July were less likely to hold a civil libertarian view than were those interviewed before.

This may, however, be a result of other characteristics of the two groups of people possess – the two are not random sub-samples of our respondents. Those interviewed early in the fieldwork period will tend to be those most easily contactable and most willing to take part in the survey, and there is every reason to suspect they may differ in their attitudes from those interviewed later.

Moreover, the events of 7th July may have had either a direct or an indirect effect. We have already seen that the perception of the terrorist threat appears to have an impact on attitudes to civil liberties. Not surprisingly, the events of that day affected perceptions of the risk of a terrorist attack: of those people interviewed before 7th July, more agreed that people exaggerated the risk of a terrorist attack than disagreed – 44 per cent compared to 39 per cent. In contrast, only 20 per cent of those interviewed after 7th July agreed with that proposition whilst 68 per cent disagreed.

It is important to identify whether the two factors have independent effects, or whether they are both measuring the same thing. If it is 7th July in itself that is more important, then it may have caused a permanent shift in attitudes; if it is the fear of terrorism that is the key, then public attitudes may well settle down once the immediate shock and associated heightened security has passed. To investigate this we carried out a multivariate analysis where we controlled for the other relevant characteristics – age, political party supported, gender, level of education, social class and fear of terrorism. In fact, those interviewed pre- and post-7th July show very few differences in their attitudes once these other factors were taken into account. The only exceptions were the questions concerning the rights of revolutionaries and the rights of the police to question suspects without a solicitor. In both cases, people interviewed after 7th July were significantly less libertarian in their views. Otherwise, 7th July played very little role in the attitudes of the public to these civil liberties.[14]

Moreover, people's fear of terrorism was not important for their attitudes to any of these issues, once we controlled for other socio-demographic characteristics using logistic regression. This casts some doubt on the role of recent events in shaping underlying public attitudes to civil liberties. This is, of course, in line with our finding that the biggest change in attitudes predates the recent global terrorist events.

The trade-off between civil liberties and tackling terrorism

So far, then, we have looked at views about civil liberties. We turn now to the views of the public about ways to tackle the threat of terrorism. Clearly the two are strongly related, as many of the measures that have been proposed involve curtailing existing civil liberties. We asked a series of eight questions in the following format:

> *A number of measures have been suggested as ways of tackling the threat of terrorism in Britain. Some people oppose these because they think they reduce people's freedom too much. Others think that the reduction in freedom is a price worth paying*

Respondents were presented with four answer options:

> *Definitely unacceptable as it reduces people's freedom too much*
> *Probably unacceptable as it reduces people's freedom too much*
> *Probably a price worth paying to reduce the terrorist threat*
> *Definitely a price worth paying to reduce the terrorist threat*

Table 7.13 shows the wording for each of the measures covered and the balance of opinion.

Table 7.13 Per cent viewing anti-terrorist measures as unacceptable or a price worth paying

		Un-acceptable	Price worth paying
Torturing people held in British jails who are suspected of involvement in terrorism to get information from them, if this is the only way this information can be obtained	%	76	22
Banning certain peaceful protests and demonstrations	%	63	35
Denying the right to trial by jury to people charged with a terrorist-related crime	%	50	45
Banning certain people from saying whatever they want in public	%	46	52
Having compulsory identity cards for all adults	%	26	71
Allowing the police to detain people for more than a week or so without charge if the police suspect them of involvement in terrorism	%	20	79
Putting people suspected of involvement with terrorism under special rules, which would mean they could be electronically tagged, prevented from going to certain places, or prevented from leaving their homes at certain times	%	18	80
Following people suspected of involvement with terrorism, tapping their phones and opening their mail	%	17	81

Base: 1058

Only two of the eight measures have clear majorities who think they are unacceptable: torture and the banning of peaceful protests and demonstrations.[15] Two measures show a fairly even split among the public: banning free speech and denying a trial by jury to people charged with terrorist-related crimes. The four remaining measures have large majorities of people believing that they are a price worth paying, despite the quite fundamental change to the British legal system that they would entail. Moreover, the three measures that have the highest proportions believing them to be a price worth paying are intended for people merely *suspected* of involvement in terrorism. Nor do respondents think these measures are needed only for foreigners. In further questioning, we found that a majority of 62 per cent think that the measures should apply to everyone in Britain no matter where they are from, whilst only 37 per cent think that stricter measures should apply to those people who are from other countries.

Interestingly, we can observe the role that the mention of terrorism appears to have on people's views by comparing five of these questions with similar ones asked elsewhere in the questionnaire that did not mention terrorism. And mentioning the 'T' word does appear to have an effect: of those people who thought that protest marches against a government action should definitely be allowed, 20 per cent now said that banning certain peaceful protests and demonstrations was a price worth paying to help tackle the threat of terrorism. Similarly, of those who thought that the right to protest against government decisions was important for democracy, 31 per cent thought that banning protests was a price worth paying if it was tackling terrorism. And 43 per cent of those people who thought that it was important for democracy that every adult in Britain had the right to say whatever they think in public, also thought that banning certain people from saying whatever they want in public was a price worth paying to tackle the threat of terrorism. Of those who disagreed with making identity cards mandatory when terrorism was not mentioned, 21 per cent actually felt it was a price worth paying to fight terrorism. And of those who disagreed that the police should be allowed to question suspects for up to a week without access to a solicitor, over half (54 per cent) felt that the police should be able to hold terror suspects for more than a week or so without charge.16 Of those people who thought that it was important that every adult had the right not to be detained by the police for more than a week without charge, a staggering 73 per cent thought that allowing the police to do just that to terror suspects was a price worth paying. Finally, of those people who thought that it was important for democracy that every adult had the right to a trial by jury, 44 per cent thought denying it to terror suspects was a price worth paying.

Fear, and experience, of terrorism

Given the discussion above, we would expect those with more fear of terrorism to be more willing to think limiting freedom to be a price worth paying. To assess people's fear of terrorism we use the same measure as earlier based on whether they saw the threat of terrorism as exaggerated. Comparing those who thought the threat of terrorism was exaggerated with those who did not (Table 7.14), we consistently find that those who believe the threat to be exaggerated are more likely to view each of the trade-off measures as unacceptable. The one exception to this is in respect of torture, where there are no differences according to people's level of fear. Two measures stand out as having particularly large differences – allowing the police to detain terror suspects for more than a week or so without charge, and compulsory identity cards. In both cases those who do not think that the terror threat has been exaggerated are twenty points more likely to think the measures are a price worth paying.

Moreover, respondents interviewed after 7th July were consistently less likely to think that each of the various measures were definitely unacceptable, with the exception of following terror suspects and putting terror suspects under house arrest.

Table 7.14 Per cent thinking various measures are unacceptable, by views on whether people exaggerate the risk of terrorism

% unacceptable	Risk of terrorism is exaggerated	Risk of terrorism is not exaggerated	Difference
Allowing the police to detain people for more than a week or so without charge if the police suspect them of involvement in terrorism	34	12	-21
Having compulsory identity cards for all adults	41	21	-20
Banning certain people from saying whatever they want in public	57	42	-15
Following people suspected of involvement with terrorism, tapping their phones and opening their mail	27	12	-15
Putting people suspected of involvement with terrorism under special rules, which would mean they could be electronically tagged, prevented from going to certain places, or prevented from leaving their homes at certain times	26	14	-12
Denying the right to trial by jury to people charged with a terrorist-related crime	59	50	-10
Banning certain peaceful protests and demonstrations	68	63	-6
Torturing people held in British jails who are suspected of involvement in terrorism to get information from them, if this is the only way this information can be obtained	78	77	0
Base	*235*	*135*	

Social characteristics

On these trade-offs we do not have any previous measures to assess change over time. What we can do, however, is see how different subgroups in the population vary in their views. In particular, we look at differences by age, level of education, social class, media consumption and political interest. We have good grounds for thinking there will be some quite substantial differences given what we found earlier in attitudes to civil liberties. In particular, the groups we might expect to be more likely to think the measures are unacceptable are the young, those with higher levels of education, and those in professional jobs. We might also expect that Labour supporters are less likely to think they are unacceptable given that it is a Labour government that has been leading the way in proposing many of these measures, and that Liberal Democrat supporters, in particular, are more likely to think they are unacceptable, in view of their party's traditional stance on such things.

Looking at the proportion saying the various measures are definitely unacceptable, we do indeed find that age is important for attitudes to three of them, with the youngest significantly more likely to think they are definitely unacceptable than the oldest. These measures are banning peaceful protests, banning people from saying whatever they want, and torture.

Our suspicions about education are confirmed with significant differences between those with degrees and those with no qualifications on all of the measures, with the exception of identity cards. However, the direction of these differences is not always as we would predict. On peaceful protests, detaining terror suspects for more than a week without charge, 'house arrest' and torture, the differences are in the predicted direction, namely that those with degrees are more likely than those with no qualifications to think they are definitely unacceptable. But on banning certain people from saying whatever they want in public, denying terror suspects the right to a trial by jury, and following terror suspects, tapping their phones and opening their mail, those with no qualifications are more likely than those with degrees to think it definitely unacceptable.

Most surprisingly, given what we found earlier, there is only one significant difference between Conservative supporters and Labour supporters. That is on the issue of allowing the police to detain terror suspects for more than a week without charge, where Labour supporters are actually more likely to think this definitely unacceptable than Conservative supporters. Liberal Democrat supporters, however, stand out as being particularly pro-civil liberties, as expected. They are significantly more likely than Conservative supporters to think each of the measures are definitely unacceptable except identity cards and denying terror suspects a trial by jury. And, similarly, for three measures they are more likely than Labour supporters to think they are definitely unacceptable – banning peaceful protests, compulsory identity cards and following terror suspects.

Table 7.15 Attitudes to trade-offs, by party identification

% saying "definitely unacceptable"	Party identification		
	Conservative	Labour	Liberal Democrat
Banning certain peaceful protests and demonstrations	32	36	48
Banning certain people from saying whatever they want in public	13	16	22
Having compulsory identity cards for all adults	14	12	19
Allowing the police to detain people for more than a week or so without charge if the police suspect them of involvement in terrorism	4	9	3
Denying the right to trial by jury to people charged with a terrorist-related crime	26	28	29
Following people suspected of involvement with terrorism, tapping their phones and opening their mail	4	6	13
Putting people suspected of involvement with terrorism under special rules, which would mean they could be electronically tagged, prevented from going to certain places, or prevented from leaving their homes at certain times	2	5	6
Torturing people held in British jails who are suspected of involvement in terrorism to get information from them, if this is the only way this information can be obtained	54	59	68
Base	*249*	*414*	*128*

We had also expected to find that professionals are more likely to think the measures are unacceptable than those working in routine manual occupations, but, in fact, this is true only for banning peaceful protests. For banning certain people from saying what they want and following terror suspects, it was actually those in routine manual jobs who were more likely than those in professional jobs to think they were definitely unacceptable.

Media consumption and political interest

As well as people's social and demographic characteristics, it also seems highly likely that their media consumption will influence their views on these issues. After all, it is predominantly through the media that we hear about terrorist threats, government and security service proposals, and critiques and counter-proposals from other political parties, interest groups, and so on. We use a crude distinction of the printed media into tabloid and broadsheet, with the former more inclined to sensationalism and less nuanced reporting than the latter. Given that the issues we are discussing are very complex, it seems likely that the simplicity with which tabloids report the issues and their general hostility to civil liberty ideas means their readers will be more likely to take the view that the measures are a price worth paying.

Table 7.16 Acceptability of trade-offs, by newspaper readership

	Tabloid readers	Broadsheet readers	Non-readers
% saying "definitely unacceptable"			
Torturing terror suspects	53	68	58
Banning peaceful protests	29	47	36
Deny terror suspects trial by jury	24	33	25
Banning people saying what they want in public	18	14	18
Compulsory identity cards	15	16	19
Following terror suspects, tapping phones, opening mail	7	5	7
Detain terror suspects for more than a week without charge	5	15	10
Putting terror suspects under special rules, including tagging	3	9	4
Base	*576*	*252*	*213*

Table 7.16 shows that there are a number of significant differences between readers of tabloids and readers of broadsheets, and all are in the direction we predicted – banning protests, detention without charge, denying terror suspects a trial by jury, putting terror suspects under special rules, and torture. There are also some differences between readers and non-readers. Non-readers were more likely than tabloid readers to think it definitely unacceptable to detain terror suspects for more than a week without charge. Non-readers were less likely than broadsheet readers to think it definitely unacceptable to ban protests, to put

terror suspects under special rules and to torture terror suspects. In general, it seems that the views of non-readers are in between those of tabloid and broadsheet readers (perhaps because many of them are not truly non-readers, just infrequent readers).

Related to an extent to news consumption is interest in politics. On the one hand we might think that those with more interest will be more aware of the terrorist threat as proclaimed by politicians. On the other we might also expect those with more interest to be less easily swayed by the views of politicians and perhaps more sceptical as to their motives, and more aware of the debates taking place in the policy arena. What we find is that those with higher levels of political interest are more likely than those with low levels to think that it is definitely unacceptable to ban peaceful protests, to allow the police to detain terror suspects for more than a week without charge, to deny terror suspects the right to a trial by jury and to torture terror suspects. For the other measures, there were no differences according to political interest.

Multivariate analysis

Whilst the findings reported above are revealing, we must undertake multivariate analysis which controls for other factors simultaneously to be sure about their importance. We used logistic regression to determine the factors associated with thinking that each of the trade-offs was "definitely unacceptable". Further details of the regression model can be found in the appendix. Table 7.17 shows which factors were significantly related to thinking that each of the trade-off measures were definitely unacceptable.

Interestingly, we find that being interviewed after 7th July made a difference on only three measures – banning certain people from saying whatever they want in public, allowing the police to detain terror suspects for more than a week without charge, and torturing terrorist suspects. As would be predicted, those interviewed after 7th July were less likely to think these were definitely unacceptable than those interviewed before. People's fears about terrorism were also important for three of the trade-offs, with those who thought that the terrorist threat was exaggerated being more likely to think the measures were definitely unacceptable. Party identification was important for the first four trade-offs, but the effect was not consistent. On banning protests and detaining terror suspects, supporters of the Conservative Party were least likely to think it was definitely unacceptable. For banning people from saying what they want in public and for every adult having a compulsory identity card, Labour supporters were less likely than Conservative supporters to think the measures were definitely unacceptable.

Political interest is also important for a number of the trade-offs: those with higher levels of political interest being more likely to say the measures were definitely unacceptable. For each of the three measures where newspaper readership was important, it was the non-readers who were the least likely to think that the trade-offs were definitely unacceptable.

Table 7.17 Factors significant in regression model for believing the trade-offs are definitely unacceptable

Trade-off measure	Factors significant in regression model
Banning peaceful protests	Age Party identification Level of education Political interest
Banning people saying what they want in public	Age Party identification 7th July
Compulsory identity cards	Party identification Terrorism risk exaggerated
Detain terror suspects for more than a week without charge	Party identification Sex 7th July Terrorism risk exaggerated Newspaper read Political interest
Deny terror suspects trial by jury	Political interest
Following terror suspects, tapping phones, opening mail	None
Putting terror suspects under special rules, including tagging	Terrorism risk exaggerated Newspaper read
Torturing terror suspects	7th July Newspaper read Political interest

It is difficult to summarise these findings succinctly, but the tendency of newspaper readership, political interest, fear of terrorism and/or pre-/post-7th July interview date to crop up in the models suggests that views on counter-terrorism measures are very much being shaped by current events. This fits well with our earlier finding that responses to the questions that mentioned terrorism were to an extent in opposition to the respondents' own underlying views on civil liberties in general.

Human rights, international law and the threat of terrorism

Finally, we briefly discuss attitudes to human rights and international law, which have been subject to a fair amount of criticism from many media quarters for preventing effective measures to tackle terrorism. Our aim is to gauge the extent of public commitment to them, to try to discern whether greater fear of terrorism produces more hostile views towards them, and, further, to see whether consumers of particular media have distinctive views.

People were asked how much they agreed or disagreed with the following propositions.

> *When a country is at war it must **always** abide by international human rights law*

> *International human rights law prevents the armed forces from doing their job properly*

> *During a war it is acceptable for the armed forces to torture people*

> *If someone is suspected of involvement with terrorism they should not be protected by international human rights law*

Table 7.18 shows a considerable amount of inconsistency in attitudes. For instance, 84 per cent agree that when a country is at war it should always abide by international human rights law, but 39 per cent then agree that terror suspects should not be protected by the very same law. Overall, though, the public does seem to value human rights law, with majorities taking viewpoints that favour it for three out of the four questions. The one question where there were more mixed views concerned possible conflicts between human rights law and effective armed force action. This does not, however, necessarily indicate that the public want to ignore international law in order for the armed forces to be able to do their job. Rather, they are prepared to accept the possibility that such law may make it more difficult for the armed forces, but that it is worth it.

Table 7.18 Attitudes to international human rights law

		Agree	Neither agree nor disagree	Disagree
When a country is at war it must always abide by human rights law	%	84	8	7
Terror suspects should not be protected by human rights law	%	39	13	46
Human rights law prevents armed forces doing job	%	35	26	34
During a war it is acceptable for armed forces to torture	%	10	11	78

Base: 1075

What can we say about these attitudes according to people's perception of the terror threat and their media consumption? Very interestingly, there are no differences in the views of those who think the terrorist threat is exaggerated and those who do not. This suggests that the commitment to international human rights law will not reduce if the threat of terrorism, or more accurately, the public perceptions of the threat, increases.

We do, however, find differences according to the type of newspaper people read. Tabloid readers are more likely than broadsheet readers to think that human rights law prevents the armed forces from doing their job properly, that torture is acceptable, and that terror suspects should not be protected by human rights law. Indeed, they are approximately twice as likely as broadsheet readers to take these views. However, support for the fact that a country at war should always abide by international human rights law was shared by both groups.

Conclusions

There is a great deal of nostalgia surrounding debates about civil liberties and freedom in the United Kingdom, with frequent references back to successive golden ages of liberty when the executive is supposed not to have been as abusive of freedom or as repressive of individual choice as the regime of the day. Even at Runnymede in 1215, the barons who gathered around King John derived a large part of their revolutionary fervour from a shared memory of the 'good times' under Henry II: this is an instinct that is deeply embedded in at least the English, and possibly also the British, constitutional culture. Such backward-looking idealism rarely survives critical scrutiny, however. Scholars of each successive candidate for a 'golden age' are invariably able to point to levels of repression that would not be tolerated by exactly the same people who look back fondly on the freedoms that they – wrongly – believe then existed for all at exactly that time (Ewing and Gearty, 2000). The truth of the matter is that broadly speaking the curve on the civil liberties graph has been moving steadily upwards over time in Britain. True, there have been occasional blips for this or that conflict or national emergency but generally speaking we have as a culture and as a collection of individuals within a culture become freer, more able to engage in politics and to do what we want with our lives. This is largely because of the unfolding of the democratic project which has been the big constitutional event since the middle of the 19th century, establishing first a universal right to vote and then delivering a series of basic liberties, such as expression, assembly and association, which have made possible a democratic culture in which votes are cast by an informed rather than ignorant or cowed electorate.

The question posed by the data generated by this survey is whether this progressive trend is at risk of being put in reverse. Our findings show that there has been a marked decline in societal commitment to civil liberties in the course of the last twenty to twenty-five years, and this cannot fully be explained away by age, party affiliation or education. The extent to which this decline has been influenced by a growing fear of terrorist attack is difficult to gauge accurately in the absence of figures from earlier surveys. But what we can say with confidence is that the general public is generally less convinced about civil liberties than they were twenty-five years ago.

This trend long predates 11th September 2001 and 7th July 2005. But these events also play a role in current attitudes: even where civil liberties ideals persist, the very mention of something being a counter-terrorism measure makes people more willing to contemplate the giving up of their freedoms. It may be that this reflects the assumption of those surveyed that suspected terrorists (rather than suspected criminals) are always going to be 'other people' and so it is not their own freedom that they are sacrificing but rather that of people who are already in some ways of doubtful ethical provenance. Nevertheless, the fact remains that the label 'counter-terrorism' does carry this strongly exculpatory dimension, inoculating its contents from a civil libertarian attack that might otherwise be thought to be devastating.

The temptation this offers to political leaders is obvious. There have been many examples of pieces of legislation passed in the aftermath of a terrorist atrocity which have contained powers dealing with far more than the specific terrorist problem that has generated the perceived need for immediate legislative action.[17] If they care about preserving Britain's civil libertarian culture, politicians of all parties need to be disciplined about their deployment of the counter-terrorism card in public debate: it is a trump, certainly, but overplayed it has the potential completely to distort the whole game.

There are lessons in our survey for the civil liberties groups as well. The arguments for the importance of human rights and civil liberties cannot be taken as read: they need to be articulated and then repeated. It is not any longer enough (if it ever were enough) merely to say that human rights law demands this or that our commitment to civil liberties requires that. Our survey shows a general public that remains on the whole committed to civil liberties, albeit with less enthusiasm than in the past and with a greater susceptibility to be persuaded to dispense with them. It is as though society is in the process of forgetting why past generations thought these freedoms to be so very important. Like the secular grandchildren of devout church-going believers, they know they should care – and want to for the sake of their own offspring – but cannot for the life of them articulate why. Civil libertarians need to re-evangelise the British public if they want to turn the graph back in what they would say (and many would agree) is the right direction. That it can be done is evident from the survey's findings on the importance of international law and the slowly decreasing public support for the death penalty. But politicians need also to be part of the more mature discussion of civil liberties and the threat of terrorism that Britain now requires if it is to come through its current anxieties with the graph of freedom continuing on its traditional upward trajectory.

Notes

1. See, most recently, the Prevention of Terrorism Act 2005 and the Terrorism Act 2006. For a statement of the government position in general terms, see Home Office (2004).

2. For a general assessment of the interrelationship between terrorism and human rights and civil liberties concerns see Gearty (2005).
3. One obvious explanation for the difference between this and the other civil liberties we ask about might be the proliferation of protests that took place before and around the time of this survey on issues that many people may have much sympathy with, such as the Iraq war and world poverty.
4. In this section we do not discuss attitudes to protest marches and demonstrations to protest against the government, or attitudes to the death penalty, as these did not become less libertarian over our period of interest.
5. Education may also have been thought relevant given what is known about attitudinal differences between those with higher education qualifications and those with lower levels of qualifications (Hyman and Wright, 1979; Bobo and Licari, 1989; Nie *et al.*, 1996), and in view of the increase in the proportion of the population with higher education over the last twenty years. However, the relationship is in the wrong direction: people with higher education tend to be more libertarian than those with no qualifications. For instance, 61 per cent of those with higher education thought public meetings to protest against the government should definitely be allowed, compared with only 41 per cent of those with no qualifications. Therefore, the growth in higher education cannot explain the decline in libertarian attitudes.
6. This is used for illustrative purposes, the pattern is similar for the right to hold public meetings to protest against the government, for the right for revolutionaries to publish books and for the police not to have the right to hold suspects for up to a week without letting them see a solicitor.
7. Bases for Table 7.8 are as follows:

			1985	2005
All			*1530*	*860*
Cohort	**Age 1985**	**Age 2005**		
1978–87		18–27		*83*
1968–77		28–37		*142*
1958–67	18–27	38–47	*336*	*181*
1948–57	28–37	48–57	*297*	*147*
1938–47	38–47	58–67	*278*	*149*
1928–37	48–57	68+	*217*	*158*
1918–27	58–67		*214*	
Pre-1917	68+		*188*	

8. For a detailed account of the various positions adopted by the mainstream political parties in the period from the end of the Second World War though to the mid 1990s see Gearty (1997). The changes in political perspective since then are well covered by Bradley and Ewing (2007: 419-441); see also Gearty (2004: 21-30).

9. When Labour won its landslide election victory of 1997, it attracted the support of many people who had not previously voted Labour and this obviously changed the attitude profile of Labour *voters*. However, the proportion of the sample who were Labour *supporters* (people who said they generally thought of themselves as a supporter of a political party) only increased from 36 per cent in 1985 to 40 per cent in 2005, making this a more stable group.

10. Bases for Table 7.9 are as follows:

% who think public protest meetings definitely should be allowed	1985	1990	1996	2005
All	1472	1197	989	860
Conservative supporters	495	419	285	210
Labour supporters	550	462	418	353
Liberal Democrat supporters	244	98	112	113
Not party supporter	110	98	85	108

11. Bases for Table 7.10 are as follows:

% agree police should be allowed to hold suspects without solicitor	1990	1994	1996	2004	2005
All	1197	970	2047	853	860
Conservative supporters	419	281	565	240	210
Labour supporters	462	402	879	261	353
Liberal Democrat supporters	98	139	232	100	113
Not party supporter	98	73	191	138	108

12. Bases for Table 7.11 are as follows:

% agree that every adult should carry identity card	1990	1994	1996	2004	2005
All	1197	970	2047	853	860
Conservative supporters	419	281	565	240	210
Labour supporters	462	402	879	261	353
Liberal Democrat supporters	98	139	232	100	113
Not party supporter	98	73	191	138	108

13. Another contention is that four of the questions were asking about either protesting against the *government* or overthrowing the *government* by revolution. This could lead party supporters to think about the government of the day when answering. However, given that the trends were also evident for the other questions we asked, this seems of marginal importance at most.

14. We were unable to include fear of terrorism in the analysis for the rights of revolutionaries due to small sample sizes.
15. It is likely that these two are rejected for rather different reasons – torture would seem to be the ultimate infringement on a person's freedom and many would argue is useless in obtaining reliable information, whereas banning protests may seem to be rather tenuously linked to combating terrorism.
16. Clearly, the two questions do ask about slightly different concepts – without access to a solicitor compared to without charge – so it may be that people assume the terror suspects have access to a solicitor, which is why they are more likely to view it as acceptable.
17. One outstanding example is in the Anti-terrorism, Crime and Security Act 2001 passed in the immediate aftermath of 11th September 2001, but containing many broad powers that would otherwise have been difficult to get through Parliament: some indeed had been rejected when they had appeared in earlier bills.

References

Bobo, L. and Licari, F.C. (1989), 'Education and political tolerance', *Public Opinion Quarterly*, **53**: 285–308

Bradley, A.W. and Ewing, K.D. (2007), *Constitutional and Administrative Law* (14th edition), Harlow: Pearson Longman

Brooke, L. and Cape, E. (1995), 'Libertarianism in retreat?', in Jowell, R., Curtice, J., Park, A., Brook, L. and Ahrendt, D. (eds.), *British Social Attitudes: the 12th Report*, Aldershot: Dartmouth

Evans, G. (2002), 'In search of tolerance', in Park A., Curtice, J., Thomson, K., Jarvis, L. and Bromley, C. (eds.), *British Social Attitudes: the 19th Report*, London: Sage

Ewing, K.D. and Gearty, C.A. (2000), *The Struggle for Civil Liberties. Political Freedom and the Rule of Law in Britain, 1914–1945*, Oxford: Oxford University Press

Gearty, C.A. (1997), 'The United Kingdom' in Gearty, C. A., (ed), *European Civil Liberties and the European Convention on Human Rights: A Comparative Study*, The Hague: Martinus Nijhoff Publishers

Gearty, C.A. (2004), *Principles of Human Rights Adjudication*, Oxford: Oxford University Press

Gearty, C.A. (2005) '11 September 2001, Counter-terrorism, and the Human Rights Act', *Journal of Law and Society*, **32(1)**: 18–33

Home Office (2004), *Counter-Terrorism Powers: Reconciling Security and Liberty in an Open Society: A Discussion Paper*, White Paper Cm 6147, London: The Stationery Office

Hyman, H.H. and Wright, C.R. (1979), *Education's Lasting Influence on Values*, Chicago: University of Chicago Press

Nie, N.H., Junn, J. and Stehlik-Barry, K. (1996), *Education and Democratic Citizenship in America*, Chicago: University of Chicago Press

Park, A. (2000), 'The generation game', in Jowell, R., Curtice, J., Park, A., Thomson, K., Jarvis, L., Bromley, C. and Stratford, N. (eds.), *British Social Attitudes: the 17th Report*, London: Sage

Acknowledgements

The *National Centre for Social Research* and the authors are grateful to the Economic and Social Research Council (grant number RES–228–25–0027) for their financial support which enabled us to ask the questions reported in this chapter.

Appendix

The multivariate analysis technique used is logistic regression. The coefficients for categorical variables are presented compared with a baseline category.

Table A.1 "Definitely unacceptable" to ban certain peaceful protests

	Adjusted Wald	Sig.	Odds ratio	Linearised s.e.
Age	2.28	0.0498		
18–24			1.000	(baseline)
25–34			1.100	0.405
35–44			0.660	0.228
45–54			1.206	0.435
55–64			0.656	0.246
65+			0.584	0.212
Party identification	2.75	0.0308		
Conservative			1.000	(baseline)
Labour			1.336	0.279
Liberal Democrat			1.964	0.465
No party			1.071	0.327
Other party			2.065	0.656
Sex	0.01	0.9281		
Male			1.000	(baseline)
Female			0.987	0.147
Education	2.70	0.0480		
Degree/higher education			1.000	(baseline)
A levels or equiv.			1.328	0.348
GCSEs or equiv.			0.637	0.177
No qualifications			0.781	0.227
7th July	2.21	0.1397		
Pre-			1.000	(baseline)
On/post-			0.746	0.147
Social class	0.44	0.7763		
Professional/managerial			1.000	(baseline)
Intermediate			1.034	0.278
Employer			1.503	0.481
Lower supervisory			1.010	0.268
Semi-routine/routine			1.114	0.277
Terrorism risk exaggerated	3.70	0.0563		
Agree			1.000	(baseline)
Disagree			0.744	0.114
Newspaper read	2.60	0.0780		
Do not read			1.000	(baseline)
Tabloid			1.634	0.372
Broadsheet			1.383	0.297
Political interest	10.93	0.000		
Great deal/quite a lot			1.000	(baseline)
Some			0.601	0.110
Not much/none			0.346	0.079

Table A.2 "Definitely unacceptable" to ban certain people from saying whatever they want in public

	Adjusted Wald	Sig.	Odds ratio	Linearised s.e.
Age	3.51	0.005		
18–24			1.000	(baseline)
25–34			0.478	0.224
35–44			0.562	0.245
45–54			0.465	0.220
55–64			0.161	0.077
65+			0.373	0.179
Party identification	2.93	0.023		
Conservative			1.000	(baseline)
Labour			0.899	0.249
Liberal Democrat			1.886	0.619
No party			1.175	0.432
Other party			2.147	0.701
Sex	0.36	0.550		
Male			1.000	(baseline)
Female			1.136	0.241
Education	1.82	0.146		
Degree/higher education			1.000	(baseline)
A levels or equiv.			0.996	0.355
GCSEs or equiv.			1.544	0.472
No qualifications			2.162	0.785
7th July	7.78	0.006		
Pre-			1.000	(baseline)
On/post-			0.487	0.126
Social class	1.95	0.105		
Professional/managerial			1.000	(baseline)
Intermediate			1.135	0.396
Employer			2.514	0.865
Lower supervisory			1.233	0.428
Semi-routine/routine			1.145	0.321
Terrorism risk exaggerated	2.82	0.095		
Agree			1.000	(baseline)
Disagree			0.714	0.143
Newspaper read	0.32	0.725		
Do not read			1.000	(baseline)
Tabloid			0.907	0.251
Broadsheet			0.783	0.238
Political interest	2.65	0.074		
Great deal/quite a lot			1.000	(baseline)
Some			0.583	0.139
Not much/none			0.694	0.186

Table A.3 "Definitely unacceptable" to have compulsory identity cards for all adults

	Adjusted Wald	Sig.	Odds ratio	Linearised s.e.
Age	2.08	0.0717		
18–24			1.000	(baseline)
25–34			0.341	0.179
35–44			0.533	0.234
45–54			0.554	0.231
55–64			0.685	0.308
65+			1.092	0.479
Party identification	4.10	0.0036		
Conservative			1.000	(baseline)
Labour			0.737	0.199
Liberal Democrat			1.122	0.378
No party			1.253	0.407
Other party			2.835	0.963
Sex	1.39	0.2408		
Male			1.000	(baseline)
Female			0.777	0.167
Education	1.91	0.1303		
Degree/higher education			1.000	(baseline)
A levels or equiv.			1.557	0.476
GCSEs or equiv.			0.729	0.250
No qualifications			0.737	0.240
7th July	1.69	0.1956		
Pre-			1.000	(baseline)
On/post-			0.715	0.185
Social class	1.20	0.3144		
Professional/managerial			1.000	(baseline)
Intermediate			1.092	0.468
Employer			1.695	0.686
Lower supervisory			0.730	0.303
Semi-routine/routine			1.411	0.469
Terrorism risk exaggerated	13.97	0.0003		
Agree			1.000	(baseline)
Disagree			0.435	0.097
Newspaper read	0.91	0.4061		
Do not read			1.000	(baseline)
Tabloid			1.386	0.376
Broadsheet			0.958	0.273
Political interest	1.36	0.2589		
Great deal/quite a lot			1.000	(baseline)
Some			0.665	0.164
Not much/none			0.798	0.239

Table A.4 "Definitely unacceptable" to allow police to detain people for more than a week or so without charge if the police suspect them of involvement in terrorism

	Adjusted Wald	Sig.	Odds ratio	Linearised s.e.
Age	0.15	0.9806		
18–24			1.000	(baseline)
25–34			1.051	0.706
35–44			1.409	0.938
45–54			1.460	0.899
55–64			1.273	0.787
65+			1.376	0.956
Party identification	2.48	0.0469		
Conservative			1.000	(baseline)
Labour			2.488	1.068
Liberal Democrat			2.915	1.425
No party			3.441	1.738
Other party			4.086	2.052
Sex	4.87	0.0289		
Male			1.000	(baseline)
Female			0.517	0.155
Education	0.08	0.9731		
Degree/higher education			1.000	(baseline)
A levels or equiv.			1.023	0.474
GCSEs or equiv.			0.820	0.392
No qualifications			0.929	0.518
7th July	5.82	0.0171		
Pre-			1.000	(baseline)
On/post-			0.450	0.149
Social class	2.03	0.0928		
Professional/managerial			1.000	(baseline)
Intermediate			1.735	1.044
Employer			0.974	0.567
Lower supervisory			1.562	0.725
Semi-routine/routine			3.025	1.274
Terrorism risk exaggerated	16.09	0.0001		
Agree			1.000	(baseline)
Disagree			0.272	0.088
Newspaper read	5.27	0.0062		
Do not read			1.000	(baseline)
Tabloid			2.218	0.790
Broadsheet			3.912	1.653
Political interest	5.07	0.0075		
Great deal/quite a lot			1.000	(baseline)
Some			0.517	0.176
Not much/none			0.227	0.109

Table A.5 "Definitely unacceptable" to deny the right to a trial by jury to people charged with a terrorist-related crime

	Adjusted Wald	Sig.	Odds ratio	Linearised s.e.
Age	1.50	0.1923		
18–24			1.000	(baseline)
25–34			1.293	0.479
35–44			0.894	0.317
45–54			0.984	0.380
55–64			1.054	0.395
65+			0.611	0.247
Party identification	1.33	0.2629		
Conservative			1.000	(baseline)
Labour			1.126	0.246
Liberal Democrat			1.126	0.353
No party			0.890	0.293
Other party			1.875	0.584
Sex	1.66	0.2003		
Male			1.000	(baseline)
Female			0.783	0.149
Education	0.23	0.8768		
Degree/higher education			1.000	(baseline)
A levels or equiv.			0.829	0.208
GCSEs or equiv.			0.853	0.217
No qualifications			0.878	0.242
7th July	2.94	0.0887		
Pre-			1.000	(baseline)
On/post-			0.689	0.150
Social class	2.33	0.0585		
Professional/managerial			1.000	(baseline)
Intermediate			1.941	0.594
Employer			1.375	0.439
Lower supervisory			0.686	0.206
Semi-routine/routine			1.349	0.316
Terrorism risk exaggerated	2.80	0.0964		
Agree			1.000	(baseline)
Disagree			0.723	0.140
Newspaper read	0.44	0.6458		
Do not read			1.000	(baseline)
Tabloid			1.106	0.281
Broadsheet			1.256	0.307
Political interest	10.33	0.0001		
Great deal/quite a lot			1.000	(baseline)
Some			0.427	0.088
Not much/none			0.415	0.102

Table A.6 "Definitely unacceptable" to follow people suspect of involvement with terrorism, tapping their phones and opening their mail

	Adjusted Wald	Sig.	Odds ratio	Linearised s.e.
Age	2.10	0.0692		
18–24			1.000	(baseline)
25–34			0.896	0.601
35–44			0.555	0.337
45–54			0.268	0.218
55–64			0.608	0.427
65+			1.171	0.816
Party identification	1.56	0.1891		
Conservative			1.000	(baseline)
Labour			1.439	0.705
Liberal Democrat			3.480	1.876
No party			1.621	1.064
Other party			1.731	1.017
Sex	0.02	0.8886		
Male			1.000	(baseline)
Female			0.958	0.296
Education	2.15	0.0962		
Degree/higher education			1.000	(baseline)
A levels or equiv.			0.749	0.612
GCSEs or equiv.			2.719	1.496
No qualifications			2.416	1.360
7th July	0.58	0.4494		
Pre-			1.000	(baseline)
On/post-			0.749	0.286
Social class	0.90	0.4631		
Professional/managerial			1.000	(baseline)
Intermediate			2.402	1.339
Employer			1.677	0.982
Lower supervisory			1.579	0.838
Semi-routine/routine			2.319	1.132
Terrorism risk exaggerated	2.10	0.1499		
Agree			1.000	(baseline)
Disagree			0.612	0.207
Newspaper read	0.45	0.6373		
Do not read			1.000	(baseline)
Tabloid			1.310	0.560
Broadsheet			1.524	0.738
Political interest	0.04	0.9650		
Great deal/quite a lot			1.000	(baseline)
Some			0.997	0.425
Not much/none			1.100	0.511

Table A.7 "Definitely unacceptable" to put people suspected of involvement with terrorism under special rules, so they could be electronically tagged, prevented from going to certain places, or from leaving their homes at certain times

	Adjusted Wald	Sig.	Odds ratio	Linearised s.e.
Age	0.82	0.5366		
18–24			1.000	(baseline)
25–34			0.338	0.319
35–44			1.007	0.699
45–54			0.474	0.358
55–64			1.011	0.735
65+			0.850	0.632
Party identification	0.75	0.5609		
Conservative			1.000	(baseline)
Labour			1.783	1.025
Liberal Democrat			1.700	1.122
No party			2.869	1.872
Other party			2.655	1.921
Sex	0.21	0.6497		
Male			1.000	(baseline)
Female			1.197	0.474
Education	0.78	0.5067		
Degree/higher education			1.000	(baseline)
A levels or equiv.			0.369	0.257
GCSEs or equiv.			0.861	0.501
No qualifications			0.672	0.450
7th July	1.08	0.3005		
Pre-			1.000	(baseline)
On/post-			1.813	1.038
Social class	1.04	0.3906		
Professional/managerial			1.000	(baseline)
Intermediate			2.479	1.374
Employer			1.174	0.933
Lower supervisory			0.586	0.521
Semi-routine/routine			1.612	0.938
Terrorism risk exaggerated	8.97	0.0032		
Agree			1.000	(baseline)
Disagree			0.276	0.119
Newspaper read	6.76	0.0016		
Do not read			1.000	(baseline)
Tabloid			1.553	0.787
Broadsheet			5.327	2.531
Political interest	0.54	0.5849		
Great deal/quite a lot			1.000	(baseline)
Some			0.657	0.295
Not much/none			0.661	0.346

Table A.8 "Definitely unacceptable" to torture people held in British jails who are suspected of involvement in terrorism to get information from them, if this is the only way this information can be obtained

	Adjusted Wald	Sig.	Odds ratio	Linearised s.e.
Age	2.26	0.0518		
18–24			1.000	(baseline)
25–34			1.115	0.374
35–44			1.578	0.482
45–54			2.224	0.685
55–64			2.034	0.611
65+			1.777	0.535
Party identification	1.66	0.1621		
Conservative			1.000	(baseline)
Labour			1.415	0.291
Liberal Democrat			1.828	0.467
No party			1.445	0.434
Other party			1.645	0.481
Sex	0.77	0.3831		
Male			1.000	(baseline)
Female			1.164	0.202
Education	0.63	0.5964		
Degree/higher education			1.000	(baseline)
A levels or equiv.			0.783	0.193
GCSEs or equiv.			0.769	0.164
No qualifications			0.864	0.239
7th July	4.95	0.0277		
Pre-			1.000	(baseline)
On/post-			0.583	0.141
Social class	2.00	0.0971		
Professional/managerial			1.000	(baseline)
Intermediate			0.820	0.239
Employer			0.794	0.239
Lower supervisory			0.568	0.136
Semi-routine/routine			1.071	0.231
Terrorism risk exaggerated	0.01	0.9255		
Agree			1.000	(baseline)
Disagree			0.985	0.154
Newspaper read	3.44	0.0347		
Do not read			1.000	(baseline)
Tabloid			1.278	0.284
Broadsheet			1.724	0.358
Political interest	4.79	0.0097		
Great deal/quite a lot			1.000	(baseline)
Some			0.600	0.100
Not much/none			0.781	0.160

8 New Labour, New unions?

Alex Bryson[*]

In 1997 New Labour swept to power after 18 years in the political wilderness. It did so with the full financial and organisational backing of a trade union movement keen on a change in the political climate. The unions had reached the zenith of their power in the late 1970s. Trade union membership and union density (defined as the percentage of workers in membership) peaked in 1980 just after Margaret Thatcher became Prime Minister (Charlwood and Metcalf, 2005). The intervening years were a period of unremitting decline in the union movement's membership and political influence. Although academic research has identified a number of different reasons for union decline over the period to 1997, union leaders pinned the blame squarely on successive Conservative governments. Little wonder, then, that they campaigned so hard for the return of a Labour government.

Although Tony Blair had made it clear that the relationship between the union movement and the Labour Party in government would be more 'arm's length' than in earlier decades, the incoming government had made a number of pledges to the union movement that it was now under a lot of pressure to deliver. These included the repeal of some, but by no means all, Conservative trade union legislation, the introduction of new rights for unions and their members, embarkation upon a new social agenda emphasising individual workers' rights to fair treatment, and substantial new investment in public sector services where so many union members work.

In spite of speculation about a 'falling-out' between trade unions and the Labour Party, the government has delivered on many of its pledges. Perhaps most significantly, in 2000 it introduced a statutory right for unions to be recognised by employers for bargaining where a majority of workers wish for this. This signalled the government's view that unions were legitimate

[*] Alex Bryson is a Principal Research Fellow at the Policy Studies Institute and the Manpower Fellow at the Centre for Economic Performance at the London School of Economics.

'partners' of management in UK PLC. This message has been emphasised time and again in government Green and White Papers pointing to the value of 'partnership at work' in improving Britain's productivity (for example, Department of Trade and Industry, 1998). The Labour government also removed some of the restrictions on industrial action and extended the legal protection of trade union members against employer discrimination. Furthermore, it created opportunities for unions to enhance their influence in the workplace through initiatives such as support for Union Learning Representatives and the enactment of a right for employees to be accompanied by someone of their choosing in grievance and disciplinary hearings, including a union representative, even where unions are not recognised by the employer for bargaining. There was a *quid pro quo*: unions had to 'modernise', by which the government meant ditching the old adversarial image associated with the 1979 Winter of Discontent and the 1984–1985 Miners' Strike and instead cultivating a 'partnership' image in which unions could be seen as legitimate partners in social dialogue with employers in the construction of a modern productive economy with fair rewards for all. Under the stewardship of John Monks as General Secretary of the Trades Union Congress, the union movement shifted some way in this direction. It was further encouraged to do so with financial assistance from government in the form of grants from the Partnership at Work Fund and the Union Modernisation Fund, both administered by government.[1]

Talk in the union movement had been about the prospects for union 'revitalisation' under a Labour government. This 'revitalisation' would entail halting and then reversing the decline in membership, heightened political influence, greater union effectiveness within the workplace, and a growing recognition on the part of workers and employers that unions were an important stakeholder in the economy and were here to stay. All did not go smoothly to plan, however. First, the high expectations that the union movement had had of the incoming government and what it would do for workers were not met in full. This resulted in grumblings and discontent with the Labour government within the union movement and talk of disaffiliation from the Labour Party within some unions. This mood may also have contributed to the election in some key trade unions of a new breed of union leaders who were less enthusiastic about the modernisation agenda. These leaders, pejoratively known as the 'awkward squad', were driven by a desire to represent what they saw as their members' interests, first and foremost, whether these accorded with the hopes and wishes of the Labour government or not (Charlwood, 2004). Secondly, where partnership with employers was tried, it was far from a resounding success for unions and their members (Kelly, 2004), raising doubts about its value in future. Thirdly, the modernisation of public services and the reorganisation of working practices it entailed, although negotiated in great detail with trade unions, most notably through Agenda for Change, proved to be a bruising experience (Bewley, 2006).

Although this broad picture is familiar, it is only recently that evidence has started to emerge about the changing fortunes of trade unions over the period since Labour came to power. There is some evidence from existing surveys that union density has stabilised, though there are few signs of any renewed membership growth (Grainger, 2006). Similarly, new union recognition agreements exceed union de-recognitions (Gall, 2004; Blanden *et al.*, 2006; Kersley *et al.*, 2006) but there has been no breakthrough in the workplace presence of trade unions (Kersley *et al.*, 2006).

The 2005 *British Social Attitudes* survey provides an opportunity to learn more about how unions have fared under a Labour government because it replicates and adds to a special module of questions on trade unions and employment relations that was last asked in 1998, shortly after the Labour government came to power. This chapter reviews those changing fortunes by looking at change between 1998 and 2005 in four areas. First, the chapter considers changes in union membership between 1998 and 2005, identifying rates of union membership across different segments of the population and comparing them to 1998. Secondly, it uses a range of measures to establish how effective employees think unions are now, and how this has changed since 1998. Thirdly, the chapter looks at unions' ability to 'deliver' in two spheres: their effect on the climate of industrial relations at the workplace and the wage premium members receive relative to 'like' non-members. The final substantive section of the chapter investigates the desire for union representation among employees by exploring why so many employees do not join their workplace union and establishing the extent of unmet demand for unions among those who are not in unionised workplaces. The last section focuses on the implications of the analysis for public policy, on the one hand, and union organising, on the other.

Union membership

In 2005, a fifth (20 per cent) of those who had ever worked were union members, down from 23 per cent in 1998.[2] This is a decline of 15 per cent over the period, or roughly two per cent per annum. Among employees, membership rates fell four percentage points from 33 per cent in 1998 to 29 per cent in 2005. Membership also fell among non-employees who make up a quarter of the union members among *British Social Attitudes* respondents. For instance, it fell from 18 per cent to 12 per cent among retired people, who are the largest group of non-employed members. Figure 8.1 below shows the declining percentage of employees who were union members over the period 1983–2005. Since 1997, the rate of decline has slowed considerably compared with the 1980s and first half of the 1990s (Charlwood and Metcalf, 2005) and there have been some ups and downs in recent years. Nevertheless, there is still a clear downward drift in membership, which is also replicated in other data such as the Labour Force Survey (Grainger, 2006). What is more, the percentage of people who have never been union members drifted upwards over the period from 48 per cent to 52 per cent.[3] This rise in 'never-membership' was also apparent among employees (42 per cent in 1998 to 48 per cent in 2005), continuing a trend that has been apparent for many years (Bryson and Gomez, 2002, 2005).

Figure 8.1 Union membership density among employees, 1983–2005

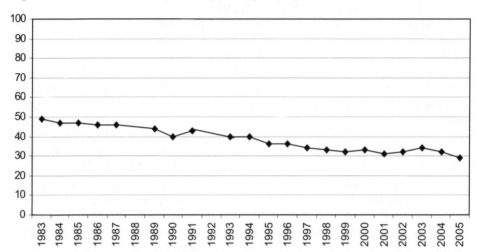

Figures are percentage of all employees working 10 or more hours per week who were union members. Union membership includes staff association membership. The survey was not conducted in 1988 and 1992

The first two columns of Table 8.1 show the composition of the workforce in 1998 and 2005 on a number of different variables. The last two columns show union membership within these groups of employees. It is immediately apparent that there is no group represented in the table where union membership has shown a significant rise, though the rate of decline has differed across groups. Big falls in union membership have occurred among those in manufacturing, the highest social classes, the highly educated, the better paid, non-white ethnic groups, and those resident in Wales. In contrast, there are other groups where membership has remained roughly stable, such as the public sector, the low paid, those with no qualifications, the lowest social classes and those on the right of the political spectrum.[4]

The only notable change in workforce composition between 1998 and 2005 is the increase in the percentage of employees on the political right and the commensurate reduction in the percentage on the left – a general trend among the population which has been observed before on the *British Social Attitudes* survey (see, for example, Curtice and Fisher, 2003).

Table 8.1 Workforce composition and union membership,[5] 1998 and 2005

	Workforce composition (employees)		% of employees who are union members	
	1998	**2005**	**1998**	**2005**
Gender	%	%		
Male	48	52	35	30
Female	52	48	31	29
Age	%	%		
18–24	11	12	16	15
25–34	29	24	30	24
35–44	24	27	39	31
45–54	25	22	36	38
55–64	11	13	39	35
Ethnicity	%	%		
White	94	92	33	30
Non-white	6	8	38	26
Qualifications	%	%		
Degree/HE	36	39	41	34
Other qualifications	47	48	30	27
No qualifications	17	13	25	25
Region	%	%		
Scotland	8	10	37	33
Wales	6	4	51	40
Midlands	17	17	33	34
North	24	25	33	32
South	33	32	30	25
Greater London	11	12	35	31
Left–right scale	%	%		
Right	27	37	25	26
Centre	35	33	34	31
Left	38	29	41	36
Hours	%	%		
Full-time	75	78	35	31
Part-time	25	23	27	22
Occupational class	%	%		
Professional/managerial/technical	36	39	41	32
Skilled, non-manual	26	24	27	26
Skilled, manual	19	20	38	31
Partly skilled/unskilled manual	19	16	23	26
Earnings	%	%		
Low	36	36	21	21
Not low	64	64	40	34
Workplace tenure	%	%		
10+ years	32	31	54	51
<10 years	68	69	25	24

table continued on next page

	Workforce composition (employees)		% of employees who are union members	
	1998	2005	1998	2005
Workplace size	%	%		
<25 employees	28	31	19	18
25–99 employees	26	26	32	29
100–499 employees	26	24	30	27
500+ employees	19	18	48	41
Sector	%	%		
Public	30	30	59	58
Private/voluntary	70	70	22	17
Industry	%	%		
Manufacturing	21	17	28	22
Non-manufacturing	79	83	34	31
Unionisation	%	%		
Recognition	49	48	61	58
No union recognition	51	52	8	8
Base for ethnicity	*1420*	*1946*		
Base for left–right scale	*1184*	*1611*		
Base for unionisation	*1428*	*1476*		
Base for all other variables: all employees	*1428*	*1952*		

See the chapter appendix for definitions
See end note 5 for bases in columns three and four

Table 8.1 shows only part of the story, because changes in the various variables interact. Multivariate analyses presented in the appendix to the chapter estimate the probability of union membership while controlling for all the other factors, and shed light on two issues that cannot be tackled with descriptive analyses. First, the analysis indicates that union membership declined by 0.5 per cent per year over the period 1998 to 2005, but this proved not to be statistically significant once we control for employee, job and workplace characteristics (see Model 1 in the appendix to the chapter). In other words, having accounted for the characteristics of employees and their workplaces, membership has remained broadly constant over the period.

Secondly, a comparison of the models for 1998 and 2005 (Models 2 and 3 in the chapter appendix) shows which segments of the employee population experienced the fastest rates of decline in membership, having controlled for other factors.

For example, as we have already seen in the previous table, union membership fell substantially in Wales. The multivariate analysis in the chapter appendix shows that in 1998, living in Wales increased the probability of an employee being a union member by 20 per cent over someone living in the south of England (once other factors such as workforce composition had been taken into account). By 2005, this had fallen to nine per cent, which was no longer statistically significant.

The lower rate of membership among the low-paid in 1998 was no longer significant in 2005 because, as Table 8.1 indicates, membership fell among the higher paid but not among the low paid.

Although this is not apparent from the descriptive analysis in the previous table, the probability of being a union member actually rose significantly for full-timers relative to part-timers, such that it was 11 per cent greater in 2005, once other factors were taken into account (Model 3 in the chapter appendix).

Political leanings were independently associated with membership probabilities in 1998, but this was no longer the case in 2005, in spite of substantial differences in political ideology indicated in the descriptive table above. This fits well with the finding in *The 22nd Report* that trade unionists are no longer as distinctive in their political views as they used to be (Curtice and Mair, 2005).

The most pronounced change was the increased probability of being a union member in the public sector relative to the private and voluntary sectors: public sector employment increased the probability of membership by nine per cent in 1998 once other factors are taken into account, but this had more than doubled to 23 per cent in 2005 (Models 2 and 3 in the chapter appendix).

In both years, union recognition had the largest effect on membership probabilities, raising them by around 40 per cent. Although it had dropped slightly by 2005, the change was not statistically significant.

In sum, there is little sign of revival in union membership, although the precipitate decline of recent decades has been arrested. This may be due, at least in part, to Labour policies supportive of union organising, a conjecture supported by recent workplace survey evidence (Kersley *et al.*, 2006).

Union effectiveness

In theory, workers' preparedness to join unions and be active members rises with the problems they have at work, since this can trigger the desire for a union solution. The problems at work may translate into a desire for unions if management are blamed for these shortcomings, rather than unions, and if unions are seen as instrumental in solving those problems (Kelly, 1998). Only recently have studies sought to 'rate' union effectiveness in Britain. These studies indicate that unions are perceived to be more effective in the USA and New Zealand than in Britain (Bryson, 2006; Bryson and Freeman, 2006a) and that "there is room for unions to improve their effectiveness on all fronts" (Bryson, 2005: 37). Nevertheless, these studies confirm that non-members' desire for union membership and members' satisfaction with representation by their union are higher where unions are perceived to be effective (Bryson, 2003, 2006; Bryson and Freeman, 2006b). But what has happened to union effectiveness in Britain under New Labour? The *British Social Attitudes* survey in 2005 contains a wide array of union effectiveness items, perhaps more than any other previous survey. We focus primarily on those items that also appeared in 1998, permitting analysis of change over time.

We asked employees in unionised settings:

> *Do you think that your workplace would be a better or worse place to work if there was no trade union, or would it make no difference?*

Those in non-union settings were asked whether they thought their workplace would be better or worse *with* a union. In a unionised environment there was a strong preference for retaining the union, with over half the employees thinking it made the workplace a better place to work, and only around one in twenty believing it made matters worse (Table 8.2). Even so, around two-fifths thought the loss of the union would make "no difference" to the workplace. In non-union settings, two-thirds of employees thought a union would make no difference, with the remainder split roughly equally between those who thought a union might make things better and those who thought it might make things worse. The implication is that, while workers in unionised workplaces believe that unions are doing a reasonable job, workers at non-union sites are not convinced unions would make enough of a difference to attract them. This finding is consistent with other recent research using the British Worker Representation and Participation Survey 2001 and previous *British Social Attitudes* surveys (Bryson, 2005; Bryson and Freeman, 2006b).

There are no statistically significant differences in the figures over the period 1998–2005, suggesting that unions have neither been able to 'up their game' where they have a presence on the ground, nor been able to reach out to those in non-union workplaces.

Table 8.2 The difference a union makes to the workplace, 1998 and 2005

Union makes/would make workplace ...	Union workplaces		Non-union workplaces		All	
	1998	**2005**	**1998**	**2005**	**1998**	**2005**
	%	%	%	%	%	%
A lot better	24	27	7	7	16	17
A little better	27	30	10	11	19	20
No difference	42	36	65	66	53	51
A little worse	4	3	8	7	6	5
A lot worse	1	2	9	7	5	4
Base	*759*	*749*	*669*	*727*	*1428*	*1476*

Base: all employees

A second 'global' question about union effectiveness was directed at employees in unionised workplaces who, unlike those in non-union workplaces, had direct experience of how unions operated. Around three-fifths (62 per cent) said "yes" when we asked:

On the whole, do you think these unions do their job well or not?

Responses were unchanged over the period (61 per cent in 1998) and are directly in line with figures from earlier years, which have remained more or less unchanged since 1983 (Bryson, 2005).

Other questions relate to specific aspects of union activity. The first relates to unions' responsiveness as membership organisations. We asked employees how strongly they agreed or disagreed with the statement:

Trade unions at my workplace take notice of members' problems and complaints

Some 59 per cent of employees in unionised workplaces agreed with this statement in both years, although the proportion who "agreed strongly" fell from 13 per cent in 1998 to nine per cent in 2005. Among union members, those agreeing strongly fell from 17 to 12 per cent, while the overall per cent in agreement was stable (62 per cent in 1998 and 64 per cent in 2005).

Unions' futures depend on their relationships with management, as well as employees, for two reasons. First, British employees are keen for management and unions to operate in a collaborative, constructive manner (Bryson and Freeman, 2006a). Secondly, employers can do much to facilitate or obstruct unions' efforts to organise workers. These considerations have fuelled a vigorous debate about how closely unions should align themselves with management. On one side of the debate are advocates of 'partnership' who maintain that, by showing what they can offer to management, unions will increase the likelihood of management reciprocating through the creation of an environment that is more conducive to unionisation than it might otherwise be. On the other side of the debate are those who maintain that unions can only mobilise the workforce where they keep their distance from management, thus ensuring that they are not implicated in managerial failings. Only then, it is argued, can they establish a bargaining powerbase that is independent of management.

In spite of government efforts to encourage union–employer partnership, little has changed in terms of employees' perceptions of unions' preparedness to assist in the smooth running of the workplace. Now, as in 1998, 39 per cent agree that the trade unions at their workplace help "make things run more smoothly at work".

A more mixed picture emerges from employee perceptions of managements' orientation towards unions over the period. There seems to have been little change in the perception of the seriousness with which management engages with unions where they are present. Asked whether the trade unions at their workplace are "usually ignored by management", one fifth (20 per cent) agreed in both 2005 and 1998. The percentage disagreeing was also static (51 per cent in 2005 compared with 52 per cent in 1998). Yet, as the next table shows, management attitudes toward union membership appear to have changed since 1998. In both 2005 and 1998 employees were asked:

How would you describe the management's attitude to trade unions at the place where you work? Would you say that management **encourages** *trade union membership, accepts it or would accept it,* **discourages** *trade union membership, or, isn't it really an issue at your workplace?*

Table 8.3 Management attitudes to union membership, 1998 and 2005

	Union workplaces		Non-union workplaces		All	
Management view on membership	1998	2005	1998	2005	1998	2005
	%	%	%	%	%	%
Encourages	11	18	1	1	6	9
Accepts	53	53	6	12	30	32
Discourages	6	7	17	16	11	11
Not an issue	28	19	69	64	48	41
Base	759	749	669	727	1428	1476

Base: all employees

Overall, the increase in the percentage of employees who thought management encouraged or accepted membership, and the decline in the percentage who thought it was "not an issue" are statistically significant. This more favourable attitude to membership reverses a trend apparent in the previous decade (Bryson, 1999). Splitting the analysis by whether the employee worked in a unionised or non-unionised environment shows that employees saw little change in the small percentage of employers who actually discouraged membership. Instead, the decline in the percentage who thought membership was not an issue was driven by an increase in the percentage perceiving management encouragement in unionised settings and an increase in the percentage of employers accepting membership where there was no union present.

Although this change in managerial attitudes towards union membership might appear promising from a union perspective, caution is merited. The evidence is somewhat at odds with employer survey evidence which indicates very little change in management attitudes to unions over the period 1998–2004 (Kersley *et al.*, 2006).[6] Furthermore, unions can only really capitalise on a more favourable environment if they have the organisational capacity to do so. *British Social Attitudes* contains three measures of this organisational capacity. The first measure is whether unions are actually recognised by management for pay bargaining purposes. As we saw in Table 8.1, there has been little change in this respect over the period, a finding which is in keeping with other research (Kersley *et al.*, 2006).[7] Secondly, unions rely on on-site representation to voice members' opinions to management and represent them in grievance, disciplinary and bargaining matters, as well as to recruit and retain members. The percentage of unionised workers who know who the worker representative is at their workplace remained constant over the period (63 per cent in 2005 compared with 62 per cent in 1998).[8] Although workers in unionised workplaces are much more likely to know of a worker representation than those in non-union workplaces (where only one tenth of employees knew of representatives), there was no progress on this score under the Labour government, in spite of new initiatives such as the introduction of Union Learning Representatives.[9]

The third measure available is employee perceptions of the power unions have at the workplace. Without a modicum of power, there is no reason to suspect that management will listen to trade unions. It is, perhaps, for this reason that over two-thirds of employees in the British Worker Representation and Participation Survey 2001 believed "strong unions are needed to protect the working conditions and wages of employees" (Bryson, 2005: 29). We asked employees:

> *Do you think that trade unions* **at your workplace** *have too much or too little power?*

Table 8.4 Employee perceptions of union power at the workplace, 1989, 1998 and 2005

	1989	1998	2005
Unions have ...	%	%	%
... far too much power	*	*	1
... too much power	4	2	3
... about the right amount	51	45	51
... too little power	31	40	33
... far too little power	6	7	3
Base	*862*	*759*	*749*

Base: employees in unionised workplaces

Table 8.4 shows that since 1998 there has been a statistically significant increase in the percentage of employees in unionised workplaces who think unions have "about the right amount of power", with a commensurate decline in the percentage thinking unions have "too little" or "far too little power". The 2005 responses are very similar to those given in 1989 (Bryson, 2005), suggesting that union power at the workplace may have returned to the point it had reached at the end of the 1990s.

To get a clearer picture of the trend in employee perceptions of union effectiveness under the Labour government we produced a simple summary scale running from zero to five based on the responses of employees in unionised workplaces. A point was scored for each of the following employee responses:

- respondent says "yes" when asked if the union "does its job well or not";
- respondent believes the workplace would be better if it retained the union;
- respondent disagrees that the union is "usually ignored by management";
- respondent agrees the union "helps make things run more smoothly at work"; and
- respondent agrees that the union "takes notice of members' problems and complaints".

The scale is presented in the next table.

Table 8.5 Additive scale of employee perceptions of union effectiveness, 1998 and 2005

	1998	2005
Union effectiveness scale	%	%
0 Low	11	10
1	13	15
2	18	17
3	23	21
4	21	22
5 High	15	16
Base	*759*	*749*

Base: employees in unionised workplaces

The scores are bunched a little towards the top end of the distribution: around one quarter of employees score their union poorly (a zero or a one) compared with a little over one third giving them a score of four or five. The scores for the two years are very similar indeed, indicating no trend in improved union effectiveness over the period. This lack of change is confirmed in multivariate analysis.[10]

Three other findings emerging from multivariate analyses are worthy of note. First, union members have significantly higher perceptions of union effectiveness than non-members. Although this might simply reflect the preponderance of non-members in workplaces with weaker unions, the effect is still apparent when we control for union recognition and the presence of on-site worker representatives. An alternative explanation is that it may indicate unions' ability to target services at their members. Secondly, there is a strong, significant independent association between employer recognition of unions for pay bargaining and employee perceptions of union effectiveness, even after controlling for other factors – an association which was particularly strong where the union also had on-site worker representation. Thirdly, unions were perceived to be most effective where management encouraged membership and least effective where union membership was thought not to be an issue.

Union effects on employment relations

Whether New Labour has been right to emphasise partnership at work between unions and employers depends, in part, on whether unions deliver a climate that is conducive to employers and employees alike. One way of testing this is to establish their impact on the climate of employment relations. Other studies suggest that perceptions of the climate now are at least as good as they were in 1998 and, on some measures, may have improved (Kersley et al., 2006). But what effect are trade unions having?

We asked respondents:

> In general how would you describe relations between management and other employees at your workplace ...very good, quite good, not very good or not at all good?

The next table seems to show that employee perceptions of relations between employees and management have improved a little over the period when looking at the economy as a whole. Although the improvement seems to have occurred both in the union and non-union sectors, the change is only statistically significant in the non-union sector.

Table 8.6 The climate of employment relations, 1998 and 2005

Relations between management and employees	Union workplaces		Non-union workplaces		All	
	1998	2005	1998	2005	1998	2005
	%	%	%	%	%	%
Very good	18	22	39	43	28	33
Quite good	55	55	44	42	50	48
Not very good	20	17	11	10	16	14
Not at all good	5	5	5	3	5	4
Base	759	749	669	727	1428	1476

Base: all employees

It is also notable that, in both years, perceptions of relations are considerably worse in a union setting than in a non-union setting. However, it does not follow that this is an effect of unionisation. There are a number of reasons why one might expect relations to be poorer in a unionised workplace than a non-unionised one. Unions tend to take root where workers have more problems at the workplace (Bryson and Freeman, 2006a), and so it is not surprising to find an association between unions and poorer climate. Moreover, as has often been noted (Freeman and Medoff, 1984), part of the function of trade unions is to raise awareness of problems at work in the hope of rectifying them through negotiation with management. This function, often referred to as unions' 'voice' function, can increase the flow of information to workers, thus heightening their awareness of employer shortcomings, and politicising them so that they become more critical of employment relations than they might otherwise have been. Also, it is possible that the sort of workers who feel disgruntled enough to join a union are also those who are more liable to express dissatisfaction with their working life.

To tease out the independent association between unions and employee perceptions of employment relations we estimated multivariate models for the whole economy, and then for employees in the union sector alone.[11] The analysis reveals five findings. First, once other factors were taken into account, there has been no statistically significant trend in perceptions of climate, either in the whole economy or the union sector, suggesting that the trend in Table 8.6 is an artefact of other changes in the structure of the labour force.

Secondly, union members had poorer perceptions of the employment relations' climate than non-members, both in the whole economy and within unionised workplaces. Furthermore, their perceptions have deteriorated compared with non-members over the period since 1998. Thirdly, the multivariate analysis confirmed that employees in workplaces recognising unions for pay bargaining have poorer perceptions of the employment relations' climate than those in non-unionised workplaces, particularly if the workplace contained an on-site worker representative.[12] Fourthly, management's response to unions mattered, with perceptions of climate at their best where employees thought management encouraged membership and worst where they were thought to discourage membership. This was apparent in 1998 and 2005 in the whole economy and within the union sector. Finally, employee perceptions of union effectiveness – as measured by the five-point measure discussed earlier – were positively associated with better climate in unionised workplaces, the effect being similar in 1998 and 2005.

Taken together, these findings suggest that unions can have a negative effect on employee perceptions of the employment relations' climate where management oppose the unions. However, unions can be beneficial for employment relations where they are supported by management. Indeed, all other things being equal, employee perceptions of the employment relations' climate were more positive in unionised workplaces where management supported membership than they were in non-unionised workplaces.

Union effects on wages

As analyses of previous *British Social Attitudes* surveys in *The 19th Report* show, union members have tended to earn more than non-members, a gap that narrows but persists after taking into account differences in demographic, job and workplace characteristics (Bryson and Gomez, 2002). This wage difference, commonly referred to as the 'union wage premium', has traditionally averaged around 10 per cent in Britain (Blanchflower and Bryson, 2003). However, some have recently come to question whether, in the face of declining union bargaining power and a more plentiful supply of non-union labour, unions are capable of raising members' wages at all relative to 'like' non-members (Metcalf, 2005). This claim is disputed by others who argue that most of the recent decline in the premium is cyclical rather than reflecting a long-term underlying trend (Blanchflower and Bryson, 2003; Blanchflower, 2006). Nevertheless, any diminution in the union wage premium, for whatever reason, signals a reduction in what is the clearest, most palpable, benefit of union membership. If it persists, it may feed through to a lower propensity for employees to become or remain union members. So what does the latest evidence indicate?

The full analysis is shown in the appendix to this chapter. In summary, the findings are these. If we do not control for factors such as demographic, job and workplace characteristics, we find that union members earn roughly 20 per cent more per hour than non-members. This rises to around 30 per cent when comparing weekly wages. However, union members tend to be in better-paid jobs, so these differences drop to a statistically non-significant three per cent hourly wage premium once we do control for other factors. The equivalent weekly wage premium is six per cent, which is still statistically significant.

We can take this analysis one stage further by accounting for union recognition (as well as individual membership). Union recognition is interesting in its own right since it denotes whether or not an individual is in a workplace where at least some workers have their pay set through collective bargaining. (Indeed some argue that this is the more appropriate measure for estimating union wage effects.) With union recognition in the model, the union membership variable is picking up the effect of membership having netted out the effect of union bargaining coverage. However, we find that union recognition is not statistically significant and makes little difference to the union membership wage premium.

When looking separately at 1998 and 2005, we find that the 'raw' union membership wage premium (before taking other factor into account) declined significantly over the period, whether measured in hourly or weekly wages. When controls are added, the hourly wage premium is no longer statistically significant in either year. The eight per cent weekly wage premium in 1998 falls to a statistically non-significant four per cent by 2005.

Taken together, these results indicate that, having accounted for observable differences across members and non-members, the membership wage premium apparent in 1998 was no longer there in 2005. Whether this is a cyclical effect or indicates a true long-term trend is not possible to discern from these data.

Other questions in the survey support the notion that employees are sceptical about a significant wage premium. Trade union members were asked:

> *On the whole, do you think the service you receive from your union represents ...*
> *... good value for money,*
> *reasonable value for money,*
> *or, poor value for money?*

Only 31 per cent thought that they were getting good value for money. And when asked to rate the union's performance on five items, only three per cent of employees in unionised workplaces rated the union as "excellent" at "winning pay increases and bonuses" – the lowest of the five scores. These questions were new in 2005, so, unfortunately, we cannot tell whether there has been change since 1998.

The 'representation gap'

We have shown that union membership is continuing to edge downwards while never-membership rises in spite of a more benign environment facing unions, as indicated by a perceived increase in union power at the workplace and a softening of employer attitudes to union membership. Part of the problem unions face seems to be the uncertainty employees express about the difference unions really make, a concern that is borne out by the disappearance of the union wage premium by 2005. The question arises, therefore, whether there really is an unmet demand for union representation in Britain – what some have referred to as a 'representation gap' – or whether employees are simply losing their appetite for unions, as others have suggested (Millward *et al.,* 2000). In approaching this issue, we look at two sets of employees: non-members in non-unionised workplaces; and non-members in unionised workplaces who are eligible to join their workplace union. These are very different groups, of course, since the former would need to incur the costs of setting up a union at the workplace from scratch if they wished to join a union, whereas the latter have a union available to them yet have not joined.

In 1998 and 2005 we asked workers in non-unionised workplaces:

> *If there were a trade union at your workplace, how likely or unlikely do you think you would be to join it?*

As the next table indicates, around one in seven employees in non-union workplaces say it is "very likely" that they would join, with a further one quarter saying it is "fairly likely". These percentages, which are very similar to those obtained in the British Worker Representation and Participation Survey

2001, do seem to indicate a substantial representation gap.[13] However, there has been no change in the desire for unions between 1998 and 2005. Furthermore, as Bryson and Freeman (2006a, 2006b) note, this question is usually a purely hypothetical one for such employees, since they are very rarely asked to join a union. If they were to consider the issue more thoroughly they might attach greater weight to the costs of joining. In addition, many of these employees also said that they did not think a union would make any difference at their workplace. In 1998 only six per cent of non-members in non-unionised workplaces said they would be "very likely" to join if there was a union and also said a union would make the workplace "a lot better". In 2005, the figure was four per cent. This finding resembles Bryson and Freeman's analysis (2006a, 2006b) of the British Worker Representation and Participation Survey 2001 and brings into question just how large the real representation gap in Britain is.

Table 8.7 Likelihood that employees in non-union workplaces would join a union if there was one, 1998 and 2005

	1998	2005
Likelihood of joining union	%	%
Very likely	14	15
Fairly likely	25	26
Not very likely	30	32
Not at all likely	29	25
Base	*632*	*694*

Base: employees in non-unionised workplaces

Multivariate analyses were run to identify which factors were associated with the desire to join a union.[14] Five findings emerged. First, there was no change in the desire to join over the period once we controlled for demographic, job and workplace characteristics. Secondly, the likelihood of joining was significantly lower for those on the right of the 'left–right' scale. The size of this effect increased significantly over the period 1998–2005. There was also a shift towards the right of the scale among non-members in non-union workplaces.[15] Thus both the changing political complexion of unorganised employees and the increasing importance of political ideology reduced desire for union representation, all other things being equal.

Thirdly, employees' likelihood of joining a union increased with the number of problems they said they had at work, confirming the proposition that problems at work can help trigger desire for unions.[16] The size of these effects on the likelihood of joining rose significantly under the Labour government. However, the number of problems expressed by non-members in non-union workplaces fell, making it harder for potential union organisers to capitalise on problems at work.

Fourthly, the perception of whether a union would make the workplace a better or worse place to work had a very large effect on non-members' professed likelihood of joining a union. However, the negative effect of believing a union would make the workplace "a lot worse" strengthened significantly between 1998 and 2005, while the positive effect of believing a union would make things "a lot better" weakened significantly. Nevertheless, the effects remained very large, emphasising the importance of union instrumentality in employees' unionisation decisions.

Finally, management played an important role in determining non-union workers' orientation towards union membership. Paradoxically, non-members were significantly more likely to say they would join a union where they thought management "discourages trade union membership" compared to the scenario in which employees thought management attitudes to union membership was not really an issue at the workplace. This finding is a little surprising in that it suggests that potential employer recrimination against union organisers is unlikely to dissuade employees from organising. However, the finding echoes recent work by Bryson and Freeman (2006a) who suggest that employee perceptions of employer opposition to unions may signify a particularly harsh employment regime which creates the sorts of problem that fuel support for unions.

Turning to employees in unionised workplaces, one of the biggest problems unions have faced since the early 1990s is the rise in the percentage of employees in unionised workplaces who do not join the union, a group often termed 'free-riders', since they can potentially benefit from union activities yet do not pay union membership subscriptions. There has been a big rise in union 'free-riding' since the early 1990s when the end of the closed shop meant employees had a free choice as to whether they joined a union or not (Bryson, 2006; Bryson and Freeman, 2006a). Our data suggest that this growth in free-riding has ceased. In 1998, 41 per cent of employees in unionised workplaces were non-members eligible to join the union, compared to 42 per cent in 2005. The figures for unionised workplaces where the union is recognised for pay bargaining are 40 per cent and 41 per cent respectively.

Once again, we used multivariate analyses to isolate the independent effect of variables of interest to the propensity to free-ride.[17] The main findings are as follows. First, there was no underlying increase or decrease in free-riding, having controlled for demographic, job and workplace characteristics. Secondly, although the likelihood of free-riding was greater among employees on the political right in 1998, political persuasions no longer had a significant effect in 2005. This runs counter to union-joining behaviour in the non-union sector where, as we have seen, political persuasions played a growing role. Thirdly, the probability of free-riding fell with the number of workplace problems employees identified, as one might expect, the magnitude of this effect rising over the period. Fourthly, union organisation and union effectiveness played a role. Free-riding was significantly less likely where unions were recognised for pay bargaining and the employee knew of an on-site union representative. It was also less likely if the union was rated as being more effective (as measured by the variable presented in Table 8.5). This effect increased significantly over the period.

Finally, perceptions of management attitudes to unions had some influence in 1998, with free-riding less likely where management was thought to support membership compared to scenarios in which it was thought to simply 'accept' membership. However, this effect was no longer significant in 2005, suggesting that workers in a unionised environment are attaching less importance to what management thinks when making their union-joining decisions – as we might expect given the new legislation that strengthens the protection against discrimination on the grounds of union membership. In both years, those most likely to free-ride were those who said they did not know what their management's attitude was to union membership.

Conclusions

A simple story emerges from this chapter. Under the Labour government the rapid demise of trade unionism has been arrested. Union membership continues to drift down a little, and never-membership has risen, but the rate of change has slowed considerably compared with the Thatcher and Major years. However, there are few signs of a union revival, in spite of a raft of legislation intended to assist unions and their members to prosper and grow. This picture is consistent with other recent survey evidence (Kersley et al., 2006).

There are some crumbs of comfort for trade unions. Perceptions of union power have returned to the levels of the late 1980s. Although their power is considerably reduced relative to that which they wielded in the pre-Thatcher era, this finding is certainly at odds with academics' perception of an underlying long-term decline in union power. There also appears to have been a shift in management attitudes towards unions, at least as perceived by their employees. It is possible that some employers are taking their cue from the government, which has been pushing partnership between managers and unions.

New Labour has thrown down the gauntlet to employers and unions by encouraging closer relationships between the parties than might otherwise exist, but it is unclear whether the two sides of industry are up to the challenge. Consider the climate of employment relations, for example. Employees tend to view employment relations as poorer in the presence of a union, yet, where management actively supports unions, employment relations are perceived to be better than in non-union settings. This is consistent with the New Labour proposition that union–management partnership can bring real benefits to the workplace. The message has gone largely unheeded, however, since only a minority of unionised workers perceive management as being supportive of the union. Unions have not played their part, either. They are no more likely to be perceived as helping in the smooth running of the workplace than they were in 1998. Of course, unions have members to serve and their interests may not always align with those of management. And yet the analysis shows that employees' perceptions of the employment relations' climate improve with perceptions of union effectiveness. This sends an important message to trade unions, since it suggests that unions can continue to appeal to their membership whilst delivering an environment that is attractive to both employees and employers.

From a union organising perspective the story is a grim one. There has been no improvement in unionised workers' perceptions of union effectiveness since 1998, two-fifths of those eligible to join their workplace union do not, and there is no sign that this is changing. While a sizeable percentage of non-members in non-union workplaces say they might join a union if one were available, only one sixth of unorganised workers actually believe a union would make their workplace a better place to work.

The one thing unions have been able to deliver to their members over the years is a wage premium, yet even this appears to have disappeared by 2005. This is perhaps all the more surprising given the small upswing in employee perceptions of union power at the workplace. But perhaps it explains why less than a third of members think the service they receive from the union is good value for money and why members' ratings of the union are poorest on the issue of pay. As yet it remains unclear whether the absence of a union wage premium reflects an underlying long-term decline in unions' bargaining power, or is a cyclical phenomenon. In any event, its absence is bad news for unions trying to sell the benefits of membership right now.

What happens next will be intriguing. So far unions have been unable to 'up their game'. The government made a number of pledges to the unions just before the 2005 General Election in what has come to be known as the Warwick Agreement (Bewley, 2006). If pursued with vigour, this agenda offers a lot to the union movement but, even then, it remains uncertain how employees and employers will respond to what unions have to offer.

Notes

1. The Partnership at Work Fund is now defunct. For details of the Union Modernisation Fund, see:
   http://www.dti.gov.uk/employment/trade-union-rights/modernisation/what-is-the-fund/page20774.html.
2. In 2005 all respondents were asked: "Are you **now** a member of a trade union or staff association?" In 1998, the question was filtered on ever having a job. To make the data comparable, the figure for 2005 is limited to those who have ever had a job. Note that the question refers to "trade union or staff association". Similarly, the first question on workplace recognition reads, "At your place of work are there any unions or staff associations?" The wording of subsequent questions was tailored to

whether respondents reported membership/recognition of trade unions or of a staff association. However, staff associations account for only two–three per cent of the workforce. For the purposes of this chapter, staff association membership/recognition has been included within union membership/recognition and the wording of the staff association version of the questions is not reported. For a full record of the wording of the questions, please see the questionnaires in the Appendix to this Report.

3. 'Never-members' are identified if they say "No" to the question "Have you **ever** been a member of a trade union or staff association?" (which is filtered on saying "No" or "Don't know" to the question in note 2).

4. Our employee questions are confined to those in paid work for 10 hours or more per week so that analyses of the employee population are confined to employees satisfying this definition. This should be borne in mind when comparing results to those from other surveys.

5. Bases for Table 8.1, columns 3 and 4 are as follows:

	% of employees who are members	
	1998	**2005**
Gender		
Male	661	926
Female	767	1026
Age		
18–24	123	169
25–34	429	420
35–44	371	580
45–54	334	450
55–64	153	303
Ethnicity		
White	1335	1812
Non-white	85	134
Qualifications		
Degree/HE	534	751
Other qualifications	656	933
No qualifications	229	260
Region		
Scotland	123	205
Wales	79	79
Midlands	242	308
North	343	539
South	477	639
Greater London	164	182
Left–right scale		
Right	319	596
Centre	404	553
Left	461	462
Hours		
Full-time	1072	1487
Part-time	356	465

table continued on next page

	% of employees who are members	
	1998	**2005**
Occupational class		
Professional/managerial/		
technical	529	771
Skilled, non-manual	370	482
Skilled, manual	264	373
Partly skilled/unskilled manual	262	315
Earnings		
Not low	948	1253
Low	480	699
Workplace tenure		
10+ years	465	464
<10 years	960	1008
Workplace size		
<25 employees	401	608
25–99 employees	374	509
100–499 employees	371	467
500+ employees	275	355
Sector		
Public	451	606
Private/voluntary	977	1346
Industry		
Manufacturing	300	324
Non-manufacturing	1128	1628
Unionisation		
Recognition	714	674
No union recognition	714	802

6. When comparing *British Social Attitudes* evidence with that from the Workplace Employment Relations Survey (WERS) of workplaces reported in Kersley *et al.* (2006), one needs to bear in mind that we are comparing employee perceptions of management attitudes in *British Social Attitudes* with actual expressed management attitudes in WERS. In addition, there are differences in survey questions and the sample frames are different.

7. For evidence of a recent increase in new union recognition agreements at company level see Blanden *et al.*, 2006.

8. Employees in a workplace with a union or staff representative were asked: "Do you know who the *(trade union/staff association/worker or staff)* representative is at your workplace *(or is there not one based where you work)*?" with responses coded "yes", "no", "there is no representative based at my workplace" and "I am the representative".

9. Evidence from workplace surveys of managers indicates a decline in the percentage of on-site union representatives over the period 1998–2004 (Kersley *et al.*, 2006: 123–125). For more information on the role of Union Learning Representatives see Kersley *et al.*, 2006: 153–154.

10. These models are available from the author on request.

11. We ran ordered probits where the dependent variable was an ordered outcome signalling employees' perceptions of management–employee relations as indicated

in Table 8.6. The models, which use the same control variables as those used for the analyses of membership and union effectiveness, are available from the author on request.

12. Kersley *et al.* (2006: 283) also find a negative association between union recognition and employee perceptions of the employment relations' climate in 2004.

13. The British Worker Representation and Participation Survey question is: "If a group of workers at your workplace formed a union and asked you to join, how likely is it that you would join that union?"

14. We ran ordered probits where the dependent variable was the likelihood of joining a union with responses running from "not at all likely" to "very likely". With the exception of union recognition, these analyses use the same control variables as those used in the analysis of the union wage premium. The models are available from the author on request.

15. The mean score rose from 2.56 in 1998 to 2.74 in 2005.

16. The variable capturing problems is an additive scale running from zero to five with employees scoring one point for each of the following: they say they want "more say in decisions affecting your work"; agree with the statement "management will always try to get the better of employees if it gets the chance"; and describe "relations between management and other employees at your workplace" as "not very good". Employees scored additional points if they "strongly agree" that management tries to get the better of employees and if they think management–employee relations are "not at all good". The percentage of non-members in non-union workplaces scoring zero on this scale rose from 33 per cent to 38 per cent between 1998 and 2005.

17. We used linear estimation models, incorporating the control variables used in the union joining models. Depending on the precise specification of the model, models explained between 18 and 28 per cent of the variance in free-riding. The models are available from the author on request.

References

Bewley, H. (2006), 'Raising the standard? The regulation of employment and public sector employment policy', *British Journal of Industrial Relations*, **44(2)**: 351–372

Blanchflower, D. (2006), *A Cross-country study of union membership*, IZA Discussion Paper No. 2016

Blanchflower, D. and Bryson, A. (2003), 'Changes over time in union relative wage effects in the UK and the US revisited', in Addison, J.T. and Schnabel, C. (eds.), *International Handbook of Trade Unions*, Cheltenham, UK and Northampton, Mass., USA: Edward Elgar

Blanden, J., Machin, S. and Van Reenen, J. (2006), 'Have unions turned the corner? New evidence on recent trends in union recognition in UK firms', *British Journal of Industrial Relations*, **44(2)**: 169–190

Bryson, A. (1999), 'Are unions good for industrial relations?', in Jowell, R., Curtice, J., Park, A. and Thomson, K. (eds.), *British Social Attitudes: the 16th Report – Who shares New Labour values?*, Aldershot: Ashgate

Bryson, A. (2003), *Employee Desire for Unionisation in Britain and its Implications for Union Organising*, PSI Discussion Paper Number 12

Bryson, A. (2005), 'Working with Dinosaurs? Union Effectiveness in Britain', in Gall, G. (ed.), *Union Recognition: Organising and Bargaining Outcomes*, London: Routledge

Bryson, A. (2006), *Union Free-riding in Britain and New Zealand*, CEP Discussion Paper No. 713, London School of Economics

Bryson, A. and Freeman, R. (2006a), *Worker Needs and Voice in the US and the UK*, NBER Working Paper No. 12310, Cambridge, Mass.

Bryson, A. and Freeman R. (2006b), *What Voice Do British Workers Want?*, CEP Discussion Paper No. 731, London School of Economics

Bryson, A. and Gomez, R. (2002), 'Marching on together? Recent trends in union membership', in Park, A., Curtice, J., Thomson, K., Jarvis, L. and Bromley, C. (eds.), *British Social Attitudes: the 19th Report*, London: Sage

Bryson, A. and Gomez, R. (2005), 'Why have workers stopped joining unions?: Accounting for the rise in never-membership in Britain', *British Journal of Industrial Relations*, **43(1)**: 67–92

Charlwood, A. (2004), 'The new generation of trade union leaders and prospects for union revitalisation', *British Journal of Industrial Relations*, **42(2)**: 379–397

Charlwood, A. and Metcalf, D. (2005), 'Trade union numbers, membership and density', in Fernie, S. and Metcalf, D. (eds.), *Trade Unions. Resurgence or demise?* London: Routledge

Curtice, J. and Fisher, S. (2003), 'The power to persuade: a tale of two Prime Ministers', in Park, A., Curtice, J., Thomson, K., Jarvis, L. and Bromley, C. (eds.), *British Social Attitudes: the 20th Report – Continuity and change over two decades*, London: Sage

Curtice, J. and Mair, A. (2005), 'Are trade unionists left-wing any more?', in Park, A., Curtice, J., Thomson, K., Bromley, C., Phillips, M. and Johnson, M. (eds.), *British Social Attitudes: the 22nd Report – Two terms of New Labour: the public's reaction*, London: Sage

Department of Trade and Industry (1998), *Fairness at Work*, White Paper Cm 3968, London: HMSO

Freeman, R. and Medoff, J. (1984), *What Do Unions Do*, New York: Basic Books

Gall, G. (2004), 'Trade union recognition in Britain, 1995–2002: turning a corner?', *Industrial Relations Journal*, **35(3)**: 249–270

Grainger, H. (2006), *Trade Union Membership 2005*, London: Department of Trade and Industry

Kelly, J. (1998), *Rethinking Industrial Relations*, London: Routledge

Kelly, J. (2004), 'Social partnership agreements in Britain: Labor cooperation and compliance', *Industrial Relations*, **43(1)**: 267–292

Kersley, B., Alpin, C., Forth, J., Bryson, A., Bewley, H., Dix, G. and Oxenbridge, S. (2006), *Inside the Workplace: Findings from the 2004 Workplace Employment Relations Survey*, London: Routledge

Metcalf, D. (2005), 'Trade unions: resurgence or perdition? An economic analysis', in Fernie, S. and Metcalf, D. (eds.), *Trade Unions. Resurgence or demise?* London: Routledge

Millward, N., Bryson, A. and Forth, J. (2000), *All Change at Work?*, London: Routledge

Stewart, M. (1983), 'On Least Squares Estimation when the Dependent Variable is Grouped', *Review of Economic Studies*, **50(4)**: 737–753

Acknowledgements

The *National Centre for Social Research* is grateful to the Department of Trade and Industry for their financial support which enabled us to ask the questions reported in this chapter, although the views expressed in the chapter are those of the authors.

The author would also like to thank the Nuffield Foundation (grant number OPD/00244/G) and the Policy Studies Institute's Strategic Development Fund for financial assistance.

Appendix

This is a description of the derivation of variables where this is not self-evident.

Earnings
Respondents are asked to identify which of a number of gross earnings bands covers their own earnings. These bands have been reconciled to be consistent for 1998 and 2005, the lowest being less than £4,000 per annum, the highest being £44,000 or more. We recoded the gross earnings bands into an ordinal variable with five categories ranging from 'much below average' to 'much above average'. The 'low paid' are those with earnings 'much below' and 'below average'.

Qualifications
These relate to individuals' highest qualification. 'High' means degree or higher education below degree. Other qualifications are those with 'A level', 'O level', 'CSE' or their equivalents.

Left–right scale
The left–right scale is an additive index which is described in more detail in Appendix I to this Report. This well-tried and tested index measures an underlying ('latent') attitudinal dimension relating to employees' perceptions of distributive justice. Those with lower scores on the continuous scale running from 1 to 5 are more likely to favour government economic intervention and the reduction of inequality than are those with higher scores. We distinguish between 'left', 'centre' and 'right' according to scores on the index. Those on the 'left' score below 2.26 on the scale, those in the 'centre' score 2.26–2.79 and those on the 'right' are those with 2.8 or more.

Union recognition
This relates to the question "Does management recognise (these unions/this staff association) for the purposes of negotiating pay and conditions of employment?" (asked of those employees in unionised workplaces). Employees in non-unionised workplaces are classified as 'no union recognition'.

Linear probability models estimating union membership

	Model 1	Model 2	Model 3
	Pooled	1998	2005
2005	-0.002		
	(0.65)		
Union recognition	0.402	0.435	0.363
	(17.47)**	(13.80)**	(11.18)**
Female	0.002	-0.001	-0.001
	(0.09)	(0.04)	(0.02)
Age (ref.: 35–64 years)			
18–24 years	-0.035	-0.010	-0.054
	(1.11)	(0.22)	(1.23)
25–34 years	-0.009	0.006	-0.024
	(0.44)	(0.24)	(0.82)
65+ years	-0.086	-0.212	-0.080
	(1.40)	(1.99)*	(1.16)
Non-white	0.009	0.059	-0.023
	(0.26)	(1.26)	(0.50)
Registrar General's Social Class (ref.: classes 1–2)			
Class 3, non-manual	0.005	-0.061	0.061
	(0.22)	(1.87)	(1.95)
Class 3, manual	0.053	0.031	0.061
	(2.06)*	(0.85)	(1.74)
Classes 4–5	0.023	-0.038	0.074
	(0.82)	(0.94)	(1.83)
Qualifications (ref.: mid-level)			
High qualifications	0.005	-0.015	0.029
	(0.26)	(0.52)	(1.06)
No qualifications	-0.028	-0.051	0.005
	(1.09)	(1.45)	(0.12)
Political persuasion (ref.: left)			
Centre	-0.032	-0.051	-0.006
	(1.54)	(1.86)	(0.21)
Right	-0.081	-0.123	-0.046
	(3.74)**	(4.16)**	(1.46)
Region (ref.: South)			
Scotland	0.038	0.055	0.005
	(1.30)	(1.27)	(0.13)
North	0.022	0.014	0.023
	(0.99)	(0.43)	(0.77)
Midlands	0.078	0.076	0.078
	(3.19)**	(2.34)*	(2.17)*
Wales	0.152	0.197	0.092
	(3.38)**	(3.31)**	(1.46)
Greater London	-0.011	0.019	-0.042
	(0.33)	(0.44)	(0.91)

table continued on next page

Full-timer	0.068	-0.012	0.113
	(2.74)**	(0.31)	(3.48)**
Workplace tenure 10+ years	0.135	0.131	0.137
	(6.56)**	(4.55)**	(4.77)**
Low paid	-0.073	-0.131	-0.038
	(3.18)**	(3.73)**	(1.27)
Public sector	0.159	0.091	0.225
	(6.24)**	(2.56)*	(6.34)**
Manufacturing	-0.056	-0.031	-0.085
	(2.50)*	(0.97)	(2.65)**
Workplace size (ref.: <25 employees)			
25–99	0.023	0.040	0.012
	(1.12)	(1.40)	(0.41)
100–499	-0.002	0.026	-0.026
	(0.06)	(0.74)	(0.81)
500+	-0.023	0.008	-0.062
	(0.85)	(0.21)	(1.64)
Size missing	0.089	0.048	0.144
	(0.73)	(0.25)	(1.14)
Constant	3.152	0.145	-0.049
	(0.66)	(2.54)*	(1.07)
Observations	2378	2378	2378
R-squared	0.37	0.40	0.38

Notes:
1. These are linear probability models estimating the (0,1) outcome of being a union member
2. Coefficients are percentage changes in the probability of membership
3. T-statistics are in parentheses
4. * = significant at 5% level; ** = significant at 1% level
5. Unweighted sample size is 3,380 with the following exceptions:
   (a) Non-white N=3366
   (b) Left–right scale N=2795
   (c) Union recognition N=2904

Union membership wage premium

	Pooled 1998 and 2005			No controls + controls				+ controls + union recognition	
	+ year dummy	Year dummy + controls	Year dummy + controls + union recognition	1998	2005	1998	2005	1998	2005
Log Hourly wage	.19**	.04	.04	.23**	.14**	.06	.02	.07*	.00
Log weekly wage	.29**	.06*	.07**	.34**	.23**	.08*	.04	.11**	.04

Notes:
1. *British Social Attitudes* collects banded weekly earnings data and continuous hours data. We assume each employee receives a wage at the mid-point of their banded earnings. The earnings band for the top-coded highest earners is closed by introducing an upper ceiling which is 1.5 times the lower band
2. As an alternative to the 'mid-point' assumption we fitted models using the interval regression technique developed by Stewart (1983). The results do not differ much from those presented; they are available from the author upon request. For further details on the application of the interval regression technique to *British Social Attitudes* data see Bryson and Gomez (2002)
3. To obtain hourly wages we take the mid-point of the respondent's earnings band and divide this by the continuous variable of hours worked inclusive of overtime hours. Previous analyses of *British Social Attitudes* surveys indicate that this results in a lower union premium than estimates excluding overtime
4. The figures in the table are the coefficients for a union membership dummy variable from multivariate regressions of log wages. The *ceteris paribus* percentage increase in wages from membership is the exponentiated coefficient minus 1, that is, exp(coef)-1
5. * = significant at 5% level; ** = significant at 1% level
6. Controls are: gender, age (6 dummies), non-white, any partner, any children, social class (5 dummies), education (8 dummies), owner-occupier, region (6 dummies), full-timer, workplace tenure (5 dummies), public sector, industry (13 dummies), establishment size (5 dummies)
7. All estimates are based on survey weighted data

9 Disabling attitudes? Public perspectives on disabled people

*John Rigg**

There are around 10 million disabled adults in Great Britain, one in five of the adult population (DRC, 2006). Yet disabled people often describe how society's negative attitude and lack of awareness of disability result in psychological and physical barriers. A recent survey carried out by the Disability Rights Commission (DRC) found that almost half of all respondents believe that disabled people are not treated fairly in society (DRC, 2003; see also Brent and Knight, 1999; Grewal *et al.*, 2002). The same DRC survey also found that approximately one in five respondents who were disabled have experienced harassment in public in relation to their impairment. Indeed, a survey of disabled people commissioned by Leonard Cheshire, a disabilities organisation, cited negative social attitudes as the main reason why three-fifths of disabled people said that their disability prevented them from participating in everyday social activities (Knight *et al.*, 2002). This was also a key finding to emerge in a recent report commissioned by the Mayor of London which found that people's attitudes and assumptions about disability and disabled people's capabilities was a clear barrier in disabled Londoners' experience of housing, employment and post-16 education (Greater London Authority, 2006).

Despite evidence of negative social attitudes towards disabled people – and the considerable barriers these create – there has been remarkably little research aimed at understanding attitudes towards disabled people. It is hoped that the module of questions carried in the 2005 *British Social Attitudes* survey will go some way in addressing this shortfall in our knowledge.

Attitudes towards disabled people are formed by one's understanding of the nature and cause of disability. Traditionally, many people's views were based on a 'medical' model of disability – disabled people were thought of as unable to participate in society as a direct result of their impairment or illness. In other words, impairment caused disability. Objections to this view by the civil rights

* John Rigg is Research Officer at the *Centre for Analysis of Social Exclusion* (CASE), an Economic and Social Research Council Research Centre at the London School of Economics

movement of disabled people has promoted a wider spread of a 'social' model of disability. In this approach, the 'problem' of disability results from social structures and attitudes, rather than from a person's impairment or medical condition. Disability is characterised as resulting from the exclusionary way in which society organises itself. For example, a person using a wheelchair is disabled, not because of his or her physical impairment, but because society has not ensured that all buildings are accessible.

> If [people] behave as if the problem is with the individual, they will take a different approach than if they regard the problem as being with the attitudes, systems and practices that create disabling barriers. (Clark and Marsh, 2002: 1)

There is some evidence that this 'social' model has taken root in recent government thinking (Prime Minister's Strategy Unit, 2005). There have, in fact, been significant changes in government policies towards disabled people over the last decade or so. An important legislative development has been the introduction of the 1995 Disability Discrimination Act (DDA), which has created statutory rights and obligations in a number of areas, including employment, provision of goods, facilities and services, and education. The DRC was set up in 2000 as an independent body with the dual aim of eliminating discrimination and securing equal opportunities for disabled people. There has also been a raft of initiatives aimed at promoting employment of disabled people (such as the New Deal for Disabled People), and further labour market and benefit changes are forthcoming as part of the Pathways to Work programme. The emphasis behind many of the initiatives is itself indicative of a change in the government's approach towards disabled people, reflecting a more inclusive philosophy.

According to the DDA, the legal definition of a disabled person is any person who has a physical or mental impairment or long-term health condition which has a substantial and long-term adverse effect on their ability to carry out normal day-to-day activities. 'Long-term' means that it has lasted for twelve months or more, or is likely to last for more than twelve months. In general, a person's impairment or health condition should be considered without treatment or correction (such as medication or prosthesis).[1]

The *British Social Attitudes* questionnaire asked about disability in several different ways. In this chapter we have chosen to use a set of questions which take an impairment perspective, as this provides the most detailed information about our disabled respondents:

> *[Do] you yourself have any of the health conditions or impairments on this card, which has a substantial and long-term adverse effect on your ability to carry out normal day-to-day activities? ...*[2]
>
> *... Physical impairment, such as using a wheelchair to get around and/or difficulty using [your] arms or hands*

... *Sensory impairment such as blind/having a serious visual impairment or deaf/serious hearing impairment*

... *Mental health condition, such as depression, schizophrenia or severe phobia*

... *Learning disability, such as Down's syndrome*

... *Other long-standing illness or health condition*

As seen in Table 9.1, using this question, 16 per cent of the respondents define themselves to be disabled.

Table 9.1 Whether respondent has any pre-defined health condition or disability

Whether respondent has ...	%
Physical impairment	4
Sensory impairment	3
Mental health condition	3
Learning disability	*
Other long-standing illness	7
Any type of disability mentioned	16
No disability mentioned	84
Base	*3210*

Respondents could mention more than one health condition or disability if applicable

In addition, respondents were asked if they knew anyone in any of the different impairment groups and, if so, who this was (partner, child, close relative, close friend, colleague, boss or someone else). Using this as our definition of knowing someone who is disabled, we find that approximately four-fifths of non-disabled respondents have some direct contact with a disabled person.

In this chapter, we consider three main topics. We start by looking at who is considered to be a 'disabled person'. We then examine attitudes towards disabled people in general, both by society at large and by the respondent themselves. Finally, we focus on how attitudes vary towards people with different types of impairment.

In each case, we ask whether are there any groups in the population that are distinctive in their views. We focus on three factors in particular. First, we consider people's experience of and exposure to disability, comparing people who are themselves disabled, with those who are *not* disabled but know someone who is, and with those who are *not* disabled and do *not* know anyone who is. A key theme of the chapter is to explore the ways in which 'experience of disability' shapes people's attitudes towards disabled people. There are various ways in which this might happen. One possibility is that knowing a disabled person might create positive attitudes towards that person in particular, without affecting one's attitudes towards disabled people in general. If so, we would not expect any difference in general attitudes between those who know a disabled person and those who do not. Alternatively, it could be that knowing a disabled person makes people more likely to have positive attitudes towards – and be more comfortable with – disabled people in general. If the latter scenario is true, we would expect the link to show up in our data. This would suggest that policies designed to promote inclusion of disabled people into different spheres of everyday life will also lead to less prejudice over time, and may therefore have important implications for public policy.

The second characteristic we might expect to be associated with differences in views on disability is age. Clearly, with older age, health tends to decline and life experiences accumulate, so we might anticipate a more nuanced understanding of the difficulties and disabling effect of various impairments. On the other hand, young people may be more open to new ideas and less prejudiced in general. There is a particular reason for our interest in age. If it can be shown that young people are consistently more inclusive and less prejudiced in their views, then it is likely that general attitudes in society will move in this direction over time.[3]

Thirdly, we compare the attitudes of those with degree level education with those who have no educational qualifications. Previous *British Social Attitudes Reports* have repeatedly shown the link between education and lower levels of prejudice in other areas (see, for example, Evans, 2002; Rothon and Heath, 2003). Could the same be true for prejudice against disabled people?

Perceptions of what constitutes being disabled

So what do people think it is to be disabled? As we have seen, the DDA has a wide conception of the people covered by the anti-discrimination legislation and it is worth finding out whether this is shared by the population in general. If this is not the case, then the message from campaigners and government bodies about rights for disabled people may not be interpreted correctly by a general audience. The DRC has, in fact, decided not to use the umbrella term 'disabled people' on its own in some of its communications because of the risk of it being misunderstood.

In order to establish how respondents defined disability, we asked:

> *People have different ideas about what it means to be disabled.*
> *Which of the people on this card would you think of as a disabled person?*

On the card were eleven different conditions, all of which can fall under the DDA definition, except "a person with a broken leg, using crutches while it heals". The results are shown in Table 9.2.

Clearly, there are some notable discrepancies between the legal definition of disability and what the majority of the public, including disabled people themselves, consider to be a disability. Only four of the impairments are considered disabilities by a majority of people. Notably, neither of the mental health conditions is among these, perhaps reflecting a lack of understanding about these conditions. We return to this issue later. Note that HIV/AIDS and severe facial disfigurement were considered to be disabilities by fewer people than picked the temporary broken leg scenario.

Table 9.2 Proportions thinking a person with each impairment is disabled, by exposure to disability

% who think a person with the impairment is disabled	All	Disabled	Exposure to disability	
			Not disabled, knows someone who is	Not disabled, doesn't know anyone who is
Uses wheelchair most of the time	91	87	92	89
Blind	87	84	88	82
Severe arthritis	81	86	83	68
Down's syndrome	70	62	73	67
Schizophrenia	48	53	50	37
Cancer	44	57	43	34
Older person who cannot hear without a hearing aid	44	40	47	38
Severe depression	40	53	39	27
Broken leg, on crutches while it heals	31	31	33	26
HIV/AIDS	27	34	27	19
Severe facial disfigurement	25	30	26	18
Average number of impairments thought of as a disability	5.9	6.2	6.0	5.1
Base	*3193*	*563*	*2164*	*458*

Table 9.2 also shows that personal or second-hand experience of disability tends to make people more likely to regard a person with a given impairment as disabled. For six of the eleven impairments there is a gradual decrease in the proportions considering them to be disabilities as we move from disabled people themselves, to those knowing someone who is disabled, to those who do

not know anyone who is disabled. For example, almost nine out of ten disabled people regard someone with severe arthritis as disabled, while only two-thirds of people who do not know anyone who is disabled do so. Interestingly, in a number of cases, there is a tendency for those who know a disabled person to be *more* likely than disabled people themselves to view an impairment as a disability.

A further breakdown of perceptions of disability by age and educational qualifications is shown in Table 9.3. The results indicate that both these characteristics are important factors in shaping people's ideas about what constitutes a disability. We might expect people with higher education to have more information about disability and therefore to pick more impairments from the list. This is indeed the case, with graduates picking an average of 6.7 items, compared with 5.3 among those with no educational qualifications.[4] With the exception of cancer, more graduates picked each of the impairments than those without educational qualifications and this is particularly noticeable for the two mental health conditions. This suggests that an understanding of mental health problems as a disability is related to one's level of education.

Table 9.3 Proportions thinking a person with each impairment is disabled, by age and education

% who think a person with the impairment is disabled	Age				Education	
	18–34	35–44	45–64	65+	Degree or higher	None
Uses wheelchair most of the time	93	93	92	85	95	85
Blind	90	89	87	81	91	79
Severe arthritis	75	82	86	81	86	77
Down's syndrome	78	75	69	59	81	59
Schizophrenia	47	52	52	41	63	37
Cancer	30	43	49	56	39	51
Older person who cannot hear without a hearing aid	50	51	42	33	60	33
Severe depression	31	41	46	41	51	36
Broken leg, on crutches while it heals	29	33	35	28	40	26
HIV/AIDS	19	30	31	29	33	24
Severe facial disfigurement	22	28	28	24	32	25
Average number of impairments thought of as a disability	5.6	6.2	6.2	5.6	6.7	5.3
Base	735	630	1074	752	507	882

The pattern with regards to age is more complicated, without a clearly consistent relationship. If there is any picture to be discerned from Table 9.3, it seems to be that it is the middle age groups that are most likely to pick various impairments as disabilities. This suggests that neither the increased exposure of older people to disabilities (both for oneself and among one's contemporaries), nor the generally lower prejudice of young people are the dominant factors here. Perhaps older people simply do not regard various ailments that they themselves and their friends have as warranting the label 'disability' – in particular, only a third of the over-65s thought an older person with a hearing aid was disabled, compared with half of the 18–44 year olds. Meanwhile, younger people may lack the life experience to understand the impact of various impairments – with, for example, fewer than a third picking cancer, compared with half of the 45s and over. Or they may be part of a generation where the concept of a 'disabled identity' is on its way out. It may also be that different processes are at work for different impairments. For example, the much greater integration into society nowadays of people with Down's syndrome may lie behind the tendency for young people to be more likely to regard this as a disability than older people. However, paradoxically, young people are least likely to regard people with HIV/AIDS as disabled. So, whereas exposure to disabled people and level of education have strong and largely consistent relationships with identifying various impairments as making people disabled, age does not.

Views on the extent of prejudice against disabled people

How much prejudice against disabled people is there thought to be in Britain today? We can address this directly using the following question:

> *Generally speaking, do you think there is a lot of prejudice in Britain against disabled people in general, a little, hardly any or none?*

This question has been asked twice before on *British Social Attitudes* so we can look not only at the position now, but at how it has changed over time. This is shown in Table 9.4.

Table 9.4 Perceptions of prejudice against disabled people, 1998, 2000, 2005

	1998	2000	2005
	%	%	%
A lot	25	35	25
A little	51	51	50
Hardly any	15	9	17
None	6	3	8
Base	*3146*	*3426*	*3193*

Large majorities of the population have always identified some prejudice against disabled people. However, the biggest fluctuation is in the proportion who say there is "a lot" of prejudice. This stood at a quarter in 1998. By 2000, at the time of the foundation of the DRC, it had risen to over a third. In 2005, it was back down to a quarter, perhaps as the implementation of many of the measures in the DDA has been seen to address some of the problems faced by disabled people.

In the previous section, we identified that experience of disability was a key determinant in shaping people's views on what constitutes a disability. We now examine whether experience of disability affects views on the extent of prejudice against disabled people. We investigate these issues by constructing a sixfold hierarchy in an attempt to capture the 'proximity' of a person's relationship to a disabled person. Disabled people themselves are at one end of the scale, with people who do not know anyone who is disabled at the other. The four intermediate categories, in order of descending proximity to a disabled person, comprise people who have a disabled family member (a partner or child), a close relative, a close friend or someone else (including a work colleague or boss).[5] Whilst this classification does not fully capture the depth and quality of individual relationships, it provides a reasonable proxy for how well a non-disabled person may know a disabled person.

Views on the extent of prejudice by experience of disability are reported in the next table.

Table 9.5 Views on extent of prejudice against disabled people, by exposure to disability

| | All | Disabled | Not disabled but ... | | | | Not disabled, doesn't know anyone who is |
			... partner/ child(ren) is	... close relative is	... close friend is	... know someone else who is	
	%	%	%	%	%	%	%
A lot	25	29	34	24	26	23	18
A little	50	43	43	53	51	51	49
Hardly any/ none	25	26	23	22	23	26	30
Base	3193	563	249	1051	446	417	458

Proximity to a disabled person does seem to be associated with believing that prejudice against disabled people is more widespread. In fact, people who have a close family member who is disabled think that prejudice is more widespread even than disabled people themselves. Thus just under a third of disabled people themselves believe there is a lot of prejudice, compared with just over a third of those who have a disabled partner or child and less than two-fifths of those who do not know anyone who is disabled. Conversely, just under a third of people who do not know anyone who is disabled believe there is hardly any or no discrimination, compared with only around a quarter of people who know a disabled person, irrespective of how closely they know them. Although these differences are statistically significant, it has to be said that they are not very large. Being disabled or knowing a disabled person has an impact on perceptions of prejudice in society, but those who do not know anyone who is disabled also agree that there is at least some prejudice.

Table 9.6 shows views on the extent of prejudice against disabled people by age and highest educational qualification. This shows that older people are less likely to believe there is prejudice against disabled people even though they are more likely to be disabled themselves. For instance, only around a fifth of respondents aged under 65 believe that there is hardly any or no prejudice against disabled people, compared with over a third of respondents aged 65 or more. Further, people with higher levels of educational qualifications think that prejudice against disabled people is more extensive. For instance, 29 per cent of respondents with a degree or higher think that a lot of prejudice exists towards disabled people, compared to 22 per cent of people with no educational qualifications.

Table 9.6 Views on extent of prejudice against disabled people, by age and education

	Age				Education	
	18–34	35–44	45–64	65+	Degree or higher	None
	%	%	%	%	%	%
A lot	27	24	28	18	29	22
A little	50	54	50	44	50	45
Hardly any/none	22	21	22	36	20	31
Base	*735*	*630*	*1074*	*752*	*507*	*882*

Thus people with experience of disability, people aged below 65 and graduates are more likely to think that prejudice against disabled people is widespread.[6] One explanation could be that these groups of people are more sensitive to, and aware of, prejudice. An alternative explanation could simply be that they have a broader view of what constitutes a disability, and this broader view encompasses types of impairment that experience more prejudice, such as schizophrenia. However, further analysis does not appear to support this explanation as being younger and a graduate remain related to believing that there is a lot of prejudice against disabled people, even after we take into account the number of impairments respondents regard as a disability.[7]

Respondents' own attitudes towards disabled people

The previous section discussed people's views on the extent of prejudice against disabled people in society at large. We focus in this section on people's own attitudes towards disabled people. First, we examine people's general attitudes, then explore more specifically whether people tend to hold inclusionary or exclusionary views about disabled people.

'Negative' feelings about disabled people

We begin by examining responses to a set of questions which, at least at first glance, may be thought to reveal 'negative' attitudes towards disabled people. (The extent to which these questions do, in fact, capture 'negative' attitudes is discussed below.) Respondents were asked:

> *How many people in Britain do you think tend to think of disabled people in general in the following ways:*
>
> *... as getting in the way?*
>
> *... with discomfort and awkwardness?*

The answer options were "nearly all people think of disabled people like this", "quite a lot of people think of disabled people like this", "a few people think of disabled people like this" and "hardly anyone thinks of disabled people like this". Respondents were then asked about their *own* feelings towards disabled people – whether they thought of disabled people in general like this "most of the time", "some of the time", "hardly ever" or "never".

The results are shown in Table 9.7. Even though these questions were asked in a self-completion format, we would expect people to be reluctant to owning up to negative views of disabled people. It is much easier, however, to ascribe such views to 'other people'. And this proves to be the case. Seventeen per cent of respondents believe that nearly all or quite a lot of people think of disabled people as "getting in the way". By contrast, only nine per cent of respondents said that they themselves think of disabled people in this way most or some of the time. Similarly, over a third of people believe that nearly all or quite a lot of people think of disabled people "with discomfort and awkwardness", compared with less than a quarter who said that they themselves think of disabled people in this way most or some of the time.

As we might expect, there is a strong correlation between what people say about society in general and their own views. For instance, a respondent is four times more likely to believe that nearly all or quite a lot of people think of disabled people as "getting in the way" if they themselves think of disabled people in this way, at least some of the time. Therefore, we suspect that answers to the first questions reveal a fair amount of unvoiced prejudice. Note also that less than half of respondents said they *never* thought of disabled people with discomfort and awkwardness. Thus, whilst strong 'negative' feelings about disabled people are not common, more mild 'negative' feelings are perhaps more widely held than might have been anticipated.

Table 9.7 Views on societal attitudes to disabled people and personal views on disabled people

		Nearly all	Quite a lot	A few	Hardly any
How many people in Britain think of disabled people ...					
... as getting in the way?	%	2	15	51	27
... with discomfort and awkwardness?	%	3	33	47	12
		Most of the time	Some of the time	Hardly ever	Never
Do you personally think of disabled people ...					
... as getting in the way?	%	1	8	31	57
... with discomfort and awkwardness?	%	1	20	33	42

Base: 2699

Table 9.8 shows the extent to which these 'negative' feelings depend on experience of disability. The influence of proximity to a disabled person can once again be detected, although it is not as strong as in the earlier analysis of perceptions of prejudice in society. In general, people with close relations to a disabled person are *more* likely to believe that negative feelings are widespread in society, but *less* likely to report holding these feelings themselves. For instance, fewer than one in six people who do not know anyone with a disability think that nearly all or quite a lot of people in general think of disabled people as getting in the way. This compares with almost a quarter of disabled people themselves. However, the differences are less when it comes to people's own views. A quarter of non-disabled people admitted to thinking of disabled people with discomfort or awkwardness at least some of the time, but so do almost a fifth of disabled people themselves.[8]

Table 9.8 Societal and personal attitudes to disabled people, by exposure to disability

			Exposure to disability		
% thinking nearly all/ quite a lot of people think of disabled people ...	All	Disabled	Not disabled but family member is	Not disabled, know someone who is (not family)	Not disabled, doesn't know anyone who is
... as getting in the way	17	23	20	16	15
... with discomfort and awkwardness	36	39	39	36	29
% who personally think of disabled people most/some of time ...					
... as getting in the way	9	9	7	8	14
... with discomfort and awkwardness	22	18	17	22	25
Base	*2699*	*466*	*226*	*1650*	*351*

As we might anticipate from our earlier analyses, graduates and those aged under 65 are more willing to acknowledge the existence of negative feelings towards disabled people in the form of being viewed with "discomfort and awkwardness" – though not as "getting in the way" (see Table 9.9). But contrary to our expectations, though in line with our finding that those who report negative feelings in other people are also more likely to report them in themselves, graduates (and to a lesser extent younger people) are also more likely to admit that they themselves think of disabled people with discomfort and awkwardness.

A possible explanation for this seemingly counter-intuitive finding might be found from the results of qualitative research, such as Grewal *et al.* (2002), which describes how non-disabled people sometimes feel embarrassed and uncertain how to behave with a disabled person. People sometimes fear causing offence by offering to help, for example, and fear a possible negative reaction from the disabled person. If younger people and people with higher educational qualifications are more aware of the possible difficulties disabled people face, they may end up feeling more uncomfortable and awkward when encountering a disabled person. For a subset of people, thinking of disabled people "with discomfort and awkwardness" may not so much reflect a 'negative' feeling, as an expression of uncertainty, motivated in some instances by a willingness to 'do the right thing'. For other people by contrast, thinking of disabled people "with discomfort and awkwardness" may indeed be negative, if it arises from an exclusionary attitude towards disabled people. Thus, the survey question is likely to be picking up elements of both attitudes, and care should therefore be exercised when interpreting these results.

Table 9.9 Societal and personal attitudes to disabled people, by age and education

	Age				Education	
% thinking nearly all/quite a lot of people think of disabled people ...	18–34	35–44	45–64	65+	Degree or higher	None
... as getting in the way	20	16	18	14	15	16
... with discomfort and awkwardness	41	40	37	25	45	24
% who personally think of disabled people most/some of time ...						
... as getting in the way	10	10	7	8	7	9
... with discomfort and awkwardness	25	23	20	18	29	15
Base	*594*	*521*	*946*	*638*	*431*	*727*

Inclusionary and exclusionary attitudes

To gauge a measure of people's inclusionary and exclusionary attitudes[9] towards disabled people, we asked how much people agreed or disagreed with the following two statements:

Disabled people make just as good parents as people who are not disabled

Disabled people should never have to live in a residential home if they do not want to

Agreeing that disabled people should never have to live in a residential home if they do not want to can be interpreted as an inclusionary view of disabled people, perhaps extending to an endorsement of the current care in the community strategy for people with mental health problems. Similarly, agreeing that most disabled people make just as good parents as people who are not disabled is indicative of an inclusionary, positive perspective on the role of disabled people as parents.

Table 9.10 suggests that most respondents have an inclusive view of disabled people. Approximately three-quarters of people agree with each statement, whilst only one in twenty or less disagree with them.

The proportion of people who agree that disabled people should never have to live in a residential home increases with experience of disability, as might be expected. Seventy-five per cent of non-disabled people who do not know anyone with a disability agree with the statement, compared to 83 per cent of disabled people. Whilst this difference is statistically significant, experience of disability accounts for less of the variation in this attitude than most other attitudes discussed earlier. Experience of disability is even less important in explaining the responses to the statement on the ability of disabled people to make good parents.[10]

Table 9.10 Views on participation of disabled people, by exposure to disability

	All	Disabled	Exposure to disability		
			Not disabled but family member is	Not disabled, know someone who is (not family)	Not disabled, doesn't know anyone who is
% agreeing that ...					
... disabled people should never have to live in a residential home if they don't want to	76	83	80	74	75
... disabled people make just as good parents as people who aren't disabled	73	76	69	73	72
Base	*2699*	*466*	*226*	*1650*	*351*

We might expect that people with a broader definition of disability might hold more inclusive views about disabled people. We can investigate the extent to which this is true in Figure 9.1. The scope (or breadth) of individuals' definition of disability is represented by the number of impairment types that they counted as a disability (see Table 9.2). Respondents who quoted a higher number of types of impairment are regarded as holding a broader definition of disability. Figure 9.1 shows the relationship between the scope of the definition of disability and the extent of inclusionary views towards disabled people, in terms of agreeing with the two statements above.

Figure 9.1 The relationship between inclusionary attitudes towards disability and scope of definition of disability

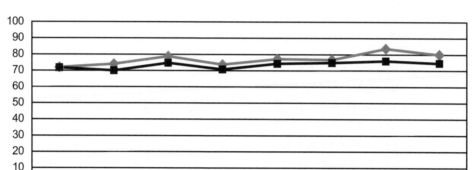

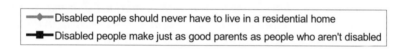
Disabled people should never have to live in a residential home
Disabled people make just as good parents as people who aren't disabled

Figure 9.1 confirms that people who hold a broad definition of disability are more likely to hold inclusionary views about disabled people – the overall shape of both lines is upward-sloping. However, only the line showing the proportion who agree that disabled people should never be made to live in residential homes against their wishes is statistically significant at conventional levels, and both series are relatively volatile. Thus, whilst broader views of disability are associated with more inclusionary views about disabled people, the extent of the association depends on the nature of inclusion in question and the association is not necessarily linear.

Attitudes towards different impairment types

So far, the chapter has largely examined attitudes towards disabled people in general. However, disabled people experience a wide range of impairments. Attitudes towards disabled people are likely to vary considerably according to the type of impairment. It is widely recognised, for example, that people with mental health impairments experience particular prejudice (see, for example, Grewal *et al.*, 2002). We now examine how attitudes vary between different impairment types and explore whether experience of disability, age and educational qualifications are important in shaping these attitudes.

Views on the extent of prejudice against different impairment types

To assess this we asked respondents the following questions:[11]

> *Generally speaking, how much prejudice do you think there is in Britain against...*
>
> *... people with physical impairments, such as someone who uses a wheelchair?*
>
> *... people who are deaf?*
>
> *... people who are blind?*
>
> *... people with learning disabilities, such as someone with Down's syndrome?*
>
> *... people with schizophrenia?*
>
> *... people with depression?*
>
> *... people who have long-term health conditions that may seriously affect their ability to carry out normal day-to-day activities, such as HIV/AIDS?*
>
> *... people who have long-term health conditions that may seriously affect their ability to carry out normal day-to-day activities, such as multiple sclerosis (MS) and severe arthritis?*

Table 9.11 Views on amount of prejudice against different impairment groups

		Amount of prejudice			
Impairment group		**A lot**	**A little**	**Hardly any/none**	*Base*
Disabled people in general	%	25	50	25	3193
Schizophrenia	%	46	32	12	772
Long-term health condition, e.g. HIV/AIDS	%	44	38	13	772
Learning disability, e.g. Down's syndrome	%	34	41	24	825
Depression	%	29	40	25	837
Physical impairment	%	20	50	29	759
Long-term health condition, e.g. MS, severe arthritis	%	15	41	40	837
Deaf	%	13	44	42	759
Blind	%	10	32	55	825

Table 9.11 shows that people believe prejudice is most widespread against people with mental health problems and learning disabilities, along with HIV/AIDS. For example, almost half of the respondents thought there was a lot of prejudice against people with schizophrenia, compared with only one in ten who thought there was a lot of prejudice against blind people. It has been argued that this prejudice against mental illness and learning disabilities is founded in a lack of understanding and fear of these conditions (although that is not the whole story: other studies show that knowledge can be increased without prejudice being reduced). Non-visible, 'hidden' disabilities are also thought to fuel prejudice, since people are less aware of them (Grewal *et al.*, 2002).[12] People clearly feel that there is considerable stigma still attached to HIV/AIDS.

Table 9.12 shows that, like for perceptions of prejudice in general, greater exposure to disabled people tends to promote greater perception of prejudice against each of the groups. However, there are some variations. Experience of disability does not affect views on the extent of prejudice against someone with a long-term health condition such as HIV/AIDS. This may well stem from it not being typically regarded as a disability (see Tables 9.2 and 9.3). Also, we should bear in mind that our measure of 'exposure to disability' is rather a blunt measure – there is really no reason why someone who is deaf or who has a boss who uses a wheelchair should have a different view of HIV/AIDS from someone who does not know any disabled people.

Table 9.12 Proportion who think there is a lot of prejudice against different impairment groups, by exposure to disability

			Exposure to disability	
% thinking there is a lot of prejudice against each impairment	All	Disabled	Not disabled but know someone who is	Not disabled, doesn't know anyone who is
Schizophrenia	46	53	47	32
Long-term health condition, e.g. HIV/AIDS	44	44	44	44
Learning disability, e.g. Down's syndrome	34	39	36	18
Depression	29	38	29	21
Physical impairment	20	26	20	14
Long-term health condition, e.g. MS, severe arthritis	15	19	15	9
Deaf	13	16	12	13
Blind	10	14	10	8
Base	*772–837*	*129–144*	*509–572*	*107–133*

Table 9.13 shows that only in the case of schizophrenia do graduates believe prejudice to be more widespread than people without educational qualifications. One explanation might be that prejudice against schizophrenia, in particular, is fuelled by ignorance and that people with more educational qualifications may have more information and therefore be more aware of prejudice.

The relationship between perceived prejudice and age is a complex one, which varies between different impairment groups, but in general there is a tendency for those over 65 to perceive less prejudice. This does not hold for the sensory impairments, where there was little variation by age.

Table 9.13 Views on amount of prejudice against different impairment groups, by age and education

	Age				Education	
	18–34	35–44	45–64	65+	Degree or higher	None
	%	%	%	%	%	%
Schizophrenia	47	40	52	40	57	47
Long-term health condition, e.g. HIV/AIDS	47	44	48	33	45	46
Learning disability, e.g. Down's syndrome	36	40	34	25	39	36
Depression	24	30	37	23	31	32
Physical impairment	17	23	26	12	18	21
Long-term health condition, e.g. MS, severe arthritis	14	13	18	11	10	17
Deaf	10	14	12	14	14	10
Blind	9	10	10	11	12	19
Base	155–213	152–164	258–275	158–205	116–139	185–241

People's own attitudes towards different impairment types

But how do people's own attitudes towards different impairment groups vary? To answer this, we make use of a series of questions in this format:

> ... how do you think you would feel if a person who uses a wheelchair were to move in next door?

> ... how do you think you would feel if one of your close relatives were to marry a person who uses a wheelchair?

These questions were further asked about the following scenarios:

- *a person who cannot hear without a hearing aid*
- *a blind person*
- *a person who has a long-term health condition which seriously affects their ability to carry out normal day-to-day activities, such as multiple sclerosis (MS) or severe arthritis*
- *a person with Down's syndrome*
- *a person who has a diagnosis of schizophrenia, which you know that he or she has managed successfully for several years*
- *a person that you know has had a diagnosis of depression in the recent past*[13]

Respondents were invited to say whether they would be "very comfortable", "fairly comfortable", "fairly uncomfortable" or "very uncomfortable" with each of these scenarios. The results are shown in Table 9.14.

Table 9.14 Level of comfort by impairment group and situation

Impairment group	Situation		Comfortable		Uncom-	
			Very	Fairly	fortable	*Base*
Person who ...						
... uses a wheelchair	Moves in next door	%	89	11	1	*759*
	Married close relative	%	59	32	8	*772*
... cannot hear without a hearing aid	Moves in next door	%	83	15	2	*759*
	Married close relative	%	62	34	4	*772*
... is blind	Moves in next door	%	79	20	1	*825*
	Married close relative	%	51	39	9	*837*
... has a long-term health condition, e.g. MS or severe arthritis	Moves in next door	%	62	32	5	*825*
	Married close relative	%	21	48	29	*837*
... has Down's syndrome	Moves in next door	%	59	34	6	*825*
... has depression	Moves in next door	%	44	40	14	*825*
	Married close relative	%	14	41	42	*837*
... has schizophrenia	Moves in next door	%	29	46	23	*759*
	Married close relative	%	19	38	40	*772*

Three features of interest stand out from the results in Table 9.14. First, most people said that they would feel fairly or very comfortable with all scenarios. This points to a broadly positive attitude towards disabled people, supporting the findings from the previous sections. However, there is clearly substantial unease with the prospect of coming into contact with certain types of impairment, notably mental-health problems, and especially in a highly personal circumstance. Approximately two-fifths of people said they would feel fairly or very uncomfortable if a close relative were to marry a person with depression or schizophrenia (and this despite respondents having been told that the schizophrenia has been successfully managed for several years).

Secondly, there is a strong overlap between the types of impairment people said they would feel uncomfortable coming into contact with themselves and the types of disabled people they believe experience most prejudice (see Table 9.11). In particular, people expressed greatest discomfort with the hypothetical situations involving people with mental health impairments. For instance, practically no one said that they would feel fairly or very uncomfortable if a person using a wheelchair or a person who was blind or deaf moved in next door, whereas 14 per cent said they would feel fairly or very uncomfortable if a person with depression were to move in next door, and the figure was almost a quarter for schizophrenia.

Thirdly, a distinctive feature of the results is that the level of discomfort increases markedly according to the personal nature of the situation. For instance, five per cent of people said they would feel fairly or very uncomfortable if a person with a long-term health condition moved in next door, compared with 28 per cent if it was a case of them marrying a close relative. Although the level of comfort varies for different types of impairment, the pronounced gradient with the degree of proximity of the situation is striking for all impairment types.

Table 9.15 Proportion who would not feel very comfortable[14] if disabled person were to move in next door, by exposure to disability

% who would not feel very comfortable if neighbour moved in next door who ...	Exposure to disability		
	Disabled	Not disabled, knows someone who is	Not disabled, doesn't know anyone who is
... uses a wheelchair	8	11	18
... cannot hear without a hearing aid	15	16	23
... is blind	14	21	27
... has a long-term health condition, e.g. MS or severe arthritis	28	39	44
... has Down's syndrome	35	41	46
... has depression	50	56	57
... has schizophrenia	62	71	82
Base	*129–149*	*509–572*	*107–133*

We now examine whether there are notable subgroup differences in the feelings of respondents to people with different types of impairments moving in next door. Table 9.15 shows the proportion of people who would not feel very comfortable with a person with a particular impairment moving in next door, broken down by individual characteristics.[15] Once more, the influence of experience of disability in reducing levels of discomfort with the hypothetical situations is apparent in most of the cases. For example, just under a quarter of people who do not know a disabled person said they would not feel very comfortable with a deaf person moving in next door, compared with only 15 per cent of disabled people.

Table 9.16 shows that people over 65 and those who have no educational qualifications tend to express higher levels of discomfort with the hypothetical situations (although not in every single case). This is despite the fact that older people and those with no educational qualifications expressed *lower* levels of discomfort and awkwardness when they were asked how they thought of disabled people in general. It may be that the explanation for this apparent paradox is that these groups are less able to grasp the purpose of the earlier, more general question, but respond more truthfully to this, more realistic, style of the scenario question.[16]

Table 9.16 Proportion who would not feel comfortable if disabled person were to move in next door, by age and education

% who would not feel comfortable if neighbour moved in next door who ...	Age				Education	
	18–34	35–44	45–64	65+	Degree or higher	None
... uses a wheelchair	6	13	12	16	8	17
... cannot hear without a hearing aid	12	21	13	25	8	30
... is blind	25	23	17	21	20	23
... has a long-term health condition, e.g. MS or severe arthritis	45	31	29	46	34	43
... has Down's syndrome	46	35	32	52	33	47
... has depression	60	55	49	61	47	61
... has schizophrenia	65	75	74	72	75	76
Base	*155–190*	*152–161*	*258–269*	*194–205*	*116–129*	*185–234*

Conclusions

This chapter has explored the nature and character of attitudes towards disabled people. The evidence has highlighted that disabled people are generally perceived to be those with physical conditions that are long-lasting or permanent and may lead to incapacity. The general public tend not to draw the definition as wide as the Disability Discrimination Act does. Mental health conditions are often not seen as disabilities. Nor are long-standing illnesses such as cancer or HIV/AIDS included by most people. This should be borne in mind by public policy makers and campaigners. When they speak of 'disabled people', the public at large – and even disabled people themselves – are unlikely to be thinking of the same groups. This has profound implications for communications on disability and echoes earlier research suggesting that people defined as disabled under the DDA often do not consider themselves 'disabled' – and often do not want to. This has led some organisations, including the DRC, to use different language in its communications campaigns, in order to reach and refer to people more effectively.

Most people think that prejudice against disabled people exists but that it is not very extensive. However, whilst respondents rarely express strong 'negative' feelings about disabled people, milder 'negative' feelings are more widely held than might have been anticipated. Negative attitudes are especially pronounced in relation to people with mental health impairments. There is widespread unease among respondents at the prospect of coming into contact with people with mental health impairments, particularly in personal settings. Policy makers need to take note of this and emphasise policies building on the best evidence on how to foster positive understanding and reduce prejudice.

A consistent and striking theme to emerge from the analysis is the positive influence that knowing a disabled person appears to have on people's attitudes towards disabled people. Those who have personal or second-hand experience of disability tend to perceive prejudice against disabled people as being more widespread, while they are significantly less likely to hold negative attitudes themselves towards disabled people.

There are a number of implications for policy that can be drawn from these findings. In particular, they support the benefits of the wider inclusion of disabled people into different walks of society. Not only is this likely to be directly beneficial to the disabled people themselves, but by fostering greater contact between disabled and non-disabled people, will tend to reduce prejudice and 'negative' attitudes in the longer term. This includes policies such as mainstream educational provision for disabled people, community participation, disabled people's leadership and policies to facilitate greater employment of disabled people. The evidence is also consistent with time-limited initiatives aimed at positive discrimination in favour of disabled people. As disabled people become gradually more integrated into different domains of everyday life and positive attitudes become more commonplace, the prevalence of discriminatory practices should ease over time.

There is some suggestion this will be helped by generational change, as older, less educated, less tolerant age groups are replaced by younger ones. However, the evidence on this is not straightforward, as the relationship between prejudice on the one hand and age and education on the other is not always consistent.

Notes

1. An exception applies to people with a visual impairment who normally wear glasses or contact lenses.
2. Interviewers were provided with these further explanations to use, if asked:

   'Long-term' means it has lasted for 12 months or more, or is likely to last for more than 12 months.
   Please think what the situation would be like without treatment or correction (e.g. without medication or hearing aid) – except for visual impairment where you should think of what the situation should be like with any glasses or contact lenses that you normally use.

3. We should also be aware of the possibility that distinctive attitudes among the young change as they grow older and gain more experience. However, other analysis of *British Social Attitudes* data suggests that greater support among the young for anti-discriminatory legislation is a cohort and not a lifecycle effect (for example, Rothon and Heath, 2003).
4. We should note the possibility, however, that graduates are simply more able to deal with a complex survey question like this, and therefore will tend to pick a larger number of answers than respondents without formal educational qualifications. With that in mind, it should be noted that graduates were more likely to pick also the temporary broken leg scenario, which is not defined as disabled under the DDA.
5. Many people know more than one disabled person. Respondents are grouped into the category which represents their closest relationship with a disabled person.
6. This pattern of results broadly corresponds with findings from other studies on attitudes towards disabled people as well as prejudice against other groups such as racial minorities, gay men and lesbians (Stonewall, 2003).
7. Multivariate analysis showed that people aged under 55 and graduates were more likely to believe there is a lot of prejudice against disabled people. The importance of these individual characteristics were substantively unaffected after controlling for number of health conditions and the importance of the young age group actually increased slightly. As anticipated, the number of impairments is positively related to believing that a lot of prejudice exists against disabled people. However, this relationship is nonlinear – it applies only to people who have an especially broad definition of disability (the 26 per cent of people who regard eight or more of the health conditions as a disability) – but where it exists, the strength of this association is particularly pronounced. Compared even to people with a moderately broad definition of disability (people who regard seven of the health conditions as a

disability, for example), people with this especially broad definition of disability are approximately seven percentage points (almost a third) more likely to think that there is a lot of prejudice against disabled people.

8. People who have a disabled family member are actually less likely than disabled people themselves to think of disabled people "as getting in the way" or "with discomfort and awkwardness". These differences are small but statistically significant at conventional levels. This pattern of results mirrors those in relation to views on the extent of prejudice in the previous section, where people with a disabled family member believe there is more prejudice in society against disabled people than disabled people think themselves.

9. See Burchardt *et al.* (2002) for a definition of social exclusion and a discussion of relevant domains of participation in normal day-to-day activities.

10. Rather unexpectedly, people who have a disabled family member are least likely to agree with this statement. However, this is not statistically significantly different from the other groups.

11. In order to make the task for respondents manageable, not all questions were asked of everyone. The respondents were divided into four random groups. Group 1 were asked about someone with a physical impairment, such as being in a wheelchair, and someone who was deaf. Group 2 were asked about someone who was blind and someone with a learning disability like Down's syndrome. Group 3 were asked about schizophrenia and long-term illnesses like HIV/AIDS. Group 4 were asked about depression and long-term illnesses like MS and severe arthritis. The bases of the questions reported in this section are therefore lower than elsewhere in the chapter.

12. The belief that prejudice is so widespread against people with depression is particularly surprising given that it is a condition that is fairly common and therefore prejudice is to some degree less driven by ignorance.

13. Again, not all respondents were asked all the questions (see end note 11). Respondents in group 1 were asked about neighbours in wheelchairs, with schizophrenia and with hearing aids. (They were also asked about bosses with these impairments.) Respondents in group 2 were asked about neighbours who were blind, had depression, or had long-term illnesses such as MS and arthritis and Down's syndrome (and also about bosses with the first three of these). Respondents in group 3 were asked about a close relative marrying someone in a wheelchair, someone with schizophrenia and someone with a hearing aid. Respondents in group 4 were asked about a close relative marrying a blind person, someone with depression and someone with a long-term illness such as MS or arthritis.

14. "Not very comfortable" means that respondents said they would feel either "fairly comfortable", "fairly uncomfortable", "very uncomfortable" or "don't know".

15. We present evidence for "moving in next door" only – subgroup differences for "marrying a close relative' are broadly similar.

16. This is similar to the finding in relation to racism from an earlier *British Social Attitudes* survey: older respondents were no more likely to describe themselves as racist than younger respondents when asked a general question, but when asked a specific question on equal opportunities legislation, older respondents were much less supportive than younger ones (Rothon and Heath, 2003).

References

Brent, M. and Knight, J. (1999), *Excluding Attitudes: Disabled people's experience of social exclusion*, London: Leonard Cheshire

Burchardt, T., LeGrande, J. and Piachaud, D. (2002), 'Degrees of Social Exclusion: Developing a Dynamic, Multi-Dimensional Measure', in Hills, J., LeGrand, J. and Piachaud, D. (eds.), *Understanding Social Exclusion*, Oxford: Oxford University Press

Clark, L. and Marsh, S. (2002), *Patriarchy in the UK: The Language of Disability*, Leeds: Leeds University Disability Archive

Disability Rights Commission (DRC) (2003), *Attitudes and awareness survey 2003*, London: DRC

Disability Rights Commission (2006), *Disability Briefing Spring 2006*, London: Disability Rights Commission

Evans, G. (2002), 'In search of tolerance', in Park, A., Curtice, J., Thomson, K., Jarvis, L. and Bromley, C. (eds.), *British Social Attitudes: the 19th Report*, London: Sage

Greater London Authority (2006), *Towards joined up lives: Disabled and deaf Londoners' experience of housing, employment and post-16 education from a Social Model perspective*, Report produced by Equal Ability Ltd, London: Mayor of London Public Liaison Unit

Grewal, I., Joy, S., Lewis, J., Swales, K. and Woodfield, K. (2002), *'Disabled for Life?' Attitudes Towards, and Experiences of Disability in Britain*, London: Corporate Document Services DWP

Knight, J., Heaven, C., with Christie, I. (2002), *Inclusive Citizenship. The Leonard Cheshire Social Exclusion Report 2002*, London: Leonard Cheshire

Prime Minister's Strategy Unit (2005), *Improving the life chances of disabled people*, London: Prime Minister's Strategy Unit

Rothon, C. and Heath, A. (2003), 'Trends in racial prejudice', in Park, A., Curtice, J., Thomson, K., Jarvis, L. and Bromley, C. (eds.), *British Social Attitudes: the 20th Report - Continuity and change over two decades*, London: Sage

Stonewall (2003), *Profiles of Prejudice: The Nature of Prejudice in England*, London: Stonewall/Citizenship 21 Project

Acknowledgements

The *National Centre for Social Research* is grateful to the Disability Rights Commission for their financial support which enabled us to ask the questions reported in this chapter.

We also wish to thank Chloe Robinson for her help and advice.

10 Isolates or socialites? The social ties of internet users

John Curtice and Pippa Norris[*]

The advent of the internet has been one of the biggest developments in the history of communications technology. Like the railways and the telephone before it, the internet has helped to make the world a smaller place, making it easier to undertake both business and pleasure with individuals and organisations located far away. At the same time it has enabled individuals to acquire from the comfort of their office or front room access to both a hive of information and a wide range of commercial services, activities that previously would have necessitated a trip to the high street. Seemingly the internet has both made it easier to maintain contact with our fellow human beings, especially those who do not live locally, and, at the same time, reduced the need to engage in social contact with others in order to conduct the everyday business of commercial or private life.

These apparently divergent features of the internet have resulted in a lively debate about whether its advent has strengthened or weakened the social bonds and ties between individuals. One school of thought argues that it has had a beneficial impact. It points out that the internet makes it much easier to get into contact with individuals who have similar interests to oneself, irrespective of where they live, thereby making it possible to create 'virtual communities'. Contact with friends and relatives who live some distance away can more easily be maintained too –not just using words but also exploiting the ability to send photos, video clips and scanned images via the internet too. These apparent consequences derive principally from the opportunity afforded by e-mail to communicate asynchronously and to do so at no greater cost with someone halfway round the world than with a neighbour living next door (Hauben and

[*] John Curtice is Research Consultant at the *Scottish Centre for Social Research*, part of NatCen, Deputy Director of CREST, and Professor of Politics at Strathclyde University. Pippa Norris is the McGuire Lecturer in Comparative Politics at the John F Kennedy School of Government, Harvard University and is currently working on secondment as the Director of the Democratic Governance Group at the United Nations Development Program in New York.

Hauben, 1997; Wellman and Gulia, 1999; Wellman *et al.*, 2001; Horrigan, 2002).

These arguments, though, do not address the possible impact of the internet on face-to-face communication. It is often argued that face-to-face communication helps develop bonds of trust and reciprocity between individuals in a manner that no other form of communication can achieve (Putnam, 2000; though for a dissenting view see Uslaner, 2002). Such bonds, fostered by and embedded in social networks, provide a stock of 'social capital' that helps make societies healthier, more caring and more efficient. Thus, whether or not the internet makes it easier for people to organise face-to-face meetings rather than just maintain electronic contact with those living far away is a vital question. Certainly, those who are optimistic about the impact of the internet think it does. After all, it can be used to make an appointment to meet a friend in the local pub or to advertise and encourage people to attend a communal social activity. Moreover, friends initially made on-line may subsequently be met face to face. In short, the ability to engage in 'on-line' social activity could help to stimulate greater 'off-line' social activity too (Robinson *et al.*, 2000; Shah *et al.*, 2001; Hampton and Wellman, 2002) – with consequential beneficial impacts on the stock of social capital

On the other hand 'on-line' activity could serve to displace 'off-line' activity. Those engaged in a virtual network may spend less time participating in their local social networks. Even if they are not particularly predisposed to withdraw from face-to-face contact, time spent on the internet is time not spent doing something else, and one of the activities that might be displaced is socialising with friends and family (Nie and Erbring, 2000; Nie, 2001). Similar arguments have been, indeed, previously made about the growth in the second half of the 20th century of television watching (Steiner, 1963, Putnam, 2000); but whereas watching television can, in fact, be turned into a communal activity, using a computer is usually a solitary activity. Indeed, it has been argued that the solitary nature of internet use may result in people becoming lonely and depressed, thereby undermining their ability to form or sustain friendships (Kraut *et al.*, 1998).

In this chapter we examine which, if either, of these perspectives appears to be correct so far as Britain's experience of the internet to date is concerned. In particular, we are interested in the impact of the internet on, first, face-to-face social interaction with family and friends and through involvement in community organisations, and, second, on the incidence of social trust and social capital, phenomena that, according to Putnam at least, are engendered by such social face-to-face interactions. In so doing we bring a fresh body of evidence to a debate that is so far largely dominated by data from North America (though see Gardner and Oswald, 2001), the generalisability of which to the rest of the world is far from certain.[1]

The chapter thus falls into two main parts. In the first part we look at whether users of the internet are more or less likely to engage in social activity with friends and family, and whether or not they are more or less likely to join or get involved in the activities of community organisations. In short, this section asks what impact, if any, does access to the internet have on the degree to which people in Britain are engaged in face-to-face interaction? In the second part we ask what impact, if any, the advent of the internet has had on the stock of social capital, whether through its influence on face-to-face interaction or otherwise. In particular, we consider whether those who use the internet are more or less trusting of their fellow citizens than others, and whether they feel able to call upon their neighbours when in need – that is, how they might feel in certain everyday situations where the existence of social capital might well help to overcome life's difficulties.

However, one important issue that we will have constantly to keep in mind is that users of the internet are not representative of the British public at large. If, say, we find that users of the internet are more likely to socialise with friends than non-users, this alone does not demonstrate that access to the internet encourages face-to-face contact. It may simply be the case that the kind of people who use the internet are the kind of people who are more likely to socialise with friends anyway – and that this was true even before they had access to the internet. We thus use both multivariate analysis that takes into account the difference between the social character of internet users and non-users, and looking at trends over time amongst different categories of internet users, to try and unravel the direction of the relationship between internet use and socialising, membership of organisations, social trust and social capital.[2] But as a prelude to our two analyses we should examine the demographic profile of internet users nowadays, and how this has changed over recent years.

Who uses the internet?

Five years ago, users of the internet still constituted no more than a minority of British adults, comprising just one in three of the population (see Table 10.1).

Table 10.1 Growth of internet use, 2000–2005

	2000	2003	2005
	%	%	%
Access at home and use internet	26	41	53
No access at home and use internet	7	9	8
Total users	33	50	61
Access at home and don't use internet	9	10	8
No access at home and don't use internet	57	40	31
Total non-users	66	50	39
Base	*2293*	*4432*	*4268*

Now a clear majority use the internet – just over three in five. The growth in use has been entirely fuelled by an increase in the proportion of people who have access to the internet at home.[3] Less than one in ten use the internet despite not having access at home, a figure that has changed little over the last five years. Indeed, as many people (37 per cent) now live in households that have broadband access to the internet as five years ago lived in households with any kind of access to the internet (36 per cent).

Nevertheless, those with access to the internet remain highly unrepresentative of British society as a whole. Users of the internet continue to be disproportionately younger and well educated, while male users continue to outnumber female ones somewhat (see Table 10.2). Indeed, while there is some evidence that those aged between 35 and 54 have been catching up to some degree with younger people in their level of internet use (something we would expect to happen eventually anyway as younger people enter middle age), the level of use remains very low (at less than one in five) amongst those aged 65 and older. Indeed, the difference between older people and younger people in their level of internet use is even wider now than it was five years ago. Equally, the internet revolution seems largely to be leaving those without any educational qualifications behind, too.

Table 10.2 Social profile of internet users

	2005	Base	Change since 2003	Change since 2000
Gender				
Men	60	1901	+7	+20
Women	54	2367	+6	+26
Age				
18–24	80	330	+6	+22
25–34	79	627	+10	+28
35–44	74	870	+9	+34
45–54	68	713	+17	+32
55–64	47	730	+11	+26
65+	18	996	+3	+13
Highest educational qualification				
Degree	90	681	+6	+18
HE below degree	74	521	+6	+27
A level	77	604	+8	+28
GCSE A–C	63	817	+10	+33
GCSE D–G	48	381	+10	+28
None	19	1166	+7	+10

Thus, so far, the rapid growth in internet use has done little to reduce the so-called 'digital divide' in Britain (see also Bromley, 2004). For our purposes in this chapter it means that we have to continue to bear in mind that if, say, younger people are more likely than older people to spend time with friends, then it is probably going to be true, too, that internet users are more likely to spend time with friends than non-users – and that this could simply be because internet users are disproportionately young rather than because of anything to do with their use of the internet itself. We have, if possible, to take into account the socially unrepresentative nature of internet users before drawing any conclusions about the impact of the internet itself.

Indeed, this understates our difficulty. If the internet does have any impact on the degree to which people interact with others face to face, we might expect its effect to be most evident amongst those who have been using the internet longest. It is they, after all, who have been 'exposed' to the internet for the greatest period of time, while in practice they also tend to spend more time on the internet than do other users.[4] Yet it is this group that is the least socially representative of all. For example, we can establish from Table 10.2 that while overall more men use the internet than women, those who have started to use the internet over the last two years comprise more or less equal numbers of men and women. Equally, the educational profile of more recent internet users is if anything slightly skewed towards those whose highest qualification is a GCSE or its equivalent – whereas graduates are strongly over-represented amongst those who have been using the internet for five years or more.

Meeting friends and family

One approach to trying to determine whether the internet has an impact on the amount of time that people spend talking face to face with other people is to ask people themselves (Nie and Erbring, 2000; see also Dutton *et al.*, 2005). Doing so reveals that there is a widespread impression that the internet can have a deleterious impact on face-to-face contact. Overall no less than 44 per cent agree that "using the internet a lot makes people less likely to go out and talk to other people" while only 24 per cent disagree. However, support for this proposition is lower amongst longer-term users of the internet than it is amongst the remainder of the population. Only 40 per cent of those who have used the internet for five or more years agree with it compared with 48 per cent of non-users and – intriguingly – 52 per cent of those who have used the internet for less than two years. Equally, those who use the internet most heavily, that is for five or more hours a week (other than for work) are less likely to agree, too, with only 37 per cent doing so.[5]

The problem with this approach, however, is that internet users may not be aware of – or perhaps may prefer to conceal – the impact that their use of the internet is having on themselves and fellow users. A better approach is to ask people how often they spend time socialising with friends and family, and then try to establish whether there are any differences between the answers given by those who use the internet and those who do not (after, of course, taking into account what we have seen are their distinctive social characteristics). We thus asked all respondents to the 2005 *British Social Attitudes* survey how often they spent time with, first, members of their family or other relatives (excluding any with whom they actually live) and, second, friends. Overall, such socialising appears to be quite common. As many as 61 per cent said that they spent time with other family members around once a week or more, while 60 per cent said they spent time with friends. Britain is evidently not an atomised society in this respect.

Table 10.3 Time spent with family and friends, and length of internet use

	Length of internet use			
% who spend time each week with …	**Non-users**	**Less than 2 years**	**2–5 years**	**More than 5 years**
Family or other relatives	65	62	63	53
Friends	54	62	64	62
Base	*1064*	*249*	*626*	*707*

Even so, at first glance at least, there appears to be some sign that long-term users of the internet are less likely to spend time with other family members. As Table 10.3 shows, only just over half of those who have used the internet for more than five years say that they spend time weekly with other family members compared with nearly two-thirds of the remainder of the population. However, this is an example of where we have to bear in mind the distinctive social profile of long-term internet users. Disproportionately consisting of graduates, many of whom sell their labour in a national rather than a local labour market, members of this group are particularly likely to live some distance from other relatives. Only 24 per cent say that most of their relatives and family members live in the same local neighbourhood or area as themselves while as many as 45 per cent say that most live elsewhere. In contrast, at 42 per cent and 31 per cent respectively, the equivalent figures for those who do not use the internet at all exhibit the reverse pattern. And, unsurprisingly, those who say that most of their relatives live close by are far more likely to say that they spend time with them weekly (84 per cent do so) than are those whose relatives largely live further away (34 per cent). When this pattern is taken into account the relationship between long-term use of the internet and time spent with relatives simply disappears.[6]

Moreover, there is little evidence to support the argument that those who spend most time on the internet are particularly less likely to spend time with family. Amongst those who use the internet for five or more hours a week, 56 per cent say they spend time weekly with family, only a little below the 60 per cent figure reported by those who spend no more than an hour a week. Such difference as does exist is again easily accounted for by the fact that the family of heavier users of the internet are more likely to live further away.

Meanwhile, it will be noted from Table 10.3 that if anything it is those that do not use the internet who are less likely to say they spend time at least once a week with friends. However, this simply reflects the markedly older age profile of internet non-users and the fact that older people in general are less likely to spend time with friends. Moreover, those who spend most time on the internet are almost just as likely to say they spend time with friends weekly (62 per cent) as are those who spend least time (64 per cent).

Table 10.4 Trends in time spent with family and friends, by internet use, 2003–2005

% who spend time each week with...	Non-users in 2003/Non-users in 2005 or used less than 2 years in 2005			Users in 2003/Users for more than 2 years in 2005		
	2003	2005	Change 2003–2005	2003	2005	Change 2003–2005
Family or other relatives	66	64	-2	61	58	-3
Friends	60	56	-4	67	63	-4
Base	1369	1313		1378	1333	

We in fact asked exactly the same questions about how much time people spend with family and friends in the 2003 *British Social Attitudes* survey, as indeed we also did with our questions about use of the internet (Curtice and Norris, 2004). We can therefore compare our results in 2005 with those obtained two years earlier. In particular, we can compare our 2005 results for all those who have been using the internet for two or more years with those for everyone who was using the internet two years earlier in 2003. If we assume that few people stop being internet users once they have started, then these two groups constitute the same set of people.[7] At the same time we can also compare the figures in our 2005 survey for those who either do not use the internet at all or who have only done so for less than two years with those who in 2003 were not internet users at all. If the internet makes a difference to the amount of face to face contact that people have then the difference between the 2003 and 2005 readings for the first of these two groups – that is, the one that has used the internet longest – should be dissimilar to the equivalent difference for the other group (one consisting of those with little if any experience of the internet).

Table 10.4 undertakes this comparison. In the first column we show the proportion of all non-users of the internet in 2003 who in that same year said that they spent time with family and friends each week. In the second column we show the equivalent 2005 figure for those who in 2005 were either not users of the internet or had been users for less than two years. The third column shows the difference between these two figures. The remaining columns then undertake the equivalent analysis for those who were internet users in 2003 and those who by 2005 had been users for more than two years. The crucial point to note from this table is that while there has been a small decline in time spent with family and friends, in both cases this decline is more or less exactly the same amongst longer-term internet users as it is amongst short-term or non-users. There is no apparent evidence here of the internet having had any impact in either direction on the incidence of face to face interaction.

Joining in

We now turn to a second potential indicator of the degree to which people interact with others. This is involvement in a community organisation, an important means by which social capital is generated according to Putnam. Moreover, as previously noted, Putnam has argued that the advent of television has helped bring about a decline in such involvement – and has suggested that the same might indeed be true of the internet (Putnam, 2000: Ch. 13). Putnam's claim about the impact of television is itself far from uncontested (Norris, 1996, 2000; Uslaner, 1998; Newton, 1999), so whether or not the internet is implicated needs to be considered carefully.

In order to acquire a measure of involvement in community organisations, we presented respondents with a card that listed a wide range of types of organisation ranging from an environmental group to a sports club to a group for older people such as a lunch club.[8] While some of the kinds of organisation that we listed (such as trade unions) might be national in scope rather than necessarily local, all were ones that would usually be expected to have a network of local branches. Membership of them was thus likely to provide an opportunity to interact face to face with other members. In any event, having presented respondents with the card we then asked them:

> *Are you currently a member of, or do you regularly join in the activities of, any of the organisations on this card?*

It should be noted that our question asked respondents to identify any organisation of which they were a 'member' and not just any in which they were active (irrespective of whether or not they were formally a 'member'). However, many of the kinds of organisation that we listed were ones, such as a sports club, where most members would be expected to be active. We thus anticipate that, in practice, those who indicated one or more memberships are relatively likely actually to be active in a local community organisation.

Overall, just over half (54 per cent) indicated membership of, or involvement with, at least one of our kinds of organisation. Some, of course, belonged to more than one, but as the average respondent only belonged to one organisation, multiple memberships were not common. But more importantly, as the first row of Table 10.5 shows, those who have been users of the internet for more than five years were most likely to say they were a member of at least one organisation (66 per cent did so) while non-users were least likely (just 43 per cent). Of the various kinds of organisation that we listed, only in the case of social clubs/working men's clubs, women's organisations and groups for older people were non-users of the internet more likely to be members. There seems little reason here to fear that the advent of the internet has undermined community activism.[9]

Indeed, if anything, our evidence would seem to support the claim that access to the internet makes it easier for under-resourced community groups to organise effectively (Etzioni, 1993; Tsagarousianou et al., 1998; but see also Bimber, 1998). Certainly, as we can see from the remaining rows in Table 10.5, the longer that someone has been a user of the internet the more likely they are to report both that they are aware that at least one of the groups to which they belong uses the internet to keep in contact with its members and that they themselves use the internet to keep in touch with groups to which they belong. Perhaps the longer that someone uses the internet the more likely it is that the on-line world stimulates them into off-line activity.

Table 10.5 Membership of organisations, by length of internet use

	Length of internet use			
	Non-users	Less than 2 years	2–5 years	More than 5 years
% member of at least one group	43	55	55	66
% use internet to keep in touch with group(s) they belong to	-	8	14	24
% say any group(s) they belong to uses internet to keep in contact	13	23	32	44
Base	1317	292	715	843

We do, of course, need to remember the distinctive social profile of long-term internet users. They are disproportionately well educated, a group that in general is more likely to get involved in local organisational activity (Curtice and Seyd, 2003; Pattie et al., 2004). On the other hand they are also disproportionately younger – not a group known for its community involvement. Indeed, when we undertake a multivariate analysis of the relationship between internet use and membership of at least one organisation while taking into account the varying propensity of people in different social groups to be members (details of which can be found in the appendix to this chapter), we still find that length of internet use is significantly associated with membership of an organisation.

Still, it may be that people's propensity to join and get involved in community organisations irrespective of their use of the internet is not adequately taken into account by our measures of social background. Perhaps those who were first to become internet users were simply the kind of people who have always been more inclined to be 'joiners' (Uslaner, 2004). We would feel more secure in arguing that using the internet actually increased involvement in community organisations if we could demonstrate that such involvement is greater amongst longer-term internet users now than it was in the past.

Table 10.6 Membership of organisations, by internet use, 2003–2005

	Non-users in 2003/Non-users in 2005 or used less than 2 years in 2005			Users in 2003/Users for more than 2 years in 2005		
	2003	2005	Change 2003–2005	2003	2005	Change 2003–2005
Member of at least one group	46	48	+2	61	64	+3
Base	*1656*	*1609*		*1641*	*1558*	

Table 10.6, however, suggests that this is not possible. Undertaking exactly the same kind of analysis we performed earlier in Table 10.4, it shows that there has indeed been a three point increase since 2003 in the proportion of longer-term internet users who are members of at least one group. But at the same time a similar two-point increase has also occurred amongst those who are still non-users or who have only started to use the internet within the previous two years. It thus seems quite possible that longer-term internet users have always been more involved in their community rather than that access to the internet has resulted in them becoming substantially more active.

Social trust and social capital

We now turn to the second main task of this chapter, that is, to establish what impact, if any, the internet has had on the stock of social capital. First we look at the incidence of a phenomenon that is thought to be vital if social capital is to be maintained and created, that is, the degree to which people trust each other. We asked two questions to assess this. The first is perhaps the best known indicator of 'social trust', being a question that has been asked regularly on the

General Social Survey in the US and analysis of which played a key role in Putnam's claim that social trust and social capital have declined in that country (Putnam, 2000). It reads:

Generally speaking, would you say that most people can be trusted, or that you can't be too careful in dealing with people?

Those who are inclined to trust their fellow human beings are expected to answer that they think most people can be trusted. Meanwhile, our second question asks:

How often do you think that people would try to take advantage of you if they got the chance and how often would they try to be fair?

Try to take advantage almost all of the time

Try to take advantage most of the time

Try to be fair most of the time

Try to be fair almost all of the time

Those who tend to trust others would be expected to say that people try to be fair most or almost all of the time.

Table 10.7 shows that in fact the proportion who answer these questions in a manner that suggests they are inclined to trust other people has changed little in recent years. Around 45 per cent have consistently said that "most people can be trusted" – an apparent decline in 2002 had been reversed by the time of our most recent survey. Indeed, not dissimilar figures of 43 per cent and 44 per cent respectively were also obtained by the first two rounds of the World Values Survey in Britain, conducted earlier than the surveys in Table 10.7, that is, in 1981 and 1990 respectively (Hall, 1999). Only a much earlier reading, taken as long ago as 1959 by Almond and Verba's Civic Culture study, has ever produced a markedly higher figure of 59 per cent (Almond and Verba, 1963).

Table 10.7 Trends in social trust, 1997–2005

	1997	1998	2000	2002	2004	2005
% think most people can be trusted	42	44	45	39	n/a	45
Base	*1355*	*2071*	*2293*	*2287*		*3167*
% think people try to be fair almost all/most of the time	n/a	57	56	n/a	55	66
Base		*1724*	*2008*		*1756*	*2646*

n/a = not asked

Of course, this still means that on this measure rather less than half seem inclined to trust others. However, on our alternative measure a clear majority have consistently said that people are either mostly or almost always fair in their dealings with others; indeed, this proportion is now at a record high of 66 per cent. In short, whatever impact the internet may have had on how trusting are those who use it, there is evidently little reason to believe that Putnam's claims about the decline of social trust have any validity in Britain (Hall, 1999)

Equally, there seems little reason to believe that the stock of social capital has declined in recent years. One of the advantages of living in a society where, for the most part, people trust each other is that they feel able to turn to others when they are in trouble or need help – thereby making it easier for them to overcome such difficulties when they do occur. To tap how far people feel able to turn to others for help – and, in particular, those living immediately around them – we asked three questions:

> Suppose you found your sink was blocked, but you did not have a plunger to unblock it. How comfortable would you be asking a neighbour to borrow a plunger?

> Suppose that you were ill in bed and needed someone to go to the chemist to collect your prescription while they were doing their shopping. How comfortable would you be asking a neighbour to do this?

> Suppose the milkman called for payment. The bill was £5 but you had no cash. How comfortable would you be asking a neighbour if you could borrow £5?

In each case the answers offered to respondents were "very comfortable", "fairly comfortable", "fairly uncomfortable" and "very uncomfortable". Table 10.8 shows for various occasions over the past seven years the proportion that has said they would feel "very comfortable" doing each of these things.

Not surprisingly, people are most likely to feel comfortable asking a neighbour to borrow a plunger, while they are by far the least likely to feel comfortable asking to borrow £5 to pay the milkman. Doubtless in the latter case, to the fear of refusal is added the embarrassment of having to admit not having any cash to hand. But in each case there is no consistent evidence of a continuous secular decline in the proportion who say that they feel "very comfortable". True, there is some evidence of decline since 2000, but the proportion feeling very comfortable in that year was apparently particularly high. In the case of borrowing a plunger and borrowing £5 to pay the milkman, at just over half and under a fifth respectively, the proportion who feel very comfortable is much the same now as it was in 1998. Only in respect of asking a neighbour to get a prescription does the most recent reading, at 40 per cent, seem particularly low as compared with earlier years.

Table 10.8 Trends in indicators of social capital, 1998–2005

% feel very comfortable asking neighbour...	1998	2000	2003	2005
To borrow plunger to unblock sink	53	60	53	52
To collect prescription when ill	47	54	45	40
To borrow £5 to pay milkman	18	22	18	19
Base	*2071*	*2293*	*3299*	*3167*

Still, even if the overall stock of social trust and social capital shows little decline, perhaps the internet has had some impact on those individuals who have been using it. If it has, then it would appear to have been a beneficial one. True, Table 10.9 reveals there is no consistent relationship between length of internet use and the proportion that feel that people try to be fair most or almost all of the time. But the longer that someone has been using the internet the more likely it is that they say that most people can be trusted.

Table 10.9 Social trust and length of internet use

	Length of internet use			
	Non-users	Less than 2 years	2–5 years	More than 5 years
% think most people can be trusted	38	40	50	53
Base	*1317*	*292*	*715*	*843*
% think people try to be fair almost all/most of the time	65	61	65	68
Base	*1064*	*249*	*626*	*707*

Moreover, this latter relationship is not simply the result of the distinctive social character of those who have used the internet longest. Certainly, if we undertake a multivariate analysis of whether our respondents felt that most people can be trusted rather than feeling that you cannot be too careful in dealing with people, those who have used the internet for two or more years are significantly more likely to say that most people can be trusted than are those who are not internet users. (Further details can be found in the appendix to this chapter.) Indeed, as we would anticipate from Putnam, those who belong to at least one group and those who spend time at least once a week with friends are more likely to say most people can be trusted. And, as we saw earlier, both of these qualities are more common amongst longer-term users of the internet. However, this relationship between internet use and trust still remains in place even when these other factors are taken into account.[10.]

However, when we look at how levels of social trust have changed over time amongst different categories of internet users, we do not get any confirmation that levels of social trust have increased particularly markedly amongst those who have used the internet longest. In Table 10.10 we perform much the same kind of analysis that we first undertook at Table 10.4 except that we can undertake our analysis over a five-year period rather than a two-year one. Thus in the first three columns of Table 10.10 we show for 2000 the level of social trust (on both our measures) amongst those who were not using the internet that year, the equivalent figures for 2005 amongst those in that year who either were not internet users at all or had been using it for less than five years, followed by the difference between these two figures. In the final three columns we undertake the equivalent analysis for those who were internet users in 2000 and those who had been users for five or more years in 2005.

We can see that on our first measure the level of social trust held steady between 2000 and 2005 amongst both groups. Meanwhile, although the proportion who feel that people try to be fair most or almost all of the time rose between 2000 and 2005 by eight points amongst longer-term internet users, it rose by even more amongst those who either were non-users or had only used the internet for a shorter period of time. We thus cannot safely rule out the possibility that those who have become internet users were more likely to trust others even before they started to use the internet, and that, indeed, their willingness to interact with others over the internet is but a reflection of their pre-existing higher level of trust.

Table 10.10 Social trust by internet use, 2000–2005

	Non-users in 2000/Non-users or used less than 5 years in 2005			Users in 2000/Users for more than 5 years in 2005		
	2000	2005	Change 2000–2005	2000	2005	Change 2000–2005
% most people can be trusted	42	42	0	52	53	+1
Base	1595	2324		684	843	
% people try to be fair most/almost all of the time	53	64	+11	60	68	+8
Base	1390	1939		613	707	

In any event, there is not any evidence that the higher level of social trust amongst longer-term internet users translates into being more likely to have a stock of social capital to draw upon in time of need (see Table 10.11). Indeed, so far as asking a neighbour to collect a prescription is concerned longer-term users of the internet are actually less likely to say that they would feel "very comfortable". In fact, multivariate analysis (not shown) reveals that this is for one very simple reason – because younger people (who are more likely to be internet users) are far less likely to say they would feel very comfortable asking a neighbour to collect a prescription. Thus, for example, whereas as many as 57 per cent of those aged 65 plus say they would feel very comfortable, only 22 per cent of those aged 18–24 would be. Perhaps, in part, this is because an older person may be more likely to think that a neighbour would accept they might need help if they are ill, but doubtless it also reflects the fact that younger people are more likely to be geographically mobile and thus less likely to know their neighbours well. Indeed, much the same pattern is also true in respect of our other two indicators of social capital and, in fact, once we take the differences in their age composition into account, those who have used the internet for five years or more are significantly *more* likely than those who do not use the internet at all to say that they are very comfortable asking a neighbour to borrow either a plunger or £5 to pay the milkman.

Table 10.11 Indicators of social capital by length of internet use

% feel very comfortable asking neighbour …	Non-users	Length of internet use		
		Less than 2 years	2–5 years	More than 5 years
To borrow plunger to unblock sink	51	54	54	52
To collect prescription when ill	47	45	38	34
To borrow £5 to pay milkman	21	19	17	16
Base	*1317*	*292*	*715*	*843*

Again, however, looking at trends over time amongst different categories of internet users does not sustain any claim that long-term internet users are more likely to feel comfortable asking their neighbour for help simply because they are an internet user. Table 10.12 shows what proportion of those who are now long-term users felt very comfortable asking a neighbour for help during the course of the last five years and how this compares with the equivalent trend amongst the rest of the population. In fact, if anything, the proportion who feel very comfortable asking for help has fallen rather more over the last five years amongst those who are now long-term internet users than it has amongst the remainder of the population – though even here the pattern is not entirely consistent.

Table 10.12 Indicators of social capital, by internet use, 2000–2005

% feel very comfortable asking neighbour...	Non-users in 2000/Non-users or used less than 3 years in 2003/Non-users or used less than 5 years 2005				Users in 2000/Users 3 or more years in 2003/Users 5 or more years in 2005			
	'00	'03	'05	Change 2000–2005	'00	'03	'05	Change 2000–2005
To borrow plunger to unblock sink	60	53	52	-8	62	54	52	-10
To collect prescription when ill	56	46	43	-13	51	41	34	-17
To borrow £5 to pay milkman	23	18	19	-4	19	17	16	-3
Base	1595	2412	2324		684	815	843	

Conclusions

Our analysis has certainly failed to implicate the internet of responsibility for any significant erosion of social ties in Britain. We have been unable to demonstrate that longer-term or heavy use of the internet leads people to spend less time face to face with friends and family, to be less likely to get involved in local organisations, or to distrust other people. If anything, the picture we have found is one that suggests that internet users are more likely to be socially connected, not less. In particular, they seem more likely to be joiners and to trust other people.

However, it is doubtful whether we should interpret our data to mean that access to electronic connections stimulates social connections. Given the difficulties there are in demonstrating that differences between the social ties of internet users and non-users are a *cause* of the differences we have found rather than a *consequence*, we would want to be able to demonstrate not only that these differences still exist when we control for as wide a range as possible of other potential influences on the strength of someone's social connections, but also that when we compare internet users with non-users over time, a distinctive trend towards stronger social ties is evident amongst the former. Not once in this chapter have we been able to demonstrate that both these patterns are evident.

In truth it would appear to make more sense to regard the internet as a facility that people integrate into their social lives according to their pre-existing motivations and preferences – and as something that perhaps then makes it easier for them to act effectively on those motivations and preferences – rather than as something that changes social lives (Wellman *et al.*, 2001; Katz and

Rice, 2002; Wellman and Haythornthwaite, 2002). Technological change does not necessarily change human beings – but human beings certainly shape how technological innovations are used.

Notes

1. Quan-Haase and Wellman (2004), for example, note that the use of the internet to facilitate socialising is far lower in Catalonia than in the United States or Hong Kong. Meanwhile, involvement in communal organisations has long been a more important feature of civic life in the USA than in Britain.
2. For a more extended discussion of the advantages and disadvantages of these two approaches see Curtice and Norris (2004).
3. Note that these figures exclude use of the internet for work purposes. In fact, in 2005 just two per cent said that they used the internet at work but did not use it for any other purpose. These respondents are regarded as users of the internet in later analyses in this chapter.
4. Those who have used the internet for five or more years claim on average to spend 6.3 hours a week on the internet (other than for their work). In contrast, those who have used the internet for two or less years, on average spend only 3.3 hours a week on the internet, while those who have been internet users for between two and five years spend 4.7 hours a week.
5. There is, however, widespread recognition of how the internet may be put to use to keep in touch with people you would not otherwise meet. No less than 70 per cent agree (and only 10 per cent disagree) that "the internet helps people keep in touch with people who they could not normally talk to very often". This perception is even more common amongst those who have used the internet the longest and amongst those who use it most.
6. This comment is based on the results of a logistic regression of whether a respondent reported spending time with relatives weekly or not, where apart from length of internet use respondent's social background as well as distance lived from relatives were included as independent variables.
7. Indeed, the proportions who in our 2005 survey fall into our three categories of length of use are not dissimilar to what we would expect given the growth of internet use over the last five years as detailed in Table 10.1. Thirty per cent said they had used the internet for five or more years, 24 per cent for between two and five years and nine per cent for two years or less.
8. Full details of the list may be found at Qs 392–406 in the face to face questionnaire to be found at Appendix III at the back of this book.
9. We might note, too, that those who use the internet for five or more hours a week are no less likely than those who use it for one hour a week or less to claim membership of at least one community organisation.
10. As many as 51 per cent of those who belong to at least one organisation say that most people can be trusted compared with just 39 per cent of those who do not belong to any organisation. Equally, 49 per cent of those who spend time with friends once a week say that most people can be trusted, whereas only 39 per cent of

those who spend time with friends less often that this do so. This, of course, does not necessarily mean that spending time with friends or being involved in the activities of an organisation necessarily make people trustful; it may be those who trust others are more likely to spend time with friends or to get involved in organisations.

References

Almond, G. and Verba, S. (1963), *The Civic Culture: Political Attitudes and Democracy in Five Nations*, Princeton, NJ: Princeton University Press

Bimber, B. (1998), 'The internet and political transformation: Populism, community and accelerated pluralism', *Polity*, **30**: 133–160

Bromley, C. (2004), 'Can Britain close the digital divide?', in Park, A., Curtice, J., Thomson, K., Bromley, C. and Phillips, M. (eds.), *British Social Attitudes: the 21st Report*, London: Sage

Curtice, J. and Norris, P. (2004), 'e-politics? The impact of the internet on political trust and participation', in Park, A., Curtice, J., Thomson, K., Bromley, C. and Phillips, M. (eds.), *British Social Attitudes: the 21st Report*, London: Sage

Curtice, J. and Seyd, B. (2003), 'Is there a crisis of political participation', in Park, A., Curtice, J., Thomson, K., Jarvis, L. and Bromley, C. (eds.), *British Social Attitudes: the 20th Report – Continuity and change over two decades*, London: Sage

Dutton, W., di Gennaro, C. and Hargrave, A. (2005), *The Oxford Internet Survey (Oxis) Report 2005: The Internet in Britain*, Oxford: Oxford Internet Institute

Etzioni, A. (1993), *The spirit of community*, New York: Crown Publications

Gardner, J. and Oswald, A. (2001), 'Internet use: The digital divide', in Park, A., Curtice, J., Thomson, K., Jarvis, L. and Bromley, C. (eds.), *British Social Attitudes: the 18th report: Public Policy, Social Ties*, London: Sage

Hall, P. (1999), 'Social Capital in Britain', *British Journal of Political Science*, **29**: 417–462

Hampton, R. and Wellman, B. (2002), 'The not so global village of a cyber society: contact and support beyond Netville', in Haythornthwaite, C. and Wellman, B. (eds.), *The Internet in Everyday Life*, Oxford: Blackwell

Hauben, M. and Hauben, R. (1997), *Netizens*, Los Alamitos, Calif.: IEEE Computer Society Press

Horrigan, J. (2002), *Online communities: Networks that mature long-distance relationships and local ties*, Washington, DC: Pew Internet and American Life Study

Katz, J, and Rice, R. (2002), *Social Consequences of Internet Use: Access, Involvement and Interaction*, Cambridge, Mass.: MIT Press

Kraut, R., Patterson, M., Lundmark, V., Kiesler, S., Mukopadhyay, T. and Scherlis, W. (1998), 'Internet paradox: A social technology that reduces social involvement and psychological well-being?', *American Psychologist*, **53**: 1017–1031

Newton, K. (1999), 'Mass media effects: Mobilization or media malaise?', *British Journal of Political Science*, **27**: 577–599

Nie, N. (2001), 'Sociability, Interpersonal Relations and the Internet: Reconciling Conflicting Findings', *American Behavioral Scientist*, **45**: 420–435

Nie, N. and Erbring, L. (2000), *Internet and society: a preliminary report*, Stanford, Calif.: Stanford Institute for the Quantitative Study of Society

Norris, P. (1996), 'Does television erode social capital? A reply to Putnam', *PS: Political Science and Politics*, **29**: 474–480

Norris, P. (2000), *A virtuous circle: Political communication in postindustrial societies*, Cambridge: Cambridge University Press

Pattie, C., Seyd, P. and Whiteley, P. (2004), *Citizenship in Britain: Values, Participation and Democracy*, Cambridge: Cambridge University Press

Putnam, R. (2000), *Bowing Alone: The collapse and revival of American community*, New York: Simon & Schuster

Quan-Haase, A. and Wellman, B. (2004), 'How does the internet affect social capital?', in Huysman, M. and Wulf, V. (eds.), *Social Capital and Information Technology*, Cambridge, Mass.: MIT Press

Robinson, J., Kestnbaum, M., Neustadtl, A. and Alvarez, A. (2000), 'Mass Media Use and Social Life among Internet Users', *Social Science Computer Review*, **18**: 490–501

Shah, D., Kwak, N. and Holbert, R. (2001), '"Connecting" and "disconnecting" with social life: Patterns of internet use and social capital', *Political Communication*, **18**: 141–162

Steiner, G. (1963), *The people look at television: a study of audience attitudes*, New York: Knopf

Tsagarousianou, R., Tambini, D. and Bryan, C. (1998), *Cyberdemocracy*, London: Routledge

Uslaner, E. (1998), 'Social capital, television and the "mean world": Trust, optimism and civic participation', *Political Psychology*, **19**: 441–467

Uslaner, E. (2002), *The moral foundations of trust*, New York: Cambridge University Press

Uslaner, E. (2004), 'Trust, Civic Engagement and the Internet', *Political Communication*, **21**: 223–242

Wellman, B. and Gulia, M. (1999), 'Net surfers don't ride alone: virtual communities as communities', in Kollock, P. and Smith, M. (eds.), *Communities and Cyberspace*, New York: Routledge

Wellman, B. and Haythornthwaite, C. (eds.) (2002), *The Internet in Everyday Life*, Oxford: Blackwell

Wellman, B., Quan-Haase, A., White, J. and Hampton, K. (2001), 'Does the internet increase, decrease or supplement social capital? Social networks, participation, and community involvement', *American Behavioral Scientist*, **45**: 437–456

Acknowledgements

We are grateful to the Economic and Social Research Council's E-Society research programme for funding the module of questions on which this chapter is based (grant number RES–335–250–0010). Responsibility for the analysis of these data lies solely with the authors.

Appendix

The following tables show the results of two logistic regression analyses to which reference is made in the text. In each case a variable was only included in the model if overall it was significantly associated with the dependent variable at the five per cent level. Social class is measured using the National Statistics Socio-Economic Classification, about which further details may be found in Appendix I of this book.

Logistic regression of organisational membership (member of at least one group *versus* not a member of any group)

	Coefficient	Standard error
Age		
18–24	-0.89*	(.17)
25–34	-0.95*	(.15)
35–44	-0.69*	(.14)
45–54	-0.35*	(.14)
55–64	0.02	(.14)
(65 +)		
Highest educational qualification		
Degree	1.53*	(.16)
HE below degree	1.01*	(.15)
A level	1.16*	(.14)
GCSE A–C	0.72*	(.13)
GCSE D–G	0.67*	(.15)
(None)		
Social class (NS-SEC)		
Professional/managerial	0.13	(.11)
Intermediate	-0.10	(.13)
Small employers	-0.36*	(.15)
Supervisory/technical	-0.04	(.12)
(Routine/semi-routine)		
Internet user		
5+ years	0.57*	(.13)
2–5 years	0.24*	(.12)
Less than 2 years	0.42*	(.15)
(Non-user)		

* = significant at 5% level. N=3052. Nagelkerke R^2 = 13 per cent. Coefficients are simple contrast coefficients. In each case the category in brackets is the reference category

Logistic regression of social trust (most people can be trusted *versus* cannot be too careful in dealing with people)

	Coefficient	Standard error
Gender		
Male	0.28*	(.08)
(Female)	-0.68*	(.17)
Age		
18–24	-.68	(.17)
25–34	-0.55*	(.15)
35–44	-0.34*	(.14)
45–54	-0.14*	(.14)
55–64	-0.20	(.13)
(65 +)		
Highest educational qualification		
Degree	0.94*	(.15)
HE below degree	0.39*	(.15)
A level	0.49*	(.14)
GCSE A–C	-0.18*	(.13)
GCSE D–G	0.29	(.15)
(None)		
Social class (NS-SEC)		
Professional/managerial	0.34*	(.11)
Intermediate	0.29*	(.13)
Small employers	0.19	(.15)
Supervisory/technical	-0.20	(.13)
(Routine/semi-routine)		
Ethnic origin		
Black/Asian	-0.39*	(.15)
(White)		
Internet user		
5+ years	0.29*	(.12)
2–5 years	0.36*	(.12)
Less than 2 years	0.08	(.15)
(Non-user)		

* = significant at 5% level. N=3022. Nagelkerke R^2 = 9 per cent. Coefficients are simple contrast coefficients. In each case the category in brackets is the reference category

Appendix I
Technical details of the survey

In 2005, the sample for the *British Social Attitudes* survey was split into four sections: versions A, B C and D each made up a quarter of the sample. Depending on the number of versions in which it was included, each 'module' of questions was thus asked either of the full sample (4,268 respondents) or of a random quarter, half or three-quarters of the sample.

The structure of the questionnaire is shown at the beginning of Appendix III.

Sample design

The *British Social Attitudes* survey is designed to yield a representative sample of adults aged 18 or over. Since 1993, the sampling frame for the survey has been the Postcode Address File (PAF), a list of addresses (or postal delivery points) compiled by the Post Office.[1]

For practical reasons, the sample is confined to those living in private households. People living in institutions (though not in private households at such institutions) are excluded, as are households whose addresses were not on the PAF.

The sampling method involved a multi-stage design, with three separate stages of selection.

Selection of sectors

At the first stage, postcode sectors were selected systematically from a list of all postal sectors in Great Britain. Before selection, any sectors with fewer than 500 addresses were identified and grouped together with an adjacent sector; in Scotland all sectors north of the Caledonian Canal were excluded (because of the prohibitive costs of interviewing there). Sectors were then stratified on the basis of:

- 37 sub-regions
- population density with variable banding used, in order to create three equal-sized strata per sub-region
- ranking by percentage of homes that were owner-occupied.

Two hundred and eighty-six postcode sectors were selected, with probability proportional to the number of addresses in each sector.

Selection of addresses

Thirty addresses were selected in each of the 286 sectors. The issued sample was therefore 286 x 30 = 8,580 addresses, selected by starting from a random point on the list of addresses for each sector, and choosing each address at a fixed interval. The fixed interval was calculated for each sector in order to generate the correct number of addresses.

The Multiple-Occupancy Indicator (MOI) available through PAF was used when selecting addresses in Scotland. The MOI shows the number of accommodation spaces sharing one address. Thus, if the MOI indicates more than one accommodation space at a given address, the chances of the given address being selected from the list of addresses would increase so that it matched the total number of accommodation spaces. The MOI is largely irrelevant in England and Wales, as separate dwelling units generally appear as separate entries on PAF. In Scotland, tenements with many flats tend to appear as one entry on PAF. However, even in Scotland, the vast majority of MOIs had a value of one. The remainder, which ranged between three and 13, were incorporated into the weighting procedures (described below).

Selection of individuals

Interviewers called at each address selected from PAF and listed all those eligible for inclusion in the *British Social Attitudes* sample – that is, all persons currently aged 18 or over and resident at the selected address. The interviewer then selected one respondent using a computer-generated random selection procedure. Where there were two or more 'dwelling units' at the selected address, interviewers first had to select one dwelling unit using the same random procedure. They then followed the same procedure to select a person for interview within the selected dwelling unit.

Weighting

The *British Social Attitudes* survey has previously only been weighted to correct for the unequal selection of addresses, dwelling units (DU) and individuals. However, falling response in recent years prompted the introduction of non-response weights. This weighting was carried out in 2005; in addition to the selection weights, a set of weights were generated to correct for any biases due to differential non-response. The final sample was then calibrated to match the population in terms of age, sex and region.

Selection weights

Selection weights are required because not all the units covered in the survey had the same probability of selection. The weighting reflects the relative selection probabilities of the individual at the three main stages of selection: address, DU and individual. First, because addresses in Scotland were selected using the MOI, weights were needed to compensate for the greater probability of an address with an MOI of more than one being selected, compared to an address with an MOI of one. (This stage was omitted for the English and Welsh data.) Secondly, data were weighted to compensate for the fact that a DU at an address that contained a large number of DUs was less likely to be selected for inclusion in the survey than a DU at an address that contained fewer DUs. (We use this procedure because in most cases where the MOI is greater than one, the two stages will cancel each other out, resulting in more efficient weights.) Thirdly, data were weighted to compensate for the lower selection probabilities of adults living in large households, compared with those in small households.

At each stage the selection weights were trimmed to avoid a small number of very high or very low weights in the sample; such weights would inflate standard errors, reducing the precision of the survey estimates and causing the weighted sample to be less efficient. Less than one per cent of the sample was trimmed at each stage.

Non-response model

It is known that certain subgroups in the population are more likely to respond to surveys than others. These groups can end up over-represented in the sample, which can bias the survey estimates. Where information is available about non-responding households, the response behaviour of the sample members can be modelled and the results used to generate a non-response weight. This non-response weight is intended to reduce bias in the sample resulting from differential response to the survey.

The data was modelled using logistic regression, with the dependent variable indicating whether or not the selected individual responded to the survey. Ineligible households[2] were not included in the non-response modelling. A number of area level and interviewer observation variables were used to model response. Not all the variables examined were retained for the final model: variables not strongly related to a household's propensity to respond were dropped from the analysis.

The variables found to be related to response were Government Office Region (GOR), proportion of the local population from a minority ethnic group and proportion of households owner-occupied. The model shows that the propensity for a household to not respond increases if it is located in an area where a high proportion of the residents are from a non-white ethnic group. Response is lower in areas where a low proportion of households are owner-occupied and if households are located in the West Midlands, London or the South. The full model is given in Table A.1 below.

Table A.1 The final non-response model

Variable	B	S.E.	Wald	df	Sig.	Odds
% population non-white	0.01	0.00	12.5	1	0.000	1.01
% households owner-occupied	-0.01	0.00	11.3	1	0.001	0.99
Government Office Region			40.3	10	0.000	
East Midlands	0.20	0.12	2.7	1	0.100	1.22
East of England	0.03	0.11	0.1	1	0.800	1.03
London	-0.20	0.11	3.1	1	0.076	0.82
North East	0.38	0.15	6.9	1	0.009	1.47
North West	-0.01	0.10	0.0	1	0.933	0.99
Scotland	0.02	0.11	0.0	1	0.836	1.02
South East	-0.12	0.10	1.5	1	0.225	0.88
South West	-0.13	0.11	1.2	1	0.272	0.88
Wales	0.05	0.13	0.1	1	0.710	1.05
West Midlands	-0.33	0.11	8.8	1	0.003	0.72
Yorks. and The Humber					<baseline>	
Constant	0.10	0.14	0.5	1	0.476	1.11

Notes:
1. The response is 1 = individual responding to the survey, 0 = non response
2. Only variables that are significant at the 0.05 level are included in the model
3. The model R^2 is 0.017 (Cox and Snell)
4. **B** is the estimate coefficient with standard error **S.E.**
5. The **Wald**-test measures the impact of the categorical variable on the model with the appropriate number of degrees of freedom **df**. If the test is significant (**sig.** < 0.05) then the categorical variable is considered to be 'significantly associated' with the response variable and therefore included in the model

The non-response weight is calculated as the inverse of the predicted response probabilities saved from the logistic regression model. The non-response weight was then combined with the selection weights to create the final non-response weight. The top and bottom one per cent of the weight were trimmed before the weight was scaled to the achieved sample size (resulting in the weight being standardised around an average of one).

Calibration weighting

The final stage of the weighting was to adjust the final non-response weight so that the weighted respondent sample matched the population in terms of age, sex and region. Only adults aged 18 and over are eligible to take part in the survey, therefore the data have been weighted to the British population aged 18+ based on the 2004 mid-year population estimates from the Office for National Statistics/General Register Office for Scotland.

The survey data were weighted to the marginal age/sex and GOR distributions using raking-ratio (or rim) weighting. As a result, the weighted data should exactly match the population across these three dimensions. This is shown in Table A.2.

Table A.2 Weighted and unweighted sample distribution, by GOR, age and sex

	Population	Unweighted respondents	Respondents weighted by selection weight only	Respondents weighted by un-calibrated non-response weight	Respondents weighted by final weight
Govern-ment Office Region	%	%	%	%	%
East Midlands	7.4	7.9	7.9	7.1	7.4
East of England	9.5	10.6	11.0	10.6	9.5
London	12.8	9.6	9.8	11.5	12.8
North East	4.4	5.3	5.0	4.3	4.4
North West	11.6	12.8	12.7	12.4	11.6
Scotland	8.8	9.3	9.0	8.7	8.8
South East	14.0	13.8	14.2	14.3	14.0
South West	8.8	8.6	8.4	8.5	8.8
Wales	5.1	5.3	5.3	5.0	5.1
West Midlands	9.1	7.8	7.9	9.0	9.1
Yorks. and Humber	8.6	8.9	8.7	8.6	8.6

table continued on next page

	Population	Unweighted respondents	Respondents weighted by selection weight only	Respondents weighted by un-calibrated non-response weight	Respondents weighted by final weight
	%	%	%	%	%
Age and sex					
M 18–24	5.8	3.4	4.8	4.9	5.8
M 25–34	8.5	5.9	6.4	6.5	8.5
M 35–44	9.8	8.6	8.6	8.6	9.8
M 45–54	8.1	8.1	8.9	8.9	8.1
M 55–59	4.1	4.2	4.4	4.4	4.1
M 60–64	3.2	4.2	4.2	4.2	3.2
M 65+	8.8	10.1	9.3	9.2	8.8
F 18–24	5.6	4.4	5.4	5.5	5.6
F 25–34	8.5	8.8	8.3	8.3	8.5
F 35–44	9.9	11.7	11.5	11.6	9.9
F 45–54	8.3	8.6	9.4	9.3	8.3
F 55–59	4.2	4.6	4.6	4.5	4.2
F 60–64	3.3	4.1	3.9	3.9	3.3
F 65+	11.8	13.3	10.3	10.2	11.8
Total	*45,340,600*	*4,268*	*4,268*	*4,268*	*4,268*

The calibration weight is the final non-response weight to be used in the analysis of the 2005 survey; this weight has been scaled to the responding sample size. The range of the weights is given in Table A.3.

Table A.3 Range of weights

	N	Minimum	Mean	Maximum
DU and person selection weight	4,268	0.54	1.00	2.18
Un-calibrated non-response weight	4,268	0.47	1.00	2.39
Final calibrated non-response weight	4,268	0.36	1.00	3.34

Effective sample size

The effect of the sample design on the precision of survey estimates is indicated by the effective sample size (neff). The effective sample size measures the size of an (unweighted) simple random sample that would achieve the same precision (standard error) as the design being implemented. If the effective sample size is close to the actual sample size then we have an efficient design with a good level of precision. The lower the effective sample size is, the lower the level of precision. The efficiency of a sample is given by the ratio of the effective sample size to the actual sample size. Samples that select one person per household tend to have lower efficiency than samples that select all household members. The final calibrated non-response weights have an effective sample size (neff) of 3,494 and efficiency of 82 per cent.

All the percentages presented in this Report are based on weighted data.

Questionnaire versions

Each address in each sector (sampling point) was allocated to either the A, B, C or D portion of the sample. If one serial number was version A, the next was version B, the third version C and the fourth version D. Thus, each interviewer was allocated seven or eight cases from each of versions A, B, C and D. There were 2,145 issued addresses for each version.

Fieldwork

Interviewing was mainly carried out between June and September 2005, with a small number of interviews taking place in October and November.

Table A.4 Response rate on *British Social Attitudes*, 2005

	Number	%
Addresses issued	8,580	
Vacant, derelict and other out of scope	802	
In scope	7,778	100.0
Interview achieved	4,268	54.9
Interview not achieved	3,510	45.1
Refused[1]	2,743	35.3
Non-contacted[2]	424	5.5
Other non-response	342	4.4

1 'Refused' comprises refusals before selection of an individual at the address, refusals to the office, refusal by the selected person, 'proxy' refusals (on behalf of the selected respondent) and broken appointments after which the selected person could not be recontacted

2 'Non-contacted' comprises households where no one was contacted and those where the selected person could not be contacted

Fieldwork was conducted by interviewers drawn from the *National Centre for Social Research*'s regular panel and conducted using face-to-face computer-assisted interviewing.[3] Interviewers attended a one-day briefing conference to familiarise them with the selection procedures and questionnaires.

The mean interview length was 64 minutes for version A of the questionnaire, 73 minutes for version B, 75 minutes for version C and 68 minutes for version D.[4] Interviewers achieved an overall response rate of 55 per cent. Details are shown in Table A.4.

As in earlier rounds of the series, the respondent was asked to fill in a self-completion questionnaire which, whenever possible, was collected by the interviewer. Otherwise, the respondent was asked to post it to the *National Centre for Social Research*. If necessary, up to three postal reminders were sent to obtain the self-completion supplement.

A total of 709 respondents (17 per cent of those interviewed) did not return their self-completion questionnaire. Version A of the self-completion questionnaire was returned by 83 per cent of respondents to the face-to-face interview, version B by 80 per cent, version C by 85 per cent and version D by 86 per cent. As in previous rounds, we judged that it was not necessary to apply additional weights to correct for non-response.

Advance letter

Interviewers were supplied with letters describing the purpose of the survey and the coverage of the questionnaire, which they posted to sampled addresses before making any calls.[5]

Analysis variables

A number of standard analyses have been used in the tables that appear in this Report. The analysis groups requiring further definition are set out below. For further details see Stafford and Thomson (2006).

Region

The dataset is classified by the 12 Government Office Regions.

Standard Occupational Classification

Respondents are classified according to their own occupation, not that of the 'head of household'. Each respondent was asked about their current or last job, so that all respondents except those who had never worked were coded. Additionally, all job details were collected for all spouses and partners in work.

With the 2001 survey, we began coding occupation to the new Standard Occupational Classification 2000 (SOC 2000) instead of the Standard Occupational Classification 1990 (SOC 90). The main socio-economic grouping based on SOC 2000 is the National Statistics Socio-Economic Classification (NS-SEC). However, to maintain time-series, some analysis has continued to use the older schemes based on SOC 90 – Registrar General's Social Class, Socio-Economic Group and the Goldthorpe schema.

National Statistics Socio-Economic Classification (NS-SEC)

The combination of SOC 2000 and employment status for current or last job generates the following NS-SEC analytic classes:

- Employers in large organisations, higher managerial and professional
- Lower professional and managerial; higher technical and supervisory
- Intermediate occupations
- Small employers and own account workers
- Lower supervisory and technical occupations
- Semi-routine occupations
- Routine occupations

The remaining respondents are grouped as "never had a job" or "not classifiable". For some analyses, it may be more appropriate to classify respondents according to their current socio-economic status, which takes into account only their present economic position. In this case, in addition to the seven classes listed above, the remaining respondents not currently in paid work fall into one of the following categories: "not classifiable", "retired", "looking after the home", "unemployed" or "others not in paid occupations".

Registrar General's Social Class

As with NS-SEC, each respondent's Social Class is based on his or her current or last occupation. The combination of SOC 90 with employment status for current or last job generates the following six Social Classes:

I	Professional etc. occupations	
II	Managerial and technical occupations	'Non-manual'
III (Non-manual)	Skilled occupations	
III (Manual)	Skilled occupations	
IV	Partly skilled occupations	'Manual'
V	Unskilled occupations	

They are usually collapsed into four groups: I & II, III Non-manual, III Manual, and IV & V.

Socio-Economic Group

As with NS-SEC, each respondent's Socio-Economic Group (SEG) is based on his or her current or last occupation. SEG aims to bring together people with jobs of similar social and economic status, and is derived from a combination of employment status and occupation. The full SEG classification identifies 18 categories, but these are usually condensed into six groups:

- Professionals, employers and managers
- Intermediate non-manual workers
- Junior non-manual workers
- Skilled manual workers
- Semi-skilled manual workers
- Unskilled manual workers

As with NS-SEC, the remaining respondents are grouped as "never had a job" or "not classifiable".

Goldthorpe schema

The Goldthorpe schema classifies occupations by their 'general comparability', considering such factors as sources and levels of income, economic security, promotion prospects, and level of job autonomy and authority. The Goldthorpe schema was derived from the SOC 90 codes combined with employment status. Two versions of the schema are coded: the full schema has 11 categories; the 'compressed schema' combines these into the five classes shown below.

- Salariat (professional and managerial)
- Routine non-manual workers (office and sales)
- Petty bourgeoisie (the self-employed, including farmers, with and without employees)
- Manual foremen and supervisors
- Working class (skilled, semi-skilled and unskilled manual workers, personal service and agricultural workers)

There is a residual category comprising those who have never had a job or who gave insufficient information for classification purposes.

Industry

All respondents whose occupation could be coded were allocated a Standard Industrial Classification 2003 (SIC 03). Two-digit class codes are used. As with Social Class, SIC may be generated on the basis of the respondent's current occupation only, or on his or her most recently classifiable occupation.

Party identification

Respondents can be classified as identifying with a particular political party on one of three counts: if they consider themselves supporters of that party, as closer to it than to others, or as more likely to support it in the event of a general election (responses are derived from Qs. 237–239). The three groups are generally described respectively as *partisans*, *sympathisers* and *residual identifiers*. In combination, the three groups are referred to as 'identifiers'.

Attitude scales

Since 1986, the *British Social Attitudes* surveys have included two attitude scales which aim to measure where respondents stand on certain underlying value dimensions – left–right and libertarian–authoritarian.[6] Since 1987 (except 1990), a similar scale on 'welfarism' has been asked. Some of the items in the welfarism scale were changed in 2000–2001. The current version of the scale is listed below.

A useful way of summarising the information from a number of questions of this sort is to construct an additive index (DeVellis, 1991; Spector, 1992). This approach rests on the assumption that there is an underlying – 'latent' – attitudinal dimension which characterises the answers to all the questions within each scale. If so, scores on the index are likely to be a more reliable indication of the underlying attitude than the answers to any one question.

Each of these scales consists of a number of statements to which the respondent is invited to "agree strongly", "agree", "neither agree nor disagree", "disagree" or "disagree strongly".

The items are:

Left–right scale

Government should redistribute income from the better off to those who are less well off. *[Redistrb]*

Big business benefits owners at the expense of workers. *[BigBusnN]*

Ordinary working people do not get their fair share of the nation's wealth. *[Wealth]*[7]

There is one law for the rich and one for the poor. *[RichLaw]*

Management will always try to get the better of employees if it gets the chance. *[Indust4]*

Libertarian–authoritarian scale

Young people today don't have enough respect for traditional British values. *[TradVals]*

People who break the law should be given stiffer sentences. *[StifSent]*

For some crimes, the death penalty is the most appropriate sentence. *[DeathApp]*

Schools should teach children to obey authority. *[Obey]*

The law should always be obeyed, even if a particular law is wrong. *[WrongLaw]*

Censorship of films and magazines is necessary to uphold moral standards. *[Censor]*

Welfarism scale

The welfare state encourages people to stop helping each other. *[WelfHelp]*

The government should spend more money on welfare benefits for the poor, even if it leads to higher taxes. *[MoreWelf]*

Around here, most unemployed people could find a job if they really wanted one. *[UnempJob]*

Many people who get social security don't really deserve any help. *[SocHelp]*

Most people on the dole are fiddling in one way or another. *[DoleFidl]*

If welfare benefits weren't so generous, people would learn to stand on their own two feet. *[WelfFeet]*

Cutting welfare benefits would damage too many people's lives. *[DamLives]*

The creation of the welfare state is one of Britain's proudest achievements. *[ProudWlf]*

The indices for the three scales are formed by scoring the leftmost, most libertarian or most pro-welfare position as 1 and the rightmost, most authoritarian or most anti-welfarist position as 5. The "neither agree nor disagree" option is scored as 3. The scores to all the questions in each scale are added and then divided by the number of items in the scale, giving indices ranging from 1 (leftmost, most libertarian, most pro-welfare) to 5 (rightmost, most authoritarian, most anti-welfare). The scores on the three indices have been placed on the dataset.[8]

The scales have been tested for reliability (as measured by Cronbach's alpha). The Cronbach's alpha (unstandardised items) for the scales in 2005 are 0.80 for the left–right scale, 0.80 for the 'welfarism' scale and 0.75 for the libertarian–authoritarian scale. This level of reliability can be considered "very good" for the left–right and welfarism scales and "respectable" for the libertarian–authoritarian scale (DeVellis, 1991: 85).

Other analysis variables

These are taken directly from the questionnaire and to that extent are self-explanatory. The principal ones are:

Sex (Q. 41)
Age (Q. 42)
Household income (Q. 1394)
Economic position (Q. 993)
Religion (Q. 1143)
Highest educational qualification obtained (Qs. 1273–1274)
Marital status (Q. 135)
Benefits received (Qs. 1349–1387)

Sampling errors

No sample precisely reflects the characteristics of the population it represents, because of both sampling and non-sampling errors. If a sample were designed as a random sample (if every adult had an equal and independent chance of inclusion in the sample) then we could calculate the sampling error of any percentage, p, using the formula:

$$s.e. \ (p) = \sqrt{\frac{p(100 - p)}{n}}$$

where n is the number of respondents on which the percentage is based. Once the sampling error had been calculated, it would be a straightforward exercise to calculate a confidence interval for the true population percentage. For example, a 95 per cent confidence interval would be given by the formula:

$$p \pm 1.96 \ x \ s.e. \ (p)$$

Clearly, for a simple random sample (srs), the sampling error depends only on the values of p and n. However, simple random sampling is almost never used in practice because of its inefficiency in terms of time and cost.

As noted above, the *British Social Attitudes* sample, like that drawn for most large-scale surveys, was clustered according to a stratified multi-stage design into 286 postcode sectors (or combinations of sectors). With a complex design like this, the sampling error of a percentage giving a particular response is not simply a function of the number of respondents in the sample and the size of the percentage; it also depends on how that percentage response is spread within and between sample points.

The complex design may be assessed relative to simple random sampling by calculating a range of design factors (DEFTs) associated with it, where:

$$DEFT = \sqrt{\frac{\text{Variance of estimator with complex design, sample size n}}{\text{Variance of estimator with srs design, sample size n}}}$$

and represents the multiplying factor to be applied to the simple random sampling error to produce its complex equivalent. A design factor of one means that the complex sample has achieved the same precision as a simple random sample of the same size. A design factor greater than one means the complex sample is less precise than its simple random sample equivalent. If the DEFT for a particular characteristic is known, a 95 per cent confidence interval for a percentage may be calculated using the formula:

$$p \pm 1.96 \times complex\ sampling\ error\ (p)$$

$$= p \pm 1.96 \times DEFT \times \sqrt{\frac{p(100 - p)}{n}}$$

Calculations of sampling errors and design effects were made using the statistical analysis package STATA.

Table A.5 gives examples of the confidence intervals and DEFTs calculated for a range of different questions. Most background variables were fielded on the whole sample, whereas many attitudinal variables were asked only of a half or quarter of the sample; some were asked on the interview questionnaire and some on the self-completion supplement. The table shows that most of the questions asked of all sample members have a confidence interval of around plus or minus two to three per cent of the survey percentage. This means that we can be 95 per cent certain that the true population percentage is within two to three per cent (in either direction) of the percentage we report.

Variables with much larger variation are, as might be expected, those closely related to the geographic location of the respondent (for example, whether they live in a big city, a small town or a village). Here, the variation may be as large as five or six per cent either way around the percentage found on the survey. Consequently, the design effects calculated for these variables in a clustered sample will be greater than the design effects calculated for variables less strongly associated with area. Also, sampling errors for percentages based only on respondents to just one of the versions of the questionnaire, or on subgroups within the sample, are larger than they would have been had the questions been asked of everyone.

Table A.5 Complex standard errors and confidence intervals of selected variables

	% (p)	Complex standard error of p	95% confidence interval	DEFT	Base
Classification variables					
Q240 **Party identification (full sample)**					
Conservative	24.2	1.0	22.3–26.1	1.45	4268
Labour	39.8	1.0	38.0–41.7	1.26	4268
Liberal Democrat	12.8	0.7	11.5–14.1	1.27	4268
Q1129 **Housing tenure (full sample)**					
Owns	71.5	1.1	69.3–73.7	1.59	4268
Rents from local authority	10.6	0.7	9.3–12.0	1.41	4268
Rents privately/HA	16.3	0.9	14.7–18.0	1.51	4268
Q1143 **Religion (full sample)**					
No religion	39.6	1.0	37.7–41.6	1.31	4268
Church of England	26.4	0.9	24.6–28.2	1.35	4268
Roman Catholic	9.1	0.5	8.2–10.0	1.07	4268
Q1208 **Age of completing continuous full-time education (full sample)**					
16 or under	55.5	1.1	53.4–57.6	1.38	4268
17 or 18	18.6	0.7	17.2–19.9	1.16	4268
19 or over	21.6	0.8	20.1–23.1	1.24	4268
Q340 **Home internet access (full sample)**					
Yes	60.8	1.1	58.8–62.9	1.4	4268
No	39.2	1.1	37.1–41.2	1.4	4268
Q1130 **Urban or rural residence (1/2 sample)**					
A big city	34.3	2.0	30.3–38.3	1.98	2176
A small city/town	43.5	2.4	38.8–48.2	2.23	2176
Village/countryside	21.8	1.9	17.9–25.6	2.17	2176
Attitudinal variables (face-to-face interview)					
Q255 **Benefits for the unemployed are … (3/4 sample)**					
… too low	26.2	0.9	24.4–28.1	1.21	3193
… too high	50.2	1.1	48.1–52.3	1.20	3193
Q511 **NHS should be only available to those with lower incomes (3/4 sample)**					
Support a lot	9.4	0.6	8.2–10.5	1.15	3193
Support a little	14.7	0.7	13.2–16.1	1.17	3193
Oppose a little	15.4	0.8	13.8–17.0	1.27	3193
Oppose a lot	58.6	1.2	56.3–60.9	1.34	3193

table continued on next page

		% (p)	Complex standard error of p	95% confidence interval	DEFT	Base
Q258	**Government should (1/2 sample)**					
	Reduce taxes & spend less on health, education etc.	6.6	0.6	5.3–7.8	1.18	2166
	Keep taxes & spending as it is on health, education etc.	43.1	1.3	40.6–45.6	1.19	2166
	Increase taxes & spend more on health, education etc.	45.6	1.3	43.1–48.1	1.19	2166
Q492	**Concern that building roads could damage countryside (1/4 sample)**					
	Very concerned	24.4	1.4	21.6–27.2	1.09	1101
	Fairly concerned	51.5	1.7	48.1–54.9	1.15	1101
	Not very concerned	19.0	1.3	16.3–21.6	1.14	1101
	Not at all concerned	4.8	0.7	3.4–6.2	1.10	1101
Q1088	**Prejudiced against people of other races (1/4 sample)**					
	Very/a little	32.5	1.7	29.2–35.7	1.15	1075
	Not at all	65.3	1.7	62.1–68.6	1.14	1075

Attitudinal variables (self-completion)

		% (p)	Complex standard error of p	95% confidence interval	DEFT	Base
A72a B53a C34a D37a	**Government should redistribute income from the better off to those who are less well off (full sample)**					
	Agree strongly	6.4	0.5	5.5–7.3	1.13	3559
	Agree	25.8	0.9	24.1–27.5	1.18	3559
	Neither agree nor disagree	26.9	0.9	25.2–28.7	1.17	3559
	Disagree	31.4	0.9	29.7–33.1	1.11	3559
	Disagree strongly	7.9	0.5	6.9–8.9	1.11	3559
A38 C2 D5	**Government should top up wages for couples with children (3/4 sample)**					
	Should top up	57.6	1.2	55.3–59.9	1.22	2699
	Leave to the couple	30.7	1.1	28.5–32.9	1.25	2699
B37 C22	**View of voting in the general election (1/2 sample)**					
	Not worth voting	12.2	0.9	10.4–14.1	1.17	1732
	Should vote if care who wins	22.6	1.1	20.3–24.8	1.12	1732
	Duty to vote	64.1	1.3	61.5–66.7	1.15	1732
B6	**Satisfied with the way democracy works (1/4 sample)**					
	Very satisfied	9.2	1.1	7.1–11.3	1.08	860
	Fairly satisfied	61.9	1.9	58.2–65.6	1.11	860
	Not very satisfied	22.7	1.4	19.8–25.5	1.00	860
	Not at all satisfied	4.2	0.8	2.6–5.8	1.19	860

Analysis techniques

Regression

Regression analysis aims to summarise the relationship between a 'dependent' variable and one or more 'independent' variables. It shows how well we can estimate a respondent's score on the dependent variable from knowledge of their scores on the independent variables. It is often undertaken to support a claim that the phenomena measured by the independent variables *cause* the phenomenon measured by the dependent variable. However, the causal ordering, if any, between the variables cannot be verified or falsified by the technique. Causality can only be inferred through special experimental designs or through assumptions made by the analyst.

All regression analysis assumes that the relationship between the dependent and each of the independent variables takes a particular form. In *linear regression*, it is assumed that the relationship can be adequately summarised by a straight line. This means that a one percentage point increase in the value of an independent variable is assumed to have the same impact on the value of the dependent variable on average, irrespective of the previous values of those variables.

Strictly speaking the technique assumes that both the dependent and the independent variables are measured on an interval level scale, although it may sometimes still be applied even where this is not the case. For example, one can use an ordinal variable (e.g. a Likert scale) as a *dependent* variable if one is willing to assume that there is an underlying interval level scale and the difference between the observed ordinal scale and the underlying interval scale is due to random measurement error. Often the answers to a number of Likert-type questions are averaged to give a dependent variable that is more like a continuous variable. Categorical or nominal data can be used as *independent* variables by converting them into dummy or binary variables; these are variables where the only valid scores are 0 and 1, with 1 signifying membership of a particular category and 0 otherwise.

The assumptions of linear regression cause particular difficulties where the *dependent* variable is binary. The assumption that the relationship between the dependent and the independent variables is a straight line means that it can produce estimated values for the dependent variable of less than 0 or greater than 1. In this case it may be more appropriate to assume that the relationship between the dependent and the independent variables takes the form of an S-curve, where the impact on the dependent variable of a one-point increase in an independent variable becomes progressively less the closer the value of the dependent variable approaches 0 or 1. *Logistic regression* is an alternative form of regression which fits such an S-curve rather than a straight line. The technique can also be adapted to analyse multinomial non-interval level dependent variables, that is, variables which classify respondents into more than two categories.

The two statistical scores most commonly reported from the results of regression analyses are:

A measure of variance explained: This summarises how well all the independent variables combined can account for the variation in respondent's scores in the dependent variable. The higher the measure, the more accurately we are able in general to estimate the correct value of each respondent's score on the dependent variable from knowledge of their scores on the independent variables.

A parameter estimate: This shows how much the dependent variable will change on average, given a one-unit change in the independent variable (while holding all other independent variables in the model constant). The parameter estimate has a positive sign if an increase in the value of the independent variable results in an increase in the value of the dependent variable. It has a negative sign if an increase in the value of the independent variable results in a decrease in the value of the dependent variable. If the parameter estimates are standardised, it is possible to compare the relative impact of different independent variables; those variables with the largest standardised estimates can be said to have the biggest impact on the value of the dependent variable.

Regression also tests for the statistical significance of parameter estimates. A parameter estimate is said to be significant at the five per cent level if the range of the values encompassed by its 95 per cent confidence interval (see also section on sampling errors) are either all positive or all negative. This means that there is less than a five per cent chance that the association we have found between the dependent variable and the independent variable is simply the result of sampling error and does not reflect a relationship that actually exists in the general population.

Factor analysis

Factor analysis is a statistical technique which aims to identify whether there are one or more apparent sources of commonality to the answers given by respondents to a set of questions. It ascertains the smallest number of *factors* (or dimensions) which can most economically summarise all of the variation found in the set of questions being analysed. Factors are established where respondents who give a particular answer to one question in the set, tend to give the same answer as each other to one or more of the other questions in the set. The technique is most useful when a relatively small number of factors are able to account for a relatively large proportion of the variance in all of the questions in the set.

The technique produces a *factor loading* for each question (or variable) on each factor. Where questions have a high loading on the same factor, then it will be the case that respondents who give a particular answer to one of these questions tend to give a similar answer to the other questions. The technique is most commonly used in attitudinal research to try to identify the underlying ideological dimensions which apparently structure attitudes towards the subject in question.

International Social Survey Programme

The *International Social Survey Programme* (*ISSP*) is run by a group of research organisations, each of which undertakes to field annually an agreed module of questions on a chosen topic area. Since 1985, an *International Social Survey Programme* module has been included in one of the *British Social Attitudes* self-completion questionnaires. Each module is chosen for repetition at intervals to allow comparisons both between countries (membership is currently standing at over 40) and over time. In 2005, the chosen subject was Work Orientations, and the module was carried on the A version of the self-completion questionnaire (Qs. 1–36).

Notes

1. Until 1991 all *British Social Attitudes* samples were drawn from the Electoral Register (ER). However, following concern that this sampling frame might be deficient in its coverage of certain population subgroups, a 'splicing' experiment was conducted in 1991. We are grateful to the Market Research Development Fund for contributing towards the costs of this experiment. Its purpose was to investigate whether a switch to PAF would disrupt the time-series – for instance, by lowering response rates or affecting the distribution of responses to particular questions. In the event, it was concluded that the change from ER to PAF was unlikely to affect time trends in any noticeable ways, and that no adjustment factors were necessary. Since significant differences in efficiency exist between PAF and ER, and because we considered it untenable to continue to use a frame that is known to be biased, we decided to adopt PAF as the sampling frame for future *British Social Attitudes* surveys. For details of the PAF/ER 'splicing' experiment, see Lynn and Taylor (1995).
2. This includes households not containing any adults aged 18 and over, vacant dwelling units, derelict dwelling units, non-resident addresses and other deadwood.
3. In 1993 it was decided to mount a split-sample experiment designed to test the applicability of Computer-Assisted Personal Interviewing (CAPI) to the *British Social Attitudes* survey series. CAPI has been used increasingly over the past decade as an alternative to traditional interviewing techniques. As the name implies, CAPI involves the use of lap-top computers during the interview, with interviewers entering responses directly into the computer. One of the advantages of CAPI is that it significantly reduces both the amount of time spent on data processing and the number of coding and editing errors. There was, however, concern that a different interviewing technique might alter the distribution of responses and so affect the year-on-year consistency of *British Social Attitudes* data.

   Following the experiment, it was decided to change over to CAPI completely in 1994 (the self-completion questionnaire still being administered in the conventional way). The results of the experiment are discussed in *The 11th Report* (Lynn and Purdon, 1994).
4. Interview times recorded as less than 20 minutes were excluded, as these timings were likely to be errors.

5. An experiment was conducted on the 1991 *British Social Attitudes* survey (Jowell *et al.*, 1992) which showed that sending advance letters to sampled addresses before fieldwork begins has very little impact on response rates. However, interviewers do find that an advance letter helps them to introduce the survey on the doorstep, and a majority of respondents have said that they preferred some advance notice. For these reasons, advance letters have been used on the *British Social Attitudes* surveys since 1991.
6. Because of methodological experiments on scale development, the exact items detailed in this section have not been asked on all versions of the questionnaire each year.
7. In 1994 only, this item was replaced by: Ordinary people get their fair share of the nation's wealth. *[Wealth1]*
8. In constructing the scale, a decision had to be taken on how to treat missing values ('Don't knows,' 'Refused' and 'Not answered'). Respondents who had more than two missing values on the left–right scale and more than three missing values on the libertarian–authoritarian and welfarism scale were excluded from that scale. For respondents with just a few missing values, 'Don't knows' were recoded to the midpoint of the scale and 'Refused' or 'Not answered' were recoded to the scale mean for that respondent on their valid items.

References

DeVellis, R.F. (1991), 'Scale development: theory and applications', *Applied Social Research Methods Series*, **26**, Newbury Park: Sage

Jowell, R., Brook, L., Prior, G. and Taylor, B. (1992), *British Social Attitudes: the 9th Report*, Aldershot: Dartmouth

Lynn, P. and Purdon, S. (1994), 'Time-series and lap-tops: the change to computer-assisted interviewing', in Jowell, R., Curtice, J., Brook, L. and Ahrendt, D. (eds.), *British Social Attitudes: the 11th Report*, Aldershot: Dartmouth

Lynn, P. and Taylor, B. (1995), 'On the bias and variance of samples of individuals: a comparison of the Electoral Registers and Postcode Address File as sampling frames', *The Statistician*, **44**: 173–194

Spector, P.E. (1992), 'Summated rating scale construction: an introduction', *Quantitative Applications in the Social Sciences*, **82**, Newbury Park: Sage

Stafford, R. and Thomson, K. (2006), *British Social Attitudes and Young People's Social Attitudes surveys 2003: Technical Report*, London: *National Centre for Social Research*

Appendix II
Notes on the tabulations in chapters

1. Figures in the tables are from the 2005 *British Social Attitudes* survey unless otherwise indicated.
2. Tables are percentaged as indicated by the percentage signs.
3. In tables, '*' indicates less than 0.5 per cent but greater than zero, and '–' indicates zero.
4. When findings based on the responses of fewer than 100 respondents are reported in the text, reference is made to the small base size.
5. Percentages equal to or greater than 0.5 have been rounded up (e.g. 0.5 per cent = one per cent; 36.5 per cent = 37 per cent).
6. In many tables the proportions of respondents answering "Don't know" or not giving an answer are not shown. This, together with the effects of rounding and weighting, means that percentages will not always add to 100 per cent.
7. The self-completion questionnaire was not completed by all respondents to the main questionnaire (see Appendix I). Percentage responses to the self-completion questionnaire are based on all those who completed it.
8. The bases shown in the tables (the number of respondents who answered the question) are printed in small italics. The bases are unweighted, unless otherwise stated.

Appendix III
The questionnaires

As explained in Appendix I, four different versions of the questionnaire (A, B, C and D) were administered, each with its own self-completion supplement. The diagram that follows shows the structure of the questionnaires and the topics covered (not all of which are reported on in this volume).

The four interview questionnaires reproduced on the following pages are derived from the Blaise computer program in which they were written. For ease of reference, each item has been allocated a question number. Gaps in the numbering system indicate items that are essential components of the Blaise program but which are not themselves questions, and so have been omitted. In addition, we have removed the keying codes and inserted instead the percentage distribution of answers to each question. We have also included the SPSS variable name, in square brackets, at each question. Above the questions we have included filter instructions. A filter instruction should be considered as staying in force until the next filter instruction. Percentages for the core questions are based on the total weighted sample, while those for questions in versions A, B, C or D are based on the appropriate weighted sub-samples.

The four versions of the self-completion questionnaire follow. We begin by reproducing version A of the interview questionnaire in full; then those parts of versions B, C and D that differ.

The percentage distributions do not necessarily add up to 100 because of weighting and rounding, or for one or more of the following reasons:

(i)   Some sub-questions are filtered – that is, they are asked of only a proportion of respondents. In these cases the percentages add up (approximately) to the proportions who were asked them. Where, however, a series of questions is filtered, we have indicated the reduced weighted base (for example, all employees), and have derived percentages from that base.

(ii)   At a few questions, respondents were invited to give more than one answer and so percentages may add to well over 100 per cent. These are clearly marked by interviewer instructions on the questionnaires.

As reported in Appendix I, the 2005 *British Social Attitudes* self-completion questionnaire was not completed by 17 per cent of respondents who were successfully interviewed. The answers in the supplement have been percentaged on the base of those respondents who returned it. This means that the distribution of responses to questions asked in earlier years are comparable with those given in Appendix III of all earlier reports in this series except in *The 1984 Report*, where the percentages for the self-completion questionnaire need to be recalculated if comparisons are to be made.

BRITISH SOCIAL ATTITUDES: 2005 SURVEY

Version A	**Version B**	**Version C**	**Version D**
(quarter of sample)	(quarter of sample)	(quarter of sample)	(quarter of sample)

Face-to-face questionnaires

Household grid, newspaper readership and party identification			
Public spending and social security	—	Public spending and social security	
Transport	e-Society (Internet and social networks)		
Health	Civil liberties	Health	
Disability	—	Disability	
—	Social identities		—
—		Education	
Job details			
Employment relations		—	Employment relations
Politics and Europe			
—	Political respect	—	
End of life issues		—	
Classification			

Self-completion questionnaires

ISSP (Work)	Comparative study of electoral systems	—	
Public spending and social security	—	Public spending and social security	
Transport	e-Society (Internet and social networks)		
Health	Civil liberties	Health	
Disability	—	Disability	
—	Social identities		—
—		Education	
Employment relations		—	Employment relations
End of life issues	—		
Standard scales			

BRITISH SOCIAL ATTITUDES 2005

FACE-TO-FACE QUESTIONNAIRE

Contents

Introduction	287
Household grid	287
Newspaper readership and media exposure	290
Party identification	293
Public spending and social welfare (mainly versions A, C and D)	294
e-Society (versions B, C and D)	300
Transport (version A)	307
Health (versions A, C and D)	309
Civil liberties (version B)	313
Disability (versions A, C and D)	317
Social identity (versions B and C)	328
Education (versions C and D)	335
Employment	339
Respondent's job details	339
Anti-social hours (versions A, C and D)	342
Employment relations (mainly versions A, B and D)	343
Genetic testing (versions A, B and D)	351
Retirement (versions A, C and D)	352
Politics	353
Voting	353
Constitution etc. (mainly version B)	354
Europe (mainly versions B and C)	354
Political efficacy (mainly versions B, C and D)	356
Social identities (versions B and C)	357
Political respect (version B)	358
Prejudice (mainly versions B and C)	363
End of life issues (versions A and B)	364
Classification	369
Housing	369
Religion and ethnicity	370
Education	373
Partner's/spouse's job details	376
Income and benefits	378
Administration	380

Introduction

ASK ALL

Q1   [SerialNo]   **(NOT ON SCREEN)**   N=4268
     Serial Number
     Range: 170001 ... 178578

Q18   [GOR2]   **(NOT ON SCREEN)**   N=4268
%   Government office region 2003 version
4.4   North East
11.6   North West
8.7   Yorkshire and Humberside
7.6   East Midlands
9.1   West Midlands
8.8   South West
9.3   Eastern
5.0   Inner London
7.8   Outer London
13.7   South East
5.1   Wales
8.8   Scotland

Q29   [ABCDVer]   **(NOT ON SCREEN)**   N=4268
%   A, B, C or D?
25.9   A
24.8   B
24.4   C
24.8   D

Household grid

ASK ALL

Q39   [Household]   N=4268
     (You have just been telling me about the adults that
     live in this household. Thinking now of **everyone**
     living in the household, **including children:**)
     Including yourself, how many people live here
     regularly as members of this **household**?
     CHECK INTERVIEWER MANUAL FOR DEFINITION OF HOUSEHOLD
     IF NECESSARY.
     NOTE THAT THIS MAY BE **DIFFERENT** TO THE DWELLING UNIT
     YOU ENUMERATED FOR THE SELECTION.
     IF YOU DISCOVER THAT YOU WERE GIVEN THE WRONG
     INFORMATION FOR THE RESPONDENT SELECTION ON THE ARF:
     *DO NOT REDO THE ARF SELECTION PRODECURE
     *DO ENTER THE CORRECT INFORMATION HERE
     *DO USE <CTRL + M> TO MAKE A NOTE OF WHAT HAPPENED.
     Median: 2 people
%   (Don't know)
-    (Refusal/Not answered)

Q40   **FOR EACH PERSON AT [Household]**
     [Name] **(NOT ON DATAFILE)**   N=4268
     FOR RESPONDENT: (Can I just check, what is your first
     name?
     PLEASE TYPE IN THE FIRST NAME (OR INITIALS) OF
     RESPONDENT
     FOR OTHER HOUSEHOLD MEMBERS: PLEASE TYPE IN THE FIRST
     NAME (OR INITIALS) OF PERSON NUMBER *(number)*

Q41   [RSex] *(Figures refer to respondent)*   N=4268
%   PLEASE CODE SEX OF *(name)*
48.3   Male
51.7   Female

Q42   [RAgel]   *(Figures refer to respondent)*   N=4268
FOR RESPONDENT IF ONE PERSON IN HOUSEHOLD: I would now like to ask you a few details about yourself. What was your age last birthday?
FOR RESPONDENT IF SEVERAL PEOPLE IN HOUSEHOLD: I would like to ask you a few details about each person in your household. Starting with yourself, what was your **age** last birthday?
FOR OTHER PEOPLE IN HOUSEHOLD: What was *(name's)* age last birthday?
FOR 97+, CODE 97.
Median: 46 years
%
0.0   (Don't Know)
0.1   (Refusal/Not answered)

FOR PEOPLE IN THE HOUSEHOLD OTHER THAN RESPONDENT
N=4268

Q49   [P2Rel3]   *(Figures refer to second person in household)*
PLEASE ENTER RELATIONSHIP OF *(name)* TO RESPONDENT
%
61.0   Partner/ spouse/ cohabitee
7.1   Son/ daughter (inc step/adopted)
0.1   Grandson/ daughter (inc step/adopted)
7.9   Parent/ parent-in-law
0.1   Grand-parent
2.4   Brother/ sister (inc. in-law)
0.6   Other relative
2.8   Other non-relative
-   (Don't Know)
-   (Refusal/Not answered)

Q135   [MarSta2b]   N=4268
CARD A1
Can I just check, which of these applies to you at present?
Please choose the first on the list that applies
%
53.1   Married
11.0   Living with a partner
2.1   Separated (after being married)
6.1   Divorced
7.5   Widowed
20.2   Single (never married)
-   (Don't Know)
0.0   (Refusal/Not answered)

Q138   **VERSION A: IF 'living with partner' AT [MarSta2b]**
[LegStat]   N=1107
CARD A2
And what is your legal marital status?
%
0.1   Married
0.3   Separated (after being married)
2.3   Divorced
-   Widowed
8.0   Single (never married)
0.7   (Civil partnership)
0.1   (Other (WRITE IN))
-   (Don't Know)
0.2   (Refusal/Not answered)

Q153-   CARD (A3/A2)   N=4268
Q160   Can I just check which, if any, of these types of relatives do you yourself have alive at the moment.
Please include adoptive and step relatives.
PROBE: Which others?
DO NOT INCLUDE FOSTER RELATIVES
CODE ALL THAT APPLY
Multicoded (Maximum of 8 codes)
%
47.0   Father   [RelFath]
57.8   Mother   [RelMoth]
61.9   Brother   [RelBroth]
61.5   Sister   [RelSist]
51.6   Son   [RelSon]
50.1   Daughter   [RelDaug]
21.1   Grandchild (daughter's child)   [RelGrChD]
18.9   Grandchild (son's child)   [RelGrChS]
1.8   None of these   [RelNone3]
0.0   (Don't Know)
0.1   (Refusal/Not answered)

Q170 [RelatCom]
CARD A3
VERSIONS B AND C: ASK ALL WITH A SON OR DAUGHTER AT [Relat3]
N=2101
How much do you feel you have in common with (fathers/mothers) in general, compared with other people?

%
19.8 A lot more in common with them than with other people
16.6 A little more in common with them than with other people
29.1 No more in common with them than with other people
1.3 (Don't Know)
0.2 (Refusal/Not answered)

Q949 [REconAct] (NOT ON SCREEN)
CARD A3/A4
ASK ALL
N=4268
Which of these descriptions applied to what you were doing last week, that is the seven days ending last Sunday?
PROBE: Which others? CODE ALL THAT APPLY
Priority coded

%
3.7 In full-time education (not paid for by employer, including on vacation)
0.4 On government training/employment programme
56.3 In paid work (or away temporarily) for at least 10 hours in week
0.3 Waiting to take up paid work already accepted
2.1 Unemployed and registered at a benefit office
1.1 Unemployed, **not** registered, but actively looking for a job (of at least 10 hrs a week)
0.9 Unemployed, wanting a job (of at least 10 hrs per week) but **not** actively looking for a job
4.2 Permanently sick or disabled
21.9 Wholly retired from work
8.3 Looking after the home
0.7 (Doing something else) (WRITE IN)
- (Don't Know)
- (Refusal/Not answered)

Q950 [RLastJob] (NOT ON SCREEN)
ASK ALL THOSE WHO ARE NOT WORKING OR WAITING TO TAKE UP WORK (I.E. 'in full-time education', 'on government training scheme', 'unemployed', 'permanently sick or disabled', 'wholly retired from work', 'looking after the home' OR 'doing something else' AT [REconAc2])
N=1851
How long ago did you last have a paid job of at least 10 hours a week?
GOVERNMENT PROGRAMS/SCHEMES DO NOT COUNT AS 'PAID JOBS'.

%
16.0 Within past 12 months
21.5 Over 1, up to 5 years ago
15.7 Over 5, up to 10 years ago
23.3 Over 10, up to 20 years ago
16.5 Over 20 years ago
7.1 Never had a paid job of 10+ hours a week
- (Don't Know)
- (Refusal/Not answered)

Q1275 [SEconAct] (NOT ON SCREEN)
CARD A3/A4 AGAIN
ASK ALL WHO ARE MARRIED OR LIVING WITH A PARTNER
N=2736
Which of these descriptions applied to what your (husband/wife/partner) was doing last week, that is the seven days ending last Sunday?
PROBE: Which others? CODE ALL THAT APPLY
Priority coded

%
1.1 In full-time education (not paid for by employer, including on vacation)
0.1 On government training/employment programme
63.8 In paid work (or away temporarily) for at least 10 hours in week
0.1 Waiting to take up paid work already accepted
0.5 Unemployed and registered at a benefit office
0.5 Unemployed, **not** registered, but actively looking for a job (of at least 10 hrs a week)
0.6 Unemployed, wanting a job (of at least 10 hrs per week) but **not** actively looking for a job
2.4 Permanently sick or disabled
19.2 Wholly retired from work
11.2 Looking after the home
0.4 (Doing something else) (WRITE IN)
- (Don't Know)
0.3 (Refusal/Not answered)

Newspaper readership and media exposure

Q204　ASK ALL
[Readpap]
Do you normally read any daily **morning** newspaper at least 3 times a week?　N=4268
%
50.5　Yes
49.5　No
-　(Don't Know)
-　(Refusal/Not answered)

Q205　IF 'yes' AT [Readpap]
[WhPaper]
Which one do you normally read?
IF MORE THAN ONE: Which one do you read **most** frequently?　N=4268
%
2.8　(Scottish) Daily Express
9.9　(Scottish) Daily Mail
6.2　Daily Mirror (/Scottish Mirror)
1.5　Daily Star
11.3　The Sun
1.6　Daily Record
4.1　Daily Telegraph
0.4　Financial Times
2.1　The Guardian
1.4　The Independent
3.7　The Times
0.0　Morning Star
5.1　Other Irish/Northern Irish/Scottish regional or local **daily morning** paper (WRITE IN)
0.1　Other (WRITE IN)
0.1　**EDIT ONLY:** MORE THAN ONE PAPER READ WITH EQUAL FREQUENCY
0.0　(Don't Know)
-　(Refusal/Not answered)

ASK ALL THOSE WHOSE SPOUSE/PARTNER IS NOT WORKING OR WAITING TO TAKE UP WORK (I.E. 'in full-time education', 'on government training scheme', 'unemployed', 'permanently sick or disabled', 'wholly retired from work', 'looking after the home' OR 'doing something else' AT [SEconAc2]) **(NOT ON SCREEN)**

Q1276　[SLastJob]　N=989
How long ago did (he/she) last have a paid job of at least 10 hours a week?
GOVERNMENT PROGRAMS/SCHEMES DO NOT COUNT AS 'PAID JOBS'.
%
12.2　Within past 12 months
22.5　Over 1, up to 5 years ago
20.2　Over 5, up to 10 years ago
24.0　Over 10, up to 20 years ago
14.9　Over 20 years ago
4.8　Never had a paid job of 10+ hours a week
0.6　(Don't Know)
0.8　(Refusal/Not answered)

ASK ALL THOSE WHOSE SPOUSE/PARTNER IS WORKING OR WAITING TO TAKE UP WORK

Q1309　[S2PartF1]　N=1755
%
(Is/Was) the job ... READ OUT ...
77.8　... full-time - that is, 30 or more hours per week,
21.4　or, part-time?
0.4　(Don't Know)
0.4　(Refusal/Not answered)

Q210 [InterPap]
VERSIONS A, C AND D: IF 'no' AT [ReadPap] N=3210
Can I just check, do you read a newspaper on the internet at least 3 times a week?
EXCLUDE BBC WEBSITE.

	%
Yes	2.4
No	47.2
(Don't Know)	0.1
(Refusal/Not answered)	0.1

Q211 [WhIntPap] N=3210
IF 'yes' AT [InterPap]
Which one?

	%
(Scottish) Daily Express	0.1
(Scottish) Daily Mail	0.2
Daily Mirror (/Scottish Mirror)	0.1
Daily Star	0.0
The Sun	0.1
Daily Record	0.1
Daily Telegraph	0.2
Financial Times	0.1
The Guardian	0.6
The Independent	-
The Times	0.2
Morning Star	-
Other Irish/Northern Irish/Scottish regional or local daily morning paper (WRITE IN)	0.3
Other (WRITE IN)	0.2
EDIT ONLY: MORE THAN ONE INTERNET PAPER READ WITH EQUAL FREQUENCY	0.2
(Don't Know)	-
(Refusal/Not answered)	0.2

Q216 [EverPap] N=1058
VERSION B: IF 'no' AT [Readpap]
Do you **ever** read a daily **morning** paper?

	%
Yes	20.2
No	27.9
(Don't Know)	0.2
(Refusal/Not answered)	-

Q217 [EvWhPap]
IF 'yes' AT [EverPap] N=1058
Which one do you read most often?

	%
(Scottish) Daily Express	1.3
(Scottish) Daily Mail	3.4
Daily Mirror (/Scottish Mirror)	3.2
Daily Star	0.4
The Sun	4.2
Daily Record	0.5
Daily Telegraph	1.7
Financial Times	0.3
The Guardian	1.4
The Independent	0.4
The Times	1.4
Morning Star	-
Other Irish/Northern Irish/Scottish regional or local **daily morning** paper (WRITE IN)	1.7
Other (WRITE IN)	0.1
EDIT ONLY: MORE THAN ONE PAPER READ WITH EQUAL FREQUENCY	0.2
(Don't Know)	-
(Refusal/Not answered)	0.2

Q222 [PapOft] N=1058
VERSION B: IF PAPER GIVEN AT [WhPaper] OR AT [EvWhPap]
CARD A5
How often do you read (name of newspaper)?

	%
Every day	29.8
Almost every day	9.8
Most days	5.3
A few days a week	12.0
Once a week	9.5
Less often than that	5.5
(Don't Know)	-
(Refusal/Not answered)	0.2

Q223 [ReadSun] N=1058
VERSION B: ASK ALL
Do you ever read a **Sunday** paper?

	%
Yes	61.2
No	38.8
(Don't Know)	-
(Refusal/Not answered)	-

Q224
[WhSun]   N=1058
IF 'yes' AT [ReadSun]
Which one do you read most often?
%
-      The Business
0.6   Daily Star Sunday
3.7   Sunday Express
0.7   Sunday Herald
1.1   The Independent on Sunday
16.0   (Mail on Sunday / Sunday Mail (Scotland))
6.9   Sunday Mirror
11.7   News of the World
3.1   The Observer
1.2   The People
1.8   Sunday Post
0.4   Scotland on Sunday
-      Sunday Sport
5.3   Sunday Telegraph
7.6   Sunday Times
0.2   Wales on Sunday
-      Other Sunday paper (WRITE IN)
       EDIT ONLY: MORE THAN ONE SUNDAY PAPER READ WITH EQUAL
       FREQUENCY
0.1   (Don't Know)
-      (Refusal/Not answered)

Q227
[SPapOft]   N=1058
IF 'yes' AT [ReadSun]
CARD A6
How often do you read (name of Sunday newspaper)?
%
37.9   Every week
8.8   Almost every week
8.1   Every few weeks
6.4   Occasionally
-      (Don't Know)
-      (Refusal/Not answered)

VERSION B: ASK ALL
Q228
[PolTV]   N=1058
Do you ever watch the news or current affairs
programmes on TV?
%
93.1   Yes
6.9   No
-      (Don't Know)
-      (Refusal/Not answered)

Q229
[PolTVCh]   N=1058
IF 'yes' AT [PolTV]
On which **channel** do you watch news or current affairs
programmes most frequently?
PROBE FOR CORRECT CODE
%
52.6   BBC1
1.3   BBC2
4.4   BBC News 24
15.1   (Main) ITV (not ITV News channel)
8.8   ITV News channel
2.4   Channel 4
0.7   Channel 5
6.2   Sky News Channel
0.2   Other Sky channels (not Sky News)
-      CNN
1.1   Other (WRITE IN)
0.4   (Don't Know)
-      (Refusal/Not answered)

Q232
[PolTVoft]   N=1058
IF 'yes' AT [PolTV]
CARD A7
How often do you watch the news or current affairs
programmes on (channel)?
%
56.5   Every day
17.2   Almost every day
7.2   Most days
8.2   A few days a week
2.0   Once a week
1.8   Less often than that
0.1   (Don't Know)
-      (Refusal/Not answered)

VERSIONS B, C AND D: ASK ALL
Q233
[TVHrsWk3]   N=3161
How many hours of television do you normally watch on
an ordinary day or evening during the week, that is,
Monday to Friday?
INTERVIEWER: ROUND UP TO NEAREST HOUR
IF DOES NOT WATCH TELEVISION ON WEEKDAYS, CODE 0
IF NEVER WATCHES TELEVISION AT ALL, CODE 97
Median: 3 hours
%
0.0   (Never watch TV)
0.2   (Don't Know)
-      (Refusal/Not answered)

VERSION A: ASK ALL

Q234　[Internet]
Does anyone have access to the internet or World Wide Web from this address?　N=4268

IF 'yes' AT [Internet]

Q235　[BroadBnd]
Do you have a **broadband** connection to the internet?　N=4268

ASK ALL

Q236　[WWWUse]
Do you yourself ever use the internet or World Wide Web for any reason (other than your work)?　N=4268

NOTE: This table includes respondents on versions B, C and D, who were asked these questions in the e-society module (below).

	[Internet]	[BroadBnd]	[WWWUse]
	%	%	%
Yes	60.8	37.3	60.8
No	39.2	23.0	39.2
(Don't Know)	-	0.6	-
(Refusal/Not answered)	-	-	-

Party identification

Q237　**ASK ALL**
[SupParty]
Generally speaking, do you think of yourself as a supporter of any one political party?　N=4268

IF 'no' OR DON'T KNOW AT [SupParty]

Q238　[ClosePty]
Do you think of yourself as a little closer to one political party than to the others?　N=4268

	[SupParty]	[ClosePty]
	%	%
Yes	36.9	26.8
No	63.0	36.1
(Don't Know)	0.0	0.1
(Refusal/Not answered)	0.1	0.1

IF 'yes' AT [SupParty] OR 'yes', 'no' OR DON'T KNOW AT [ClosePty]

Q239　[Partyid1]
IF 'yes' AT [SupParty] OR AT [ClosePty]: Which one?
IF 'no' OR DON'T KNOW AT [SupParty] OR AT [ClosePty]: If there were a general election tomorrow, which political party do you think you would be most likely to support?　N=4268
DO NOT PROMPT

%	
24.2	Conservative
39.8	Labour
12.8	Liberal Democrat
1.5	Scottish National Party
0.4	Plaid Cymru
1.5	Green Party
0.6	UK Independence Party (UKIP)/Veritas
0.5	British National Party (BNP)/ National Front
0.3	RESPECT/ Scottish Socialist Party (SSP)/ Socialist Party
0.1	Other party (WRITE IN)
0.7	Other answer (WRITE IN)
12.9	None
2.5	(Don't Know)
2.2	(Refusal/Not answered)

Q247 [Idstrng]
IF PARTY GIVEN AT [PartyID1]   N=4268
Would you call yourself very strong (party), fairly strong, or not very strong?

%
6.9   Very strong (party)
28.1 Fairly strong
46.5 Not very strong
0.2   (Don't Know)
5.5   (Refusal/Not answered)

ASK ALL
Q248 [Politics]   N=4268
How much interest do you generally have in what is going on in politics
...READ OUT ...

%
10.5 ... a great deal,
22.9 quite a lot,
35.2 some,
22.3 not very much,
9.2   or, none at all?
-     (Don't Know)
-     (Refusal/Not answered)

VERSION B: ASK ALL
Q249 [DfWnGE]   N=1058
CARD A8
Some people say that it makes no difference which party wins in elections, things go on much the same. Using this card, please say how much of a difference you think it makes who wins in elections to the **House of Commons?**

%
16.7 A great deal
25.5 Quite a lot
23.8 Some
25.8 Not very much
6.7   None at all
1.3   (Don't Know)
0.2   (Refusal/Not answered)

Public spending and social welfare (mainly versions A, C and D)

VERSIONS A AND D: ASK ALL   N=2167
Q251 [Spend1]
CARD B1
Here are some items of government spending. Which of them, if any, would be your highest priority for **extra** spending? Please read through the whole list before deciding.
ENTER ONE CODE ONLY FOR HIGHEST PRIORITY

IF NOT 'none', DON'T KNOW OR REFUSAL AT [Spend1]   N=2167
Q252 [Spend2]
CARD B1 AGAIN
And which next?
ENTER ONE CODE ONLY FOR NEXT HIGHEST

	[Spend1]	[Spend2]
	%	%
Education	26.8	32.0
Defence	2.2	3.3
Health	47.1	27.6
Housing	4.3	7.7
Public transport	4.8	6.9
Roads	3.0	4.2
Police and prisons	5.2	8.8
Social security benefits	1.7	3.3
Help for industry	2.2	3.2
Overseas aid	1.8	1.4
(None of these)	0.8	0.4
(Don't Know)	0.2	0.1
(Refusal/Not answered)	0.1	1.1

VERSION A, C AND D: ASK ALL   N=3210
Q253 [SocBen1]
CARD (B2/B1)
Thinking now only of the government's spending on **social benefits** like those on the card. Which, if any, of these would be your highest priority for **extra** spending?
ENTER ONE CODE ONLY FOR HIGHEST PRIORITY

Q254
IF ANSWER GIVEN AT [SocBen1]   N=3210
[SocBen2]
CARD (B2/B1) AGAIN
And which next?
ENTER ONE CODE ONLY FOR NEXT HIGHEST

	[SocBen1]	[SocBen2]
	%	%
Retirement pensions	60.9	18.6
Child benefits	15.0	24.0
Benefits for the unemployed	2.4	5.4
Benefits for disabled people	13.9	38.3
Benefits for single parents	5.9	9.0
(None of these)	1.3	2.5
(Don't Know)	0.5	0.4
(Refusal/Not answered)	-	-

VERSION A, C AND D: ASK ALL   N=3210
Q255 [Dole]
Opinions differ about the level of benefits for
unemployed people.
Which of these two statements comes closest to your
own view

% ...READ OUT...
26.2 ...benefits for unemployed people are **too low** and
      cause hardship,
50.2 or, benefits for unemployed people are **too high** and
      discourage them from finding jobs?
15.8 (Neither)
0.1   **EDIT ONLY:** BOTH: UNEMPLOYMENT BENEFIT CAUSES HARDSHIP
      BUT CAN'T BE HIGHER OR THERE WOULD BE NO INCENTIVE TO
      WORK
0.4   **EDIT ONLY:** BOTH: UNEMPLOYMENT BENEFIT CAUSES HARDSHIP
      TO SOME, WHILE OTHERS DO WELL OUT OF IT
0.6   **EDIT ONLY:** ABOUT RIGHT/IN BETWEEN
2.4   Other answer (WRITE IN)
4.3   (Don't Know)
 -    (Refusal/Not answered)

VERSION A AND D: ASK ALL   N=2167
Q258 [TaxSpend]
CARD B3
Suppose the government had to choose between the three
options on this card. Which do you think it should
choose?
%
6.6 Reduce taxes and spend **less** on health, education and
     social benefits
43.1 Keep taxes and spending on these services at the **same**
     level as now
45.6 Increase taxes and spend **more** on health, education and
     social benefits
3.5 (None)
1.2 (Don't Know)
 -   (Refusal/Not answered)

VERSION B, C AND D: ASK ALL   N=3161
Q259 [HIncDiff]
CARD (B1/B2/B4)
Which of the phrases on this card would you say comes
closest to your feelings about your household's income
these days?
%
39.9 Living comfortably on present income
43.9 Coping on present income
11.5 Finding it difficult on present income
4.2 Finding it very difficult on present income
0.2 (Other answer (WRITE IN))
0.2 (Don't Know)
0.1 (Refusal/Not answered)

VERSION A, C AND D: ASK ALL   N=3210
Q262 [ImpBen1]
CARD (B4/B3/B5)
There are different things the government can do to
improve the benefit system. Which, if any, of these do
you think should be the government's highest priority?
ENTER ONE CODE ONLY FOR HIGHEST PRIORITY

IF NOT 'none of these', DON'T KNOW OR REFUSAL AT
[ImpBen1]
Q263 [ImpBen2]   N=3210
CARD (B4/B3/B5) AGAIN
And which next?
ENTER ONE CODE ONLY FOR NEXT HIGHEST PRIORITY

	[ImpBen1]	[ImpBen2]
	%	%
Making sure those who are entitled to money claim it	14.8	14.7
Targeting benefits only at those who really need them	25.5	19.9
Rewarding those who work or look for work	15.7	14.8
Making sure those who save are not penalised	14.9	15.7
Providing benefits for those who cannot work	5.1	9.1
Making sure payments are fast and accurate	3.5	6.2
Reducing fraud	19.7	18.1
(None of these)	0.5	0.3
(Don't Know)	0.4	0.2
(Refusal/Not answered)	-	-

VERSION A, C AND D: ASK ALL

Q264 [HealResp] *   N=3210
CARD (B5/B4/B6)
Please say from this card who you think should **mainly** be responsible for paying for the cost of health care when someone is ill?

Q265 [RetResp] *   N=3210
CARD (B5/B4/B6) AGAIN
Still looking at this card, who do you think should **mainly** be responsible for ensuring that people have enough money to live on in retirement?

Q266 [SickResp] *   N=3210
CARD (B5/B4/B6) AGAIN
And who do you think should **mainly** be responsible for ensuring that people have enough to live on if they become sick for a long time or disabled?

	[HealResp]	[RetResp]	[SickResp]
	%	%	%
Mainly the government	86.4	56.2	83.2
Mainly a person's employer	6.2	10.2	7.8
Mainly a person themselves and their family	6.3	31.6	7.6
(Don't Know)	1.0	2.0	1.2
(Refusal/Not answered)	0.0	0.1	0.1

Q267 [UBCPoor]   N=3210
Think of a couple living together without children who are both unemployed. Their only income comes from state benefits. Would you say that they ...READ OUT...

Q268 [PenCPoor]   N=3210
Now think about a pensioner couple living together. Their only income comes from the state pension and other benefits specially for pensioners. Would you say that they ...READ OUT...

Q269 [UBCon88]   N=3210
Now thinking again of that couple living together without children who are both unemployed. After rent, their income is £88 a week. Would you say that they ...READ OUT...

Q270 [PenCO171]   N=3210
And thinking again about that pensioner couple living together. After rent, their income is £171 a week. Would you say that they ...READ OUT...

	[UBCPoor]	[PenCPoor]	[UBCon88]	[PenCO171]
	%	%	%	%
have more than enough to live on,	7.5	1.5	3.7	11.2
have enough to live on,	40.7	25.4	25.8	58.8
are hard up,	34.9	58.8	56.0	26.6
or, are really poor?	4.1	9.4	12.6	2.0
(Don't Know)	12.7	4.9	1.9	1.3
(Refusal/Not answered)	0.0	0.0	-	-

Q271   [SavFrRet]
CARD (B6/B5/B7)   N=3210
Please tell me, from this card, how much you agree or disagree with the following statements...
...The government should encourage people to provide something for their own retirement instead of relying only on the state pension.

Q272   [StPnWor2]
CARD (B6/B5/B7) AGAIN   N=3210
...State pensions used to provide a better standard of living than they do nowadays.
(How much do you agree or disagree?)

	[SavFrRet]	[StPnWor2]
	%	%
Agree strongly	26.9	10.3
Agree	54.6	40.4
Neither agree nor disagree	8.7	22.8
Disagree	7.5	16.1
Disagree strongly	1.6	0.9
(Don't Know)	0.7	9.5
(Refusal/Not answered)	-	-

Q273   [PenBase]
CARD (B7/B6/B8)   N=3210
Which of the statements on this card comes closest to your view?

%

51.8   The amount of state pension a person gets should be based on their **contributions** through taxation, even if this means that those who take time out from working, for example to bring up children, get less money, OR

43.5   The amount of state pension a person gets should be based on their **need**, even if this means someone who has periods of not working might get more than someone who has worked all their life.

4.5   (Don't Know)
0.2   (Refusal/Not answered)

Q274   [Worseoff]
CARD (B8/B7/B9)   N=3210
Please look at this card and say, as far as money is concerned, what you think happens when a marriage breaks up?

%

12.4   The woman nearly always comes off worse than the man
16.3   The woman usually comes off worse
21.7   The woman and the man usually come off about the same
26.1   The man usually comes off worse
11.8   The man nearly always comes off worse than the woman
8.3   (Varies/depends)
0.2   Other answer (WRITE IN)
3.3   (Don't Know)
-    (Refusal/Not answered)

VERSION A, C AND D: ASK ALL

Q277   [CoupUB]   N=3210
Thinking about a couple living together without children. One person is working and the other person is looking for work. Should the person looking for work ...READ OUT...

%

39.1   ..be able to claim unemployment benefits regardless of their partner's income,

52.4   only be able to claim if their partner has a low income,

6.6   or, not be able to claim unemployment benefits at all?
1.8   (Don't Know)
0.0   (Refusal/Not answered)

Q278   [CareEmp]
CARD (B9/B8/B10)   N=3210
Suppose someone in full-time work is considering giving up their job to become the carer for a close relative with a long-term illness or disability. Taking your answer from this card, how much, if at all, are you in favour of...
...the employer being required to give up to six months paid leave to allow the person to care for their relative?

Q279   [CareGCar]
       CARD (B9/B8/B10) AGAIN   N=3210
       ...the government using tax payers' money to provide
       good quality, affordable care for the relative,
       allowing the carer to continue working?
       (How much, if at all, are you in favour of this?)

Q280   [CareGBen]
       CARD (B9/B8/B10) AGAIN   N=3210
       ...the government using tax payers' money to pay
       benefits to the carer, allowing them to stop working?
       (How much, if at all, are you in favour of this?)

	[CareEmp]	[CareGCar]	[CareGBen]
	%	%	%
A great deal	26.7	32.0	25.0
Quite a lot	27.6	43.0	38.3
Some	20.2	17.8	23.3
Not very much	13.6	4.5	9.2
Not at all	10.0	1.5	2.8
(Don't Know)	2.0	1.1	1.4
(Refusal/Not answered)	0.0	0.1	0.0

Q281   [CareGCh]
       CARD (B10/B9/B11)   N=3210
       And suppose the government **had** to make a choice, which
       of the options on this card do you think it should
       choose?
%
57.6   Using tax payers' money to provide good quality,
       affordable care for the relative, allowing the carer
       to continue working, OR
37.2   Using tax payers' money to pay benefits to the carer,
       allowing them to stop working
5.1   (Don't Know)
0.1   (Refusal/Not answered)

VERSION A: ASK ALL
       CARD B11   N=1107
Q282- Imagine an unmarried couple who split up. They have a
Q288   child at primary school who remains with the mother.
       The father has been judged to have sufficient income
       to pay maintenance. If he **doesn't** pay it, which, if
       any, of these do you think should
       happen?
       PROBE: Which others?
       CODE ALL THAT APPLY
       Multicoded (Maximum of 7 codes)
%
2.3   No action should be taken   [MPenNonA]
77.7   He should have the money deducted from his
       earnings   [MPenMoDA]
22.2   He should be encouraged to pay the money,
       but it should not be deducted from his
       earnings   [MPenMoEA]
10.8   His access to the child should be stopped   [MPenAccA]
3.1   He should be sent to prison   [MPenPriA]
3.7   His driving licence should be withdrawn   [MPenDriA]
4.9   His passport should be withdrawn   [MPenPasA]
2.2   Other answer (WRITE IN)   [MPenOthA]
0.5   (Don't Know)
-      (Refusal/Not answered)

VERSION C: ASK ALL

Q289-
Q295 CARD B10   N=1044

Imagine an unmarried couple who split up. They have a child at primary school who remains with the mother. The father has been judged to have sufficient income to pay maintenance. If he **doesn't** pay it, which, if any, of these do you think should happen?
PROBE: Which others?
CODE ALL THAT APPLY
Multicoded (Maximum of 7 codes)

%		
1.4	No action should be taken	[MPenNonC]
3.6	His driving licence should be withdrawn	[MPenDriC]
5.8	His passport should be withdrawn	[MPenPasC]
14.5	His access to the child should be stopped	[MPenAccC]
4.0	He should be sent to prison	[MPenPriC]
81.9	He should have the money deducted from his earnings	[MPenMoDC]
16.9	He should be encouraged to pay the money, but it should not be deducted from his earning	[MPenMoEC]
2.6	Other answer (WRITE IN)	[MPenOthC]
1.0	(Don't Know)	
0.1	(Refusal/Not answered)	

VERSION D: ASK ALL

Q296-
Q302 CARD B12   N=1059

Imagine an unmarried couple who split up. They have a child at primary school who remains with the mother. The father has been judged to have sufficient income to pay maintenance. If he **doesn't** pay it, which, if any, of these do you think should happen?
PROBE: Which others?
CODE ALL THAT APPLY
Multicoded (Maximum of 7 codes)

%		
1.5	No action should be taken	[MPenNonD]
11.5	His access to the child should be stopped	[MPenAccD]
4.1	He should be sent to prison	[MPenPriD]
82.1	He should have the money deducted from his earnings	[MPenMoDD]
16.6	He should be encouraged to pay the money, but it should not be deducted from his earnings	[PenMoED]
2.9	His driving licence should be withdrawn	[MPenDriD]
4.7	His passport should be withdrawn	[MPenPasD]
2.0	Other answer (WRITE IN)	[MPenOthD]
0.4	(Don't Know)	
0.1	(Refusal/Not answered)	

e-Society (versions B, C and D)

VERSIONS B, C AND D: ASK ALL

Q340   [Internet]   N=4268
Does anyone have access to the internet or World Wide Web from this address?

IF 'yes' AT [Internt]

Q341   [BroadBnd]   N=4268
Do you have a **broadband** connection to the internet?

Q342   [WWWUse]   N=4268
Do you yourself ever use the internet or World Wide Web for any reason *(other than your work)*?

NOTE: This table includes respondents on version A, who were asked these questions in the Media Exposure section (above).

	[Internet]	[BroadBnd]	[WWWUse]
	%	%	%
Yes	60.8	37.3	60.8
No	39.2	23.0	39.2
(Don't Know)	-	0.6	-
(Refusal/Not answered)	-	-	-

VERSIONS B, C AND D: IF 'yes' AT [WWWUse]

Q343   [WWWHrsWk]   N=3161
How many **hours** a week on average do you spend using the internet or World Wide Web *(other than for your work)*?
INTERVIEWER: ROUND UP TO NEAREST HOUR
Median: 2 hours
%
0.2   (Don't Know)
-   (Refusal/Not answered)

Q344   [PCLearn]   N=3161
CARD C1
Where did you first learn to use a computer?
%
20.7   At school, college/university
16.0   At work
21.7   At home (e.g. self-taught or taught by someone else)
1.7   Some other way
-   (Don't Know)
-   (Refusal/Not answered)

Q345   [PCHelpU]   N=3161
Do you have any friends or relatives who you could call on for help if there were any problems with your computer or with using the internet?
%
48.3   Yes
6.8   No
4.8   (Respondent could fix any problems him/herself)
0.1   (Don't Know)
-   (Refusal/Not answered)

Q346-   CARD C2
Q360   For which of the following do you personally use the internet or World Wide Web *(other than for your work)*?
PROBE: Which others?
CODE ALL THAT APPLY.
Multicoded (Maximum of 15 codes)

%		
35.3	Shopping	[WWWShop]
4.7	Chat rooms	[WWWChat]
46.5	E-mail	[WWWEmail]
23.1	News and current affairs	[WWWNews]
21.2	Training, education and learning	[WWWEduc]
34.0	Travel and weather information	[WWWTrav]
10.9	Keeping in touch with groups I belong to	[WWWGroup]
35.6	General information	[WWWInfo]
27.7	Banking and bill-paying	[WWWBank2]
14.1	Downloading music	[WWWMusi2]
13.8	Sports information	[WWWSpor2]
10.2	Games	[WWWGame2]
17.7	Job search	[WWWJobs2]
17.1	Accessing local/central government information/services	[WWWGovt]
2.4	Other (PLEASE SPECIFY)	[WWWOth2]
0.3	(None of these)	[WWWNone2]
-	(Don't Know)	
-	(Refusal/Not answered)	

VERSIONS B, C AND D: IF IN WORK OR ON GOVERNMENT TRAINING SCHEME   N=3161

[WWWWork]
Q363 And do you yourself ever use the internet or World Wide Web for your work?

%
29.5 Yes
27.5 No
0.0   (Don't Know)
0.0   (Refusal/Not answered)

IF 'yes' AT [WWWWork]

[WWWHrWk2]   N=3161
Q364 How many hours a week on average do you spend using the internet or World Wide Web for your work?
INTERVIEWER: ROUND UP TO NEAREST HOUR
Median: 4 hours

%
0.1   (Don't Know)
0.1   (Refusal/Not answered)

VERSIONS B, C AND D: ASK ALL WHO USE THE INTERNET (WHETHER FOR WORK OR NOT) ('yes' AT [WWWUse] OR AT [WWWWork])   N=3161

Q365 [WWWLong2]
CARD C3
Thinking now about all the times you use the internet, either for work or for your own personal use. Can you tell me when you first started using the internet?

%
1.5   Within the last 6 months
2.4   Over 6 months, up to 1 year ago
5.3   Over 1 year, up to 2 years ago
7.0   Over 2 years, up to 3 years ago
16.7 Over 3 years, up to 5 years ago
29.7 More than 5 years ago
-     (Don't Know)
-     (Refusal/Not answered)

Q366 [MeetWWW]
Have you ever got to know someone personally whom you first happened to make contact with through e-mail or via the internet (, other than through your work)?
IF YES: is this just one person or several people?

%
2.8   Yes, one person
5.1   Yes, several people
54.6 No
-     (Don't Know)
-     (Refusal/Not answered)

VERSIONS B, C AND D: ASK ALL WHO DO NOT USE THE INTERNET (OTHER THAN FOR WORK) ('no' AT [WWWUse])   N=3161

Q367- CARD C4
Q375   Here are some reasons why people might not use the internet (other than for work).
Which of these reasons, if any, apply to you?
PROBE: Which others?
CODE ALL THAT APPLY
Multicoded (Maximum of 9 codes)

%
7.1   Don't like using the internet or computers [NWWWLik]
14.8 Don't need to use the internet [NWWWNee]
14.6 Don't know how to use the internet or computers [NWWWDKUs]
1.6   Don't know anyone who could help me to use the internet [NWWWHelp]
11.3 Don't have or can't afford a computer [NWWWAfC]
7.0   I am too old to learn how to use a computer [NWWWROld]
1.2   Not many people I know use the internet either [NWWWNeig]
7.6   There's not much on the internet I am interested in [NWWWInrs]
2.8   Other reason (PLEASE SPECIFY) [NWWWOth2]
1.3   (None of these reasons apply) [NWWWNon2]
0.0   (Don't Know)
-     (Refusal/Not answered)

Q378 [ProxUseI] N=3161
Thinking back over the past twelve months or so, have you ever got someone you know to send an e-mail or find something on the internet for you?
IF YES: Did you do this a number of times or just once or twice?
%
7.6 Yes - a number of times
8.9 Yes - just once or twice
23.5 No - have not done this
- (Don't Know)
- (Refusal/Not answered)

Q379 [Use1day] N=3161
How likely do you think it is, if at all, that you will start using the internet one day (other than for work) ..READ OUT...
%
4.9 ...very likely,
8.6 fairly likely,
8.1 not very likely,
18.3 or, not at all likely?
0.1 (Don't Know)
- (Refusal/Not answered)

Q380 [WdLkUse] N=3161
Regardless of whether you think you ever will, would you like to use the internet (other than for work) one day, or not?
%
18.3 Yes
21.2 No
0.4 (Don't Know)
0.0 (Refusal/Not answered)

Q381 [PCHelpNU] N=3161
If you were to start using the internet (other than for work) do you have any friends or relatives who you could call on for help with any problems you might have with your computer or with using the internet?
%
30.7 Yes
8.7 No
0.4 (Respondent could fix any problems him/herself)
0.1 (Don't Know)
- (Refusal/Not answered)

VERSIONS B, C AND D: ASK ALL
Q382 [FriUsWWW] N=3161
CARD C5
Thinking about all the people you know reasonably well, how many would you say use the internet or email?
%
29.4 All or nearly all of them
32.9 Most
15.5 About half
16.1 Some, but not many
5.1 None or hardly any at all
1.0 (Don't Know)
- (Refusal/Not answered)

Q383 [VoteChoi] N=3161
CARD C6
There are many different ways of voting in elections. If you had a choice, which **one** of the ways on this card would be your **preferred** way of voting in British elections?
%
13.8 By pressing a button on a computer at a polling station
46.6 By filling in a paper ballot paper at a polling station
12.3 By sending in a ballot paper by post
4.3 By voting over the telephone
15.5 By voting over the internet
4.8 By sending a text message from a mobile phone
0.3 (None of these)
2.3 (Don't vote at elections)
0.2 (Don't Know)
- (Refusal/Not answered)

Q384 [PassPApp]
CARD C7
N=3161
Say you needed to apply for a new passport. Which one of the ways on this card would be your **preferred** way of doing this?
%
37.7 In person (e.g. at a post office or passport office)
29.6 By post
22.4 Over the internet
7.8 Over the telephone
0.1 Another way (PLEASE SPECIFY)
2.3 (Does not apply / wouldn't want a passport)
0.1 (Don't Know)
- (Refusal/Not answered)

VERSIONS B, C AND D: ASK ALL
Q387 [BankBal]
CARD C8
N=3161
And what if you needed to check your bank balance? Which one of the ways on this card would be your **preferred** way of doing this?
%
49.5 In person (e.g. at a cash machine or at a bank branch)
3.0 By post
29.4 Over the internet
16.6 Over the telephone
0.4 Another way (PLEASE SPECIFY)
1.1 (Does not apply / don't have a bank account)
0.1 (Don't Know)
0.0 (Refusal/Not answered)

VERSIONS B, C AND D: ASK ALL
Q390 [NghBrHd]
N=3161
Can I just check, how long have you lived in your present neighbourhood?
ENTER YEARS. ROUND TO NEAREST YEAR.
PROBE FOR BEST ESTIMATE.
IF LESS THAN ONE YEAR, CODE 0.
MEDIAN: 14 years
%
0.0 (Don't Know)
- (Refusal/Not answered)

VERSIONS B, C AND D: IF USE THE INTERNET (WHETHER FOR WORK OR NOT) ('yes' AT [WWWUse OR AT [WWWork])
Q391 [MemWWW]
N=1975
Are you a member of, or do you ever join in the activities of, any **internet based** discussion groups, interest groups or online gaming groups?
%
12.2 Yes
87.8 No
- (Don't Know)
- (Refusal/Not answered)

VERSIONS B, C AND D: ASK ALL
Q392- CARD C9
N=3161
Q406 Are you currently a member of, or do you regularly join in the activities of, any of the organisations on this card?
IF YES: Which ones? PROBE: Which others?
CODE ALL THAT APPLY
Multicoded (Maximum of 15 codes)
%
46.1 None of these [MemNoGrp]
8.8 Political parties or trade unions (inc student unions) [MemPtyTU]
5.4 An environmental or conservation group [MemEnvC]
2.8 A pressure group or campaigning organisation [MemPress]
5.4 Parent-teachers' / school parents association / Board of Governors etc [MemPTA2]
3.3 Youth groups (e.g. scouts, guides, youth clubs etc) [MemYouth]
9.6 Education, arts, drama, reading or music group / evening class [MemArtEd]
11.3 Religious group or church organisation [MemRelg]
20.3 A sports or recreation club [MemSport]
6.2 Tenants' / Residents' group / Neighbourhood watch [MemResd2]
6.8 Social club / working men's club [MemSClub]
2.8 Women's group / Women's Institute [MemWomen]
2.8 Group for older people (e.g. lunch clubs) [MemOlder]
5.1 Local groups which raise money for charity (e.g. The Rotary Club) [MemChari]
5.5 Other local community or voluntary group (PLEASE SPECIFY) [MemOthL]
2.8 Other national or international group (PLEASE SPECIFY) [MemOthNI]
- (Don't Know)
- (Refusal/Not answered)

IF NOT 'mentioned' AT [MemNoGrp]

Q427 [GrpWWW]   N=3161
As far as you know, (does this/do any of these)
group(s) or organisation(s) use e-mail or the internet
to keep in contact with (its/their) members?

	%
Yes	27.7
No	22.6
(Don't Know)	3.6
(Refusal/Not answered)	-

VERSIONS B, C AND D: ASK ALL

Q428 [NeigIll] *   N=3161
CARD C10
Suppose that you were in bed ill and needed someone to
go to the chemist to collect your prescription while
they were doing their shopping.
How comfortable would you be asking a neighbour to do
this?

Q429 [NeigSink] *   N=3161
CARD C10 AGAIN
Now suppose you found your sink was blocked, but you
did not have a plunger to unblock it.
How comfortable would you be asking a neighbour to
borrow a plunger?

Q430 [NeigMilk] *   N=3161
CARD C10 AGAIN
Now suppose the milkman called for payment. The bill
was £5 but you had no cash.
How comfortable would you be asking a neighbour if you
could borrow £5?

	[NeigIll]	[NeigSink]	[NeigMilk]
	%	%	%
Very comfortable	40.4	52.4	18.5
Fairly comfortable	30.7	29.7	13.8
Fairly uncomfortable	14.6	8.8	19.0
Very uncomfortable	13.5	8.2	47.8
(Don't Know)	0.7	1.0	0.9
(Refusal/Not answered)	0.0	0.0	-

VERSIONS B, C AND D: ASK ALL WHO USE THE INTERNET (WHETHER
FOR WORK OR NOT) ('yes' AT [WWWUse OR AT [WWWWork])
                                                                  N=1975
Q431 [GovInfoW] *
CARD C11
How often do you use the internet to look up
information about national or local government or the
services they provide, or do you never do this?

Q432 [PolInfoW] *   N=1975
CARD C11 AGAIN
And how often do you use the internet to look up
information about political parties, campaigns or
events, or do you never do this?

Q433 [NewsWeb] *   N=1975
CARD C11 AGAIN
And how often do you use the internet to visit a news
or current affairs web site, including the web sites
for any newspapers, radio or television news
programmes, or do you never do this?

	[GovInfoW]	[PolInfoW]	[NewsWeb]
	%	%	%
Every day, or nearly every day	2.6	0.6	15.7
2-5 days a week	1.3	0.4	7.6
At least once a week	4.9	1.2	9.2
At least once a fortnight	3.4	1.2	5.2
Less often but at least once a month	13.5	3.1	9.5
Less often than that	22.1	13.7	14.5
Never do this	52.1	79.7	38.3
(Don't Know)	-	-	-
(Refusal/Not answered)	0.1	0.1	0.1

VERSIONS B, C AND D: ASK ALL

N=3161

Q434-
Q443

CARD C12

During the campaign in the run up to the general election on May the 5th, did you do any of the things listed on this card?
PROBE: Which others?
CODE ALL THAT APPLY
Multicoded (Maximum of 10 codes)

%

55.8	Read a leaflet or other printed material produced by a party or candidate	[GECmLeaf]
56.4	Watched a Party Election Broadcast or film produced by a party or candidate	[GECmPEB]
4.1	Contacted someone from a political party or a candidate in person, by phone, or by letter	[GECmCont]
51.0	Watched a TV programme or listened to a radio show specifically about the election	[GECmTVPr]
47.0	Read articles in a newspaper specifically about the election	[GECmNPap]
0.5	Wrote to or telephoned a newspaper, television or radio programme about the election	[GECmWrot]
1.6	Attended a public meeting or event about the election	[GECmMeet]
14.7	Was contacted by someone from a party or candidate in person or by phone	[GECmWCon]
45.9	Discussed the election with friends or family in person or by phone	[GECmDisc]
5.5	Tried to persuade someone else to vote for a particular party or candidate by phone	[GECmPers]
16.9	None of these	[GECmNone]
0.0	(Don't Know)	
-	(Refusal/Not answered)	

VERSIONS B, C AND D: ASK ALL WHO USE THE INTERNET (WHETHER FOR WORK OR NOT) ('yes' AT [WWWUse OR AT [WWWWork])

N=1975

Q444-
Q452

CARD C13

Still thinking about the general election campaign, did you do any of the things listed on this card?
PROBE: Any others?
CODE ALL THAT APPLY
Multicoded (Maximum of 8 codes)

%

10.1	Looked at the official website of a political party or candidate	[GECWPWeb]
0.8	Read or joined in a weblog ("blog") about the election	[GECWBlog]
8.9	Looked at any other kind of website for information about the election	[GECWOWeb]
1.6	Emailed a political party or candidate	[GECWSEM1]
2.1	Was emailed by a political party or a candidate	[GECWWEM1]
0.5	Emailed a newspaper, television or radio programme about the election	[GECWNPap]
11.8	Discussed the election with friends or family via the internet or email	[GECWFrie]
2.1	Tried to persuade someone else to vote for a particular party or candidate via email or the internet	[GECWPers]
78.8	None of these	[GECWNone]
-	(Don't Know)	
0.1	(Refusal/Not answered)	

VERSIONS B, C AND D: ASK ALL

Q453- CARD C14   N=3161
Q459 Suppose a law was being considered by parliament which you thought was really unjust and harmful. Which, if any, of the things on this card do you think you would do?

PROBE: Which others?
CODE ALL THAT APPLY

%
Multicoded (Maximum of 8 codes)
43.7 Contact my MP or MSP   [DoMP]
15.3 Speak to an influential person   [DoSpk]
10.9 Contact a government department   [DoGov]
13.6 Contact radio, TV or a newspaper   [DoTV]
73.7 Sign a petition   [DoSign]
8.0   Raise the issue in an organisation I
      already belong to   [DoRais]
17.0 Go on a protest or demonstration   [DoProt]
4.5   Form a group of like-minded people   [DoGrp]
10.1 (None of these)   [DoNone]
0.2   (Don't Know)
-     (Refusal/Not answered)

VERSIONS B, C AND D: IF USE THE INTERNET (WHETHER FOR WORK OR NOT) ('yes' AT [WWWUse OR AT [WWWWork]): IF NOT 'mentioned' AT [DoNone]

Q469 [EvDoWWW]   N=3161
      And do you think you would use email or the Internet to help you do (this/any of these things)?
      IF WOULD/WOULD NOT: Definitely or probably?

%
15.3 Definitely would
21.4 Probably would
7.4   Probably would not
11.8 Definitely would not
1.9   (Depends)
0.2   (Don't Know)
0.0   (Refusal/Not answered)

VERSIONS B, C AND D: ASK ALL

Q470- CARD C14 AGAIN   N=3161
Q477 And have you ever done any of the things on this card about a government action which you thought was unjust and harmful?
      Which ones? Any others?
      CODE ALL THAT APPLY

%
Multicoded (Maximum of 8 codes)
13.5 Contact my MP or MSP   [DoneMP]
4.9   Speak to an influential person   [DoneSpk]
3.1   Contact a government department   [DoneGov]
3.6   Contact radio, TV or a newspaper   [DoneTV]
37.0 Sign a petition   [DoneSign]
3.9   Raise the issue in an organisation I
      already belong to   [DoneRais]
9.8   Go on a protest or demonstration   [DoneProt]
1.4   Form a group of like-minded people   [DoneGrp]
52.7 (None of these)   [DoneNone]
0.2   (Don't Know)
-     (Refusal/Not answered)

VERSIONS B, C AND D: IF USE THE INTERNET (WHETHER FOR WORK OR NOT) ('yes' AT [WWWUse OR AT [WWWWork]): IF NOT 'mentioned' AT [DoneNone]

Q487 [EvDonWWW]   N=3161
      And did you use email or the internet to help you do (this/any of these things)?

Q488 [WWWProt]   N=3161
      Has anyone ever contacted you by email or via the internet asking you to join in a protest or campaign about an issue?

	[EvDonWWW]	[WWWProt]
	%	%
Yes	6.3	9.3
No	25.0	53.1
(Don't Know)	0.1	0.1
(Refusal/Not answered)	0.0	0.0

Transport (version A)

VERSION A: ASK ALL

Q489 [TrfPb6U] * N=1107
CARD C1
Now thinking about traffic and transport problems, how serious a problem for you is congestion on motorways?

Q490 [TrfPb9U] * N=1107
CARD C1 AGAIN
(And how serious a problem for you is ...) traffic congestion in towns and cities?

Q491 [TrfPb10U] * N=1107
CARD C1 AGAIN
(And how serious a problem for you are ...) exhaust fumes from traffic in towns and cities?

	[TrfPb6U]	[TrfPb9U]	[TrfPb10U]
	%	%	%
A very serious problem	12.7	18.0	24.4
A serious problem	20.3	33.2	36.4
Not a very serious problem	36.4	34.1	24.8
Not a problem at all	30.3	14.6	13.6
(Don't Know)	0.3	0.1	0.6
(Refusal/Not answered)	-	-	0.3

Q492 [TrfConc1] * N=1107
CARD C2
Transport like cars, buses, trains and planes can affect the environment in a number of ways. How concerned are you about damage to the countryside from building roads?

Q493 [TrfConc2] * N=1107
CARD C2 AGAIN
And how concerned are you about the effect of transport on climate change?

Q494 [TrfConc3] * N=1107
CARD C2 AGAIN
And how concerned are you about exhaust fumes from traffic?

	[TrfConc1]	[TrfConc2]	[TrfConc3]
	%	%	%
Very concerned	24.4	36.5	41.5
Fairly concerned	51.5	43.8	39.4
Not very concerned	19.0	14.9	15.6
Not at all concerned	4.8	3.5	3.4
(Don't Know)	0.3	1.3	0.2
(Refusal/Not answered)	-	-	-

Q495 [Drive] N=1107
May I just check, do you yourself drive a car at all these days?
%
70.3 Yes
29.7 No
 -    (Don't Know)
 -    (Refusal/Not answered)

IF 'Yes' AT [Drive]
Q496 [TRAVEL1] N=1107
CARD C3
How often nowadays do you usually travel ...by car as a driver?

VERSION A: ASK ALL
Q497 [Travel2] N=1107
CARD C3 AGAIN
(How often nowadays do you usually) ...travel by car as a passenger?

Q498 [Travel3] N=1107
CARD C3 AGAIN
(How often nowadays do you usually) ...travel by local bus?

Q499 [Travel4] N=1107
CARD C3 AGAIN
(How often nowadays do you usually) ...travel by train?

	[Travel1] %	[Travel2] %	[Travel3] %	[Travel4] %
Every day or nearly every day	46.2	9.4	7.5	1.8
2-5 days a week	17.8	22.4	11.6	3.8
Once a week	4.2	26.0	7.0	2.9
Less often but at least once a month	1.2	16.8	9.7	15.0
Less often than that	0.6	13.3	13.5	35.2
Never nowadays	0.3	11.9	50.6	41.2
(Don't Know)	-	0.2	-	-
(Refusal/Not answered)	-	-	-	-

	[CliCar] %	[CliPlane] %
Agree strongly	26.8	23.5
Agree	49.9	40.6
Neither agree nor disagree	15.0	23.6
Disagree	6.0	7.7
Disagree strongly	0.4	0.6
(Don't Know)	1.8	4.0
(Refusal/Not answered)	-	-

Q500 [AirTrvl]   N=1107
And how many trips did you make by plane during the
last 12 months? Please count the outward and return
flight and any transfers as one trip.
INTERVIEWER WRITE IN ANSWER
ACCEPT BEST ESTIMATE IF NECESSARY
CODE 'NONE' AS 0

%   **MEDIAN: 1 trip**
-    (Don't Know)
-    (Refusal/Not answered)

Q501 [CliCar] *   N=1107
CARD C4
Please tell me how much you agree or disagree with
each of these statements:
The current level of **car use** has a serious effect on
climate change.

Q502 [CliPlane] *   N=1107
CARD C4 AGAIN
(Please tell me how much you agree or disagree with
this statement)
The current level of **air travel** has a serious effect
on climate change.

Health (versions A, C and D)

VERSIONS A, C AND D: ASK ALL

Q503 [NHSSat] *
N=3210
CARD D1
All in all, how satisfied or dissatisfied would you say you are with the way in which the National Health Service runs nowadays?
Choose a phrase from this card.

Q504 [GPSat] *
N=3210
CARD D1 AGAIN
From your own experience, or from what you have heard, please say how satisfied or dissatisfied you are with the way in which each of these parts of the National Health Service runs nowadays:
First, local doctors or GPs?

Q505 [DentSat] *
N=3210
CARD D1 AGAIN
(And how satisfied or dissatisfied are you with the NHS as regards...)
... National Health Service dentists?

Q506 [InpatSat] *
N=3210
CARD D1 AGAIN
(And how satisfied or dissatisfied are you with the NHS as regards...)
... being in hospital as an **in**-patient?

Q507 [OutpaSat] *
N=3210
CARD D1 AGAIN
(And how satisfied or dissatisfied are you with the NHS as regards...)
... attending hospital as an **out**-patient?

Q508 [AESat] *
N=3210
CARD D1 AGAIN
(And how satisfied or dissatisfied are you with the NHS as regards...)
... Accident and Emergency departments?

Q509 [NDirSat] *
N=3210
CARD D1 AGAIN
(And how satisfied or dissatisfied are you with the NHS as regards...)
... (NHS Direct/NHS 24), the telephone or internet advice service?

Q510 [CYPSat] *
N=3210
CARD D1 AGAIN
Now from your own experience, **or from what you have heard**, please say how satisfied or dissatisfied you are with ....
... NHS services for children and young people?

	[NHSSat]	[GPSat]	[DentSat]	[InpatSat]
	%	%	%	%
Very satisfied	9.8	28.2	14.7	15.7
Quite satisfied	38.4	45.6	29.9	34.1
Neither satisfied nor dissatisfied	20.2	9.1	16.5	21.8
Quite dissatisfied	20.9	11.9	15.4	14.0
Very dissatisfied	10.2	4.6	18.2	6.4
(Don't Know)	0.4	0.6	5.3	8.1
(Refusal/Not answered)	0.0	-	-	-

	[OutpaSat]	[AESat]	[NdirSat]	[CYPSat]
	%	%	%	%
Very satisfied	14.8	15.9	11.4	11.4
Quite satisfied	45.9	35.1	20.6	33.6
Neither satisfied nor dissatisfied	18.6	19.5	32.1	27.2
Quite dissatisfied	11.5	14.5	5.8	5.1
Very dissatisfied	4.7	7.4	4.2	1.8
(Don't Know)	4.5	7.6	25.9	20.8
(Refusal/Not answered)	-	-	-	0.0

Q511 [NHSLimit]   N=3210
It has been suggested that the National Health Service should be available **only to those with lower incomes**. This would mean that contributions and taxes could be lower and most people would then take out medical insurance or pay for health care.
Do you support or oppose this idea?
IF 'SUPPORT' OR 'OPPOSE': A lot or little?
%
9.4   Support a lot
14.7 Support a little
15.4 Oppose a little
58.6 Oppose a lot
2.0   (Don't know)
0.0   (Not answered)

Q512 [InPat1] *   N=3210
CARD D2
Now, suppose you had to go into a local NHS hospital for observation and maybe an operation. From what you know or have heard, please say whether you think the hospital doctors would tell you all you feel you need to know?

Q513 [InPat2] *   N=3210
CARD D2 AGAIN
(And please say whether you think ...)
...the hospital doctors would take seriously any views you may have on the sorts of treatment available?

Q514 [InPat3] *   N=3210
CARD D2 AGAIN
(And please say whether you think ...)
...the operation would take place on the day it was booked for?

Q515 [InPat4] *   N=3210
CARD D2 AGAIN
(And please say whether you think ...)
...you would be allowed home only when you were really well enough to leave?

Q516 [InPat5] *   N=3210
CARD D2 AGAIN
(And please say whether you think ...)
...the nurses would take seriously any complaints you may have?

Q517 [InPat6] *   N=3210
CARD D2 AGAIN
(And please say whether you think ...)
...the hospital doctors would take seriously any complaints you may have?

Q518 [InPat7] *   N=3210
CARD D2 AGAIN
(And please say whether you think ...)
...there would be a particular nurse responsible for dealing with any problems you may have?

	[InPat1]	[InPat2]	[InPat3]	[InPat4]
	%	%	%	%
Definitely would	21.6	14.2	7.4	13.4
Probably would	52.6	51.8	45.3	45.7
Probably would not	20.0	25.5	36.5	30.3
Definitely would not	4.1	5.0	7.7	8.2
(Don't Know)	1.6	3.5	3.1	2.4
(Refusal/Not answered)	-	-	0.0	0.0

	[InPat5]	[InPat6]	[InPat7]
	%	%	%
Definitely would	15.5	14.8	11.3
Probably would	57.3	58.5	40.1
Probably would not	20.5	19.9	33.6
Definitely would not	4.1	3.9	7.1
(Don't Know)	2.6	2.9	7.9
(Refusal/Not answered)	0.0	-	-

Q519 [HosSaySh] *   N=3210
CARD D3
How much say do you think NHS patients **should have** over which hospital to go to if they need treatment?

Q520 [HosSayDs] *
CARD D3 AGAIN
And how much say do you think NHS patients **actually**
have over which hospital to go to if they need
treatment?
N=3210

Q521 [TimSaySh] *
CARD D3 AGAIN
How much say **should** NHS hospital out-patients have
over the time of their appointments?
N=3210

Q522 [TimSayDs] *
CARD D3 AGAIN
And how much say do you think NHS hospital out-
patients **actually have** over the time of their
appointments?
N=3210

Q523 [TreSaySh] *
CARD D3 AGAIN
How much say **should** NHS patients have over the kind of
treatment they receive?
N=3210

Q524 [TreSayDs] *
CARD D3 AGAIN
And how much say do you think NHS patients **actually**
have over the kind of treatment they receive?
N=3210

	[HosSaySh]	[HosSayDs]	[TimSaySh]
	%	%	%
A great deal	24.2	1.6	12.1
Quite a lot	43.8	10.1	44.4
A little	25.4	49.8	34.9
None at all	5.5	35.0	7.5
(Don't Know)	1.1	3.5	1.2
(Refusal/Not answered)	-	-	-

	[TimSayDs]	[TreSaySh]	[TreSayDs]
	%	%	%
A great deal	1.5	21.7	1.9
Quite a lot	15.0	47.6	18.3
A little	47.2	22.6	54.5
None at all	33.5	5.9	21.2
(Don't Know)	2.9	2.2	4.1
(Refusal/Not answered)	-	0.0	-

Q525 [CareNeed]
At some point in their lives people can need regular
help looking after themselves because of illness,
disability or old age. This can include help with
things like getting washed and dressed, shopping,
cooking or cleaning. Have either you or someone you
are close to been in need of any regular help like
this over the last ten years?
PROBE FOR CORRECT CATEGORY
N=3210

	%
Yes, respondent only	6.7
Yes, someone else only	46.1
Yes, respondent and someone else	3.4
No	43.7
(Don't know)	0.0
(Not answered)	0.0

Q526-
Q527 Are you currently providing, or have you ever
provided, unpaid regular help for someone who needs
help looking after themselves because of their
illness, disability or old age?
INTERVIEWER: INCLUDE ANY REGULAR HELP TO A FAMILY
MEMBER.
CODE ALL THAT APPLY
Multicoded (Maximum of 2 codes)
N=3210

		%
Yes, currently providing help	[CarePCur]	11.5
Yes, have provided help in the past	[CarePPst]	21.1
No	[CarePNon]	68.1
(Don't know)		0.1
(Not answered)		-

Q528 [CareSat]
CARD D4
From your own experience, or from what you have heard,
please say how satisfied or dissatisfied you are with
the services provided to people who need this kind of
regular help with looking after themselves whose
family cannot provide it?
N=3210

	%
Very satisfied	6.7
Quite satisfied	32.5
Neither satisfied nor dissatisfied	26.7
Quite dissatisfied	18.1
Very dissatisfied	6.6
(Don't know)	9.4
(Not answered)	-

Q529   [CareStHm] *
       CARD D5   N=3210
       I'd now like you to imagine an elderly person who
       needs this kind of **regular** help with looking after
       themselves. From what you know or have heard please
       say whether you think that enough help would be
       available for this person so that they could stay
       in their own home if they wanted to?

Q530   [CareArng] *   N=3210
       CARD D5 AGAIN
       Now imagine that you, or someone you knew, needed this
       kind of help.
       Please say whether you think you would know how to go
       about arranging this?

	CareStHm[]	CareArng[]
	%	%
Definitely would	9.9	18.8
Probably would	43.6	32.4
Probably would not	32.4	27.6
Definitely would not	8.9	19.5
(Don't Know)	5.2	1.7
(Refusal/Not answered)	0.0	0.0

Q531   [CareCost]   N=3210
       CARD D6
       Still thinking about an elderly person who needs
       regular help with looking after themselves. Which of
       these statements comes closest to what you believe
       about who should **pay** for this help?

       %
42.5   The government should pay, no matter how much money
       the person has
2.3   The person should pay, no matter how much money he/she
       has
53.6   Who pays should depend on how much money the person
       has

1.5   (Don't know)
0.1   (Not answered)

       VERSION A: ASK ALL
       NOTE: The following 3 questions were also asked for
       version B in the Social Identities module (Q805 to
       Q807)
Q532   [NHSTrust]   N=2165
       CARD D7
       How much do you trust hospital doctors always to put
       the interests of their patients above the convenience
       of the hospital?

       %
12.9   Always
49.9   Most of the time
29.6   Only some of the time
5.2   Just about never
2.4   (Don't know)
0.1   (Not answered)

Q533   [DieShdSy] *   N=2165
       CARD D8
       I'd like you to think now of a patient who is nearing
       the end of his or her life. How much say do you think
       someone in this situation **should** have in the decisions
       that are made about their medical treatment?

Q534   [DieDsSy] *   N=2165
       CARD D8 AGAIN
       And from what you know or have heard, how much say do
       you think a patient like this **actually has** in the
       decisions that are made about their medical treatment
       towards the end of their life?

	[DieShdSy]	[DieDsSy]
	%	%
A great deal	57.8	4.3
Quite a lot	32.3	20.4
A little	6.2	53.6
None at all	1.6	16.9
(Don't Know)	1.8	4.6
(Refusal/Not answered)	0.3	0.1

Q535 **VERSIONS A, C AND D: ASK ALL**
[SRHealth] N=3210
How is your health in general for someone of your age?
Would you say that it is ... READ OUT ...
%
44.4 ... very good,
37.5 fairly good,
12.9 fair,
3.9 bad,
1.4 or, very bad?
0.0 (Don't know)
- (Not answered)

Civil liberties (version B)

Q537 **VERSION B: ASK ALL**
[ObeyLaw] N=1058
In general, would you say that people should obey the law without exception, or are there exceptional occasions on which people should follow their consciences even if it means breaking the law?
%
40.5 Obey law without exception
56.5 Follow conscience on occasions
2.9 (Don't know)
0.2 (Not answered)

Q538 [DemSocR1] * N=1058
CARD D1
There are different views about people's rights in a democratic society.
On a scale of 1 to 7, where 1 is not at all important and 7 is very important, how important to democracy is it that **every** adult living in Britain has...READ OUT...
...the right to protest against government decisions they disagree with?

Q539 [DemSocR2] * N=1058
CARD D1 AGAIN
(And how important is it that **every** adult living in Britain has...)
...the right **not** to be detained by the police for more than a week or so without being charged with a crime?

Q540 [DemSocR3] * N=1058
CARD D1 AGAIN
(And how important is it that **every** adult living in Britain has...)
...the right to keep their life private from government?

Q541 [DemSocR4] * N=1058
CARD D1 AGAIN
And how important is it that **every** adult living in Britain has...READ OUT...
...the right **not** to be exposed to offensive views in public?

Q542 [DemSocR5] *   N=1058
CARD D1 AGAIN
(And how important is it that **every** adult living in Britain has...)
...the right to a trial by jury if they are charged with a serious crime?

Q543 [DemSocR6] *   N=1058
CARD D1 AGAIN
(And how important is it that **every** adult living in Britain has...)
...the right to say whatever they think in public?

	[DemSocR1]	[DemSocR2]	[DemSocR3]
	%	%	%
1:Not at all important	2.3	5.3	2.9
2	1.2	4.7	1.6
3	2.2	6.3	3.5
4	7.2	12.1	11.2
5	13.7	14.3	12.9
6	16.8	12.6	16.5
7:Very important	55.7	41.1	50.1
(Don't Know)	1.0	3.7	1.2
(Refusal/Not answered)	-	-	-

	[DemSocR4]	[DemSocR5]	[DemSocR6]
	%	%	%
1:Not at all important	4.5	0.7	4.4
2	3.0	0.6	5.6
3	4.1	1.0	6.9
4	11.2	2.7	16.3
5	12.9	6.8	19.5
6	19.2	14.9	14.4
7:Very important	42.7	71.7	31.4
(Don't Know)	2.5	1.7	1.5
(Refusal/Not answered)	-	-	-

Q544 [TradeOf1] *   N=1058
CARD D2
A number of measures have been suggested as ways of tackling the threat of terrorism in Britain. Some people oppose these because they think they reduce people's freedom too much. Others think that the reduction in freedom is a price worth paying. For each of the measures I mention, please say which of the views on this card comes closest to your own. Firstly, banning certain peaceful protests and demonstrations.

Q545 [TradeOf2] *   N=1058
CARD D2
(Still thinking about measures that have been suggested as ways of tackling the threat of terrorism in Britain.)
(Which of the views on the card comes closest to your own?)
Banning certain people from saying whatever they want in public.

Q546 [TradeOf3] *   N=1058
CARD D2
(Still thinking about measures that have been suggested as ways of tackling the threat of terrorism in Britain.)
(Which of the views on the card comes closest to your own?)
Having compulsory identity cards for all adults.

Q547 [TradeOf4] *   N=1058
CARD D2
(Still thinking about measures that have been suggested as ways of tackling the threat of terrorism in Britain.)
(Which of the views on the card comes closest to your own?)
Allowing the police to detain people for more than a week or so without charge if the police suspect them of involvement in terrorism.

	[TradeOf1]	[TradeOf2]	[TradeOf3]
	%	%	%
Definitely unacceptable as it reduces people's freedom too much	35.5	17.2	15.7
Probably unacceptable as it reduces people's freedom too much	27.1	28.5	10.7
Probably a price worth paying to reduce the terrorist threat	23.4	28.0	29.5
Definitely a price worth paying to reduce the terrorist threat	11.4	23.7	41.8
(Don't Know)	2.6	2.5	2.4
(Refusal/Not answered)	-	-	-

	[TradeOf4]	[TradeOf5]	[TradeOf6]
	%	%	%
Definitely unacceptable as it reduces people's freedom too much	9.0	26.9	6.7
Probably unacceptable as it reduces people's freedom too much	10.6	23.4	10.3
Probably a price worth paying to reduce the terrorist threat	26.6	21.9	36.8
Definitely a price worth paying to reduce the terrorist threat	52.0	23.0	44.3
(Don't Know)	1.7	4.6	1.9
(Refusal/Not answered)	-	0.2	0.1

Q548 [TradeOf5] *
CARD D2   N=1058
Still thinking about measures that have been suggested as ways of tackling the threat of terrorism in Britain.
Which of the views on the card comes closest to your own for...READ OUT...
...denying the right to a trial by jury to people charged with a terrorist-related crime.

Q549 [TradeOf6] *
CARD D2   N=1058
(Still thinking about measures that have been suggested as ways of tackling the threat of terrorism in Britain.)
(Which of the views on the card comes closest to your own?)
Following people suspected of involvement with terrorism, tapping their phones and opening their mail.

Q550 [TradeOf7] *
CARD D2   N=1058
(Still thinking about measures that have been suggested as ways of tackling the threat of terrorism in Britain.)
(Which of the views on the card comes closest to your own?)
Putting people suspected of involvement with terrorism under special rules, which would mean they could be electronically tagged, prevented from going to certain places, or prevented from leaving their homes at certain times.

Q551 [TradeOf8] *
CARD D2   N=1058
(Still thinking about measures that have been suggested as ways of tackling the threat of terrorism in Britain.)
(Which of the views on the card comes closest to your own?)
Torturing people held in British jails who are suspected of involvement in terrorism to get information from them, if this is the only way this information can be obtained.

	[TradeOf7]	[TradeOf8]
	%	%
Definitely unacceptable as it reduces people's freedom too much	5.2	57.7
Probably unacceptable as it reduces people's freedom too much	13.1	18.4
Probably a price worth paying to reduce the terrorist threat	32.1	12.8
Definitely a price worth paying to reduce the terrorist threat	48.1	8.8
(Don't Know)	1.6	2.3
(Refusal/Not answered)	-	-

Q552 [BritNon]   N=1058
CARD D3
Thinking again of all of these measures that have been suggested as ways of tackling the threat of terrorism in Britain.
Some people say that the same measures should apply to everyone in Britain, no matter where they are from.
Others say stricter measures should apply to people who are from other countries.
What about you?

%
61.5 Everyone in Britain should be treated the same
36.9 Stricter measures should apply to people from other countries

1.5   (Don't know)
0.1   (Not answered)

Q553 **IF NOT DON'T KNOW OR REFUSAL AT [BritNon]**
[BritNonS]   N=1058
CARD D4
And how strongly do you think that?
(Please take your answer from this card)

%
50.1 Very strongly
44.5 Quite strongly
3.5   Not very strongly
0.4   Not at all strongly
0.1   (Don't know)
1.6   (Not answered)

VERSION B: ASK ALL

Q554 [TerrorLk] *   N=1058
CARD D5
Please say whether you agree or disagree with each of the following statements.
It is very likely that there will be a major terrorist attack in Britain in the next couple of years.

Q555 [TerrConc] *   N=1058
CARD D5 AGAIN
(Please say whether you agree or disagree with this statement.)
The threat of a terrorist attack in Britain is of great concern to me.

Q556 [WarHumRi] *   N=1058
CARD D5 AGAIN
(Please say whether you agree or disagree with this statement.)
When a country is at war it must **always** abide by international human rights law.

Q557 [RiskTer] *   N=1058
CARD D5 AGAIN
(Please say whether you agree or disagree with this statement.)
People exaggerate the risks of there being a major terrorist attack in Britain.

Q558 [HumRiJob] *   N=1058
CARD D5 AGAIN
(Please say whether you agree or disagree with this statement.)
International human rights law prevents the armed forces from doing their job properly.

Q559 [TortWar] *   N=1058
CARD D5 AGAIN
(Please say whether you agree or disagree with this statement.)
During a war it is acceptable for the armed forces to torture people.

Q560 [TerHumRi] * N=1058
CARD D5 AGAIN
(Please say whether you agree or disagree with this statement.)
If someone is suspected of involvement with terrorism they should not be protected by international human rights law.

Q561 [TerInno] * N=1058
CARD D5 AGAIN
(Please say whether you agree or disagree with this statement.)
Britain must take the strongest measures possible to tackle terrorism, even if this means some innocent people get caught up in them by mistake.

	[TerrorLk] %	[TerrConc] %	[WarHumRi] %	[RiskTer] %
Agree strongly	48.9	47.6	43.6	3.6
Agree	35.2	37.3	40.2	18.9
Neither agree nor disagree	9.6	7.5	8.3	12.7
Disagree	4.1	6.1	5.5	42.8
Disagree strongly	1.0	0.9	1.2	20.5
(Don't Know)	1.0	0.6	1.2	1.5
(Refusal/Not answered)	0.2	-	-	-

	[HumRiJob] %	[TortWar] %	[TerHumRi] %	[TerInno] %
Agree strongly	7.1	1.9	10.8	14.2
Agree	27.5	8.4	28.0	44.6
Neither agree nor disagree	25.5	10.9	13.0	15.0
Disagree	29.2	41.7	34.1	19.4
Disagree strongly	4.7	36.3	11.7	5.1
(Don't Know)	5.8	0.6	2.3	1.7
(Refusal/Not answered)	-	-	0.1	0.1

Disability (versions A, C and D)

VERSIONS A, C AND D: ASK ALL
[DisNew2] N=3210
Q563 Do you have a long-standing physical or mental health condition or disability? By long-standing, I mean anything that has lasted at least 12 months or that is likely to last at least 12 months?

IF 'yes' AT [DisNew2]
[DisAct] N=3210
Q564 Does this condition or disability have a substantial adverse effect on your ability to carry out normal day-to-day activities?

	[DisNew2] %	[DisAct] %
Yes	32.9	16.4
No	67.0	16.5
(Don't Know)	0.0	-
(Refusal/Not answered)	0.1	0.1

VERSIONS A, C AND D: ASK ALL
Q565-
Q575 CARD E1   N=3210

People have different ideas about what it means to be disabled.

Which of the people on this card would you think of as a disabled person?
PROBE: Which others?
CODE ALL THAT APPLY

Multicoded (Maximum of 11 codes)

%
0.5 (None of these)   [WDisNone]
80.8 A person with severe arthritis   [WDisArth]
27.0 A person who has HIV/AIDS   [WDisAIDS]
48.2 A person who has a diagnosis of
     schizophrenia   [WDisSchi]
39.7 A person who has a diagnosis of
     severe depression   [WDisDepr]
70.5 A person who has Down's Syndrome   [WDisDown]
43.8 A person who has cancer   [WDisCanc]
44.3 An older person who cannot hear without
     a hearing aid   [WDisOldH]
86.8 A blind person   [WDisBlin]
91.1 A person who uses a wheelchair most of
     the time   [WDisWhlC]
31.4 A person with a broken leg, using
     crutches while it heals   [WDisBrok]
25.3 A person with a severe facial
     disfigurement   [WDisFacD]
0.1 (Don't know)
 -   (Not answered)

Q588 [DisWhlC]
     CARD E2   N=3210

In law, a person is disabled if he or she has a physical or mental impairment which has a substantial and long-term adverse effect on their ability to carry out normal day-to-day activities.
This might include people in each of the groups on the upper section of this card.

Thinking first of someone with a **physical impairment**, such as someone who uses a wheelchair to get around or who has problems using their arms or hands.

Thinking of people you know other than yourself, do you personally know anyone who is disabled in this way?

IF ASKED: 'Long-term' means it has lasted for 12 months or more, or is likely to last for more than 12 months.

IF ASKED: Please think what the situation for the person would be like **without** treatment or correction, e.g. without medication, prosthesis.

%
47.8 Yes
52.1 No
0.1 (Don't know)
 -   (Not answered)

IF 'yes' AT [DisWhlC]
Q589 [DisWhlCR]
     CARD E2 AGAIN   N=3210

What is this person's relationship to you? (If you know several, please think of the person who you know best. Please take your answer from the lower section of this card.)

%
1.8 My partner
1.4 My child/One of my children
16.1 Another close relative
11.4 A close friend
2.2 A colleague or co-worker
0.2 My boss
14.6 Someone else I know
 -   (Don't know)
0.1 (Not answered)

Q590 **VERSIONS A, C AND D: ASK ALL**
[DisBlDf]   N=3210
CARD E2 AGAIN
And do you personally know anyone (other than
yourself) who has a sensory impairment, such as being
blind or deaf?
INCLUDE SERIOUS VISUAL / HEARING IMPAIRMENTS
IF ASKED: Please think what the situation for the
person would be like **without** treatment or correction,
e.g. without hearing aid, **except** for visual
impairment, where you should think of what the
situation for the person is like **with** any glasses or
contact lenses they normally use.

%
39.6   Yes
60.4   No
0.0   (Don't know)
 -      (Not answered)

IF 'yes' AT [DisBlDf]

Q591 [DisBlDfR]   N=3210
CARD E2 AGAIN
What is this person's relationship to you? (If you
know several, please think of the person who you know
best. Please take your answer from the lower section
of this card.)

%
1.7   My partner
0.8   My child/One of my children
14.8   Another close relative
7.8   A close friend
2.2   A colleague or co-worker
0.1   My boss
12.2   Someone else I know
 -      (Don't know)
0.0   (Not answered)

Q592 **VERSIONS A, C AND D: ASK ALL**
[DisMent]   N=3210
CARD E2 AGAIN
And do you personally know anyone (other than
yourself) who has a **mental health condition**, such as
depression, schizophrenia or severe phobias?
IF ASKED: Please think what the situation for the
person would be like **without** treatment, e.g. without
medication.

%
40.0   Yes
59.8   No
0.2   (Don't know)
 -      (Not answered)

IF 'yes' AT [DisMent]

Q593 [DisMentR]   N=3210
CARD E2 AGAIN
What is this person's relationship to you? (If you
know several, please take your answer from the lower section
best. Please take your answer from the lower section
of this card.)

%
2.0   My partner
2.2   My child/One of my children
11.9   Another close relative
11.5   A close friend
2.0   A colleague or co-worker
0.0   My boss
10.2   Someone else I know
0.0   (Don't know)
0.3   (Not answered)

Q594 **VERSIONS A, C AND D: ASK ALL**
[DisDown]   N=3210
CARD E2 AGAIN
And do you personally know anyone (other than
yourself) who has a **learning disability** - what used to
be called a **mental handicap** - such as Down's Syndrome?

%
31.5   Yes
68.5   No
0.1   (Don't know)
 -      (Not answered)

Q595

IF 'yes' AT [DisDown] N=3210
[DisDownR]
CARD E2 AGAIN
What is this person's relationship to you? (If you
know several, please think of the person who you know
best. Please take your answer from the lower section
of this card.)

%	
0.0	My partner
1.4	My child/one of my children
6.7	Another close relative
5.4	A close friend
0.8	A colleague or co-worker
–	My boss
17.2	Someone else I know
–	(Don't know)
0.1	(Not answered)

Q596

VERSIONS A, C AND D: ASK ALL N=3210
[DisLIll]
CARD E2 AGAIN
And do you personally know anyone (other than
yourself) who has any other **long-standing illness or
health condition** which prevents them from carrying out
normal day-to-day activities. This may include, for
example, some people with multiple sclerosis
(MS), severe arthritis, cancer or HIV/AIDS.
IF ASKED: 'Long-term' means it has lasted for 12
months or more, or is likely to last for more than 12
months.
IF ASKED: Please think what the situation for the
person would be like **without** treatment (e.g. without
medication).

%	
49.0	Yes
51.0	No
0.0	(Don't know)
–	(Not answered)

Q597

IF 'yes' AT [DisLIll] N=3210
[DisLIllR]
CARD E2 AGAIN
What is this person's relationship to you? (If you
know several, please think of the person who you know
best. Please take your answer from the lower section
of this card.)

%	
1.9	My partner
0.8	My child/One of my children
18.6	Another close relative
12.5	A close friend
2.0	A colleague or co-worker
0.1	My boss
12.9	Someone else I know
–	(Don't know)
0.0	(Not answered)

Q598-
Q602

VERSIONS A, C AND D: ASK ALL   N=3210
[RDisFW] NOT ON DATAFILE
CARD E2 AGAIN
And do you yourself have any of the health conditions
or impairments on this card, which has a substantial
and long-term adverse effect on your ability to carry
out normal day-to-day activities?
PROBE: Which others?
CODE ALL THAT APPLY
IF ASKED:'Long-term' means it has lasted for 12 months
or more, or is likely to last for more than 12 months.
IF ASKED:Please think what the situation would be like
without treatment or correction (e.g. without
medication or hearing aid) - **except** for visual
impairment where you should think of what the
situation would be like **with** any glasses or contact
lenses that you normally use.
Multicoded (Maximum of 5 codes)

%
4.4   Physical impairment, such as using a   [RDisWhlc]
       wheelchair to get around and/or
       difficulty using your arms or hands
2.6   Sensory impairment such as blind/serious   [RDisBlDf]
       visual impairment or deaf/serious
       hearing impairment
3.4   Mental health condition, such as   [RDisMent]
       depression, schizophrenia or severe
       phobia
0.3   Learning disability, such as Down's   [RDisDown]
       syndrome
7.4   Other long-standing illness or health   [RDisLIl1]
       condition (WRITE IN)
84.2   (None of these)   [RDisNone]
0.1   (Don't know)
0.1   (Not answered)

Q611   [DPRand]   N=3210
       Random number for DPrj
       Range: 1 ... 4

       VERSIONS A, C AND D: ASK ALL
Q613   [DisPrj] *   N=3210
       Generally speaking, do you think there is a lot of
       prejudice in Britain against **disabled people in
       general**, a little, hardly any or none?

Q614   **VERSIONS A, C AND D: ASK ALL IN RANDOM GROUP 1**   N=761
       [DPrjWhlC] *
       CARD E3
       And generally speaking, how much prejudice do you
       think there is in Britain against **people with physical
       impairments**, such as someone who uses a wheelchair?

Q615   [DPrjDeaf] *   N=761
       CARD E3 AGAIN
       And generally speaking, how much prejudice do you
       think there is in Britain against **people who are deaf?**

Q616   **VERSIONS A, C AND D: ASK ALL IN RANDOM GROUP 2**   N=830
       [DPrjBlin] *
       CARD E3
       And generally speaking, how much prejudice do you
       think there is in Britain against **people who are
       blind?**

Q617   [DPrjDown] *   N=830
       CARD E3 AGAIN
       And generally speaking, how much prejudice do you
       think there is in Britain against **people with learning
       disabilities**, such as someone with Down's syndrome?

Q618   **VERSIONS A, C AND D: ASK ALL IN RANDOM GROUP 3**   N=783
       [DPrjSchi] *
       CARD E3
       And generally speaking, how much prejudice do you
       think there is in Britain against **people with
       schizophrenia?**

Q619   [DPrjAIDS] *   N=783
       CARD E3 AGAIN
       And generally speaking, how much prejudice do you
       think there is in Britain against **people who have
       long-term health conditions** that may seriously affect
       their ability to carry out normal day-to-day
       activities, such as **HIV/AIDS?**

VERSIONS A, C AND D: ASK ALL IN RANDOM GROUP 4

Q620 [DPrjDepr] * N=836
CARD E3
And generally speaking, how much prejudice do you think there is in Britain against **people with depression?**

Q621 [DPrjLill] * N=836
CARD E3 AGAIN
And generally speaking, how much prejudice do you think there is in Britain against **people who have long-term health conditions** that seriously affect their ability to carry out normal day-to-day activities, such as multiple sclerosis (MS) and severe arthritis?

	[DisPrj]	[DPrjWhlC]	[DPrjDeaf]	[DPrjBlin]
	%	%	%	%
A lot	24.8	20.0	12.5	10.2
A little	49.5	49.8	43.6	31.9
Hardly any	17.0	19.0	27.5	33.5
None	7.6	10.3	14.2	21.3
(Don't Know)	1.1	0.9	2.2	2.9
(Refusal/Not answered)	-	-	-	0.2

	[DprjDown]	[DPrjSchi]	[DPrjAIDS]
	%	%	%
A lot	33.7	45.8	44.1
A little	41.0	31.9	38.0
Hardly any	14.3	8.4	9.2
None	9.6	4.0	3.8
(Don't know what this means)	0.3	3.7	0.8
(Don't Know)	1.1	6.2	4.0
(Refusal/Not answered)	-	-	-

	[DprjDepr]	[DprjIll]
	%	%
A lot	28.9	14.7
A little	40.0	40.8
Hardly any	18.6	26.7
None	6.4	13.2
(Don't know what this means)	2.6	2.1
(Don't Know)	3.5	2.5
(Refusal/Not answered)	-	-

VERSIONS A, C AND D: ASK ALL IN RANDOM GROUP 1

Q622 [DNeiWhlC] N=761
CARD E4
Taking your answer from this card, how do you think you would feel if a person who **uses a wheelchair** were to move in next door?

Q623 [DNeiSchi] N=761
CARD E4 AGAIN
And what if it was a person **who has a diagnosis of schizophrenia**, which you know that he or she has managed successfully for several years (who moved in next door)?
(How comfortable or uncomfortable do you think you would feel with this?)

Q624 [DNeiDeaf] * N=761
CARD E4 AGAIN
And what if it was a person **who cannot hear without a hearing aid** (who moved in next door)?
(How comfortable or uncomfortable do you think you would feel with this?)

	[DNeiWhlC]	[DNeiSchi]	[DNeiDeaf]
	%	%	%
Very comfortable with this	88.7	28.7	83.0
Fairly comfortable with this	10.6	45.6	14.5
Fairly **uncomfortable** with this	0.1	18.6	1.8
Very **uncomfortable** with this	0.5	4.8	0.4
(Don't know what this means)	-	1.0	-
(Don't Know)	0.2	1.2	0.2
(Refusal/Not answered)	-	-	-

Q625 [DBosWhlC] * N=761
CARD E4 AGAIN
Thinking now of a different situation, how do you think you would (feel/have felt) if a person who (uses/used) a wheelchair (was/had been) appointed as your boss (when you were working)?

Q626 [DBosSchi] N=761
CARD E4 AGAIN
And what if it was a person who (has/had) a diagnosis of schizophrenia which you (know/knew) that he or she (has/had) managed successfully for several years (who (was/had been) appointed as your boss (when you were working))?
(How comfortable or uncomfortable do you think you would (feel/have felt) with this?)

Q627 [DBosDeaf] N=761
CARD E4 AGAIN
And what if it was a person who (cannot/could not) hear without a hearing aid (who (was/had been) appointed as your boss (when you were working))?
(How comfortable or uncomfortable do you think you would (feel/have felt) with this?)

	[DBosWhlC]	[DBosSchi]	[DBosDeaf]
	%	%	%
Very comfortable with this	83.1	30.9	68.2
Fairly comfortable with this	14.5	38.2	24.0
Fairly uncomfortable with this	0.6	18.1	3.9
Very uncomfortable with this	0.3	8.8	2.5
(Don't know what this means)	-	0.9	-
(Don't Know)	1.3	3.1	1.5
(Refusal/Not answered)	0.2	-	-

VERSIONS A, C AND D: ASK ALL IN RANDOM GROUP 2

Q628 [DNeiBlin] N=830
CARD E4
Taking your answer from this card, how do you think you would feel if a blind person were to move in next door?

Q629 [DNeiDepr] * N=830
CARD E4 AGAIN
And what if it was a person that you know has had a diagnosis of depression in the recent past (who moved in next door)?
(How comfortable or uncomfortable do you think you would feel with this?)

Q630 [DNeiLill] * N=830
CARD E4 AGAIN
And what if it was a person who has a long-term health condition which seriously affects their ability to carry out normal day-to-day activities, such as multiple sclerosis (MS) or severe arthritis (who moved in next door)?
(How comfortable or uncomfortable do you think you would feel with this?)

Q631 [DNeiDown] * N=830
CARD E4 AGAIN
And what if it was a person with Down's syndrome (who moved in next door)?
(How comfortable or uncomfortable do you think you would feel with this?)

	[DNeiBlin]	[DNeiDepr]	[DNeiLill]	[DNeiDown]
	%	%	%	%
Very comfortable with this	78.8	44.4	62.0	59.2
Fairly comfortable with this	19.9	40.5	32.3	34.2
Fairly uncomfortable with this	1.1	12.7	4.7	4.8
Very uncomfortable with this	0.1	1.4	0.7	1.0
(Don't know what this means)	-	0.1	0.1	0.5
(Don't Know)	0.1	0.8	0.2	0.4
(Refusal/Not answered)	-	-	-	-

Q632 [DBosBlin]   N=830
CARD E4 AGAIN
Thinking now of a different situation, how do you think you would (feel/have felt) if a blind person (was/had been) appointed as your boss (when you were working)?
(How comfortable or uncomfortable do you think you would (feel/have felt) with this?)

Q633 [DBosDepr] *   N=830
CARD E4 AGAIN
And what if it was a person that you (know/knew) (has/had) had serious depression in the recent past (who (was/had been) appointed as your boss (when you were working))?
(How comfortable or uncomfortable do you think you would (feel/have felt) with this?)

Q634 [DBosLill] *   N=830
CARD E4 AGAIN
And what if it was a person who (has/had) a long-term health condition which seriously (affects/affected) their ability to carry out normal day-to-day activities, such as multiple sclerosis (MS) or severe arthritis (who (was/had been) appointed as your boss (when you were working))?
(How comfortable or uncomfortable do you think you would (feel/have felt) with this?)

	[DBosBlin]	[DBosDepr]	[DBosLill]
	%	%	%
Very comfortable with this	61.2	30.3	41.5
Fairly comfortable with this	29.3	37.5	38.2
Fairly uncomfortable with this	4.9	24.2	14.0
Very uncomfortable with this	2.5	6.0	4.3
(Don't know what this means)	-	0.1	0.2
(Don't Know)	2.0	1.8	1.7
(Refusal/Not answered)	0.1	0.1	0.1

VERSIONS A, C AND D: ASK ALL IN RANDOM GROUP 3
Q635 [RelMWhlC]   N=783
CARD E4
Taking your answer from this card, how do you think you would feel if one of your close relatives were to marry a person who uses a wheelchair?

Q636 [RelMSchi]   N=783
CARD E4 AGAIN
And what if it was a person who has a diagnosis of schizophrenia which you know that he or she has managed successfully for several years (who was marrying your close relative)?
(How comfortable or uncomfortable do you think you would feel with this?)

Q637 [RelMDeaf] *   N=783
CARD E4 AGAIN
And what if it was a person who cannot hear without a hearing aid (who was marrying your close relative)?
(How comfortable or uncomfortable do you think you would feel with this?)

VERSIONS A, C AND D: ASK ALL IN RANDOM GROUP 4
Q638 [RelMBlin] *   N=836
CARD E4
Taking your answer from this card, how do you think you would feel if one of your close relatives were to marry a blind person?

Q639 [RelMDepr] *   N=836
CARD E4 AGAIN
And what if it was a person that you know who has had serious depression in the recent past (who was marrying your close relative)?
(How comfortable or uncomfortable do you think you would feel with this?)

Q640 [RelMLill] *   N=836
CARD E4 AGAIN
And what if it was a person who has a long-term health condition which seriously affects their ability to carry out normal day-to-day activities, such as multiple sclerosis (MS) or severe arthritis (who was marrying your close relative)?
(How comfortable or uncomfortable do you think you would feel with this?)

	[RelMWhlC]	[RelMSchl]	[RelMDeaf]
	%	%	%
Very comfortable with this	59.3	18.7	61.5
Fairly comfortable with this	31.9	38.3	33.6
Fairly **uncomfortable** with this	6.8	26.4	3.8
Very **uncomfortable** with this	1.3	13.8	0.5
(Don't know what this means)	-	1.4	-
(Don't Know)	0.7	1.5	0.5
(Refusal/Not answered)	-	-	-

	[RelMBlin]	[RelMDepr]	[RelMLIll]
	%	%	%
Very comfortable with this	51.1	14.4	21.1
Fairly comfortable with this	38.8	40.6	47.7
Fairly **uncomfortable** with this	7.3	34.5	23.6
Very **uncomfortable** with this	1.6	8.0	5.1
(Don't know what this means)	-	0.6	0.1
(Don't Know)	1.2	1.9	2.3
(Refusal/Not answered)	0.1	0.1	-

VERSIONS A, C AND D: ASK ALL DISABLED ('Yes' AT [DisAct] OR DISABLITY GIVEN AT [RDisFW])

Q641- CARD E5 N=676

Q648 In the last 12 months, have you personally experienced any **violent or abusive behaviour** for a reason related to your impairment or health condition in any of the settings listed on this card?
PROBE: Which others?
CODE ALL THAT APPLY
Multicoded (Maximum of 8 codes)

%		
92.4	No, have not experienced such behaviour	[RDsVNone]
0.2	Yes, at school or college	[RDsVSchC]
1.4	Yes, at work	[RDsVWork]
1.4	Yes, on public transport	[RDsVTran]
2.1	Yes, in shops or banks	[RDsVShop]
0.2	Yes, in bars, restaurants or leisure facilities	[RDsVLeis]
0.9	Yes, in doctors' surgeries or hospitals	[RDsVGP]
3.3	Yes, in the street	[RDsVStre]
1.1	Yes - somewhere else (WRITE IN)	[RDsVOth]
-	(Don't know)	
0.5	(Not answered)	

IF NOT 'mentioned' AT [RDsVNone]

[RDsVStaf]

Q660 Generally speaking, has this been ... READ OUT ... N=676

%	
1.0	... by staff,
4.7	by others,
1.3	or, by both staff and others?
0.1	(Don't know)
0.5	(Not answered)

[RDsVFreq]

Q661 Have you experienced such behaviours ... READ OUT ... N=676

%	
2.1	... frequently,
2.2	occasionally,
2.7	or, rarely?
0.2	(Don't know)
0.5	(Not answered)

[RDsVAffc]

Q662 Have these behaviours affected you ... READ OUT ... N=676

%	
3.4	... a lot,
2.8	a little,
1.0	or, have they not affected you at all?
-	(Don't know)
0.5	(Not answered)

VERSIONS A, C AND D: ASK ALL   N=3210

Q663-
Q670

CARD E5 (AGAIN)

In the last 12 months, have you personally witnessed any **violent or abusive behaviour** towards a disabled person (other than yourself) for a reason related to their impairment or health condition in any of the settings listed on this card?
PROBE: Which others?
CODE ALL THAT APPLY
Multicoded (Maximum of 8 codes)

%		
92.0	No, have not witnessed such behaviour	[DisVNone]
1.3	Yes, at school or college	[DisVSchC]
1.5	Yes, at work	[DisVWork]
2.2	Yes, on public transport	[DisVTran]
1.2	Yes, in shops or banks	[DisVShop]
1.5	Yes, in bars, restaurants or leisure facilities	[DisVLeis]
0.4	Yes, in doctors' surgeries or hospitals	[DisVGP]
4.2	Yes, in the street	[DisVStre]
0.2	Yes - somewhere else (WRITE IN)	[DisVOth]
0.1	(Don't know)	
-	(Not answered)	

Q682

IF NOT 'mentioned' AT [DisVNone]   N=3210
[DisVStaf]
Generally speaking, has this been ... READ OUT ...

%	
0.7	... by staff,
6.5	by others,
0.7	or, by both staff and others?
0.1	(Don't know)
0.1	(Not answered)

VERSIONS A, C AND D: ASK ALL DISABLED ('yes' AT [DisAct] OR DISABLITY GIVEN AT [RDisFW])   N=676

Q683-
Q690

CARD E5 AGAIN

In the last 12 months, have you personally experienced any **other unfair or unpleasant behaviour** for a reason related to your impairment or health condition in any of the settings listed on this card?
PROBE: Which others?
CODE ALL THAT APPLY
Multicoded (Maximum of 8 codes)

%		
91.0	No, have not experienced such behaviour	[RDsUNone]
1.3	Yes, at school or college	[RDsUSchC]
3.0	Yes, at work	[RDsUWork]
1.5	Yes, on public transport	[RDsUTran]
1.3	Yes, in shops or banks	[RDsUShop]
0.9	Yes, in bars, restaurants or leisure facilities	[RDsULeis]
1.1	Yes, in doctors' surgeries or hospitals	[RDsUGP]
2.8	Yes, in the street	[RDsUStre]
1.1	Yes - somewhere else (WRITE IN)	[RDsUOth]
-	(Don't know)	
0.5	(Not answered)	

Q702

IF NOT 'mentioned' AT [RDsUNone]   N=676
[RDsUStaf]
Generally speaking, has this been ... READ OUT ...

%	
3.0	... by staff,
4.4	by others,
1.1	or, by both staff and others?
0.1	(Don't know)
0.5	(Not answered)

Q703

[RDsUFreq]   N=676
Have you experienced such behaviours ... READ OUT ...

%	
1.4	... frequently,
4.0	occasionally,
3.1	or, rarely?
-	(Don't know)
0.5	(Not answered)

Q704   [RDsUAffc]
       Have these behaviours affected you ... READ OUT ...   N=676
%
5.0   ... a lot,
3.2   a little,
0.4   or, have they not affected you at all?
-      (Don't know)
0.5   (Not answered)

VERSIONS A, C AND D: ASK ALL
       CARD E5 AGAIN   N=3210
Q705- In the last 12 months, have you personally witnessed
Q712   any **other unfair or unpleasant behaviour** towards a
       disabled person *(other than yourself)* for a reason
       related to their impairment or health condition in any
       of the settings listed on this card?
       PROBE: Which others?
       CODE ALL THAT APPLY
       Multicoded (Maximum of 8 codes)
%
89.6   No, have not witnessed such behaviour   [DisUNone]
1.3   Yes, at school or college   [DisUSchC]
2.1   Yes, at work   [DisUWork]
1.8   Yes, on public transport   [DisUTran]
1.8   Yes, in shops or banks   [DisUShop]
1.9   Yes, in bars, restaurants or leisure
       facilities   [DisULeis]
0.4   Yes, in doctors' surgeries or hospitals   [DisUGP]
4.4   Yes, in the street   [DisUStre]
0.5   Yes - somewhere else (WRITE IN)   [DisUOth]
1.0   (Don't know)
0.0   (Not answered)

IF NOT 'mentioned' AT [DisUNone]
Q724   [DisUStaf]
%   Generally speaking, has this been ... READ OUT ...   N=3210
1.6   ... by staff,
7.1   by others,
1.5   or, by both staff and others?
-      (Don't know)
0.1   (Not answered)

**VERSIONS A, C AND D: ASK ALL DISABLED ('yes' AT
[DisAct] OR DISABLITY GIVEN AT [RDisFW])**
Q725   [ConfPT]   N=676
       CARD E6
       How confident do you feel in using public transport?
       Please take your answers from this card
%
33.8   Very confident
33.7   Fairly confident
13.4   Not very confident
15.8   Not at all confident
2.9   (Don't know)
0.5   (Not answered)

Social identity (versions B and C)

VERSIONS B AND C: ASK ALL

N=2101

Q726 [PtyThnk]
Generally speaking, do you usually think of yourself as Conservative, Labour, Liberal Democrat, (nationalist/Plaid Cymru) or what?

IF 'none/no' OR DON'T KNOW AT [PtyThnk]

N=2101

Q729 [PtyCls]
Do you generally think of yourself as a little closer to one of the parties than the others?
IF YES: Which party?

	[PtyThnk]	[PtyCls]
	%	%
None/No	21.3	16.5
Conservative	22.6	1.4
Labour	37.3	2.4
Liberal Democrat	10.8	1.1
Scottish National Party (SNP)	1.3	0.1
Plaid Cymru	0.4	-
Green Party	1.1	0.2
UKIP/Veritas	0.5	-
BNP/National Front	0.4	-
Scottish Socialist party/RESPECT	0.2	0.0
Other (WRITE IN)	0.6	-
Refused	2.7	0.0
(Don't Know)	0.8	0.3
(Not answered)	-	2.8

IF PARTY GIVEN AT [PtyThnk] OR AT [PtyCls]

N=2101

Q732 [IdStrng2]
Would you call yourself (party), fairly strong or not very strong?
%
8.4   Very strong
30.5   Fairly strong
41.5   Not very strong
0.1   (Don't know)
3.1   (Not answered)

Q733 [PartyCom]
CARD F1
How much do you feel you have in common with
(Conservative/Labour/Liberal Democrat/Scottish
National Party/Plaid Cymru/Green) supporters (of this
party) in general, compared with other people?
%
9.0   A lot more in common with them than with other people
22.7   A little more in common with them than with other people
47.5   No more in common with them than with other people
1.2   (Don't know)
3.1   (Not answered)

VERSIONS B AND C: ASK ALL

N=2101

Q734 [FPartyID]
Do you remember when you were young, whether your
father had any particular preference for one of the
parties?
IF YES: Which party was that?
%
23.2   Conservative
37.6   Labour
3.7   Liberal Democrats/Liberals/SDP/Alliance
1.7   Other party (WRITE IN)
16.1   No preference
0.9   Moved around
4.4   R didn't have a father/ father was dead or not around
       when R was young
2.8   Refused
9.7   (Don't know)
-      (Not answered)

Q737 **VERSIONS B AND C: ASK ALL**   N=2101
[MPartyID]
And what about your mother? (Did she have any
particular preference for one of the parties when you
were young?
  NOTE: IF ANSWER TO PREVIOUS QUESTION SUGGESTS THAT
  THIS QUESTION WILL CAUSE DISTRESS, CODE 'R didn't have
  mother' OR DON'T KNOW (Ctrl+K), AS APPLICABLE, INSTEAD
  OF ASKING
%
21.9 Conservative
33.5 Labour
4.7   Liberal Democrats/Liberals/SDP/Alliance
1.6   Other party (WRITE IN)
23.0 No preference
1.0   Moved around
1.8   R didn't have a mother/ mother was dead or not around
      when R was young
2.5   Refused
10.0 (Don't know)
-     (Not answered)

Q740 **VERSIONS B AND C: ASK ALL**   N=2101
[SRSocCl1]
Do you ever think of yourself as belonging to any
particular class?
IF YES: Which class is that?
%
19.7 Yes, middle class
25.2 Yes, working class
1.3   Yes, other (WRITE IN)
53.5 No
0.4   (Don't know)
-     (Not answered)

IF 'yes,other' OR 'no' AT [SRSocCl1]
Q743 [SRSocCl2]   N=2101
Most people say they belong either to the middle class
or the working class. If you **had** to make a choice,
would you call yourself ... READ OUT ...
%
16.9 ... middle class
32.2 or, working class
4.9   (Don't know)
1.1   (Not answered)

Q744 **VERSIONS B AND C: ASK ALL**   N=2101
[SRSoCCl]   **(NOT ON SCREEN)**
Derived from SRSocCl1 and SRSocCl2
%
36.6 Middle class
57.4 Working class
6.0   No class given
-     (Don't know)
-     (Not answered)

Q745 [MClass] (NOT ON SPSS FILE)   N=2101
What sort of people would you say belong to the middle
class?
RECORD VERBATIM. CONTINUE ON NOTEPAD IF NECESSARY
Open Question (Maximum of 120 characters)

Q746- [XMClass] **(EDIT ONLY)**
Q747   EDIT: What sort of people would you say belong to the
middle class?
MCLASS: *(text from [MClass])*
CODE UP TO TWO (FIRST TWO THINGS MENTIONED)
Multicoded (Maximum of 2 codes)
%
13.5 DK, Not answered, no distinguishing characteristics
45.8 Occupational
24.8 Income and standard of living
5.7   Educational background, level of intelligence
1.9   Family background, breeding
0.8   Manners and morals
3.8   Attitudes and hierarchical location
0.2   Political attitudes
3.5   Other answers

Q749 [WClass] (NOT ON SPSS FILE)   N=2101
What sort of people would you say belong to the
working class?
RECORD VERBATIM. CONTINUE ON NOTEPAD IF NECESSARY.
Open Question (Maximum of 120 characters)

Q750-
Q751　[XWClass]　(EDIT ONLY)　　　　　　　　　　N=2101
EDIT: What sort of people would you say belong to the working class?
WCLASS: (text from [WClass])
CODE UP TO TWO (FIRST TWO THINGS MENTIONED)
Multicoded (Maximum of 2 codes)

%
10.9　DK, Not answered, no distinguishing characteristics
59.5　Occupational
17.5　Income and standard of living
3.2　Educational background, level of intelligence
1.0　Family background, breeding
1.0　Manners and morals
3.0　Attitudes and hierarchical location
0.3　Political attitudes
3.6　Other answers

Q753　[ClassMov]　　　　　　　　　　　　　　　N=2101
How difficult would you say it is for people to move from one class to another? Is it ... READ OUT ...

%
17.4　...very difficult,
42.2　fairly difficult,
32.9　or, not very difficult?
7.2　(Don't know)
0.3　(Not answered)

IF CLASS GIVEN AT [SRSocCl1] OR [SRSocCl2]
Q754　[SRClsCom]　　　　　　　　　　　　　　N=2101
Some people feel they have a lot in common with other people of their own class, but others don't feel this way so much. How about you? Would you say you feel ... READ OUT ...

%
36.9　... pretty close to other (same class) class people,
55.3　or, that you don't feel much closer to them than you do to people in other classes?
1.8　(Don't know)
0.0　(Not answered)

VERSIONS B AND C: ASK ALL　　　　　　　　　N=2101
Q755　[ClsConfl]
On the whole, do you think there is bound to be some conflict between different social classes, or do you think they can get along together without any conflict?

%
45.7　Bound to be conflict
50.6　Can get along without conflict
3.5　(Don't know)
0.2　(Not answered)

Q756-　CARD F2　　　　　　　　　　　　　　　N=2101
Q759　Irrespective of how old you actually are, do you usually think of yourself as being in any of the categories on this card, or are none of these right for you?
CODE ALL MENTIONED, BUT DO **NOT** PROBE FOR MORE ANSWERS
Multicoded (Maximum of 4 codes)

%
25.1　A middle aged person　　　　　　　[SRAgeMid]
13.1　An older person　　　　　　　　　[SRAgeOld]
28.3　A young person　　　　　　　　　[SRAgeYou]
19.6　A thirty-something person　　　　　[SRAge30]
14.7　None of these are right for me　　[SRAgeNon]
0.0　(Don't know)
0.0　(Not answered)

Q765　IF 'mentioned' AT [SRAgeMid]
[MidCom] *　　　　　　　　　　　　　　　N=2101
CARD F3
How much do you feel you have in common with middle aged people in general, compared with other people?

Q766　IF 'mentioned' AT [SRAgeOld]
[OldCom]　　　　　　　　　　　　　　　N=2101
CARD F3　(AGAIN)
How much do you feel you have in common with older people in general, compared with other people?

Q767　IF 'mentioned' AT [SRAgeYou]
[YouCom]　　　　　　　　　　　　　　　N=2101
CARD F3　(AGAIN)
How much do you feel you have in common with young people in general, compared with other people?

Q768 [T30Com] N=2101
CARD F3 (AGAIN)
IF 'mentioned' AT [SRAge30]
How much do you feel you have in common with thirty-something people in general, compared with other people?

	[MidCom]	[OldCom]	[YouCom]	[T30Com]
	%	%	%	%
A lot more in common with them than with other people	7.4	3.0	9.8	5.4
A little more in common with them than with other people	6.3	3.8	8.7	5.6
No more in common with them than with other people	11.2	6.1	9.4	8.3
(Don't Know)	-	0.1	0.2	-
(Refusal/Not answered)	0.1	0.1	0.1	0.1

Q769 VERSIONS B AND C: ASK ALL MEN
[MenCom] N=2101
% In general, do you feel that you have ... READ OUT ...
9.0 ... a lot more in common with other men than with women,
11.8 a little more in common with other men than with women,
25.8 or, no more in common with other men than with women?
0.6 (Don't know)
0.0 (Not answered)

Q770 VERSIONS B AND C: ASK ALL WOMEN
[WomenCom] N=2101
% In general, do you feel that you have ... READ OUT ...
11.7 ... a lot more in common with other women than with men,
14.8 a little more in common with other women than with men,
26.0 or, no more in common with other women than with men?
0.1 (Don't know)
0.1 (Not answered)

Q771 VERSIONS B AND C: ASK ALL
[DesBrand] N=2101
CARD F4
Thinking about the clothes or shoes you wear, which of the statements on this card comes **closest** to how you feel about designer brands?
%
15.9 I like to wear designer brands if I can afford them
12.3 I try to avoid buying designer brands
71.5 I really don't mind whether I wear designer brands or not
0.2 (Don't know)
0.0 (Not answered)

IF 'like to wear designer brands if I can afford them' AT [DesBrand]
Q772 [DesBImp] N=2101
CARD F5
How important is it to you to be someone who wears designer brands?
(Please take your answer from this card).
%
1.1 Very important
5.5 Fairly important
7.6 Not very important
1.7 Not at all important
- (Don't know)
0.3 (Not answered)

VERSIONS B AND C: ASK ALL
Q773- Q781 CARD F6 N=2101
Which, if any, of these do you think of yourself as?
CODE ALL THAT APPLY
Multicoded (Maximum of 9 codes)
%
9.2 An animal rights campaigner [NwIDAnim]
8.2 An anti-war campaigner [NwIDAnWr]
23.4 An environmentalist [NwIDEnvi]
4.8 A feminist [NwIDFemi]
15.0 A Euro-sceptic [NwIDEUSc]
9.5 A supporter of fox hunting [NwIDFoxH]
13.9 A graduate [NwIDGrad]
3.8 A vegetarian or vegan [NwIDVege]
23.5 A supporter of a particular football team [NwIDFoot]
40.5 None of these [NwIDNone]
0.0 (Don't know)
0.1 (Not answered)

Q792 **IF 'mentioned' AT [NwIDAnim]** N=2101
[AnimCom] *
CARD F7
How much do you feel you have in common with animal rights campaigners in general, compared with other people?

Q793 **IF 'mentioned' AT [NwIDAnWr]** N=2101
[AnWrCom] *
CARD F7 (AGAIN)
How much do you feel you have in common with anti-war campaigners in general, compared with other people?

Q794 **IF 'mentioned' AT [NwIDEnvi]** N=2101
[EnviCom] *
CARD F7 (AGAIN)
How much do you feel you have in common with environmentalists in general, compared with other people?

Q795 **IF 'mentioned' AT [NwIDFemi]** N=2101
[FemiCom] *
CARD F7 (AGAIN)
How much do you feel you have in common with feminists in general, compared with other people?

Q796 **IF 'mentioned' AT [NwIDEUSc]** N=2101
[EUScCom] *
CARD F7 (AGAIN)
How much do you feel you have in common with Euro-sceptics in general, compared with other people?

Q797 **IF 'mentioned' AT [NwIDFoxH]** N=2101
[FoxHCom] *
CARD F7 (AGAIN)
How much do you feel you have in common with supporters of fox hunting, compared with other people?

Q798 **IF 'mentioned' AT [NwIDGrad]** N=2101
[GradCom] *
CARD F7 (AGAIN)
How much do you feel you have in common with graduates in general, compared with other people?

Q799 **IF 'mentioned' AT [NwIDVege]** N=2101
[VegeCom] *
CARD F7 (AGAIN)
How much do you feel you have in common with vegetarians and vegans in general, compared with other people?

Q800 **IF 'mentioned' AT [NwIDFoot]** N=2101
[FootCom] *
CARD F7 (AGAIN)
How much do you feel you have in common with supporters of your football team, compared with other people?

	[AnimCom]	[AnWrCom]	[EnviCom]
	%	%	%
A lot more in common with them than with other people	1.6	2.2	4.2
A little more in common with them than with other people	3.2	2.6	9.1
No more in common with them than with other people	4.4	3.3	9.9
(Don't Know)	0.0	0.1	0.3
(Refusal/Not answered)	0.1	0.1	0.1

	[FemiCom]	[EUScCom]	[FoxHCom]
	%	%	%
A lot more in common with them than with other people	0.7	2.9	2.6
A little more in common with them than with other people	2.3	6.0	3.0
No more in common with them than with other people	1.7	6.0	3.8
(Don't Know)	0.1	0.1	0.1
(Refusal/Not answered)	0.1	0.1	0.1

	[GradCom]	[VegeCom]	[FootCom]
	%	%	%
A lot more in common with them than with other people	3.4	1.5	7.3
A little more in common with them than with other people	5.0	0.8	6.7
No more in common with them than with other people	5.5	1.6	9.4
(Don't Know)	-	-	0.1
(Refusal/Not answered)	0.1	0.1	0.1

VERSIONS B AND C: ASK ALL

Q801 [CharOft]
CARD F8
N=2101

Generally speaking, how often, on average, do you give money to charity - please do **not** include money spent in charity shops or buying lottery or raffle tickets?
Please just tell me a letter from this card.
IF ASKED: DO NOT INCLUDE MONEY TO BEGGARS OR BUYING THE BIG ISSUE

%
8.0 A: Never
10.7 B: Occasionally but less often than once a year
20.9 C: Once or twice a year
24.9 D: Once every few months
26.0 E: Once or twice a month
9.5 F: Once a week or more
0.1 (Don't know)
0.0 (Not answered)

Q802 [OthHelp2]
CARD F9
N=2101

Thinking of people you know but who are **not** part of your household - such as relatives, friends or neighbours - in the last 12 months, how often, if at all, have you helped someone like this with housework or shopping?
INCLUDE GARDENING AND SIMILAR.

%
9.7 More than once a week
12.9 At least once a week
17.1 At least once a month
21.0 At least two or three times in the last 12 months
4.9 Once in the last 12 months
34.1 Not at all in the last 12 months
0.3 (Don't know)
0.1 (Not answered)

Q803 [VolGroup]
N=2101

During the last 12 months, have you given your time **for free** to help any groups, clubs or organisations?

%
36.3 Yes
63.5 No
0.2 (Don't know)
0.0 (Not answered)

Q804 [ShopChKp]
CARD F10
N=2101

Using this card, what comes closest to what you think about this situation:
A man gives a **£5** note for goods he is buying in a corner shop. By mistake, he is given change for a **£10** note. He notices, but keeps the change.

%
5.9 Nothing wrong
19.3 Bit wrong
39.3 Wrong
18.4 Seriously wrong
16.8 Very seriously wrong
0.3 (Don't know)
0.0 (Not answered)

VERSION B: ASK ALL
NOTE: see Q532

Q805 [NHSTrust]
CARD G1
N=2165

How much do you trust hospital doctors always to put the interests of their patients above the convenience of the hospital?

%
12.9 Always
49.9 Most of the time
29.6 Only some of the time
5.2 Just about never
2.4 (Don't know)
0.1 (Not answered)

Q806   [DieShdSy]   *   N=2165
CARD G2
I'd like you to think now of a patient who is nearing
the end of his or her life. How much say do you think
someone in this situation **should** have in the decisions
that are made about their medical treatment?

Q807   [DieDsSy]   *   N=2165
CARD G2 AGAIN
And from what you know or have heard, how much say do
you think a patient like this **actually has** in the
decisions that are made about their medical treatment
towards the end of their life?

	[DieShdSy]	[DieDsSy]
	%	%
A great deal	57.8	4.3
Quite a lot	32.3	20.4
A little	6.2	53.6
None at all	1.6	16.9
(Don't Know)	1.8	4.6
(Refusal/Not answered)	0.3	0.1

VERSION B: ASK ALL

Q808   [EDisPrb]   N=1058
Now some questions about health problems and
disabilities. Firstly, do you have any health problems
or disabilities which limit the kind of paid work you
can do?

IF 'yes' AT [EDisPrb]
Q809   [SDisTm]   N=1058
Do you expect this health problem or disability to
last for more than a year?

VERSION B: ASK ALL

Q810   [InfCare]   N=1058
May I just check, is there anyone in your household
who is sick, disabled or elderly who you look after or
give special help to (for example, a relative,
husband/wife, child, friend?).

IF 'no' OR DON'T KNOW AT [InfCare]
Q811   [EvlnCar]   N=1058
Have you ever had anyone in your household who was
sick, disabled or elderly who you looked after or gave
special help to?

	[EDisPrb]	[SDisTm]	[InfCare]	[EvlnCar]
	%	%	%	%
Yes	21.8	20.6	10.3	25.1
No	78.0	0.8	89.6	64.5
(Don't Know)	0.1	0.3	0.0	-
(Refusal/ Not answered)	0.1	0.2	-	0.1

Education (versions C and D)

VERSIONS C AND D: ASK ALL　　N=2103

Q813　[EdSpnd1c] *
CARD G1
Now some questions about education.
Which of the groups on this card, if any, would be
your highest priority for **extra** government spending on
education?

**IF ANSWER GIVEN AT [EdSpnd1c] (I.E. NOT 'none'/DON'T
KNOW/REFUSAL)**　　N=2103
Q814　[EdSpnd2c] *
CARD G1 AGAIN
And which is your next highest priority?

	[EdSpnd1c]	[EdSpnd2c]
	%	%
Nursery or pre-school children	12.1	11.0
Primary school children	21.6	22.6
Secondary school children	23.3	22.5
Children with special educational needs	25.6	21.5
Students at universities	10.2	10.0
Students in further education	4.5	8.8
(None of these)	1.3	0.6
(Don't Know)	1.5	0.2
(Refusal/Not answered)	0.0	-

VERSIONS C AND D: ASK ALL　　N=2103
Q815　[PrimImp1]
CARD G2
Here are a number of things that some people think
would improve education in our schools.
Which do you think would be the **most** useful one for
improving the education of children in **primary** schools
- aged 5- (11/12) years? Please look at the whole list
before deciding.

**IF ANSWER GIVEN AT [PrimImp1] (I.E. NOT DON'T
KNOW/REFUSAL)**　　N=2103
Q818　[PrimImp2]
CARD G2 AGAIN
And which do you think would be the **next** most useful
one for children in **primary** schools?

	[PrimImp1]	[PrimImp2]
	%	%
More information available about individual schools	1.7	1.7
More links between parents and schools	12.2	9.9
More resources for buildings, books and equipment	13.7	17.5
Better quality teachers	15.3	15.3
Smaller class sizes	35.9	21.1
More emphasis on exams and tests	0.6	2.6
More emphasis on developing the child's skills and interests	14.4	24.2
Better leadership within individual schools	2.3	4.6
Other (WRITE IN)	1.8	0.8
(Don't Know)	2.1	0.3
(Refusal/Not answered)	0.0	-

VERSIONS C AND D: ASK ALL　　N=2103
Q821　[SecImp1]
CARD G3
And which do you think would be the **most** useful thing
for improving the education of children in **secondary**
schools - aged (11/12)-18 years?

**IF ANSWER GIVEN AT [SecImp1] (I.E. NOT DON'T
KNOW/REFUSAL)**　　N=2103
Q824　[SecImp2]
CARD G3 AGAIN
And which do you think would be the **next** most useful
one for children in **secondary** schools?

	[SecImp1]	[SecImp2]
	%	%
More information available about individual schools	1.6	0.9
More links between parents and schools	7.5	6.9
More resources for buildings, books and equipment	13.0	12.6
Better quality teachers	18.9	13.4
Smaller class sizes	25.6	14.5
More emphasis on exams and tests	3.1	4.9
More emphasis on developing the child's skills and interests	13.7	19.1
More training and preparation for jobs	10.2	21.2
Better leadership within individual schools	2.5	3.3
Other (WRITE IN)	2.0	1.1
(Don't Know)	1.8	0.2
(Refusal/Not answered)	0.0	-

VERSIONS C AND D: ASK ALL

Q827 [Acad100]
CARD G4

N=2103

Once people have finished schooling at age 16 they have a number of options. Some stay on to do academic qualifications like (A-levels (or A2-levels)/ Scottish Highers (or Higher Stills)); others do more work-related qualifications like (NVQs/SVQs); and other people do neither.

Out of every 100 people finishing schooling at age 16, how many do you think go on to do academic qualifications?

MEDIAN: 50 people

%
9.1 (Don't know)
0.0 (Not answered)

Q828 [Voc100]
CARD G4 AGAIN

N=2103

And how many do you think go on to do vocational qualifications?

MEDIAN: 30 people

%
10.5 (Don't know)
0.0 (Not answered)

Q829 [VocVAcad]
In the long-run, which do you think gives people more opportunities and choice in life ... READ OUT ...

N=2103

%
..having good practical skills and training,   45.1
or, having good academic results?   21.7
(Mixture/depends)   32.7
(Don't know)   0.5
(Not answered)   0.0

Q830 [VocCantA] *
CARD G5

N=2103

For each of the following statements please say whether you agree or disagree.

Only people who can't do academic qualifications should do vocational ones.

Q831 [VocEasy] *
CARD G5 AGAIN

N=2103

(Please say whether you agree or disagree with this statement)

Vocational qualifications are easier than academic qualifications.

Q832 [VocUnder] *
CARD G5 AGAIN

N=2103

(Please say whether you agree or disagree with this statement)

Most people don't understand what vocational qualifications are.

Q833 [VocResp] *
CARD G5 AGAIN

N=2103

(Please say whether you agree or disagree with this statement)

Employers don't respect vocational qualifications enough.

Q834 [VocScEnc] *
CARD G5 AGAIN

N=2103

(Please say whether you agree or disagree with this statement)

Schools should do more to encourage young people to do vocational qualifications.

	[VocCantA]	[VocEasy]	[VocUnder]
	%	%	%
Agree strongly	2.6	2.1	4.8
Agree	17.0	25.6	53.9
Neither agree nor disagree	17.0	23.1	20.1
Disagree	45.7	39.3	18.7
Disagree strongly	16.1	6.3	0.6
(Don't Know)	1.6	3.6	1.9
(Refusal/Not answered)	0.0	0.0	0.0

	[VocResp]	[VocScEnc]
	%	%
Agree strongly	5.3	13.2
Agree	45.7	58.9
Neither agree nor disagree	22.9	18.6
Disagree	19.3	6.7
Disagree strongly	0.9	0.2
(Don't Know)	5.9	2.3
(Refusal/Not answered)	0.1	0.0

Q835   [HEdOpp]   N=2103
CARD G6
Do you feel that opportunities for young people in Britain to go on to **higher education** - to a university or college - should be increased or reduced, or are they at about the right level now?
IF INCREASED OR REDUCED: a lot or a little?
%
14.8   Increased a lot
22.0   Increased a little
45.9   About right
12.4   Reduced a little
2.3   Reduced a lot
2.5   (Don't know)
0.0   (Not answered)

Q836   [HEFee]   N=2103
CARD G7
I'm now going to ask you what you think about university or college students or their families paying towards the costs of their tuition, either while they are studying or after they have finished. Which of the views on this card comes closest to what you think about that?
%
8.7   **All** students or their families should pay towards the costs of their tuition
66.8   **Some** students or their families should pay towards the costs of their tuition, depending on their circumstances
22.9   **No** students or their families should pay towards the costs of their tuition
1.6   (Don't know)
0.0   (Not answered)

Q837   [HEFeeWhn]   N=2103
IF 'all students' OR 'some students' AT [HEFee]
And **when** should students or their families start paying towards the costs of their tuition...READ OUT...
%
29.5   ...while they are studying,
33.1   or, after they have finished studying and have got a job?
12.5   (Depends)
0.4   (Don't know)
1.6   (Not answered)

Q838   [HEDonate]   N=2103
CARD G8
VERSIONS C AND D: ASK ALL
Please tell me whether you agree or disagree with this statement.
Graduates ought to make voluntary donations to their university later in life.
%
3.7   Agree strongly
30.0   Agree
28.0   Neither agree nor disagree
29.5   Disagree
6.7   Disagree strongly
2.1   (Don't know)
0.0   (Not answered)

Q839 [HEUGo] N=2103
Did you ever, or do you now, go to a university or polytechnic?
%
33.8 Yes
66.1 No
0.1 (Don't know)
0.0 (Not answered)

Q840 [HEUDonat] N=2103
IF 'yes' AT [HEUGo]
If you were approached by your university or polytechnic asking you to give them a donation, would you...READ OUT...
%
7.5 ...never give any money,
9.1 give some money if you could afford it,
15.7 give some money if you thought it was a particularly good cause,
1.1 or definitely give regardless of the cause?
0.4 (Don't know)
0.2 (Not answered)

VERSIONS C AND D: ASK ALL
Q841 [WWWLearn] N=2103
CARD G9
How important do you think the Internet is for learning new knowledge or skills?
%
46.8 Very important
40.1 Fairly important
7.2 Not very important
1.7 Not at all important
4.2 (Don't know)
0.0 (Not answered)

Q842 [CompEver] N=2103
Do you ever use a computer for any reason?
%
67.1 Yes
32.7 No
0.1 (Don't know)
0.0 (Not answered)

IF 'yes' AT [CompEver]
Q843- CARD G10 N=2103
Q856 For which of the following do you personally use a computer (, including anything you may do at work)?
CODE ALL THAT APPLY
Multicoded (Maximum of 14 codes)
%
52.4 Writing letters or documents [CompWrit]
35.3 Pursuing hobbies or leisure interests [CompHob]
21.9 Playing games [CompGame]
38.5 Shopping [CompShop]
50.9 Email [CompEmail]
5.3 Chatrooms [CompChat]
28.6 Doing accounts or organising personal finances [CompAcc]
29.4 Training, education and learning [CompTrai]
24.6 Job searching or job applications [CompJob]
11.3 Watching or downloading DVDs [CompDVD]
19.1 Listening to, downloading or organising music [CompMusi]
50.4 Looking up information on the internet [CompNet]
31.8 Work [CompWork]
1.1 Other answer (WRITE IN) [CompOth]
0.2 (None of these) [CompNone]
0.1 (Don't know)
0.1 (Not answered)

Q873 [CompConf] N=2103
CARD G11
How confident do you feel when using a computer?
%
31.1 Very confident
26.2 Fairly confident
8.2 Not very confident
1.5 Not at all confident
0.1 (Don't know)
0.1 (Not answered)

Employment

Respondent's job details

ASK ALL WHO HAVE EVER HAD A JOB ('paid work' OR 'waiting to take up a job' AT [EconAct] OR NOT 'never had a paid job' AT [LastJob])

Q951 [Title] **NOT ON DATAFILE**   N=4137
Now I want to ask you about your *(present/last/future)* job.
PRESENT JOB: What is your job?
PAST JOB: What was your job?
FUTURE JOB: What will that job be?
PROBE IF NECESSARY: What *(is/was)* the name or title of the job?
Open Question (Maximum of 80 characters)

Q952 [Typewk] **NOT ON DATAFILE**   N=4137
What kind of work *(do/did/will)* you do most of the time?
IF RELEVANT: What materials/machinery *(do/did/will)* you use?
Open Question (Maximum of 80 characters)

Q953 [Train] **NOT ON DATAFILE**   N=4137
What training or qualifications *(are/were)* needed for that job?
Open Question (Maximum of 80 characters)

Q954 [REmployee]   N=4137
In your (main) job *(are you/ were you/ will you be)*
%   ... READ OUT ...
88.2 ... an employee,
11.4 or self-employed?
0.2 (Don't know)
0.2 (Not answered)

VERSIONS B AND C: ASK ALL EMPLOYEES IN CURRENT/LAST JOB ('employee' OR DON'T KNOW AT [REmplyee])   N=1804

Q956 [JobCom]
CARD H1
Thinking now not just of your own workplace, but more generally, how much do you feel you have in common with people who do this job, compared with other people?
%
27.9 A lot more in common with them than with other people
26.8 A little more in common with them than with other people
43.8 No more in common with them than with other people
0.7 (Don't know)
0.8 (Not answered)

VERSIONS A, B AND D: ASK ALL CURRENT EMPLOYEES ('employed' at REconAct, 'employee' OR DON'T KNOW AT [REmplyee])   N=1555

Q957 [EmpPerm]
Are you employed on a permanent, temporary or fixed-term basis?
IF UNSURE: Which best describes your employment contract, as you understand it?
%
92.0 Permanent
5.1 Temporary
2.7 Fixed-term
0.2 (Don't know)
0.1 (Not answered)

Q958 [WorkPlac]   N=1555
Does the organisation that employs you have more than one workplace?
IF ASKED: By workplaces we mean separate sites.
%
76.1 Yes - more than one
23.6 No - just the one
0.2 (Don't know)
0.1 (Not answered)

ASK ALL WHO HAVE EVER HAD A JOB ('paid work' OR 'waiting to take up a job' AT [REconAct] OR NOT 'never had a paid job' AT [RLastJob])
[Superv]   N=4137

Q959
In your job, (do/did/will) you have any formal responsibility for supervising the work of other (employees/people)?
DO NOT INCLUDE PEOPLE WHO ONLY SUPERVISE:
- CHILDREN, E.G. TEACHERS, NANNIES, CHILDMINDERS
- ANIMALS
- SECURITY OR BUILDINGS, E.G. CARETAKERS, SECURITY GUARDS

%
39.3   Yes
60.2   No
0.2   (Don't know)
0.2   (Not answered)

IF 'yes' AT [RSuperv]   N=4137

Q960
[RMany]
How many?
Median: 5 (of those supervising any)
%
0.3   (Don't know)
0.5   (Not answered)

ASK ALL EMPLOYEES IN CURRENT/LAST JOB ('employee' OR DON'T KNOW AT [REmplyee])   N=3664

Q962
[OcSect2]
CARD (H1/H2)
Which of the types of organisation on this card (do you work/did you work/will you be working) for?
%
66.2   PRIVATE SECTOR FIRM OR COMPANY Including, for example, limited companies and PLCs
3.3   NATIONALISED INDUSTRY OR PUBLIC CORPORATION Including, for example, the Post office and the BBC
26.8   OTHER PUBLIC SECTOR EMPLOYER
       Incl eg: - Central govt/ Civil Service/ Govt Agency
       - Local authority/ Local Educ Auth (INCL 'OPTED OUT' SCHOOLS)
       - Universities
       - Health Authority / NHS hospitals / NHS Trusts/ GP surgeries
       - Police / Armed forces
2.6   CHARITY/ VOLUNTARY SECTOR Including, for example, charitable companies, churches, trade unions
0.5   Other answer (WRITE IN)
0.0   (Don't know)
0.5   (Not answered)

ASK ALL WHO HAVE EVER HAD A JOB ('paid work' OR 'waiting to take up a job' AT [REconAct] OR NOT 'never had a paid job' AT [RLastJob])
[EmpMake] NOT ON DATAFILE   N=4137

Q965
IF EMPLOYEE:What (does/did) your employer make or do at the place where you (will) usually work(ed) from?
IF SELF-EMPLOYED: What (do/did/will) you make or do at the place where you (will) usually work(ed) from?
Open Question (Maximum of 80 characters)

Q967 [SEmpNum] N=485
ASK ALL SELF-EMPLOYED IN CURRENT/LAST JOB ('self-employed' AT [REmplyee])
In your work or business, (do/did/will) you have any employees, or not?
IF YES: How many?
IF 'NO EMPLOYEES', CODE 0.
FOR 500+ EMPLOYEES, CODE 500.
NOTE: FAMILY MEMBERS MAY BE EMPLOYEES ONLY IF THEY RECEIVE A REGULAR WAGE OR SALARY.
MEDIAN: 0 employees
%
0.3 (Don't know)
3.5 (Not answered)

Q972 [SNumEmp] (NOT ON SCREEN) N=319
ASK ALL CURRENTLY SELF-EMPLOYED ('paid work' at [REconAct] AND 'self-employed' AT [REmplyee])
(derived from [SEmpNum]) - does R have any employees?
%
31.0 Yes
68.0 No
- (Don't know)
1.1 (Not answered)

Q973 [WkJbTim] N=2403
ASK ALL IN PAID WORK (AT [REconAct])
In your present job, are you working ... READ OUT ...
RESPONDENT'S OWN DEFINITION
%
77.7 ... full-time,
22.1 or, part-time?
0.2 (Don't know)
0.0 (Not answered)

Q976 [WkJbHrsI] N=2403
How many hours do you normally work a week in your main job - including any paid or unpaid overtime?
ROUND TO NEAREST HOUR.
IF RESPONDENT CANNOT ANSWER, ASK ABOUT LAST WEEK.
IF RESPONDENT DOES NOT KNOW EXACTLY, ACCEPT AN ESTIMATE.
FOR 95+ HOURS, CODE 95.
FOR 'VARIES TOO MUCH TO SAY', CODE 96.
MEDIAN: 40 hours
%
0.9 (Varies too much to say)
0.3 (Don't know)
0.0 (Not answered)

Q977 [EJbHrsX] N=2087
ASK ALL CURRENT EMPLOYEES ('paid work' at [REconAct] and 'employee' OR DON'T KNOW AT [REmplyee])
What are your **basic or contractual hours** each week in your main job - **excluding** any paid and unpaid overtime?
ROUND TO NEAREST HOUR.
IF RESPONDENT CANNOT ANSWER, ASK ABOUT LAST WEEK.
IF RESPONDENT DOES NOT KNOW EXACTLY, ACCEPT AN ESTIMATE.
FOR 95+ HOURS, CODE 95.
FOR 'VARIES TOO MUCH TO SAY', CODE 96.
MEDIAN: 37 hours
%
3.1 (Varies too much to say)
1.8 (Don't know)
0.2 (Not answered)

Q978 [ExPrtFul] N=1734
ASK ALL WHO HAVE EVER WORKED BUT ARE NOT CURRENTLY WORKING ('waiting' to take up work' AT [REconAct] OR NOT 'never worked' AT [RLastJob])
(Is/Was/Will) the job (be) ... READ OUT ...
%
69.6 ... full-time - that is, 30 or more hours per week,
29.5 or, part-time?
0.5 (Don't know)
0.4 (Not answered)

Q979 [EJbHrCaI] (NOT ON SCREEN) N=2087
ASK ALL CURRENT EMPLOYEES ('paid work' at [REconAct] AND 'employee' OR DON'T KNOW AT [REmplyee])
Respondent's working time including overtime - categorised - current employees
Derived from [REconAct], [REmplyee] and [WkJbHrsI]
%
5.2 10-15 hours a week
8.7 16-23 hours a week
5.2 24-29 hours a week
80.1 30 or more hours a week
0.5 (Varies too much to say)
0.1 (Don't know)
0.2 (Not answered)

Q980 [EJbHrCaX] (NOT ON SCREEN)   N=2087
Respondent's working time excluding overtime - categorised - current employees
Derived from [REconAct], [REmplyee] and [EJbHrsX]

%
1.3 Less than 10 hours a week
4.8 10-15 hours a week
9.2 16-23 hours a week
5.3 24-29 hours a week
74.2 30 or more hours a week
3.1 (Varies too much to say)
1.8 (Don't know)
0.2 (Not answered)

Q981 **ASK ALL CURRENT SELF-EMPLOYED ('paid work' at [REconAct] AND 'self-employed' AT [REmplyee])**
[SJbHrcaI] (NOT ON SCREEN)   N=319
Respondent's working time including overtime - categorised - current self-employed
Derived from [REconAct], [REmplyee] and [WkJbHrsI].

%
6.8 10-15 hours a week
8.0 16-23 hours a week
6.8 24-29 hours a week
73.6 30 or more hours a week
3.3 (Varies too much to say)
0.4 (Don't know)
1.1 (Not answered)

Q982 **ASK ALL WHO HAVE EVER WORKED ('paid work' OR 'waiting to take up a job' AT [REconAct] OR NOT 'never had a paid job' AT [RlastJob])**
[RPartFul] (NOT ON SCREEN)   N=4137
Full-time/part-time status - all respondents who have ever worked
Derived from [REconAct], [WkJbTim] and [ExPrtFul]

%
74.3 Full-time (30+ hours)
25.2 Part-time (10-29 hours)?
0.3 (Don't know)
0.2 (Not answered)

Anti-social hours (versions A, C and D)

VERSIONS A, C AND D: ASK ALL CURRENT EMPLOYEES ('paid work' at [REconAct] AND 'employee' OR DON'T KNOW AT [REmplyee])

Q984- CARD (H2/H3)   N=1592
Q987   Please tell me which, if any, of the times on this card you have worked in the last month in your main job.
CODE ALL THAT APPLY
Multicoded (Maximum of 4 codes)

%
50.3 Evenings between 6 and 8pm   [AntSocEv]
32.1 Nights after 8pm   [AntSocNi]
45.8 Saturdays   [AntSocSa]
34.6 Sundays   [AntSocSu]
34.7 None of these   [AntSocNo]
0.1 (Don't know)
0.1 (Not answered)

Q988 **IF 'mentioned' AT [AntSocEv]**   N=1592
[WkEvning] *
CARD (H3/H4)
And about how many times did you work evenings between 6 and 8 pm last month, including Saturday or Sunday evenings?

Q989 **IF 'mentioned' AT [AntSocNi]**   N=1592
[WkNights] *
CARD (H3/H4) (AGAIN)
And about how many times did you work after 8pm last month, including Saturday or Sunday nights?

Q990 **IF 'mentioned' AT [AntSocSa]**   N=1592
[WkSatday] *
CARD (H4/H5)
And about how many times did you work during the day on Saturday last month?

Q991 **IF 'mentioned' AT [AntSocSu]**   N=1592
[WkSunday] *
CARD (H4/H5) (AGAIN)
And about how many times did you work during the day on Sunday last month?

	[WkEvning]	[WkNights]	[WkSatday]	[WkSunday]
	%	%	%	%
None	-	-	2.4	2.2
Once or twice	9.3	5.9	22.2	20.1
3 or 4 times	9.2	5.8	19.0	10.5
5-10 times	15.5	10.5	-	-
11-20 times	12.7	7.5	-	-
More than this	3.4	2.4	2.2	1.8
(Don't Know)	0.1	0.1	-	-
(Refusal/Not answered)	0.2	0.2	0.2	0.2

Employment relations (mainly versions A, B and D)

ASK ALL

Q1007 [UnionSA] *
(May I just check) are you **now** a member of a trade union or staff association?
PROBE AS NECESSARY AND CODE FIRST TO APPLY

%   N=4268
16.8 Yes, trade union
2.1   Yes, staff association
80.8 No
0.3   (Don't know)
0.0   (Not answered)

IF 'no' OR DON'T KNOW AT [UnionSA]

Q1008 [TUSAEver]
Have you **ever** been a member of a trade union or staff association?
PROBE AS NECESSARY AND CODE FIRST TO APPLY

%   N=4268
25.3 Yes, trade union
2.5   Yes, staff association
53.0 No
0.3   (Don't know)
0.1   (Not answered)

VERSIONS B AND C: ASK ALL WHO ARE MEMBERS OF TRADE UNIONS ('yes, trade union' AT [UnionSA])

Q1009 [TUCom]   N=376
Some members of trade unions feel they have a lot in common with other members: but others don't feel this way so much. How about you? Would you say that you ...
READ OUT ...

%
13.7 ... feel pretty close to trade union members in general,
82.6 or, that you don't feel much closer to them than to other kinds of people?
0.3   (Don't know)
3.3   (Not answered)

VERSION B: ASK ALL MARRIED OR COHABITING (AT [MarSta2b])

Q1010 [SUnionSA]   N=669
Is your (husband/wife/partner) **now** a member of a trade union or staff association?
PROBE AS NECESSARY AND CODE FIRST TO APPLY

%
16.9 Yes: trade union
1.9   Yes: staff association
78.7 No
2.5   (Don't know)
-     (Not answered)

ASK ALL THOSE WHO ARE NOT WORKING (I.E. 'in full-time education', 'on government training scheme', 'waiting to take up work', 'unemployed', 'permanently sick or disabled', 'wholly retired from work', 'looking after the home' OR 'doing something else' AT [REconAc2])

Q875 [NPWork10]   N=1865
In the seven days ending last Sunday, did you have any paid work of less than 10 hours a week?

%
4.1   Yes
95.5 No
0.3   (Don't know)
0.0   (Not answered)

VERSIONS A, B AND D: ASK ALL CURRENT EMPLOYEES ('employee' OR DON'T KNOW AT [EMployB])

Q876 [JobSat3] *   N=1555
CARD (H3/H5)
All in all, how satisfied are you with your main job?

Q877 [PaySatis] *
CARD (H3/H5) AGAIN
How satisfied are you with your pay, including any overtime, bonuses or tips?
N=1555

Q878 [HrsSatis] *
CARD (H3/H5) AGAIN
How satisfied are you with the number of hours you usually work each week?
N=1555

	[JobSat3]	[PaySatis]	[HrsSatis]
	%	%	%
Very satisfied	37.6	13.4	16.8
Satisfied	43.2	44.0	57.1
Neither satisfied nor dissatisfied	9.3	15.4	10.2
Dissatisfied	6.9	20.5	13.0
Very dissatisfied	2.6	6.3	2.5
(Don't Know)	0.3	0.3	0.3
(Refusal/Not answered)	-	-	-

VERSIONS A, B AND D: ASK ALL CURRENT EMPLOYEES ('employee' OR DON'T KNOW AT [EmployB])

Q881 [EmploydT]
For how long have you been continuously employed by your present employer? (MONTHS)
N=1555
MEDIAN: 48 months
%
0.3 (Don't know)
- (Not answered)

Q882 [WpUnion3]
At your place of work are there any unions or staff associations?
IF ASKED: A union or staff association is any independent organisation that represents the interests of people at work.
IF YES, PROBE FOR UNION OR STAFF ASSOCIATION. CODE FIRST TO APPLY.
N=1555
%
44.7 Yes: trade union(s)
4.9 Yes: staff association
45.0 No, none
5.5 (Don't know)
- (Not answered)

VERSIONS A, B AND D: ASK ALL CURRENT EMPLOYEES: IF IN UNIONISED WORKPLACE (IF 'yes, trade unions' OR 'yes, staff association' AT [WpUnion3])

Q883 [UnionRec]
Does management recognise (these unions/this staff association) for the purposes of negotiating pay and conditions of employment?
N=1555

Q884 [WpUnioW3]
On the whole, do you think (these unions/this staff association) (do their/does its) job well or not?
N=1555

	[UnionRec]	[WpUnioW3]
	%	%
Yes	45.3	30.8
No	2.5	12.9
(Don't Know)	1.8	5.8
(Refusal/Not answered)	5.5	5.5

Q885 [TUElig]
Are people doing your job eligible to join a union or staff association at your workplace?
IF ASKED: A union or staff association is any independent organisation that represents the interests of people at work.
IF YES, PROBE FOR UNION OR STAFF ASSOCIATION. CODE FIRST TO APPLY.
N=1555
%
41.9 Yes: trade union(s)
4.5 Yes: staff association
1.8 No
1.4 (Don't know)
5.5 (Not answered)

VERSIONS A, B AND D: ASK ALL CURRENT EMPLOYEES: IF NOT IN UNIONISED WORKPLACE (IF 'no' OR DON'T KNOW AT [WpUnion3])

Q886 [OtherRep]
Are there any other worker or staff representatives at your workplace?
N=1555
%
5.0 Yes
39.6 No
0.4 (Don't know)
5.5 (Not answered)

VERSIONS A, B AND D: ASK ALL CURRENT EMPLOYEES: IF REPRESENTATIVE AT WORKPLACE (IF 'yes, trade unions' OR 'yes, staff association' AT [WpUnion3] OR 'yes' AT [OtherRep]
N=1555

Q887 [WhoRep]
Do you know who the (trade union/staff association/worker or staff) representative is at your workplace (or is there not one based where you work)?
IF SEVERAL, CODE 'Yes' IF RESPONDENT KNOWS WHO AT LEAST ONE IS

%
35.4 Yes
10.6 No
7.5 There is no representative based at my workplace
0.2 (I am the (trade union/staff association/worker or staff) representative)
1.5 (Don't know)
5.3 (Not answered)

IF 'yes' AT [WhoRep]
Q888 [ContcRep]
In the last 12 months, have you contacted any (trade union/staff association/worker or staff) representative for information or help?
N=1555

%
11.9 Yes
23.1 No
0.3 (I am the (trade union/staff association/worker or staff) representative)
- (Don't know)
6.8 (Not answered)

VERSION A, B AND D: ASK ALL
N=3224

Q889 [TUMstImp]
CARD (H8/H10)
Listed on this card are a number of things that trade unions or staff associations can do. Which, if any, do you think should be the **most important** thing they should try to do?

%
4.5 Reduce pay differences in the workplace
10.3 Promote equality for women or for ethnic and other minority groups
30.0 Represent individual employees in dealing with their employer about problems at work
12.1 Protect existing employees' jobs
23.4 Improve working conditions across the workplace
10.5 Improve pay for all employees
2.4 Have an input into the running of the business
10.8 (None of these)
3.8 (Don't know)
0.2 (Not answered)

VERSIONS A, B AND D: ASK ALL CURRENT EMPLOYEES: IF IN UNIONISED WORKPLACE (IF 'yes, trade unions' OR 'yes, staff association' AT [WpUnion3])
N=1555

Q890 [WTUPow2]
CARD (H5/H70)
Do you think that (trade unions/the staff association) at your workplace (have/has) too much or too little power? Please use a phrase from this card.

%
0.7 Far too much power
1.5 Too much power
25.2 About the right amount of power
16.3 Too little power
1.6 Far too little power
4.2 (Don't know)
5.5 (Not answered)

Q891 [TUNotice] *
CARD (H6/H8)
N=1555
Using this card, please say how strongly you agree or disagree with the following statements about (trade unions/the staff association) at your workplace.
(Trade unions/The staff association) at my workplace

... (take/takes) notice of members' problems and complaints

Q892   [TUIgnore] *   AGAIN   N=1555
CARD (H6/H8)
(Using this card, please say how strongly you agree or disagree with the following statement about (trade unions/the staff association)at your workplace.
((Trade unions/The staff association) at my workplace
...) (are/is) usually ignored by management

Q893   [TUSmooth]   N=1555
CARD (H6/H8)   AGAIN
(Using this card, please say how strongly you agree or disagree with the following statement about (trade unions/the staff association)at your workplace.
((Trade unions/The staff association) at my workplace
...) (help/helps) make things run more smoothly at work

	[TUNotice]	[TUIgnore]	[TUSmooth]
	%	%	%
Agree strongly	4.5	0.9	0.8
Agree	29.3	8.8	18.3
Neither agree nor disagree	8.3	11.0	18.4
Disagree	2.8	23.2	8.0
Disagree strongly	0.7	2.0	1.1
(Don't Know)	3.9	3.6	2.8
(Refusal/Not answered)	5.5	5.5	5.5

Q894   [TUGdPay] *   N=1555
CARD (H7/H9)
Using this card, how would you rate the performance of the (unions/staff association) at your workplace on each of the following:
Winning pay increases and bonuses?

Q895   [TUGdAcc] *   N=1555
CARD (H7/H9) AGAIN
(Using this card, how would you rate the performance of the (unions/staff association) on the following:)
Being open and accountable to its members

Q896   [TUGdWom] *   N=1555
CARD (H7/H9) AGAIN
(Using this card, how would you rate the performance of the (unions/staff association) on the following:)
Promoting equal opportunities for women

Q897   [TUGdEth] *   N=1555
CARD (H7/H9) AGAIN
(Using this card, how would you rate the performance of the (unions/staff association) on the following:)
Promoting equal opportunities for ethnic minorities

Q898   [TUGdProt] *   N=1555
CARD (H7/H9) AGAIN
(Using this card, how would you rate the performance of the (unions/staff association) on the following:)
Protecting workers against unfair treatment

	[TUGdPay]	[TUGdAcc]	[TUGdWom]
	%	%	%
Excellent	1.4	2.8	4.7
Good	9.0	17.5	16.4
Fair	19.6	15.6	13.4
Poor	7.8	5.4	4.0
Failure	1.6	0.8	0.4
The trade union/staff association does not deal with this	3.8	0.4	2.2
(Don't Know)	6.3	7.0	8.5
(Refusal/Not answered)	5.5	5.5	5.5

	[TUGdEth]	[TUGdProt]
	%	%
Excellent	4.0	4.3
Good	16.7	22.8
Fair	13.7	11.3
Poor	3.4	3.7
Failure	0.3	0.8
The trade union/staff association does not deal with this	2.4	0.6
(Don't Know)	9.1	6.1
(Refusal/Not answered)	5.5	5.5

Q899 [TUValMon]
VERSIONS A, B AND D: ASK ALL TRADE UNION/STAFF ASSOCIATION MEMBERS ('yes' AT [UnionSA]) WHO ARE CURRENTLY IN WORK.
N=482
On the whole, do you think the service you receive from your (union/staff association) represents ...
READ OUT ...
%
30.3 ... good value for money,
48.4 reasonable value for money,
15.3 or, poor value for money?
2.6 (Don't know)
1.0 (Not answered)

Q900 [TUBetter]
VERSIONS A, B AND D: ASK ALL CURRENT EMPLOYEES: IF NOT IN UNIONISED WORKPLACE (IF 'no' OR DON'T KNOW AT [WpUnion3]
N=1555
Do you think that your workplace would be a better or worse place to work if there were a trade union, or would it make no difference?
IF 'BETTER' OR 'WORSE': Is that a lot (better/worse) or a little (better/worse)?
%
3.2 A lot better
5.5 A little better
33.0 No difference
3.4 A little worse
3.4 A lot worse
1.9 (Don't know)
- (Not answered)

Q901 [JoinTU]
CARD (H8/H10)
N=1555
If there were a trade union at your workplace, how likely or unlikely do you think you would be to join it? Please take your answer from this card.
%
7.9 Very likely
13.1 Fairly likely
15.7 Not very likely
12.0 Not at all likely
1.8 (Don't know)
- (Not answered)

Q902 [NoTUBet]
VERSIONS A, B AND D: ASK ALL CURRENT EMPLOYEES: IF IN UNIONISED WORKPLACE (IF 'yes, trade unions' OR 'yes, staff association' AT [WpUnion3])
N=1555
Do you think that your workplace would be a better or worse place to work if there was no (trade union/staff association), or would it make no difference?
IF 'BETTER' OR 'WORSE': Is that a lot (better/worse) or a little (better/worse)?
%
1.0 A lot better
1.7 A little better
17.6 No difference
14.6 A little worse
13.3 A lot worse
1.3 (Don't know)
5.5 (Not answered)

Q903
VERSIONS A, B AND D: ASK ALL CURRENT EMPLOYEES: IF ELIGIBLE TO JOIN TRADE UNION/STAFF ASSOCIATION ('yes' AT [TUElig1]) BUT NOT A MEMBER ('no' OR DON'T KNOW AT [UnionSA]
[YNTUFee] *
CARD (H9/H11)
N=1555
How important were the following factors in your decision not to join a (union/staff association):
Membership fees are too high.

Q904 [YNTUJob] *
CARD (H9/H11) AGAIN
N=1555
(How important was this in your decision not to join a (union/staff association):)
People doing my job don't join (trade unions/staff associations).

Q905 [YNTUAchN] *
CARD (H9/H11) AGAIN
N=1555
(How important was this in your decision not to join a (union/staff association):)
The (union/staff association) does not acheive anything.

Q906   [YNTUFree] *   N=1555
        CARD (H9/H11) AGAIN
        (How important was this in your decision **not** to join a
        (union/staff association):)
        There is no point joining since I get all the benefits
        anyway.

Q907   [YNTUNAsk] *   N=1555
        CARD (H9/H11) AGAIN
        (How important was this in your decision **not** to join a
        (union/staff association):)
        No one ever asked me.

	[YNTUFree]	[YNTUJob]	[YNTUAchN]
	%	%	%
Very important	1.5	0.9	1.4
Quite important	3.5	2.6	4.3
Not very important	6.2	7.6	5.9
Not at all	6.4	7.0	5.5
important			
(Don't Know)	1.3	0.9	1.8
(Refusal/Not	6.9	6.8	6.9
answered)			

	[YNTUFree]	[YNTUNAsk]
	%	%
Very important	2.4	2.5
Quite important	5.2	3.7
Not very important	6.2	5.1
Not at all	3.9	6.9
important		
(Don't Know)	1.3	0.7
(Refusal/Not	6.8	6.8
answered)		

VERSIONS A, B AND D: ASK ALL CURRENT EMPLOYEES
('employee' OR DON'T KNOW AT [EmployB])

Q908   [IndRel]   N=1555
        In general how would you describe relations between
        management and other employees at your workplace ...
        READ OUT ...
        %
32.6   ... very good,
48.1   quite good,
13.7   not very good,
 4.0   or, not at all good?
 1.6   (Don't know)
   -    (Not answered)

Q909   [ManAttTU]   N=1555
        How would you describe the management's attitude to
        trade unions at the place where you work? Would you
        say that management . . .READ OUT. . .
        %
 9.4   . . **encourages** trade union membership,
31.8   accepts it or would accept it,
11.1   **discourages** trade union membership,
41.4   or, isn't it really an issue at your workplace?
 6.3   (Don't know)
   -    (Not answered)

Q910   [SayJob]   N=1555
        Suppose there was going to be some decision made at
        your place of work that changed the way you do your
        job. Do you think that **you personally** would have any
        say in the decision about the change, or not?
        IF 'DEPENDS': Code as 'Don't know' <CTRL+K+Enter>
        %
56.4   Yes
40.5   No
 3.0   (Don't know)
   -    (Not answered)

        IF 'yes' AT [SayJob]
Q911   [MuchSay]   N=1555
        How much say or chance to influence the decision do
        you think you would have ... READ OUT ...
        %
15.4   ...a great deal,
23.7   quite a lot,
17.3   or, just a little?
 3.0   (Don't know)
   -    (Not answered)

Q912

**VERSIONS A, B AND D: ASK ALL CURRENT EMPLOYEES
('employee' OR DON'T KNOW AT [EmployB])**   N=1555
[MoreSay]
Do you think you should have more say in decisions affecting your work, or are you satisfied with the way things are?
%
44.5 Should have more say
55.1 Satisfied with way things are
0.7 (Don't know)
-    (Not answered)

Q913

[JCCAtWP]   N=1555
At some workplaces there are committees which discuss conditions at work and the employer's future plans but do **not** negotiate wages or initiate industrial action. They can be called **Works Councils, Joint Consultative Committees or Staff Forums.**
Where you work, is there a committee like this where management and employees - or their representatives - meet regularly to consult over workplace issues?
%
36.0 Yes
59.2 No
4.8 (Don't know)
-    (Not answered)

IF 'yes' AT [JCCAtWP]

Q914

[JCCApp]   N=1555
CARD (H10/H12)
How are the employee representatives appointed to this Works Council or committee?

Q915

[JCCShApp]   N=1555
CARD (H10/H12) AGAIN
And how do you think the representatives to this Works Council or committee **should** be chosen?

	[JCCApp]	[JCCShApp]
	%	%
Elected by employees	13.4	21.9
Chosen by management	4.5	1.8
Chosen by the union or staff association	2.7	1.9
Volunteers	11.3	9.2
(Don't Know)	4.0	1.2
(Refusal/Not answered)	4.8	4.8

Q916

**VERSIONS A, B AND D: ASK ALL CURRENT EMPLOYEES
('employee' OR DON'T KNOW AT [EmployB])**   N=1555
[JCCTU]
CARD (H11/H13)
All in all, which of the options on this card do you think would be best for your workplace?
%
33.2 **Both** Works Council (or similar committee) **and** trade union or staff association
13.7 Works Council (or similar committee) on its own
16.3 Trade union or staff association on its own
29.1 **Neither** Works Council (or similar committee) **nor** trade union or staff association
7.8 (Don't know)
-    (Not answered)

Q917-
Q921

CARD (H12/H14)   N=1555
Are any of the things on this card available to you at your workplace?
PROBE: Which others?
CODE ALL THAT APPLY
Multicoded (Maximum of 5 codes)
%
63.8 Team briefings   [WCnTeamB]
30.7 Problem solving groups   [WCnPrGrp]
42.4 Suggestion schemes   [WCnSuggs]
61.0 Regular meetings between management and employees   [WCnRegMe]
36.0 Regular staff survey   [WCnSurvy]
17.4 None of these   [WCnNone]
1.3 (Don't know)
-    (Not answered)

Q922

[PrefHr2]   N=1555
Thinking about the number of hours you work including regular overtime, would you prefer a job where you worked ... READ OUT ...
%
5.3 ...more hours per week,
27.6 fewer hours per week,
66.6 or, are you happy with the number of hours you work at present?
0.3 (Don't know)
0.2 (Not answered)

Q923   **IF 'fewer' AT [PrefHr2]**
[EarnHr2]   N=1555
Would you still prefer to work fewer hours, if it meant earning less money as a result?

%	
6.9	Yes
18.8	No
1.8	It depends
0.5	(Don't know)
-	(Not answered)

VERSIONS A, B AND D: ASK ALL CURRENT EMPLOYEES
('employee' OR DON'T KNOW AT [EmployB])

Q924   **[WkWorkHd]**   N=1555
CARD (H13/H15)
Which of these statements best describes your feelings about your job?

%	
9.2	I only work as hard as I have to
42.4	I work hard, but not so that it interferes with the rest of my life
47.8	I make a point of doing the best I can, even if it sometimes does interfere with the rest of my life
0.4	(Don't know)
0.2	(Not answered)

Q925   **[Replaced] ***
CARD (H14/H16)   N=1555
In your opinion, how difficult or easy would it be for your employer to replace you if you left? (Please use this card)

	[Replaced] %
Very difficult	14.8
Difficult	29.3
Neither difficult nor easy	23.3
Easy	21.0
Very easy	10.8
(Don't Know)	0.6
(Refusal/Not answered)	0.2

Q926   **[EasyJob] ***
CARD (H14/H16) AGAIN   N=1555
And how difficult or easy would it be for you to get a similar or better job with another employer if you wanted?

	[EasyJob] %
Very difficult	10.5
Difficult	25.7
Neither difficult nor easy	21.0
Easy	32.2
Very easy	9.4
(Don't Know)	1.2
(Refusal/Not answered)	0.2

Q927   **[SecurEmp]**
CARD (H15/H17)   N=1555
How secure do you feel your employment is with your present employer?

%	
37.1	Very secure
40.4	Secure
12.7	Neither secure nor insecure
7.0	Insecure
2.2	Very insecure
0.4	(Don't know)
0.2	(Not answered)

Q928   **[TrainJob]**   N=1555
If somebody with the right education and qualifications replaced you in your job, how long do you think it would take for them to learn to do the job reasonably well?
PROBE FOR CORRECT PRE-CODE

%	
3.3	1 day or less
4.7	2 - 6 days
16.0	1 - 4 weeks
23.4	1 - 3 months
32.7	More than 3 months, up to a year
9.8	More than 1 year, up to 2 years
6.0	More than 2 years, up to 5 years
2.5	More than 5 years
1.5	(Don't know)
0.2	(Not answered)

Genetic testing (versions A, B and D)

VERSIONS A, B AND D: ASK ALL   N=3224
Q933   [GenEmpl2]
        CARD (H16/H18)
        Now some questions on genetic tests.
        People can take genetic tests to tell them whether
        they are likely to develop a serious genetic condition
        in the future.
        Suppose someone who is applying for a job **has had** such
        a genetic test. Should the employer have **the right** to
        see the result of this test, or not?

VERSIONS A, B AND D: ASK ALL   N=3224
Q936   [GenTakeT]
        CARD (H16/H18) AGAIN
        Now suppose the applicant has **never** had such a test.
        Should the employer have the right to **make** the
        applicant have a test?

VERSIONS A, B AND D: ASK ALL   N=3224
Q939   [GenExist]
        CARD (H16/H18) AGAIN
        And what about an **existing** employee, should the
        employer have the right to **make** them take a test?

VERSIONS A, B AND D: ASK ALL   N=3224
Q942   [GenSens2]
        CARD (H16/H18) AGAIN
        And should the employer have the right to **make**
        applicants have a test to see if they are particularly
        sensitive to chemicals that may be used in the
        workplace?

Q929   [ReducEm]   N=1555
        Has there been a reduction in the number of employees
        at your workplace in the last 12 months?
%
37.3   Yes
59.4   No
3.1   (Don't know)
0.2   (Not answered)

Q930   [Sacked]   N=1555
        Has any employee been dismissed, or made redundant, at
        your workplace in the last 12 months?
        IF YES: (Was the employee / Were the employees)
        dismissed or made redundant?
%
21.7   Yes - dismissed
12.3   Yes - made redundant
6.6   Yes - both
2.5   Yes - not sure whether dismissed or made redundant
53.1   No
3.7   (Don't know)
0.2   (Not answered)

Q931   [ECourse]   N=1555
        In the last **two** years, have you been on any courses or
        had other formal training, which was part of your work
        or helpful to your work?
        ANY TRAINING WHICH IS RELATED TO RESPONDENT'S PAST,
        PRESENT OR FUTURE WORK MAY BE COUNTED, BUT DO NOT
        INCLUDE LEISURE COURSES OR HOBBIES WHICH ARE NOT JOB-
        RELATED.
%
66.0   Yes, had training related to work
33.4   No, had none
0.4   (Don't know)
0.2   (Not answered)

IF 'yes' AT [ECourse]
Q932   [ECourseT]
        In all, about how many full days have you spent in
        this kind of training over the last two years?
        PROBE FOR TOTAL TIME SPENT IN JOB-RELATED TRAINING IN
        PAST OR PRESENT JOB.
        IF LESS THAN HALF A DAY, CODE 0.
        MEDIAN: 7 days
%
0.4   (Don't know)
0.6   (Not answered)

	[GenEmpl2]	[GenTakeT]	[GenExist]	[GenSens2]
	%	%	%	%
Definitely should	7.7	3.2	2.6	35.3
Probably should	16.2	9.3	7.8	48.0
Probably should not	23.2	19.4	19.9	6.5
Definitely should not	49.0	64.2	65.7	7.2
(Other answer (WRITE IN))	0.7	0.4	0.6	0.3
EDIT: depends on job/type of work	0.4	0.6	0.4	0.1
(Don't Know)	2.6	2.7	2.8	2.5
(Refusal/Not answered)	0.2	0.2	0.2	0.2

Retirement (versions A, C and D)

Q945   **VERSIONS A, C AND D: ASK ALL CURRENT EMPLOYEES ('employee' OR DON'T KNOW AT [EmployB])**

[RetExp]   N=1592

At the moment when do you expect to retire from your main job? In your ...READ OUT...

	%
...40s,	2.3
50s,	20.6
60s,	63.4
70s,	4.8
80s,	0.5
or, at some other time?	1.7
(Not planning to retire)	4.4
(No main job)	0.8
(Don't know)	1.2
(Not answered)	0.2

VERSIONS A, C AND D: ASK ALL CURRENT EMPLOYEES: IF AGED 35 OR OVER OR IF UNDER 35 BUT ANSWERED '60s' OR 'at some other time' AT [RetExp]

Q946   **[RetExpb]**   N=1592

And specifically, at what age do you expect to retire from your main job?

MEDIAN: 63 years

	%
(Don't know)	3.9
(Not answered)	1.4

IF NOT 'not planning to retire' OR 'no main job' AT [RetExp]

Q947   **[FutrWrk]**   N=1592

Do you think you are likely to do any further paid work after retiring from your main job?

	%
Yes	49.0
No	39.0
(Don't know)	6.5
(Not answered)	0.2

Politics

Voting

ASK ALL

Q1022 [Voted]   N=4268
Talking to people about the general election on the
5th of May, we have found that a lot of people didn't
manage to vote. How about you - did you manage to vote
in the general election?
IF NOT ELIGIBLE / TOO YOUNG TO VOTE: CODE 'NO'.

%
68.6   Yes, voted
30.9   No
0.1   (Don't know)
0.1   (Not answered)

Q1023 IF 'yes' AT [Voted]   N=4268
[Vote]
Which party did you vote for in the general election?
DO NOT PROMPT
%
20.2   Conservative
27.9   Labour
13.2   Liberal Democrat
1.3   Scottish National Party
0.5   Plaid Cymru
0.7   Green Party
0.7   UK Independence Party (UKIP)/Veritas
0.2   British National Party (BNP)/ National Front
0.2   RESPECT/ Scottish Socialist Party (SSP)/ Socialist
       Party
0.3   Other party (WRITE IN)
3.3   Refused to say
0.3   (Don't know)
0.2   (Not answered)

Q1026 VERSION B: IF 'yes' AT [Voted]   N=1058
[VotePost]
Did you vote ...READ OUT....
%
59.5   ...in person at a polling station,
8.8   by post,
0.2   or, did someone vote on your behalf?
0.1   (Don't know)
0.1   (Not answered)

ASK ALL

Q1027 [VotedEU]   N=4268
A lot of people did not vote in the European election
in 2004. How about you? Did you vote in that election
or didn't you manage to?
%
35.4   Yes: voted
61.3   No
0.3   (Refused to say)
3.0   (Don't know)
-      (Not answered)

Q1028 IF 'yes' AT [VotedEU]   N=4268
[VoteEU]
Which party did you vote for in the European election?
DO NOT PROMPT
%
9.3   Conservative
11.5   Labour
4.8   Liberal Democrat
0.7   Scottish National Party
0.3   Plaid Cymru
1.1   Green Party
1.3   UK Independence Party (UKIP)/Veritas
0.1   British National Party (BNP)/ National Front
0.2   RESPECT/ Scottish Socialist Party (SSP)/ Socialist
       Party
0.2   Other party (WRITE IN)
2.1   Refused to say
3.9   (Don't know)
3.3   (Not answered)

Constitution etc. (mainly version B)

VERSION B: ASK ALL
N=1058

Q1031 [Lords00]
CARD J1
Which of the statements on this card comes closest to your view about what should happen to the House of Lords.

%
7.0 All or most of its members should be appointed
26.2 All or most of its members should be elected
35.3 It should contain roughly an equal number of appointed and elected members
17.9 It should be abolished
13.5 (Don't know)
0.1 (Not answered)

Q1032 [Monarchy] N=1058
How important or unimportant do you think it is for Britain to continue to have a monarchy
... READ OUT ...

%
32.7 ... very important,
35.9 quite important,
15.9 not very important,
6.7 not at all important,
8.0 or, do you think the monarchy should be abolished?
0.7 (Don't know)
0.1 (Not answered)

Q1033 [Coalitn] N=1058
Which do you think would generally be better for Britain nowadays ... READ OUT ...

%
47.5 ..to have a government at Westminster formed by one political party on its own,
43.9 or, to have a government at Westminster formed by two political parties together - in coalition?
8.2 (Don't know)
0.3 (Not answered)

Q1034 [VoteSyst] N=1058
Some people say we should change the voting system for general elections to the UK House of Commons to allow smaller political parties to get a fairer share of MPs. Others say that we should keep the voting system for the House of Commons as it is to produce effective government. Which view comes **closer** to your own ...
READ OUT ...
IF ASKED: THIS REFERS TO 'PROPORTIONAL REPRESENTATION'

%
32.2 ... that we should change the voting system for the House of Commons,
60.7 or, keep it as it is?
6.7 (Don't know)
0.4 (Not answered)

Q1035 [ConLabDf] N=1058
Now considering everything the Conservative and Labour parties stand for, would you say that ... READ OUT ...

%
12.7 ... there is a great difference between them,
42.0 some difference,
42.6 or, not much difference?
2.2 (Don't know)
0.4 (Not answered)

Europe (mainly versions B and C)

ASK ALL
Q1036 [ECPolicy] N=4268
CARD (J1/J2)
Do you think Britain's long-term policy should be...
READ OUT ...

%
16.5 ..to leave the European Union,
35.7 to stay in the EU and try to **reduce** the EU's powers,
23.8 to leave things as they are,
10.2 to stay in the EU and try to **increase** the EU's powers,
4.5 or, to work for the formation of a single European government?
9.2 (Don't know)
0.1 (Not answered)

Q1037 **VERSIONS B AND C: ASK ALL**
[EUConRef]   N=2101
How do you think you would vote in a referendum on the proposed new **European constitution**? Would you vote in favour of Britain adopting the new constitution or against?
IF 'would not vote', PROBE: If you did vote, how would you vote?
IF RESPONDENT INSISTS THEY WOULD NOT VOTE, CODE DON'T KNOW

%
18.5 To adopt the constitution
55.1 Not to adopt the constitution
26.1 (Don't know)
0.2 (Not answered)

Q1038 [EuroRef]   N=2101
And if there were a referendum on whether Britain should **join the single European currency, the Euro**, how do you think you would vote? Would you vote to join the Euro, or not to join the Euro?
IF 'would not vote', PROBE: If you did vote, how would you vote?
IF RESPONDENT INSISTS THEY WOULD NOT VOTE, CODE DON'T KNOW

%
22.4 To join the Euro
69.8 Not to join the Euro
7.7 (Don't know)
0.1 (Not answered)

Q1039 [EUQuiz1b] *   N=2101
Now a quick quiz about Europe.
For each thing I say, please say whether you think it is **true** or **false**. If you don't know, just say so and we will skip to the next one. Remember, true, false, or don't know.
The European Union now has 25 member countries
FOR DON'T KNOW, CODE Ctrl+K

Q1040 [EUQuiz3] *   N=2101
Britain's income tax rates are decided in Brussels
(True, false or don't know?)
FOR DON'T KNOW, CODE Ctrl+K

Q1041 [EUQuiz6] *   N=2101
Britain doesn't have any European Commissioners at the moment
(True, false or don't know?)
FOR DON'T KNOW, CODE Ctrl+K

Q1042 [EUQuiz2] *   N=2101
Britain is the only member of the EU that is not a member of the single European currency.
(True, false or don't know?)
FOR DON'T KNOW, CODE Ctrl+K

Q1043 [EUQuiz4] *   N=2101
The countries that have introduced the Euro are still using their own currencies as well.
(True, false or don't know?)
FOR DON'T KNOW, CODE Ctrl+K

	[EUQuiz1b]	[EUQuiz3]	[EUQuiz6]
	%	%	%
True	48.0	7.7	9.9
False	16.3	68.7	60.1
(Don't Know)	35.6	23.5	29.8
(Refusal/Not answered)	0.1	0.1	0.1

	[EUQuiz2]	[EUQuiz4]
	%	%
True	23.8	14.8
False	60.9	70.8
(Don't Know)	15.2	14.2
(Refusal/Not answered)	0.1	0.1

Political efficacy (mainly versions B, C and D)

VERSION B: ASK ALL

Q1045 [GovtWork]
CARD J3
N=1058
Which of these statements best describes your opinion
on the present system of governing Britain?

%
1.9   Works extremely well and could not be improved
39.6   Could be improved in small ways but mainly works well
44.0   Could be improved quite a lot
11.6   Needs a great deal of improvement
2.7   (Don't know)
0.2   (Not answered)

VERSIONS B, C, AND D: ASK ALL

Q1046 [GovTrust] *
CARD (J2/J4)
N=3161
How much do you trust British governments of any party
to place the needs of the nation above the interests
of their own political party?
Please choose a phrase from this card.

Q1047 [MPsTrust] *
CARD (J2/J4) AGAIN
N=3161
And how much do you trust politicians of any party in
Britain to tell the truth when they are in a tight
corner?

	[GovTrust]	[MPsTrust]
	%	%
Just about always	2.1	0.6
Most of the time	23.5	7.4
Only some of the time	46.8	39.3
Almost never	25.8	51.5
(Don't Know)	1.7	1.0
(Refusal/Not answered)	0.2	0.2

Q1048 [SocTrust]
N=3161
Generally speaking, would you say that most people can
be trusted, or that you can't be too careful in
dealing with people?

%
45.3   Most people can be trusted
53.4   Can't be too careful in dealing with people
1.1   (Don't know)
0.2   (Not answered)

Q1049 [GovNoSay] *
CARD (J3/J5)
N=3161
Please choose a phrase from this card to say how much
you agree or disagree with the following statements.
People like me have no say in what the government
does.

Q1050 [LoseTch] *
CARD (J3/J5) AGAIN
N=3161
(Using this card, please say how much you agree or
disagree with this statement:)
Generally speaking those we elect as MPs lose touch
with people pretty quickly.

Q1051 [VoteIntr] *
CARD (J3/J5) AGAIN
N=3161
(Using this card, please say how much you agree or
disagree with this statement:)
Parties are only interested in people's votes, not in
their opinions.

Q1052 [VoteOnly] *
CARD (J3/J5) AGAIN
N=3161
(Please choose a phrase from this card to say how much
you agree or disagree with this statement:)
Voting is the only way people like me can have any say
about how the government runs things.

Q1053 [GovComp] *
CARD (J3/J5) AGAIN
N=3161
(Please choose a phrase from this card to say how much
you agree or disagree with this statement:)
Sometimes politics and government seem so complicated
that a person like me cannot really understand what is
going on.

Q1054 [PtyNMat2] *
CARD (J3/J5) AGAIN   N=3161
(Using this card, please say how much you agree or disagree with this statement:)
It doesn't really matter which party is in power, in the end things go on much the same.

	[GovNoSay]	[LoseTch]	[VoteIntr]
	%	%	%
Agree strongly	14.3	15.9	17.2
Agree	44.2	54.2	52.4
Neither agree nor disagree	14.7	14.6	13.8
Disagree	24.4	13.0	15.0
Disagree strongly	1.5	0.4	0.3
(It depends on the level of government)	-	-	-
(Don't Know)	0.8	1.7	1.1
(Refusal/Not answered)	0.2	0.2	0.2

	[VoteOnly]	[GovComp]	[PtyNMat2]
	%	%	%
Agree strongly	10.8	11.6	12.4
Agree	49.5	46.2	51.4
Neither agree nor disagree	12.4	12.4	8.7
Disagree	24.3	26.4	24.2
Disagree strongly	1.9	2.6	2.3
(It depends on the level of government)	-	-	0.1
(Don't Know)	0.9	0.6	0.7
(Refusal/Not answered)	0.2	0.2	0.2

Social identities (versions B and C)

VERSIONS B AND C: ASK ALL
Q1055   [NatPriv]
CARD (J4/J6)   N=2101
Some people talk about nationalising industry. Which of the statements on this card comes **closest** to what you yourself feel should be done? If you don't have an opinion, just say so.
FOR 'NO OPINION', CODE DK (Ctrl+K)

%	
9.5	A lot more industries should be nationalised
18.2	Only a few more industries should be nationalised
31.4	No more industries should be nationalised, but industries that are now nationalised should stay nationalised
9.9	Some of the industries that are now nationalised should become private companies
30.8	(Don't know)
0.1	(Not answered)

Q1056   [Immig2Ma]   N=2101
Do you think that too many immigrants have been let into the country or not?

%	
78.1	Too many
17.7	Not too many
3.4	(Don't know)
0.4	(Not answered)

VERSIONS B AND C: ASK ALL IN ENGLAND
Q1057   [EngPar2E]   N=1815
CARD (J5/J7)
With all the changes going on in the way the different parts of Great Britain are run, which of the following do you think would be best for England ...READ OUT...

%	
54.4	...for England to be governed as it is now, with laws made by the UK parliament,
20.1	for each region of England to have its own elected assembly that makes decisions about the region's economy, planning and housing,
17.7	or, for England as a whole to have its own new parliament with law-making powers?
2.8	(None of these)
4.7	(Don't know)
0.2	(Not answered)

Political respect (version B)

Q1060 **VERSION B: ASK ALL** N=1058
[Oppose]
In modern Britain two parties have been in government, the Conservative Party and the Labour Party. Which of these two parties do you **oppose** more strongly?
%
44.4 Oppose Conservative Party more strongly
29.5 Oppose Labour Party more strongly
23.1 (Both equally/Neither)
2.6 (Don't know)
0.4 (Not answered)

IF 'both equally/neither', DON'T KNOW OR REFUSAL AT [Oppose]
Q1061 [LikeLess] N=1058
If you **had** to choose, is there one you like **less** than the other?
%
6.1 Like Conservative Party **less**
2.9 Like Labour Party **less**
14.7 (Both equally/Neither)
1.8 (Don't know)
0.5 (Not answered)

VERSION B: IF SAID 'Conservative' OR 'Labour' AT [Oppose] OR AT [LikeLess]
Q1062 [Respect1] * N=1058
CARD J10
How much do you agree or disagree with the following statements about the (Conservative/Labour) party?
The (Conservative/Labour) party doesn't have any valid point of view.

Q1063 [Respect2] * N=1058
CARD J10 AGAIN
(How much do you agree or disagree with this statement:)
The (Conservative/Labour) party looks after the genuine needs and interests of some people in our society.

Q1058 **VERSIONS B AND C: ASK ALL IN SCOTLAND** N=190
[ScotParS]
CARD (J6/J8)
%
Which of these statements comes closest to your view?
10.1 Scotland should become independent, separate from the UK and the European Union
18.9 Scotland should become independent, separate from the UK but part of the European Union
50.3 Scotland should remain part of the UK, with its own elected parliament which has **some** taxation powers
8.2 Scotland should remain part of the UK, with its own elected parliament which has **no** taxation powers
8.9 Scotland should remain part of the UK **without** an elected parliament
3.5 (Don't know)
- (Not answered)

Q1059 **VERSIONS B AND C: ASK ALL IN WALES** N=96
[WelshAsW]
CARD (J7/J9)
%
Which of these statements comes closest to your view?
5.5 Wales should become independent, separate from the UK and the European Union
4.8 Wales should become independent, separate from the UK but part of the European Union
26.9 Wales should remain part of the UK, with its own elected parliament which has law-making **and** taxation powers
34.1 Wales should remain part of the UK, with its own elected assembly which has limited law-making powers **only**
23.6 Wales should remain part of the UK **without** an elected assembly
4.6 (Don't know)
0.5 (Not answered)

	[Respect1]	[Respect2]	[Respect3]	[Respect4]
	%	%	%	%
Agree strongly	4.2	4.3	4.0	1.3
Agree	19.2	47.5	47.1	10.3
Neither agree nor disagree	22.3	15.5	15.5	17.3
Disagree	32.8	11.9	11.9	42.9
Disagree strongly	2.7	1.8	1.8	9.7
(Don't Know)	1.7	1.9	1.9	1.3
(Refusal/Not answered)	2.3	2.3	2.3	2.4

	[Respect5]	[Respect6]	[Respect7]	[Respect8]
	%	%	%	%
Agree strongly	1.5	3.6	5.0	2.4
Agree	15.0	13.5	50.3	37.5
Neither agree nor disagree	15.7	17.5	18.0	19.8
Disagree	42.0	40.3	8.2	19.5
Disagree strongly	7.6	6.1	0.8	2.4
(Don't Know)	1.0	2.0	0.6	1.2
(Refusal/Not answered)	2.4	2.3	2.3	2.3

Q1064 [Respect3] * N=1058
CARD J10 AGAIN
(How much do you agree or disagree with this statement:)
People should give careful consideration to suggestions made by the (Conservative/Labour) party.

Q1065 [Respect4] * N=1058
CARD J10 AGAIN
(How much do you agree or disagree with this statement:)
People who support the (Conservative/Labour) party deserve our contempt.

Q1066 [Respect5] * N=1058
CARD J10 AGAIN
(How much do you agree or disagree with this statement:)
If I'm honest with myself, I have to say that I don't really respect supporters of the (Conservative/Labour) party.

Q1067 [Respect6] * N=1058
CARD J10 AGAIN
(How much do you agree or disagree with this statement:)
When the (Conservative/Labour) party is in power, I'm turned off politics.

Q1068 [Respect7] * N=1058
CARD J10 AGAIN
(How much do you agree or disagree with this statement:)
It is important to treat supporters of the (Conservative/Labour) party with respect.

Q1069 [Respect8] * N=1058
CARD J10 AGAIN
(How much do you agree or disagree with this statement:)
I usually take the opinions of the (Conservative/Labour) party seriously, even if I don't agree with them.

VERSION B: IF MARRIED OR LIVING WITH A PARTNER (AT [Marsta2b]) N=1058
[Marsta2bl]
Q1070 [TkPolSp]
CARD J11
From time to time people discuss political matters or current affairs with other people. How often do you talk about politics with the following people?
Your (husband/wife/partner)?

	%
Every day	4.5
Several times a week	9.4
At least once a week	10.1
A couple of times a month	11.2
Less than a couple of times a month	14.4
Never	13.5
(Don't know)	0.2
(Not answered)	-

Q1071 **VERSION B: ASK ALL**   N=1058
[TkPolFam] *
CARD J11 (AGAIN)
(How often do you talk about politics with:)
(Other) family members?
%
1.2 Every day
4.1 Several times a week
9.9 At least once a week
16.5 A couple of times a month
30.7 Less than a couple of times a month
35.3 Never
1.6 (Not applicable - no family members)
0.5 (Don't know)
0.2 (Not answered)

Q1072 [TkPolFr]   N=1058
CARD J11 AGAIN
(How often do you talk about politics with:)
Friends?
%
1.1 Every day
6.8 Several times a week
10.8 At least once a week
18.2 A couple of times a month
27.8 Less than a couple of times a month
34.2 Never
0.4 (Not applicable - no friends)
0.4 (Don't know)
0.2 (Not answered)

Q1073 **VERSION B: IF IN PAID WORK (AT [REconAct])**   N=1058
[TkPolCol]
CARD J11 AGAIN
(How often do you talk about politics with:)
Fellow workers?
%
2.3 Every day
4.8 Several times a week
6.2 At least once a week
9.9 A couple of times a month
10.7 Less than a couple of times a month
18.3 Never
1.5 (Not applicable - no fellow workers)
0.5 (Don't know)
0.1 (Not answered)

Q1074 **VERSION B: ASK ALL**   N=1058
[TkPolNei]
CARD J11 AGAIN
(How often do you talk about politics with:)
Neighbours?
%
0.3 Every day
0.7 Several times a week
1.6 At least once a week
4.7 A couple of times a month
16.1 Less than a couple of times a month
74.8 Never
1.2 (Not applicable - no neighbours)
0.4 (Don't know)
0.2 (Not answered)

Q1075 [TkPolOth]   N=1058
CARD J11 AGAIN
(How often do you talk about politics with:)
Anyone else, for example, casual acquantainces or
strangers?
%
0.2 Every day
0.3 Several times a week
1.5 At least once a week
4.6 A couple of times a month
15.7 Less than a couple of times a month
75.5 Never
1.6 (Not applicable - no casual acquantainces)
0.4 (Don't know)
0.2 (Not answered)

Q1076 **VERSION B: IF SAID 'Conservative' OR 'Labour' AT
[Oppose] OR AT [LikeLess] AND MARRIED OR LIVING WITH
PARTNER: IF TALKS POLITICS WITH SPOUSE/PARTNER (AT
[TkPolSp])**   N=1058
[SpOppP]
Does your (husband/wife/partner) **support** the
(Conservative/Labour) party, that is, the party you
yourself (feel more opposed to/like less)?
IF ASKED: By 'support' we mean feel closer to or
usually vote for?

VERSION B: IF SAID 'Conservative' OR 'Labour' AT [Oppose] OR AT [LikeLess]: IF TALKS POLITICS WITH FAMILY MEMBERS (AT [TkPolFam])
N=1058

Q1077 [FamOppP]
Do any of your (other) family members who you talk about politics with support the (Conservative/Labour) party (that is, the party you yourself (feel more opposed to/like less))?
IF ASKED: By 'support' we mean feel closer to or usually vote for?

	[SpOppP]	[FamOppP]
	%	%
Yes	3.3	14.9
No	37.0	33.5
(Don't Know)	2.6	6.0
(Refusal/Not answered)	1.1	1.5

IF 'yes' AT [FamOppP]
Q1077b [FamOppNu]
N=1058
Is that all of them, most of them, some of them, or a few of them?
%
0.4 All of them
1.8 Most of them
3.0 Some of them
5.8 A few of them
0.3 (TELEPHONE ONLY - never talk politics with family)
- (Don't know)
11.1 (Not answered)

VERSION B: IF SAID 'Conservative' OR 'Labour' AT [Oppose] OR AT [LikeLess]: IF TALKS POLITICS WITH FRIENDS (AT [TkPolFr])
N=1058

Q1078 [FrOppP]
Do any of your friends who you talk about politics with support the (Conservative/Labour) party (that is, the party you yourself (feel more opposed to/like less))?
IF ASKED: By 'support' we mean feel closer to or usually vote for?
%
27.7 Yes
20.6 No
7.7 (Don't know)
1.7 (Not answered)

IF 'yes' AT [FrOppP]
Q1078b [FrOppNu]
N=1058
Is that all of them, most of them, some of them, or a few of them?
%
0.1 All of them
1.7 Most of them
8.8 Some of them
10.0 A few of them
- (TELEPHONE ONLY - never talk politics with friends)
- (Don't know)
16.1 (Not answered)

VERSION B: IF SAID 'Conservative' OR 'Labour' AT [Oppose] OR AT [LikeLess]: IF TALKS POLITICS WITH FELLOW WORKERS (AT [TkPolCol])
N=1058

Q1079 [ColOppP]
Do any of your fellow workers who you talk about politics with support the (Conservative/Labour) party (that is, the party you yourself (feel more opposed to/like less))?
IF ASKED: By 'support' we mean feel closer to or usually vote for?
%
14.5 Yes
7.7 No
6.7 (Don't know)
1.1 (Not answered)

IF 'yes' AT [ColOppP]
Q1079b [ColOppNu]
N=1058
Is that all of them, most of them, some of them, or a few of them?
%
- All of them
0.6 Most of them
4.1 Some of them
5.2 A few of them
0.6 (TELEPHONE ONLY - never talk politics with fellow workers)
- (Don't know)
11.8 (Not answered)

VERSION B: IF SAID 'Conservative' OR 'Labour' AT [Oppose] OR AT [LikeLess]: IF TALKS POLITICS WITH NEIGHBOURS (AT [TkPolNei])

Q1080   [NeiOppP]   N=1058

Do any of your neighbours who you talk about politics with **support** the (Conservative/Labour) party (that is, the party you yourself (feel more opposed to/like less))?

IF ASKED: By 'support' we mean feel closer to or usually vote for?

%	
6.0	Yes
6.8	No
6.9	(Don't know)
0.7	(Not answered)

IF 'yes' AT [NeiOppP]

Q1080b [NeiOppNu]   N=1058

Is that all of them, most of them, some of them, or a few of them?

%	
0.3	All of them
0.1	Most of them
1.5	Some of them
1.1	A few of them
1.1	(TELEPHONE ONLY – never talk politics with neighbours)
-	(Don't know)
9.1	(Not answered)

VERSION B: IF SAID 'Conservative' OR 'Labour' AT [Oppose] OR AT [LikeLess]: IF TALKS POLITICS WITH ANYONE ELSE (AT [TkPolOth])

Q1081   [OthOppP]   N=1058

Do any of the (other) people who you talk about politics with **support** the (Conservative/Labour) party (that is, the party you yourself (feel more opposed to/like less))?

IF ASKED: By 'support' we mean feel closer to or usually vote for?

%	
10.2	Yes
6.0	No
3.8	(Don't know)
0.8	(Not answered)

IF 'yes' AT [OthOppP]

Q1081b [OthOppNu]   N=1058

Is that all of them, most of them, some of them, or a few of them?

%	
0.1	All of them
0.5	Most of them
3.7	Some of them
3.5	A few of them
0.4	(TELEPHONE ONLY – never talk politics with (other) people)
0.0	(Don't know)
6.6	(Not answered)

Note re Q1077b – Q1081b: some respondents answered some of these questions by telephone due to a programming error in the face to face questionnaire.

Prejudice (mainly versions B and C)

Q1082 **VERSION B: ASK ALL** N=1058
[PrejNow]
Do you think there is generally more racial prejudice in Britain now than there was 5 years ago, less, or about the same amount?
%
51.7 More now
12.9 Less now
30.6 About the same
0.5 Other (WRITE IN)
4.0 (Don't know)
0.2 (Not answered)

Q1085 **VERSION B: ASK ALL** N=1058
[PrejFut]
Do you think there will be more, less, or about the same amount of racial prejudice in Britain in 5 years time compared with now?
%
59.4 More in 5 years
11.0 Less
22.1 About the same
1.2 Other (WRITE IN)
6.1 (Don't know)
0.2 (Not answered)

Q1088 **VERSION B: ASK ALL** N=1058
[SRPrej]
%
How would you describe yourself ... READ OUT ...
2.6 ... as very prejudiced against people of other races,
29.8 a little prejudiced,
65.3 or, not prejudiced at all?
0.8 Other (WRITE IN)
1.2 (Don't know)
0.2 (Not answered)

Q1091 **VERSIONS B AND C: ASK ALL** N=2101
[PMS] *
CARD (J12/J8)
Now I would like to ask you some questions about sexual relationships. If a man and woman have sexual relations before marriage, what would your general opinion be?

Q1092 [ExMS] * N=2101
CARD (J12/J8) AGAIN
What about a **married person** having sexual relations with someone other than his or her partner?

Q1093 [HomoSex] * N=2101
CARD (J12/J8) AGAIN
What about sexual relations between two adults of the same sex?

	[PMS]	[ExMS]	[HomoSex]
	%	%	%
Always wrong	6.1	56.8	27.3
Mostly wrong	7.3	28.4	11.6
Sometimes wrong	10.7	9.4	7.9
Rarely wrong	7.9	1.0	8.8
Not wrong at all	62.8	1.3	36.8
(Depends/varies)	3.5	1.9	4.6
(Don't Know)	1.4	0.9	2.9
(Refusal/Not answered)	0.3	0.4	0.3

End of life issues (versions A and B)

VERSIONS A AND B: ASK ALL

Q1094 [EuPreAm]   N=2165

Now I would like to ask some questions about voluntary euthanasia - that is, when someone ends the life of another person **at their request**.

I will read you some circumstances in which someone might ask a **doctor** to end their life. In each case please tell me whether you think a doctor should be allowed by law to do so.

IF IT BECOMES CLEAR THAT IT WOULD DISTRESS THE RESPONDENT TO COMPLETE THIS SECTION, ENTER CTRL + R HERE TO SKIP THIS SECTION.

(Press 1 and <Enter> to continue.)

(Refused)

%
97.5
2.5

Q1095 [EuPainSh] *   N=2165

VERSIONS A AND B: IF NOT REFUSAL AT [EUPreAm]

CARD K1

First, a person with an incurable and painful illness, from which they will die - for example someone dying of cancer.

Do you think that, if they ask for it, a doctor should ever be allowed by law to end their life, or not?

Please choose your answer from the top section of the card.

%
50.2 Definitely should be allowed
29.5 Probably should be allowed
6.0   Probably should **not** be allowed
9.6   Definitely should **not** be allowed
1.9   (Don't know)
0.3   (Not answered)

Q1096 [EuPainis]   N=2165

CARD K1 AGAIN

And do you think the law allows a doctor to do this at the moment, or not?

Please choose your answer from the **bottom** section of the card.

%
1.4   Definitely allows
4.1   Probably allows
20.9 Probably does **not** allow
68.5 Definitely does **not** allow
2.6   (Don't know)
0.2   (Not answered)

Q1097 [EuRelSh] *   N=2165

CARD K1 AGAIN

And if they ask a close **relative** to end their life, should the law ever allow the close relative to do so, or not?

Please choose your answer from the **top** section of the card.

Q1098 [EuPainSu] *   N=2165

CARD K1 AGAIN

And do you think that, if this person asks for it, a doctor should ever be allowed by law to give them lethal medication that will allow the person to take their own life?

Again, please look at the top section of the card.

VERSION A: IF NOT REFUSAL AT [EUPreAm]

Q1099 [EuNDiSh2] *   N=1107

CARD K1 AGAIN

Now, how about a person with an incurable and painful illness, from which they will **not** die.

Do you think that, if they ask for it, a doctor should ever be allowed by law to end their life, or not?

(Again, please look at the top section of the card.)

Q1100 [EuNDiSu2] *   N=1107

CARD K1 AGAIN

And do you think that, if this person asks for it, a doctor should ever be allowed by law to give them lethal medication that will allow the person to take their own life?

(Again, please look at the top section of the card.)

Q1101 **VERSION B: IF NOT REFUSAL AT [EUPreAm]**
[EuNDieSh] *   N=1058
CARD K1 AGAIN
Now, how about a person with an incurable and painful illness, from which they will **not** die - for example someone with severe arthritis.
Do you think that, if they ask for it, a doctor should ever be allowed by law to end their life, or not?
(Again, please look at the top section of the card.)

Q1102 [EuNDieSu] *   N=1058
CARD K1 AGAIN
And do you think that, if this person asks for it, a doctor should ever be allowed by law to give them lethal medication that will allow the person to take their own life?
(Again, please look at the top section of the card.)

Q1103 **VERSIONS A AND B: IF NOT REFUSAL AT [EUPreAm]**
[EuDepSh] *   N=2165
CARD K1 AGAIN
And now, how about a person who is **not** in much pain **nor** in danger of death, but becomes permanently and completely **dependent** on relatives for all their needs - for example someone who cannot feed, wash or go to the toilet by themselves.
Do you think that, if they ask for it, a doctor should ever be allowed by law to end their life, or not?
(Again, please look at the top section of the card.)

Q1104 [EuDepRel] *   N=2165
CARD K1 AGAIN
And if they ask **a close relative** to end their life, should the law ever allow the close relative to do so, or not?
(Again, please look at the top section of the card.)

Q1105 **VERSION A: IF NOT REFUSAL AT [EUPreAm]**
[EuUnbrSh] *   N=1107
CARD K1 AGAIN
What about someone who has an incurable illness, from which they will die, and who says their suffering is unbearable. Do you think that, if they ask for it, a doctor should ever be allowed by law to end their life, or not?
(Again, please look at the top section of the card.)

Q1106 [EuUnbrSu] *   N=1107
CARD K1 AGAIN
And do you think that, if this person asks for it, a doctor should ever be allowed by law to give them lethal medication that will allow the person to take their own life?
(Again, please look at the top section of the card.)

Q1107 **VERSION B: IF NOT REFUSAL AT [EUPreAm]**
[EuLSupSh] *   N=1058
CARD K1 AGAIN
Now think about what should happen to someone who has an incurable illness which leaves them unable to make a decision about their **own** future. For instance, imagine a person in a coma on a **life support machine** who is never expected to regain consciousness.
If their relatives agreed, do you think a doctor should ever be allowed by law to turn the machine off, or not?
(Again, please look at the top section of the card.)

Q1108 [EuLSupls]   N=1058
CARD K1 AGAIN
And do you think the law allows a doctor to do this at the moment, or not?
Please choose your answer from the **bottom** section of the card.

	%
Definitely allows	15.6
Probably allows	24.9
Probably does **not** allow	19.8
Definitely does **not** allow	30.2
(Don't know)	6.9
(Not answered)	0.2

Q1109 [EuLSupRI]   N=1058
CARD K1 AGAIN
If the person's close relatives did **not** agree with this decision do you think a doctor should ever be allowed by law to turn the machine off, or not?
Please choose your answer from the **top** section of the card.

	%
Definitely should be allowed	11.2
Probably should be allowed	23.1
Probably should **not** be allowed	24.7
Definitely should **not** be allowed	33.3
(Don't know)	5.0
(Not answered)	0.3

VERSIONS A AND B: IF NOT REFUSAL AT [EUPreAm]

Q1110 [ProxyCon] *   N=2165
CARD K2
Some patients choose a person who they would like doctors to consult about their medical treatment in case they should become unable to make these decisions themselves.
Do you think the law should require doctors to **consult** someone chosen by a patient in this **way**?
Please choose your answer from the **top** section of the card.

Q1111 [ProxyDo] *   N=2165
CARD K2 AGAIN
And do you think the law should require that doctors **carry out** the wishes of a person chosen by a patient in this way?
Again, please look at the top section of the card.

	[EuRelSh] %	[EuPainSu] %	[EuNDiSh2] %	[EuNDiSu2] %
Definitely should be allowed	18.8	30.0	17.2	16.2
Probably should be allowed	25.1	30.0	27.4	24.1
Probably should **not** be allowed	21.4	13.2	20.4	20.5
Definitely should **not** be allowed	29.6	21.7	28.8	33.8
(Don't Know)	2.5	2.4	3.1	2.4
(Refusal/Not answered)	0.2	0.3	0.5	0.4

	[EuNDieSh] %	[EuNDieSu] %	[EuDepSh] %	[EuDepRel] %
Definitely should be allowed	12.3	11.4	16.9	8.2
Probably should be allowed	20.7	20.9	26.1	16.0
Probably should **not** be allowed	25.5	21.8	20.3	24.9
Definitely should **not** be allowed	35.3	40.3	30.2	44.9
(Don't Know)	3.6	3.2	3.6	3.2
(Refusal/Not answered)	0.2	0.1	0.3	0.3

	[EuUnbrSh] %	[EuUnbrSu] %	[EuLSupSh] %
Definitely should be allowed	42.8	29.8	46.2
Probably should be allowed	31.2	28.1	32.5
Probably should **not** be allowed	8.1	14.8	7.4
Definitely should **not** be allowed	12.0	21.6	7.1
(Don't Know)	2.0	2.7	4.2
(Refusal/Not answered)	0.4	0.4	0.2

Q1112 [DNRShd] *   N=2165
CARD K2 AGAIN
You may have heard of the phrase 'do not resuscitate order'. These are used to decide whether a patient should be resuscitated in hospital if they stop breathing. Imagine a doctor has **not** been able to talk to a patient about what they would want in this situation.
Do you think the law should **require** doctors to consult with a person's family before deciding on a 'do not resuscitate order'?
(Again, please look at the top section of the card.)

Q1113 [DNRFam] *   N=2165
CARD K2 AGAIN
And what should happen if the doctors think that there should be a 'do not resuscitate order' in case a patient stops breathing, but the family disagree? Do you think the law should **require** doctors to follow the family's wishes?
(Again, please look at the top section of the card.)

	[ProxyCon]	[ProxyDo]	[DNRShd]	[DNRFam]
	%	%	%	%
Definitely should require	52.6	37.9	54.8	34.4
Probably should require	32.6	39.3	22.4	30.3
Probably should **not** require	5.6	10.8	8.8	16.6
Definitely should **not** require	3.1	4.2	7.9	8.7
(Don't Know)	3.3	4.9	3.4	7.2
(Refusal/Not answered)	0.3	0.4	0.2	0.3

Q1114 **VERSION A: IF NOT REFUSAL AT [EUPreAm]**   N=1107
[LivW1Pr2]
Some people make what is called a 'living will', saying what they would wish to happen if they have an incurable illness which left them unable to make a decision about their own future. This living will might include instructions about what medical treatment they would or would not want to be given in the future to keep them alive.

Q1115 [LivW1Sh2]   N=1107
CARD K2 AGAIN
Do you think the law should **allow** doctors to make decisions about how to treat a patient on the instructions of their living will, or not?
Please choose your answer from the **bottom** section of the card.
%
Definitely should be allowed   45.5
Probably should be allowed   36.5
Probably should **not** be allowed   7.2
Definitely should **not** be allowed   5.0
(Don't know)   2.8
(Not answered)   0.4

Q1116 [LivW1Rq2]   N=1107
CARD K2 AGAIN
And do you think the law should **require** that doctors carry out the instructions of a 'living will'?
Please choose your answer from the **top** section of the card.
%
Definitely should require   40.5
Probably should require   36.8
Probably should **not** require   10.7
Definitely should **not** require   5.0
(Don't know)   4.0
(Not answered)   0.4

Q1117 [LivWlFam]   N=1107
CARD K2 AGAIN
What if a patient has a living will but his or her
close relatives do not want doctors to follow its
instructions?
In these circumstances, do you think the law should
allow doctors to follow the instructions of the **bottom** section of the living
will, or not?
Please choose your answer from the **bottom** section of
the card.
%
40.0 Definitely should be allowed
35.6 Probably should be allowed
9.6 Probably should **not** be allowed
6.3 Definitely should **not** be allowed
5.7 (Don't know)
0.4 (Not answered)

Q1118 [LivWlFd]   N=1107
CARD K2 AGAIN
And what if a patient's living will says that, if they
fell into a coma from which they would not recover,
they would always want doctors to give them the
nutrition and liquid they needed to stay alive.
In these circumstances, do you think the law should
require doctors to follow the instructions of the
living will, or not?
Please choose your answer from the **top** section of the
card.
%
26.8 Definitely should require
28.7 Probably should require
25.2 Probably should **not** require
10.9 Definitely should **not** require
5.5 (Don't know)
0.4 (Not answered)

Q1119 [LivWlS2]   N=1107
Have you by chance made, or even considered making,
such a 'living will'?
IF YES: Have you actually made one?
%
2.2 Yes, made one
10.1 Yes, considered making one
84.4 No
0.4 (Don't know)
0.4 (Not answered)

VERSION B: IF NOT REFUSAL AT [EUPreAm]
Q1120 [LivWilPr] **(NOT ON SPSS FILE)**   N=1058
Some people make what is called a 'living will',
saying what they would wish to happen if they have an
incurable illness which leaves them unable to make a
decision about their own future. Suppose that
someone's 'living will' includes an instruction that
doctors should **not** keep them alive if they have a
painful illness from which they will die.

Q1121 [LivWilSh]   N=1058
CARD K2 AGAIN
Do you think the law should **allow** doctors to decide to
end a patient's life on the instruction of the 'living
will', or not?
Please choose your answer from the **bottom** section of
the card.
%
46.2 Definitely should be allowed
29.8 Probably should be allowed
8.4 Probably should **not** be allowed
7.6 Definitely should **not** be allowed
5.3 (Don't know)
0.2 (Not answered)

Q1122 [LivWilRg]   N=1058
CARD K2 AGAIN
And do you think the law should **require** that doctors
carry out the instructions of a 'living will'?
Please choose your answer from the **top** section of
the card.
%
43.1 Definitely should require
32.8 Probably should require
10.4 Probably should **not** require
5.8 Definitely should **not** require
5.3 (Don't know)
0.2 (Not answered)

Q1123 [LivWilSf]   N=1058
Have you by chance made, or even considered making,
such a `living will'?
IF YES: Have you actually made one?
%
4.2   Yes, made one
11.9 Yes, considered making one
80.3 No
1.1   (Don't know)
0.1   (Not answered)

VERSIONS A AND B: IF NOT REFUSAL AT [EUPreAm]
Q1124 [FutTrFam]   N=2165
Have you ever talked to a close friend or someone in
your family about the sort of medical treatment you
would or would not want in the future?
IF YES: PROBE FOR CORRECT CODE
%
15.0 Yes, once or twice
7.6   Yes, three times or more
74.1 No
0.6   (Don't know)
0.2   (Not answered)

Q1125 [FutTrDcr]   N=2165
And have you ever talked to your doctor about the sort
of medical treatment you would or would not want in
the future?
IF YES: PROBE FOR CORRECT CODE
%
1.6   Yes, once or twice
0.4   Yes, three times or more
94.9 No
0.4   (Don't know)
0.2   (Not answered)

Classification

Housing

ASK ALL
Q1126 [Tenure1]   N=4268
And now some questions about you and your household.
Does your household own or rent this accommodation?
PROBE IF NECESSARY
IF OWNS: Outright or on a mortgage?
IF RENTS: From whom?
%
31.4 Owns outright
40.1 Buying on mortgage
10.6 Rents: local authority
0.1   Rents: New Town Development Corporation
5.4   Rents: Housing Association
1.5   Rents: property company
0.5   Rents: employer
1.1   Rents: other organisation
0.6   Rents: relative
6.7   Rents: other individual
0.5   Rents: Housing Trust
0.3   Rent free, squatting
0.5   Other (WRITE IN)
0.4   (Don't know)
0.3   (Not answered)

VERSIONS A AND B: ASK ALL
Q1130 [ResPres]   N=2165
Can I just check, would you describe the place where
you live as ... READ OUT ...
%
9.4   ...a big city,
24.9 the suburbs or outskirts of a big city,
43.5 a small city or town,
18.3 a **country** village,
3.5   or, a farm or home in the country?
0.1   (Other answer (WRITE IN))
0.3   (Don't know)
0.1   (Not answered)

VERSION B AND C: ASK ALL   N=2101

Q1133   [WherBorn]
        CARD L1
        Using this card, please tell me where your parents
        were living when you were born?
%
9.2   Scotland
3.7   Wales
24.5   Northern England
19.8   Midlands or East England
7.2   South West of England
23.8   London and the South East of England
0.6   Northern Ireland
3.3   Elsewhere in Europe
0.5   Caribbean
2.2   Africa
1.4   India, Pakistan, Bangladesh or Sri Lanka
3.2   Somewhere else (WRITE IN)
0.5   (Don't know)
0.1   (Not answered)

Religion and ethnicity

ASK ALL

Q1143   [Religion]
        Do you regard yourself as belonging to any particular   N=4268
        religion?
        IF YES: Which?
        CODE ONE ONLY - DO NOT PROMPT
%
39.6   No religion
9.5   Christian - no denomination
9.1   Roman Catholic
26.4   Church of England/Anglican
0.9   Baptist
2.4   Methodist
3.2   Presbyterian/Church of Scotland
0.1   Other Christian
1.2   Hindu
0.8   Jewish
2.6   Islam/Muslim
0.8   Sikh
0.3   Buddhist
0.6   Other non-Christian
0.1   Free Presbyterian
0.0   Brethren
0.4   United Reform Church (URC)/Congregational
1.4   Other Protestant
0.2   (Refusal)
0.3   (Don't know)
0.1   (Not answered)

VERSIONS B AND C: IF GAVE RELIGION AT [Religion]   N=2101

Q1145   [RelCom] *
        CARD L2
        In general, how much do you feel you have in common
        with(people who belong to the Church of England/Roman
        Catholics/etc), compared with other people?

Q1146 **VERSION B AND C: IF SAID 'no religion' AT [Religion]**
[NRelCom] *
N=2101
CARD L2
In general, how much do you feel you have in common with people who don't belong to a religion, compared with other people?

	[RelCom]	[NRelCom]
	%	%
A lot more in common with them than with other people	10.0	2.3
A little more in common with them than with other people	10.9	4.3
No more in common with them than with other people	40.3	30.6
(Don't Know)	0.4	0.6
(Refusal/Not answered)	0.5	0.5

Q1154 **ASK ALL: If not 'refusal' at [Religion]**
[FamRelig]   N=4268
In what religion, if any, were you brought up?
PROBE IF NECESSARY: What was your family's religion?
CODE ONE ONLY - DO NOT PROMPT

%
12.9 No religion
10.4 Christian - no denomination
13.8 Roman Catholic
42.4 Church of England/Anglican
1.4 Baptist
4.5 Methodist
5.2 Presbyterian/Church of Scotland
0.2 Other Christian
1.3 Hindu
0.8 Jewish
2.6 Islam/Muslim
0.8 Sikh
0.3 Buddhist
0.1 Other non-Christian
0.1 Free Presbyterian
0.1 Brethren
0.6 United Reform Church (URC)/Congregational
1.7 Other Protestant
0.1 (Refusal)
0.4 (Don't know)
0.3 (Not answered)

Q1156 **IF RELIGION GIVEN AT [Religion] OR AT [FamRelig]**
[ChAttend]   N=4268
Apart from such special occasions as weddings, funerals and baptisms, how often nowadays do you attend services or meetings connected with your religion?
PROBE AS NECESSARY.

%
10.2 Once a week or more
2.3 Less often but at least once in two weeks
4.9 Less often but at least once a month
8.5 Less often but at least twice a year
5.1 Less often but at least once a year
4.5 Less often than once a year
51.6 Never or practically never
0.7 Varies too much to say
0.1 (Don't know)
0.6 (Not answered)

Q1157 **ASK ALL**
[Religius]   N=4268
Would you say that nowadays you are ...READ OUT...

%
6.9 ...very religious,
26.5 somewhat religious,
31.5 not very religious,
34.1 or, not at all religious?
0.6 (Don't know)
0.3 (Not answered)

Q1158 **VERSION B AND C: ASK ALL**
[StarSign]   N=2101
CARD L2 AGAIN
In general, how much do you feel you have in common with people who have the same sign of the Zodiac (star sign) as you, compared with other people?

%
6.3 A lot more in common with them than with other people
9.3 A little more in common with them than with other people
79.1 No more in common with them than with other people
5.2 (Don't know)
0.1 (Not answered)

ASK ALL

Q1159- CARD (L1/L3)   N=4268
Q1167 Please say which, if any, of the words on this card describes the way **you** think of **yourself**. Please choose as many or as few as apply.
PROBE: Any others?
Multicoded (Maximum of 9 codes)

%		
67.2	British	[NatBrit]
52.3	English	[NatEng]
12.0	European	[NatEuro]
2.1	Irish	[NatIrish]
0.6	Northern Irish	[NatNI]
9.4	Scottish	[NatScot]
0.2	Ulster	[NatUlst]
4.2	Welsh	[NatWelsh]
3.9	Other answer (WRITE IN)	[NatOth]
0.8	(None of these)	[NatNone]
2.1	**EDIT ONLY:** OTHER - ASIAN MENTIONED	[NatAsia]
1.0	**EDIT ONLY:** OTHER - AFRICAN /CARIBBEAN MENTIONED	[NatAfric]
0.3	(Don't know)	
0.1	(Not answered)	

IF MORE THAN ONE ANSWER AT [NationU]
[BNationU]   N=4268

Q1182 CARD (L1/L3) AGAIN
And if you had to choose, which one **best** describes the way you think of yourself?

%	
19.6	British
17.8	English
1.0	European
0.4	Irish
0.0	Northern Irish
3.4	Scottish
-	Ulster
1.3	Welsh
0.9	Other answer (WRITE IN)
0.0	(None of these)
0.5	**EDIT ONLY:** OTHER - ASIAN MENTIONED
0.1	**EDIT ONLY:** OTHER - AFRICAN /CARIBBEAN MENTIONED
0.1	(Don't know)
0.5	(Not answered)

VERSIONS B AND C: ASK ALL

Q1186 [EurCom] *   N=2101
CARD L4
In general, how much do you feel you have in common with people who say they are European, compared with other people?

Q1187 [BritCom] *   N=2101
CARD L4 AGAIN
And, in general, how much do you feel you have in common with people who say they are British, compared with other people?

Q1188 [ESWCom] *   N=2101
CARD L4 AGAIN
And, in general, how much do you feel you have in common with people who say they are (English/Scottish/Welsh), compared with other people?

	[EurCom]	[BritCom]	[ESWCom]
	%	%	%
A lot more in common with them than with other people	3.7	14.8	18.9
A little more in common with them than with other people	13.4	25.0	24.7
No more in common with them than with other people	80.1	58.3	54.8
(Don't Know)	2.6	1.8	1.5
(Refusal/Not answered)	0.1	0.1	0.1

ASK ALL
Q1189 [RaceOri2]   N=4268
CARD (L2/L5)
% To which of these groups do you consider you belong?
1.2 BLACK: of African origin
1.0 BLACK: of Caribbean origin
0.1 BLACK: of other origin (WRITE IN)
2.0 ASIAN: of Indian origin
0.8 ASIAN: of Pakistani origin
0.4 ASIAN: of Bangladeshi origin
0.5 ASIAN: of Chinese origin
0.9 ASIAN: of other origin (WRITE IN)
89.7 WHITE: of any European origin
1.1 WHITE: of other origin (WRITE IN)
0.9 MIXED ORIGIN (WRITE IN)
0.9 OTHER (WRITE IN)
0.4 (Don't know)
0.1 (Not answered)

VERSIONS B AND C: IF ANSWER GIVEN AT [RaceOri2]
Q1200 [EthnCom]   N=2101
CARD L6
How much do you feel you have in common with (white people/Black people/people of Asian origin/etc) in general, compared with other people?
%
21.6 A lot more in common with them than with other people
24.4 A little more in common with them than with other people
52.2 No more in common with them than with other people
1.2 (Don't know)
0.7 (Not answered)

Education

ASK ALL
Q1201 [RPrivEd] *   N=4268
Have you ever attended a fee-paying, **private** primary or secondary school in the United Kingdom?
'PRIVATE' PRIMARY OR SECONDARY SCHOOLS INCLUDE:
* INDEPENDENT SCHOOLS
* SCHOLARSHIPS AND ASSISTED PLACES AT FEE-PAYING SCHOOLS
THEY EXCLUDE:
* DIRECT GRANT SCHOOLS (UNLESS FEE-PAYING)
* VOLUNTARY-AIDED SCHOOLS
* GRANT-MAINTAINED ('OPTED OUT') SCHOOLS
* NURSERY SCHOOLS

IF RESPONDENT HAS NO CHILDREN AGED 5 OR OVER IN THE HOUSEHOLD (AS GIVEN IN THE HOUSEHOLD GRID)   N=4268
Q1202 [OthChld3]
Have you ever been responsible for bringing up any children of school age, including stepchildren?

IF RESPONDENT HAS CHILDREN AGED 5 OR OVER IN THE HOUSEHOLD OR 'yes' AT [OthChld3]   N=4268
Q1203 [ChPrivEd] *
And (have any of your children / has your child) ever attended a fee-paying, **private** primary or secondary school in the United Kingdom?
'PRIVATE' PRIMARY OR SECONDARY SCHOOLS INCLUDE:
* INDEPENDENT SCHOOLS
* SCHOLARSHIPS AND ASSISTED PLACES AT FEE-PAYING SCHOOLS
THEY EXCLUDE:
* DIRECT GRANT SCHOOLS (UNLESS FEE-PAYING)
* VOLUNTARY-AIDED SCHOOLS
* GRANT-MAINTAINED ('OPTED OUT') SCHOOLS
* NURSERY SCHOOLS

	[RprivEd] %	[othChld3] %	[ChPrivEd] %
Yes	11.1	33.9	8.6
No	88.5	35.9	55.0
(Don't Know)	0.3	0.2	0.1
(Refusal/Not answered)	0.1	0.1	0.3

ASK ALL (NOT ON SCREEN)

Q1208 [Tea]   N=4268
How old were you when you completed your continuous full-time education?
PROBE IF NECESSARY
`STILL AT SCHOOL' - CODE 95
`STILL AT COLLEGE OR UNIVERSITY' - CODE 96
`OTHER ANSWER' - CODE 97 AND WRITE IN

%
27.4 15 or under
28.1 16
8.4 17
10.2 18
21.6 19 or over
0.6 Still at school
2.9 Still at college or university
0.3 Other answer (WRITE IN)
0.4 (Don't know)
0.2 (Not answered)

Q1209 [SchQual]   N=4268
CARD (L3/L7)
Have you passed any of the examinations on this card?

%
66.1 Yes
33.4 No
0.3 (Don't know)
0.2 (Not answered)

IF 'yes' AT [SchQual]

Q1210- CARD (L3/L7) AGAIN   N=4268
Q1213 Please tell me which sections of the card they are in?
PROBE : Any other sections?
CODE ALL THAT APPLY
% Multicoded (Maximum of 4 codes)

28.1 **Section 1:**   [EdQual1]
GCSE Grades D-G/Short course GCSE/Vocational GCSE
CSE Grades 2-5
O-level Grades D-E or 7-9
Scottish (SCE) Ordinary Bands D-E
Scottish Standard Grades 4-7
SCOTVEC/SQA National Certificate modules
Scottish School leaving certificate (no grade)

47.8 **Section 2:**   [EdQual2]
GCSE Grades A*-C
CSE Grade 1
O-level Grades A-C or 1-6
School Certif/Matriculation
Scottish SCE Ord. Bands A-C or pass
Scottish Standard Grades 1-3 or Pass
Scottish School Leaving Certificate Lower Grade
SUPE Ordinary
N Ireland Junior Certificate

26.0 **Section 3:**   [EdQual3]
A-level, S-level, A2-level, AS-level
International Baccalaureate
Vocational A-level (AVCE)
Scottish Higher/ Higher-Still Grades
Scottish SCE/SLC/SUPE at Higher Grade
Scot. Higher School Certif
Certif Sixth Year Studies/ Advanced Higher Grades
N Ireland Senior Certificate

3.5 **Section 4:**   [EdQual4]
Overseas school leaving exam or certificate
- (Don't know)
0.5 (Not answered)

ASK ALL

Q1214   [PSchQual]   N=4268
        CARD (L4/L8)
        And have you passed any of the exams or got any of the
        qualifications on **this** card?

%
55.0   Yes
44.5   No
0.3   (Don't know)
0.2   (Not answered)

IF 'yes' AT [PSchQual]

Q1215- CARD (L4/L8) AGAIN   N=4268
Q1240   Which ones? PROBE: Which others?
        PROBE FOR CORRECT LEVEL

%   Multicoded (Maximum of 26 codes)
15.7   Univ/CNAA first degree   [EdQual38]
3.0   Univ/CNAA diploma / Foundation Degree   [EdQual39]
4.8   Postgraduate degree   [EdQual36]
4.6   Teacher training qualification   [EdQual12]
2.8   Nursing qualification   [EdQual13]
0.8   Foundation/advanced (modern)
        apprenticeship   [EdQual26]
2.7   Other recognised trade apprenticeship   [EdQual27]
2.2   OCR/RSA - (Vocational) Certificate   [EdQual28]
1.5   OCR/RSA - (First) Diploma   [EdQual29]
1.0   OCR/RSA - Advanced Diploma   [EdQual30]
0.9   OCR/RSA - Higher Diploma   [EdQual31]
2.4   Other clerical, commercial qualification   [EdQual32]
5.9   City&Guilds - Level 1/ Part I   [EdQual22]
6.1   City&Guilds - Level 2/ Craft/
        Intermediate/ Ordinary/ Part II   [EdQtal23]
3.1   City&Guilds - Level 3/Advanced/ Final/
        Part III   [EdQual24]
2.0   City&Guilds - Level 4/Full Technological/
        Part IV   [EdQual25]
0.7   Edexcel/BTEC First Certificate   [EdQual33]
0.9   Edexcel/BTEC First/General Diploma   [EdQual34]
4.7   Edexcel/BTEC/BEC/TEC (General/Ordinary)
        National Certif or Diploma (ONC/OND)   [EdQual10]
4.7   Edexcel/BTEC/BEC/TEC Higher National
        Certif (HNC) or Diploma (HND)   [EdQual11]
3.9   NVQ/SVQ Lev 1/GNVQ/GSVQ Foundation lev   [EdQual17]
6.8   NVQ/SVQ Lev 2/GNVQ/GSVQ Intermediate lev   [EdQual18]
4.3   NVQ/SVQ Lev 3/GNVQ/GSVQ Advanced lev   [EdQual19]
0.8   NVQ/SVQ Lev 4   [EdQual20]
0.5   NVQ/SVQ Lev 5   [EdQual21]
6.9   Other recogn academic or vocational
        qual (WRITE IN)   [EdQual37]
-       (Don't know)
0.5   (Not answered)

N=4268

Q1273 [HEdQual] **(NOT ON SCREEN)**
% Highest educational qual obtained
16.8 Degree
12.3 Higher educ below degree
15.7 A level or equiv
19.2 O level or equiv
8.6 CSE or equiv
1.9 Foreign or other
24.8 No qualification
0.6 DK/Refusal/NA

Q1274 [HEdQual2] **(NOT ON SCREEN)** N=4268
% Highest educational qual obtained (postgrad separate)
4.8 Postgraduate degree
12.0 First degree
12.3 Higher educ below degree
15.7 A level or equiv
19.2 O level or equiv
8.6 CSE or equiv
1.9 Foreign or other
24.8 No qualification
0.6 DK/Refusal/NA

Partner's/spouse's job details

ASK ALL WITH SPOUSE/PARTNER WHO IS WORKING OR WAITING TO TAKE UP WORK
N=1516
Q1277 [Title] **NOT ON DATAFILE**
Now I want to ask you about your (husband's/wife's/partner's) (present/future) job.
What (is his/her job / will that job be)?
PROBE IF NECESSARY: What is the name or title of the job?
Open Question (Maximum of 80 characters)

Q1278 [Typewk] **NOT ON DATAFILE** N=1516
What kind of work (do/will) (he/she) do most of the time?
IF RELEVANT: What materials/machinery (do/will) (he/she) use?
Open Question (Maximum of 80 characters)

Q1279 [Train] **NOT ON DATAFILE** N=1516
What training or qualifications (are/were) needed for that job?
Open Question (Maximum of 80 characters)

ASK ALL WHO ARE MARRIED OR LIVING WITH A PARTNER (AT [MatSta2b])
Q1280 [S2Employ] N=2736
In (husband's/wife's/partner's) (main) job (is/will) (he/she) (be) ... READ OUT ...
%
53.4 ... an employee,
10.1 or self-employed?
0.3 (Don't know)
0.4 (Not answered)

Q1285 [S2Superv]
In (his/her) job, (does/will) (he/she) have any formal   N=2736
responsibility for supervising the work of other
(employees/people)?
DO NOT INCLUDE PEOPLE WHO ONLY SUPERVISE:
- CHILDREN, E.G. TEACHERS, NANNIES, CHILDMINDERS
- ANIMALS
- SECURITY OR BUILDINGS, E.G. CARETAKERS, SECURITY
  GUARDS

%
25.1 Yes
38.3 No
0.5 (Don't know)
0.3 (Not answered)

**ASK ALL WITH SPOUSE/PARTNER WHO IS WORKING OR WAITING
TO TAKE UP WORK AS EMPLOYEE ('employee' OR DON'T KNOW
AT [EmployA])**
Q1288 [S2OcSec2]
CARD (L5/L9)   N=1479
Which of the types of organisation on this card (does
he/she work / will he she be working) for?
%
65.2 PRIVATE SECTOR FIRM OR COMPANY Including, for example,
limited companies and PLCs
1.8 NATIONALISED INDUSTRY OR PUBLIC CORPORATION Including,
for example, the Post Office and the BBC
29.2 OTHER PUBLIC SECTOR EMPLOYER
Incl eg: - Central govt/ Civil Service/ Govt Agency
- Local authority/ Local Educ Auth (INCL 'OPTED OUT'
SCHOOLS)
- Universities
- Health Authority / NHS hospitals / NHS Trusts/ GP
surgeries
- Police / Armed forces
1.9 CHARITY/ VOLUNTARY SECTOR Including, for example,
charitable companies, churches, trade unions
0.6 Other answer (WRITE IN)
0.5 (Don't know)
0.8 (Not answered)

**ASK ALL WITH SPOUSE/PARTNER WHO IS WORKING OR WAITING
TO TAKE UP WORK**
[S2EmpWr2]   N=1755
IF EMPLOYEE: Including your (husband/wife/partner),
how many people are employed at the place where
(he/she) (works/will work) from?
Q1296   **IF SELF-EMPLOYED:** (Does/Will) (he/she) have any
employees?
IF YES: PROBE FOR CORRECT PRECODE.
%
(DO NOT USE IF EMPLOYEE/No employees)
10.7 Under 10
18.3 10-24
13.5 25-49
12.5 50-99
8.4 100-199
8.8 200-499
13.4 500+
5.1 (Don't know)
1.0 (Not answered)

Income and benefits

ASK ALL

Q1349   [AnyBN3]   N=4268
        CARD (L6/L10)
        Do you (or your husband/wife/partner) receive any of
        the state benefits or tax credits on this card at
        present?
        %
57.0   Yes
42.4   No
 0.4   (Don't know)
 0.3   (Not answered)

        IF 'yes' AT [AnyBN3]   N=4268
Q1350- CARD (L6/L10) AGAIN
Q1367   Which ones? PROBE: Which others?
        Multicoded (Maximum of 18 codes)
        %
23.1   State retirement pension (National
        Insurance)   [BenefOAP]
 0.8   War Pension (War Disablement Pension or
        War Widows Pension)   [BenefWar]
 0.7   Bereavement Allowance/ Widow's Pension/
        Widowed Parent's Allowance   [BenefWid]
 1.8   Jobseeker's Allowance   [BenefUB]
 4.9   Income Support (not for pensioners)   [BenefIS2]
 4.1   Pension Credit / Minimum Income Guarantee
        / Income Support for pensioners   [BenefPC]
23.5   Child Benefit / Guardian's Allowance   [BenefCB]
13.3   Child Tax Credit   [BenefCTC]
 6.1   Working Tax Credit   [BenefFC]
 7.4   Housing Benefit (Rent Rebate/
        Rent Allowance)   [BenefHB]
 9.1   Council Tax Benefit (or Rebate)   [BenefCT]
 4.3   Incapacity Benefit / Sickness Benefit /
        Invalidity Benefit   [BenefInc]
 4.6   Disability Living Allowance (for people
        under 65)   [BenefDLA]
 1.9   Attendance Allowance (for people aged 65+)   [BenefAtA]
 0.4   Severe Disablement Allowance   [BenefSev]
 1.8   Care Allowance (formerly Invalid Care
        Allowance)   [BenefICA]
 0.5   Industrial Injuries Benefits   [BenefInd]
 0.4   Other state benefit (WRITE IN)   [BenefOth]
 0.1   (Don't know)
 0.8   (Not answered)

Q1389

ASK ALL　　　　　　N=4268

[MainInc3]

CARD (L7/L11)

Which of these is the **main** source of income for you (and your husband/ wife/ partner) at present?

%	
62.9	Earnings from employment (own or spouse / partner's)
7.9	Occupational pension(s) – from previous employer(s)
2.4	Private pension(s)
12.7	State retirement or widow's pension(s)
2.0	Jobseeker's Allowance/ Unemployment benefit
1.1	Pension Credit/ Minimum Income Guarantee/ Income Support for pensioners
3.0	Invalidity, sickness or disabled pension or benefit(s)
2.6	Other state benefit or tax credit (WRITE IN)
0.9	Interest from savings or investments
1.3	Student grant, bursary or loans
2.1	Dependent on parents/other relatives
0.2	Other main source (WRITE IN)
0.5	(Don't know)
0.4	(Not answered)

Q1394

[HhIncome] *　　　　　　N=4268

CARD (L8/L12)

Which of the letters on this card represents the total income of your household from **all** sources **before tax**? Please just tell me the letter.

NOTE: INCLUDES INCOME FROM BENEFITS, SAVINGS, ETC.

Q1395

ASK ALL IN PAID WORK (AT [REconAct])　　　　　　N=2403

[REarn] *

CARD (L8/L12) AGAIN

Which of the letters on this card represents your **own** gross or total **earnings**, before deduction of income tax and national insurance?

	[HhIncome] %	[REarn] %
Less than 3,999	1.9	3.4
4,000 to 5,999	4.2	3.5
6,000 to 7,999	4.5	4.9
8,000 to 9,999	4.8	5.7
10,000 to 11,999	4.7	7.0
12,000 to 14,999	5.5	10.7
15,000 to 17,999	5.5	9.3
18,000 to 19,999	3.2	6.0
20,000 to 22,999	4.6	7.4
23,000 to 25,999	5.0	6.6
26,000 to 28,999	4.5	4.8
29,000 to 31,999	3.9	4.1
32,000 to 37,999	6.3	5.6
38,000 to 43,999	5.0	3.4
44,000 to 49,999	4.4	2.0
50,000 to 55,999	3.9	1.6
56,000 and over	10.9	5.2
(Don't Know)	8.8	2.4
(Refusal/Not answered)	8.4	6.5

Administration

ASK ALL

Q1397 [SCXplain]   N=4268
The final set of questions are in this booklet. They
will probably be easier to answer if you read them.
All of them can be answered just by ticking a box.
(IF APPROPRIATE: You don't necessarily have to do them
right now. I can call back for the booklet another
day).
PLEASE MAKE SURE YOU GIVE THE RESPONDENT THE VERSION
(A/B/C/D) (**blue/green/orange/cream**) QUESTIONNAIRE
ENTER THE SERIAL NUMBER : (*serial number*)
...POINT NUMBER : (*sample point*)
...INTERVIEWER NUMBER : (*interviewer number*)
ON THE FRONT PAGE OF THE SELF COMPLETION.
THEN TELL US WHETHER IT IS TO BE ...

%
23.5   ... filled in immediately after interview in your
presence,
69.8   or, left behind to be filled in later,
6.2   or, if the respondent refused.
0.5   (Don't know)
0.1   (Not answered)

IF 'yes' AT [PhoneX]

Q1400 [PhoneBc2]   N=4268
A few interviews on any survey are checked by my
office to make sure that people are satisfied with the
way the interview was carried out. In case my office
needs to contact you, it would be helpful if we could
have your telephone number.
ADD IF NECESSARY: Your 'phone number will **not** be
passed to anyone outside the National Centre without
your consent.
IF NUMBER GIVEN, WRITE ON THE ARF
IF MORE THAN ONE NUMBER, ASK WHICH WOULD BE MOST
CONVENIENT FOR RECONTACT

%
88.5   Number given
7.2   Number refused
0.2   (Don't know)
0.7   (Not answered)

ASK ALL

Q1401 [PhoneX2]   N=4268
(*And, may we have your mobile phone number as well?*
IF NO MOBILE:) Is there another phone number where you
could (*also*) be reached?
IF NUMBER GIVEN, WRITE ON THE ARF

%
32.7   Number given
66.0   Number refused/not given (/no mobile or second phone)
1.2   (Don't know)
0.2   (Not answered)

Q1402 [ComeBac3]   N=4268
From time to time we do follow-up studies and may wish
to contact you again. Would this be all right?

%
79.0   Yes
20.2   No
0.7   (Don't know)
0.1   (Not answered)

IF 'yes' AT [ComeBac3]

Q1403 [Stable]   N=4268
Could you give us the address and phone number of
someone who knows you well, just in case we have
difficulty in getting in touch with you.
IF NECESSARY, PROMPT: Perhaps a relative or friend who
is unlikely to move?
WRITE DETAILS ON THE BACK PAGE OF THE ARF.

%
24.8   INFORMATION GIVEN
53.9   INFORMATION NOT GIVEN
0.2   (Don't know)
0.8   (Not answered)

Q1404 [OxfCmBk]
On part of this project we are working with academics N=4268
from the University of Oxford. They may want to do
follow up interviews with some people who have taken
part in this study. If **they**, or a survey organisation
on their behalf, wanted to contact you,
would it be alright for us to pass on your details to
them - by that, I mean your name, address, telephone
number and some of the answers you have given me
today?

%
57.6   Yes
21.1   No
0.0   (Don't know)
1.1   (Not answered)

BRITISH SOCIAL ATTITUDES 2005 SELF-COMPLETION QUESTIONNAIRE VERSION A

1. Suppose you could change the way you spend your time, spending more time on some things and less time on others. Which of the things on the following list would you like to spend <u>more</u> time on, and which would you like to spend <u>less</u> time on and which would you like to spend the <u>same</u> amount of time on as now?

N=911

PLEASE TICK *ONE* BOX ON EACH LINE

		Much more time	A bit more time	Same time as now	A bit less time	Much less time	Can't choose/ Doesn't apply	Not Answered
[TmPdJob] a.	Time in a paid job %	4.4	6.9	24.8	22.0	27.4	7.5	7.1
[TmHldWrk] b.	Time doing household work %	1.9	12.5	35.5	22.0	14.5	6.5	7.1
[TmFamily] c.	Time with your family %	28.4	39.3	22.6	0.6	0.6	3.8	4.8
[TmFriend] d.	Time with your friends %	14.2	44.1	31.5	0.9	0.4	3.1	5.7
[TmLeisre] e.	Time in leisure activities %	23.3	42.9	23.5	0.6	0.5	4.5	4.7

2. Please tick <u>one</u> box for <u>each</u> statement below to show how much you agree or disagree with it, <u>thinking of work in general</u>.

N=911

PLEASE TICK *ONE* BOX ON EACH LINE

		Strongly agree	Agree	Neither agree nor disagree	Disagree	Strongly disagree	Can't choose	Not answered
[JbErnMny] a.	A job is just a way of earning money - no more %	9.5	22.0	13.3	35.1	11.6	4.3	4.2
[JbEnjoy] b.	I would enjoy having a paid job even if I did not need the money %	9.0	40.0	18.3	14.5	6.4	7.3	4.4

3. For each of the following, please tick one box to show how important you personally think it is in a job.

How important is ...

PLEASE TICK ONE BOX ON EACH LINE

N=911

		Very important	Important	Neither important nor unimportant	Not important	Not important at all	Can't choose	Not answered
[JbImSecr] a. ...job security	%	49.4	41.3	3.7	0.6	0.2	1.6	3.1
[JbImHinc] b. ...high income	%	16.6	53.2	20.6	3.9	0.5	1.8	3.5
[JbImAdvc] c. ...good opportunities for advancement	%	23.4	50.2	16.5	3.2	0.7	2.2	3.8
[JbImIntr] d. ...an interesting job	%	50.1	41.3	3.6	0.5	0.1	1.3	3.1
[JbImIndp] e. ...a job that allows someone to work independently	%	19.4	48.9	20.1	5.3	0.4	1.7	4.2
[JbImHelp] f. ...a job that allows someone to help other people	%	21.0	47.4	21.4	4.0	1.0	2.6	2.5
[JbImUse] g. ...a job that is useful to society	%	21.1	42.7	24.7	4.0	1.2	3.0	3.3
[JbImDays] h. ...a job that allows someone to decide their times or days of work	%	13.4	36.7	30.2	12.2	1.1	3.1	3.3

4. Suppose you were working and could choose between different kinds of jobs. Which of the following would you personally choose?

N=911

[ChEmpSta]
a. I would choose ...

PLEASE TICK ONE BOX ONLY

	%
... being an employee	45.3
... being self-employed	39.9
Can't choose	12.9
Not answered	2.0

[ChFrmSiz]
b. I would choose ...

PLEASE TICK ONE BOX ONLY

	%
... working in a small firm	55.3
... working in a large firm	24.8
Can't choose	17.7
Not answered	2.2

[ChPrvPub]
c. I would choose ...

PLEASE TICK ONE BOX ONLY

	%
... working in a private business	51.1
... working for the government or civil service	22.8
Can't choose	23.9
Not answered	2.1

5. To what extent do you agree or disagree with the following statements?

PLEASE TICK ONE BOX ON EACH LINE

N=911

		Strongly agree	Agree	Neither agree nor disagree	Disagree	Strongly disagree	Can't choose	Not answered
[Ebsecse] a. Employees have more job security than the self-employed	%	1.1	42.6	26.2	12.1	2.2	3.2	2.5
[EInFamSE] b. Being an employee interferes more with family life than self-employment	%	4.7	26.0	26.3	32.5	4.7	3.3	2.5

6. To what extent do you agree or disagree with the following statements?

N=911

PLEASE TICK ONE BOX ON EACH LINE

	Strongly Agree	Agree	Neither agree nor disagree	Disagree	Strongly disagree	Can't choose	Not answered
[TUJobSec] a. Trade unions are very important for the job security of employees	% 12.8	35.9	28.5	15.1	2.7	2.7	2.3
[TUWrkCon] b. Without trade unions the working conditions of employees would be much worse than they are	% 15.7	42.8	24.8	10.9	1.4	2.4	2.0

[FtPtPref]
7. Suppose you could decide on your work situation at present. Which of the following would you prefer?

PLEASE TICK ONE BOX ONLY

N=911

	%
A full-time job [30 hours or more per week]	39.5
A part-time job [10-29 hours per week]	34.2
A job with less than 10 hours a week	4.6
No paid job at all	10.4
Can't choose	9.1
Not answered	2.1

[WorkNow]
8. Are you currently working for pay?

PLEASE TICK ONE BOX ONLY

N=911

	%	
Yes	57.3	→ PLEASE ANSWER QUESTIONS 9 TO 27
No	42.0	→ PLEASE GO TO QUESTION 28 ON PAGE 8
Not answered	0.7	

IF YOU ARE CURRENTLY WORKING FOR PAY:
PLEASE ANSWER QUESTIONS 9 – 27 ABOUT YOUR MAIN JOB

N=911

[WorkEarn]
9. Think of the number of hours you work, and the money you earn in your main job, including any regular overtime. If you had only one of these three choices, which of the following would you prefer?

PLEASE TICK ONE BOX ONLY

	%
Work longer hours and earn more money	11.7
Work the same number of hours and earn the same money	36.5
Work fewer hours and earn less money	4.3
Can't choose	4.0
Not answered	1.4

10. For each of these statements about your main job, please tick one box to show how much you agree or disagree that it applies to your job.

N=911

PLEASE TICK ONE BOX ON EACH LINE

	Strongly agree	Agree	Neither agree nor disagree	Disagree	Strongly disagree	Can't choose	Not answered
[JbIsSecr] a. My job is secure	% 10.3	27.7	10.2	5.9	1.6	0.4	1.8
[JbIsHInc] b. My income is high	% 2.6	8.7	13.6	24.6	5.9	0.1	2.4
[JbIsAdvc] c. My opportunities for advancement are high	% 2.8	12.3	18.4	18.5	3.1	0.4	2.4
[JbIsIntr] d. My job is interesting	% 17.7	28.0	9.6	4.7	1.7	0.2	2.2
[JbIsIndp] e. I can work independently	% 13.3	31.5	5.3	5.5	0.7	0.2	1.5
[JbIsHelp] f. In my job I can help other people	% 15.0	28.4	7.3	4.6	0.9	0.1	1.6
[JbIsUse] g. My job is useful to society	% 14.1	20.4	14.3	5.2	1.5	-	2.5
[JbImpSkl] h. My job gives me a chance to improve my skills	% 10.3	26.8	11.5	6.0	1.5	0.1	1.9

11. Now some more questions about your working conditions. Please tick one box for each item below to show how often it applies to your work.

N=911

How often ...

PLEASE TICK ONE BOX ON EACH LINE

	Always	Often	Some-times	Hardly ever	Never	Can't choose	Not answered
[WrkExhst] a. ...do you come home from work exhausted? %	5.0	18.1	27.6	4.4	1.6	0.1	1.3
[WrkPhysc] b. ...do you have to do hard physical work? %	3.3	8.4	16.9	11.3	16.5	--	1.5
[WrkStres] c. ...do you find your work stressful? %	3.9	14.4	30.1	5.6	2.1	0.2	1.7
[WrkDangr] d. ...do you work in dangerous conditions? %	1.6	3.1	8.8	15.7	26.6	0.5	1.7

[FlexTime]
12. Which of the following statements best describes how your working hours are decided? (By working hours we mean here the times you start and finish work, and not the total hours you work per week or month).

N=911

PLEASE TICK ONE BOX ONLY

%

Starting and finishing times are decided by my employer and I cannot change them on my own	28.5
I can decide the time I start and finish work, within certain limits	22.5
I am entirely free to decide when I start and finish work	5.8
Not answered	1.2

[DWorkOrg]
13. Which of the following statements best describes how your daily work is organised?

N=911

PLEASE TICK ONE BOX ONLY

%

I am free to decide how my daily work is organised	13.9
I can decide how my daily work is organised, within certain limits	27.9
I am not free to decide how my daily work is organised	13.5
Can't choose	1.0
Not answered	1.6

[HrOffPer]
14. How difficult would it be for you to take an hour or two off during working hours, to take care of personal or family matters?

N=911

PLEASE TICK ONE BOX ONLY

%

Not difficult at all	19.6
Not too difficult	20.7
Somewhat difficult	9.5
Very difficult	5.8
Can't choose	1.0
Not answered	1.4

15. How often do you feel that....

N=911

PLEASE TICK ONE BOX ON EACH LINE

	Always	Often	Some-times	Hardly ever	Never	Can't choose	Not answered
[JbIntFam] a. ...the demands of your job interfere with your family life? %	1.5	10.4	22.9	13.7	7.1	0.8	1.7
[FamInJb] b. ...the demands of your family life interfere with your job? %	0.4	2.1	13.7	23.8	14.5	0.8	2.7

[SkillUse]
16. How much of your past work experience and/or job skills can you make use of in your present job?

N=911

PLEASE TICK ONE BOX ONLY

%

Almost none	6.0
A little	14.8
A lot	17.1
Almost all	18.1
Can't choose	0.5
Not answered	1.4

[NuJbWkEx]
17. If you were to look for a new job, how helpful would your present work experience and/or job skills be?

N=911

PLEASE TICK **ONE** BOX ONLY

	%
Very helpful	23.0
Quite helpful	24.9
Not so helpful	5.2
Not helpful at all	2.3
Can't choose	1.1
Not answered	1.4

[TrnImJb1]
18. Over the past 12 months, have you had any training to improve your job skills either at the workplace or somewhere else?

N=911

PLEASE TICK **ONE** BOX ONLY

	%
Yes	34.3
No	21.9
Can't choose	0.4
Not answered	1.4

19. In general, how would you describe relations at your workplace …

N=911

PLEASE TICK **ONE** BOX ON EACH LINE

		Very good	Quite good	Neither good nor bad	Quite bad	Very bad	Can't choose	Not answered
[WkIndRel] a.	…between management and employees?	% 15.0	24.7	8.3	4.9	0.7	2.6	1.8
[WkMatRel] b.	…between workmates/ colleagues?	% 23.0	24.2	4.4	0.7	-	3.2	2.5

[PWWkSat2]
20. How satisfied are you in your main job?

N=911

PLEASE TICK **ONE** BOX ONLY

	%
Completely satisfied	8.6
Very satisfied	15.7
Fairly satisfied	22.0
Neither satisfied nor dissatisfied	4.2
Fairly dissatisfied	3.4
Very dissatisfied	1.3
Completely dissatisfied	0.9
Can't choose	0.3
Not answered	1.6

21. To what extent do you agree or disagree with each of the following statements?

N=911

PLEASE TICK **ONE** BOX ON EACH LINE

	Strongly agree	Agree	Neither agree nor disagree	Disagree	Strongly disagree	Can't choose	Not answered
[HelpFirm] a. I am willing to work harder than I have to in order to help the firm or organisation I work for succeed	% 10.2	25.3	14.1	5.1	0.3	1.3	1.6
[ProudFrm] b. I am proud to be working for my firm or organisation	% 10.0	25.4	16.6	2.1	0.7	1.2	2.1
[PrefStay] c. I would turn down another job that offered quite a bit more pay in order to stay with this organisation	% 3.4	8.5	12.3	21.9	7.4	2.4	2.1

[JbGdCurr]
22. How difficult or easy do you think it would be for you to find a job at least as good as your current one?

PLEASE TICK *ONE* BOX ONLY

N=911

	%
Very easy	5.1
Fairly easy	14.8
Neither easy nor difficult	12.4
Fairly difficult	17.6
Very difficult	5.7
Can't choose	1.2
Not answered	1.3

[ReplaceU]
23. How difficult or easy do you think it would be for your firm or organisation to replace you if you left?

PLEASE TICK *ONE* BOX ONLY

N=911

	%
Very easy	6.6
Fairly easy	15.8
Neither easy nor difficult	11.6
Fairly difficult	15.9
Very difficult	4.9
Can't choose	1.7
Not answered	1.5

[LikeFdJb]
24. All in all, how likely is it that you will try to find a job with another firm or organisation within the next 12 months?

PLEASE TICK *ONE* BOX ONLY

N=911

	%
Very likely	6.7
Likely	10.3
Unlikely	18.4
Very unlikely	19.4
Can't choose	1.8
Not answered	1.4

[LoseJob]
25. To what extent, if at all, do you <u>worry</u> about the possibility of losing your job?

PLEASE TICK *ONE* BOX ONLY

N=911

	%
I worry a great deal	2.5
I worry to some extent	9.7
I worry a little	17.7
I don't worry at all	26.7
Not answered	1.4

26. To what extent do you agree or disagree with the following statements?

In order to avoid unemployment I would be willing ....

N=911

PLEASE TICK *ONE* BOX ON EACH LINE

		Strongly agree	Agree	Neither agree nor disagree	Disagree	Strongly disagree	Can't choose	Not answered
[AvUnemp1] a. ...to accept a job that requires new skills.	%	13.1	33.7	4.6	3.1	0.6	1.1	1.9
[AvUnemp2] b. ...to accept a position with lower pay.	%	3.4	17.7	10.5	19.7	3.2	1.4	2.1
[AvUnemp3] c. ...to accept temporary employment.	%	5.1	28.5	8.7	10.0	2.1	1.0	2.5
[AvUnemp4] d. ...to travel longer to get work.	%	4.6	21.9	9.8	12.8	5.1	1.3	2.5

[WkAddInc]
27. In addition to your main job, do you do any other work for additional income?

PLEASE TICK *ONE* BOX ONLY

N=911

	%
No	50.5
Yes, mostly as an employee	2.5
Yes, mostly on a self-employed basis	2.0
Yes, other	1.6
Not answered	1.4

PLEASE GO TO QUESTION 37 ON PAGE 11

PLEASE ANSWER QUESTION 28 IF YOU ARE NOT CURRENTLY WORKING FOR PAY

[EverJob2]
28. Have you ever had a paid job for one year or more?

N=911

PLEASE TICK ONE BOX ONLY

	%	
Yes	34.5	→ *PLEASE ANSWER QUESTIONS 29 TO 36*
No	5.6	→ *PLEASE GO TO QUESTION 31 ON PAGE 9*
Don't know	0.1	
Not answered	2.5	

PLEASE ANSWER QUESTIONS 29 – 30 IF YOU HAVE EVER HAD A PAID JOB FOR AT LEAST A YEAR

[LastJob2]
29. When did your last paid job end?

N=911

PLEASE WRITE IN: (year)

[WhyNotWk]
30. What was the main reason that your job ended?

N=911

PLEASE TICK ONE BOX ONLY

	%
I reached retirement age	8.3
I retired early, by choice	8.6
I retired early, not by choice	0.9
I became (permanently) disabled	3.5
My place of work shut down	1.4
I was dismissed	0.2
My term of employment/contract ended	3.1
Family responsibilities	5.4
I got married	1.3
Not answered	4.5

PLEASE ANSWER QUESTION 31 – 36 IF YOU ARE NOT CURRENTLY WORKING FOR PAY

[LikeJob]
31. Would you like to have a paid job, either now or in the future?

N=911

PLEASE TICK ONE BOX ONLY

	%
Yes	13.5
No	25.1
Not answered	4.1

[LklyFdJb]
32. How likely do you think it is that you would find a job?

N=911

PLEASE TICK ONE BOX ONLY

	%
Very likely	6.0
Likely	6.9
Unlikely	5.5
Very unlikely	16.3
Can't choose	2.5
Not answered	5.5

[LookJob]
33. Are you currently looking for a job?

N=911

PLEASE TICK ONE BOX ONLY

	%
Yes	4.6
No	33.7
Not answered	4.4

34. Thinking about the last 12 months, have you done any of the following in order to find a job?

PLEASE TICK *ONE* BOX ON EACH LINE

N=911

		No	Yes, once or twice	Yes, more than twice	Not answered
[FindJob1] a.	Registered at a public employment agency?	% 31.8	1.7	1.1	8.1
[FindJob2] b.	Registered at a private employment agency?	% 31.8	1.6	0.8	8.5
[FindJob3] c.	Answered advertisements for jobs?	% 30.0	2.2	3.2	7.3
[FindJob4] d.	Advertised for a job in newspapers or journals?	% 32.4	0.6	0.8	9.0
[FindJob5] e.	Applied directly to employers?	% 29.7	2.1	2.8	8.1
[FindJob6] f.	Asked relatives, friends, or colleagues to help you find a job?	% 30.3	2.5	2.1	7.8

[TrnImJb2]

35. Over the past 12 months, have you had any training to improve your job skills?

PLEASE TICK *ONE* BOX ONLY

N=911

	%
Yes	4.3
No	31.9
Can't choose	1.4
Not answered	5.1

[MainInc2]

36. What is your <u>main</u> source of economic support?

PLEASE TICK *ONE* BOX ONLY

N=911

	%
Pension (private or state)	20.5
Unemployment benefits	3.0
Spouse/partner	7.4
Other family members	1.7
Social assistance/welfare	2.3
Occasional work	-
Other	2.2
Not answered	5.5

EVERYONE PLEASE ANSWER

37. Suppose the government ensured that affordable, good quality childcare was available...

N=1802

[SMumGov]

a. ...thinking about a <u>single mother</u> with a child <u>under school age</u>. Which one of these statements comes closest to your view?

PLEASE *TICK ONE BOX ONLY*

	%
She has a special duty to go out to work to support her child	17.9
She has a special duty to stay at home to look after her child	22.5
She should do as she chooses, like everyone else	51.6
Can't choose	7.0
Not answered	1.0

[SMSchGov]

b. ...and what about a single mother with a child of <u>school age</u>? (Again, suppose the government ensured that affordable, good quality childcare was available).

PLEASE *TICK ONE BOX ONLY*

	%
She has a special duty to go out to work to support her child	42.7
She has a special duty to stay at home to look after her child	6.7
She should do as she chooses, like everyone else	44.6
Can't choose	5.2
Not answered	0.7

[CMumGov]
c. Now think about a <u>married mother</u> with a child <u>under school age</u>. Again, suppose the government ensured that affordable, good quality childcare was available. Which one of these statements comes closest to your view?

PLEASE TICK *ONE BOX ONLY*

	%
She has a special duty to go out to work to support her child	13.4
She has a special duty to stay at home to look after her child	25.3
She should do as she chooses, like everyone else	55.0
Can't choose	5.2
Not answered	1.0

[CMSchGov]
d. And what about a married mother with a child of school age? (Again, suppose the government ensured that affordable, good quality childcare was available).

PLEASE TICK *ONE BOX ONLY*

	%
She has a special duty to go out to work to support her child	25.7
She has a special duty to stay at home to look after her child	10.0
She should do as she chooses, like everyone else	57.3
Can't choose	5.9
Not answered	1.1

[TopUpChn]
38. Some working couples with children find it hard to make ends meet on low wages. In these circumstances, do you think ...

PLEASE TICK *ONE BOX ONLY*

N=2697

	%
... the government should top-up their wages,	57.6
... or, is it up to the couple to look after themselves and their children as best they can?	30.7
Can't choose	11.0
Not answered	0.8

[TopUpNCh]
39. And what about working couples <u>without</u> children? If they find it hard to make ends meet on low wages, do you think ...

PLEASE TICK *ONE BOX ONLY*

N=2697

	%
... the government should top-up their wages,	25.9
... or, is it up to the couple to look after themselves as best they can?	64.3
Can't choose	8.9
Not answered	0.8

[TopUpLPa]
40. And what about working <u>lone</u> parents? If they find it hard to make ends meet on low wages, do you think ...

PLEASE TICK *ONE BOX ONLY*

N=2697

	%
... the government should top-up their wages,	66.5
... or, is it up to the parents to look after themselves and their children as best they can?	22.4
Can't choose	10.4
Not answered	0.8

[MoneyRet]
41. Which of these two statements comes closest to your own view?

PLEASE TICK *ONE BOX ONLY*

N=2697

	%
Young people should spend their money while they are young and worry about saving for retirement when they are older	17.6
OR	
Young people should start saving for their retirement as soon as they can even if they have to cut back on other things	69.5
Can't choose	12.2
Not answered	0.7

42. Please tick one box on each line to show how much you agree or disagree with each of these statements.   N=2697

PLEASE TICK ONE BOX ON EACH LINE	Agree strongly	Agree	Neither agree nor disagree	Disagree	Disagree strongly	Can't choose	Not answered
[LawSavRt] a. Everyone who works should be required by law to save for their own retirement instead of relying only on the state pension. %	9.2	32.5	19.3	24.8	7.9	2.9	3.5
[LawEmpPS] b. Employers should be required by law to contribute to a pension scheme for each employee, even if wages go down as a result. %	14.2	45.2	17.7	14.0	3.0	3.2	2.7

[CpIndNCh]
43. Think of a couple living together without children who are both unemployed. Which one of these statements comes closest to your view about how their unemployment benefits should be paid?   N=2697

PLEASE TICK ONE BOX ONLY   %

They should get paid as a couple, meaning only one of them is required to look for work   11.0

OR

They should get paid as two individuals, meaning both of them are required to look for work   82.0

Can't choose   6.4

Not answered   0.6

[CpIndUSc]
44. What if they had children under school age. What would your view be about how their unemployment benefits should be paid?   N=2697

PLEASE TICK ONE BOX ONLY   %

They should get paid as a couple, meaning only one of them is required to look for work   66.0

OR

They should get paid as two individuals, meaning both of them are required to look for work   26.0

Can't choose   7.5

Not answered   0.5

[CpIndSch]
45. And what if the children were of school age. What would your view be then?   N=2697

PLEASE TICK ONE BOX ONLY   %

They should get paid as a couple, meaning only one of them is required to look for work   37.6

OR

They should get paid as two individuals, meaning both of them are required to look for work   53.9

Can't choose   8.0

Not answered   0.5

[CpLivChp]
46. Thinking of basic living costs such as housing, heating and food. Which one of these statements comes closest to your view?   N=2697

PLEASE TICK ONE BOX ONLY   %

A couple can live more cheaply than two individuals living separately   73.3

Two individuals living separately can live more cheaply than a couple   3.2

There is no real difference   16.7

Can't choose   6.3

Not answered   0.4

47. Please tick one box for each of these statements to show how much you agree or disagree.   N=911

PLEASE TICK ONE BOX ON EACH LINE	Agree strongly	Agree	Neither agree nor disagree	Disagree	Disagree strongly	I never travel by car	Can't choose	Not answered
[CarWalk] a. Many of the short journeys I now make by car I could just as easily walk %	6.0	30.6	12.8	26.7	12.8	6.9	2.1	2.1
[CarBus] b. Many of the short journeys I now make by car I could just as easily go by bus %	3.8	22.5	9.9	38.0	14.8	6.3	2.2	2.5
[CarBike] c. Many of the short journeys I now make by car I could just as easily cycle, if I had a bike %	6.2	30.5	10.8	26.5	13.8	6.3	3.2	2.6

48. Please tick one box for each of these statements to show how much you agree or disagree.

N=911

PLEASE TICK **ONE** BOX ON EACH LINE		Agree strongly	Agree	Neither agree nor disagree	Disagree	Disagree strongly	Can't choose	Not answered
[BusNoOth]								
a.	I would only travel somewhere by bus if I had no other way of getting there	% 12.5	46.9	9.3	22.7	5.5	1.5	1.8
[CarTaxHi]								
b.	For the sake of the environment, car users should pay higher taxes	% 2.6	9.8	17.4	44.8	21.2	2.0	2.3
[Motorway]								
c.	The government should build more motorways to reduce traffic congestion	% 7.1	24.9	25.6	30.7	7.0	2.7	1.9
[BuildTra]								
d.	Building more roads just encourages more traffic	% 8.7	34.9	24.8	22.1	4.8	2.7	1.9
[CarAllow]								
e.	People should be allowed to use their cars as much as they like, even if it causes damage to the environment	% 3.9	13.9	32.1	31.1	12.6	4.5	1.9

49. Here are some things that might be done to reduce congestion. Please tick one box for each to show how much you would be in favour of or against it.

N=911

PLEASE TICK **ONE** BOX ON EACH LINE		Strongly in favour	In favour	Neither in favour nor against	Against	Strongly against	Can't choose	Not answered
[CutPetr]								
a.	Gradually doubling the cost of petrol over the next ten years	% 1.9	4.5	11.5	40.5	36.5	3.2	1.9
[CutCTCh2]								
b.	Charging all motorists £2 each time they enter or drive through a city or town centre outside London at peak times	% 4.3	25.1	14.6	28.3	22.2	3.7	1.7
[CutCMoCh]								
c.	Charging £1 for every 50 miles motorists travel on motorways	% 3.6	20.0	16.0	29.5	25.2	3.3	2.5
[CutCPark]								
d.	Increasing parking costs in town and city centres	% 2.3	15.2	14.0	36.8	26.1	3.3	2.2
[CutTaxE]								
e.	Taxing employers for each car parking space they provide for their employees	% 2.3	13.0	17.5	33.7	26.6	4.9	2.0

50. Please tick one box for each of these statements to show how much you agree or disagree.

N=911

PLEASE TICK **ONE** BOX ON EACH LINE		Agree strongly	Agree	Neither agree nor disagree	Disagree	Disagree strongly	Can't choose	Not answered
[BusPrior]								
a.	Buses should be given more priority in towns and cities, even if this makes things more difficult for car drivers	% 14.2	41.1	20.2	18.0	3.1	2.3	1.1
[CycPedPr]								
b.	Cyclists and pedestrians should be given more priority in towns and cities even if this makes things more difficult for other road users	% 16.2	44.3	19.2	14.1	2.1	2.7	1.4

51. Here are some things that could be done about traffic in residential streets that are not main roads. Please tick one box for each to show whether you would be in favour or not in favour.

N=911

PLEASE TICK *ONE* BOX ON EACH LINE		Strongly in favour	In favour	Neither in favour nor against	Against	Strongly against	Can't choose	Not answered
[ResClose]								
a.	Closing residential streets to through traffic	% 9.5	37.2	23.3	21.3	3.2	2.9	2.5
[Res20MPs]								
b.	Having speed limits of 20 miles per hour in residential streets	% 22.6	53.5	10.4	8.6	1.9	1.5	1.5
[ResBumps]								
c.	Having speed bumps to slow down traffic in residential streets	% 12.6	38.6	13.5	22.1	10.2	1.4	1.7

52. Please tick one box for each of these statements to show how much you agree or disagree.

N=911

PLEASE TICK *ONE* BOX ON EACH LINE		Agree strongly	Agree	Neither agree nor disagree	Disagree	Disagree strongly	Can't choose	Not answered
[SpeCamSL]								
a.	Speed cameras save lives	% 9.5	32.1	23.8	22.9	7.9	2.0	1.9
[SpeCamMo]								
b.	Speed cameras are mostly there to make money	% 19.7	33.4	22.4	18.4	1.5	2.2	2.4
[SpeCamTM]								
c.	There are too many speed cameras	% 14.7	27.5	29.2	20.6	2.9	2.8	2.3
[SpeedLim]								
d.	People should drive within the speed limit	% 45.9	45.1	4.8	1.5	0.2	0.9	1.6

53. Now some questions about air travel. Please tick one box for each statement to show how much you agree or disagree.

N=911

PLEASE TICK *ONE* BOX ON EACH LINE		Agree strongly	Agree	Neither agree nor disagree	Disagree	Disagree strongly	Can't choose	Not answered
[PlnAllow]								
a.	People should be able to travel by plane as much as they like	% 18.4	52.0	18.8	6.3	0.5	2.3	1.6
[PlnTerm]								
b.	People should be able to travel by plane as much as they like, even if new terminals or runways are needed to meet the demand	% 8.7	34.4	28.8	20.7	3.0	2.5	1.9
[PlnEnvl]								
c.	People should be able to travel by plane as much as they like, even if this harms the environment	% 3.5	14.4	34.4	33.4	9.7	2.8	1.8
[PlnUpPri]								
d.	The price of a plane ticket should reflect the environmental damage that flying causes, even if this makes air travel much more expensive	% 10.4	31.1	29.1	19.7	3.9	4.0	1.9

54. From what you know or have heard, please tick a box for each of the items below to show whether you think the National Health Service in your area is, on the whole, satisfactory or in need of improvement.

N=2697

PLEASE TICK ONE BOX ON EACH LINE		In need of a lot of improvement	In need of some improvement	Satis-factory	Very good	Don't know	Not answered
[HSArea3] a. Being able to choose which GP to see	%	14.2	28.2	44.3	11.9	-	1.4
[HSArea4] b. Quality of medical treatment by GPs	%	6.4	22.0	48.0	22.1	-	1.5
[HSArea9] c. Staffing level of nurses in hospitals	%	21.7	43.8	27.4	4.7	0.2	2.3
[HSArea10] d. Staffing level of doctors in hospitals	%	20.8	44.2	27.9	4.5	0.2	2.4
[HSArea11] e. Quality of medical treatment in hospitals	%	13.3	33.2	40.1	11.1	0.1	2.1
[HSArea12] f. Quality of nursing care in hospitals	%	14.6	33.6	36.5	13.2	0.1	2.0

55. In the last twelve months, have you or a close family member or close friend...

N=2697

PLEASE TICK ONE BOX ON EACH LINE		Yes, just me	Yes, not me but close family member or friend	Yes, both me and close family member or friend	No, neither	Not answered
[NHSDoc2] a. ... visited an NHS GP?	%	19.6	18.0	55.0	5.8	1.6
[NHSOutP2] b. ... been an out-patient in an NHS hospital?	%	18.1	32.5	18.8	28.0	2.6
[NHSInP2] c. ... been an in-patient in an NHS hospital?	%	9.1	28.5	6.9	51.2	4.4
[PrivPat2] d. ... had any medical treatment as a private patient?	%	5.8	11.1	2.9	76.7	3.6
[AETreat] e. ... had any medical treatment at an accident and emergency department?	%	10.9	25.2	5.5	55.8	2.6

N=2697

56. How many people in Britain do you think tend to think of disabled people in general in the following ways:

N=2697

PLEASE TICK ONE BOX ON EACH LINE		Nearly all people think of disabled people like this	Quite a lot of people think of disabled people like this	A few people think of disabled people like this	Hardly anyone thinks of disabled people like this	Don't know	Not answered
[ThDsWay] a. ... as getting in the way?	%	1.9	15.4	51.4	27.2	0.1	4.0
[ThDsAwt] b. ... with discomfort and awkwardness?	%	3.2	32.8	47.2	12.4	0.1	4.4
[ThDsCar] c. ... as needing to be cared for?	%	14.6	50.2	26.4	5.7	0.1	3.2
[ThDsSam] d. ... as the same as everyone else?	%	6.2	26.3	38.9	24.9	0.1	3.7

57. And do you personally tend to think of disabled people in general in the following ways:

PLEASE TICK ONE BOX ON EACH LINE		Most of the time	Some of the time	Hardly ever	Never	Don't know	Not answered
[RThDsWay] a. ... as getting in the way?	%	1.0	7.8	30.9	56.7	0.0	3.6
[RThDsAwk] b. ... with discomfort and awkwardness?	%	1.3	20.2	32.8	41.7	0.0	3.9
[RThDsCar] c. ... as needing to be cared for?	%	24.4	50.5	12.7	9.8	0.0	2.5
[RThDsSam] d. ... as the same as everyone else?	%	46.0	28.9	10.4	11.8	0.1	2.8

58. Please tick one box on each line to show how much you agree or disagree with each of these statements:

N=2697

PLEASE TICK ONE BOX ON EACH LINE

	Agree strongly	Agree	Neither agree nor disagree	Disagree	Disagree strongly	Can't choose	Not answered
[DissWork] a. Most disabled people should expect to work rather than rely on benefits. %	2.7	24.4	33.7	25.8	5.5	6.5	1.5
[DisGPar] b. Disabled people make just as good parents as people who are not disabled. %	16.1	56.5	18.7	3.7	0.4	3.6	1.1
[DisEduc] c. Most young disabled people will inevitably do less well at school and college than non-disabled students of the same age. %	1.9	11.5	21.3	45.3	14.7	3.8	1.5
[DisHome] d. Disabled people should never have to live in a residential home if they do not want to. %	22.8	53.4	15.0	4.1	0.7	2.8	1.1

[PDJobSc]
59. Are you currently in paid work for at least 10 hours a week?

N=2648

PLEASE TICK ONE BOX ONLY

%
Yes 56.0 → PLEASE ANSWER QUESTION 60
No 42.9 → PLEASE GO TO QUESTION 65 ON PAGE 20
Not answered 1.1

PLEASE ANSWER IF YOU ARE CURRENTLY IN PAID WORK FOR AT LEAST 10 HOURS A WEEK

[EmploySC]
60. Are you an employee or self-employed? (If you have several jobs, please answer about your main job.)

N=2648

PLEASE TICK ONE BOX ONLY

%
Employee 48.3 → PLEASE ANSWER QUESTIONS 61 TO 64
Self-employed 7.2 → PLEASE GO TO QUESTION 65 ON PAGE 20
Not answered 1.5

PLEASE ANSWER QUESTIONS 61 – 64 IF YOU ARE AN EMPLOYEE

N=2648

61. Do you agree, or disagree, with the following statements about working at your present workplace?

PLEASE TICK ONE BOX ON EACH LINE

	Agree strongly	Agree	Neither agree nor disagree	Disagree	Disagree strongly	Can't choose	Not answered
[SafeJob] a. I feel there will be a job for me where I work now for as long as I want it %	8.1	22.8	8.0	6.6	1.8	0.4	2.2
[WellInf] b. People at my workplace usually feel well-informed about what is happening there %	3.2	21.6	9.6	10.8	1.9	0.3	2.5
[ProudJb] c. I am proud to tell people which organisation I work for %	7.3	22.3	13.1	3.3	0.9	0.3	2.5
[LookBJob] d. I'm always on the look-out for a job that is better than mine %	7.3	22.3	13.1	3.3	0.9	0.3	2.5
[ShareVal] e. I share many of the values of my organisation %	2.3	11.1	11.7	16.7	5.1	0.4	2.6
[LoyalOrg] f. I feel loyal to my organisation %	7.1	22.1	12.2	3.7	1.5	0.6	2.8

62. Overall, how good would you say that managers at your workplace are at …

PLEASE TICK ONE BOX ON EACH LINE

	Very good	Good	Neither good nor poor	Poor	Very poor	Can't choose	Not answered
[GManView] a. … seeking the views of employees or employee representatives? %	5.7	19.6	11.4	7.5	2.7	0.6	2.3
[GManResp] b. … responding to suggestions from employees or employee representatives? %	5.0	18.3	12.7	7.8	2.8	0.9	2.4
[GManInfl] c. … allowing employees to influence final decisions? %	3.2	13.1	15.7	9.8	4.5	1.1	2.4

63. Please tick one box on each line to show how true each of the following statements is about your current job:

N=2648

PLEASE TICK **ONE** BOX ON EACH LINE

		Not at all true	A little true	Quite true	Very true	Can't choose	Not answered
[JbLearn] a.	My job requires that I keep learning new things.	% 4.5	13.8	10.7	18.3	0.1	2.4
[WagEffor] b.	My wage or salary depends on the amount of effort I put into my work.	% 25.3	9.0	7.8	4.5	0.8	2.4
[GdAdvan] c.	My opportunities for advancement are good.	% 13.5	13.6	13.0	5.7	1.5	2.5
[JbVarie] d.	There is a lot of variety in my job.	% 6.6	8.9	14.4	17.2	0.3	2.4
[HSatRisk] e.	My health and safety is at risk because of my work.	% 27.3	11.6	4.6	3.2	0.8	2.4

64. Still thinking about your current job, how much do you agree or disagree with each of the following statements:

N=2648

PLEASE TICK **ONE** BOX ON EACH LINE

		Agree strongly	Agree	Neither agree nor disagree	Disagree	Disagree strongly	Can't choose	Not answered
[CollSup] a.	I can get support and help from my co-workers when needed.	% 11.6	27.7	5.1	2.7	0.5	0.4	1.8
[JbNoTime] b.	I never seem to have enough time to get everything done in my job.	% 6.4	14.3	12.1	12.8	2.0	0.3	1.9
[JbIni] c.	I am able to use my own initiative.	% 14.0	26.8	4.3	2.4	0.4	0.1	1.8

EVERYONE PLEASE ANSWER

65. Here are a number of circumstances in which a woman might consider an abortion. Please say whether or not you think the law should allow an abortion with each case.

N=2644

PLEASE TICK **ONE** BOX ON EACH LINE

		Should abortion be allowed by law?			
		Yes	No	Don't know	Not answered
[Abort1] a.	The woman decides on her own she does not wish to have the child	% 60.3	32.9	0.0	6.7
[Abort4] b.	The couple cannot afford any more children	% 51.0	40.3	-	8.7
[Abort6] c.	The woman's health is seriously endangered by the pregnancy	% 91.3	4.6	-	4.1

66. Please tick one box on each line to show how much you agree or disagree with each of these statements:

N=1753

PLEASE TICK **ONE** BOX ON EACH LINE

		Agree strongly	Agree	Neither agree nor disagree	Disagree	Disagree strongly	Can't choose	Not answered
[BearPain] a.	We all have a duty to accept whatever pain and suffering life may bring.	% 6.6	30.8	22.8	24.1	9.8	4.2	1.7
[Suicide] b.	Suicide is never justified, no matter how bad things are.	% 17.8	25.6	21.9	19.4	8.7	4.8	1.9

67. And now some questions about 'living wills', in which people can say what sorts of medical treatment they would or would not want to be given in the future.
Please tick one box on each line to show how much you agree or disagree with each of these statements:

N=1753

PLEASE TICK ONE BOX ON EACH LINE	Agree strongly	Agree	Neither agree nor disagree	Disagree	Disagree strongly	Can't choose	Not answered
[DocFinal] a. Doctors should always make the final decision about what is right, even if this goes against what a patient's living will says they would want.	% 3.3	16.5	13.9	44.3	15.9	4.2	1.8
[AdvWill] b. A living will written in advance can never really predict what treatment decisions a person might make when the time comes.	% 5.6	48.1	22.5	13.8	2.6	5.1	2.2
[WillChos] c. If a person has an illness that will make it impossible for them to live as they want, they should be able to write a living will that asks for medical help to die at a time of their choosing.	% 16.9	50.2	13.7	9.6	2.8	5.0	1.7

68. Please tick one box on each line to show how much you agree or disagree with each of these statements about assisted dying – that is, when a person ends the life of another person at their request:

N=1753

PLEASE TICK ONE BOX ON EACH LINE	Agree strongly	Agree	Neither agree nor disagree	Disagree	Disagree strongly	Can't choose	Not answered
[LegalM] a. If we allow assisted dying to become legal, we will just legalise murder.	% 7.2	14.3	18.1	40.4	13.3	4.9	1.8
[DieWant] b. It is better that people are allowed to die when they want rather than having to stay alive against their wishes.	% 17.0	46.2	16.9	9.8	3.4	5.2	1.6

69. Please tick one box on each line to show how much you agree or disagree with each of these statements:

N=1753

PLEASE TICK ONE BOX ON EACH LINE	Agree strongly	Agree	Neither agree nor disagree	Disagree	Disagree strongly	Can't choose	Not answered
[DieComf] a. We need to worry more about whether people who are dying are as comfortable as possible, and less about whether it should be legal to help someone die.	% 23.4	46.2	16.5	7.6	1.0	3.9	1.5
[EmpAlive] b. There is too much emphasis nowadays on keeping people alive, and not enough on letting people die comfortably and in their own time.	% 19.4	50.2	17.2	5.5	1.6	4.5	1.5

[CommLaw]
70. As far as you know, do unmarried couples who live together for some time have a 'common law marriage' which gives them the same legal rights as married couples?

N=3539

PLEASE TICK ONE BOX ONLY

%

Definitely do	15.0
Probably do	32.7
Probably do not	24.3
Definitely do not	19.6
Can't choose	7.6
Not answered	0.8

71. Please tick one box for each statement to show how much you agree or disagree with it.

N=2697

PLEASE TICK ONE BOX ON EACH LINE	Agree strongly	Agree	Neither agree nor disagree	Disagree	Disagree strongly	Not answered
[WelfHelp] a. The welfare state encourages people to stop helping each other	4.6	27.3	36.3	27.0	2.8	1.9
[MoreWelf] b. The government should spend more money on welfare benefits for the poor, even if it leads to higher taxes	4.2	31.6	31.5	27.1	3.5	2.1
[UnempJob] c. Around here, most unemployed people could find a job if they really wanted one	16.5	53.0	18.1	9.9	0.9	1.6
[SocHelp] d. Many people who get social security don't really deserve any help	9.2	30.9	33.3	22.6	2.5	1.5
[DoleFidl] e. Most people on the dole are fiddling in one way or another	10.3	28.6	32.3	24.0	3.2	1.6
[WelfFeet] f. If welfare benefits weren't so generous, people would learn to stand on their own two feet	12.0	37.4	24.0	21.5	3.1	2.0
[DamLives] g. Cutting welfare benefits would damage too many people's lives	7.2	39.9	33.2	16.5	1.4	1.7
[ProudWlf] h. The creation of the welfare state is one of Britain's proudest achievements	16.7	37.3	31.9	10.1	2.4	1.6

72. Please tick one box for each statement below to show how much you agree or disagree with it.

N=3539

PLEASE TICK ONE BOX ON EACH LINE	Agree strongly	Agree	Neither agree nor disagree	Disagree	Disagree strongly	Not answered
[Redistrb] a. Government should redistribute income from the better-off to those who are less well off	6.4	25.8	26.9	31.4	7.9	1.6
[BigBusnN] b. Big business benefits owners at the expense of workers	10.1	41.1	28.9	16.0	1.9	2.1
[Wealth] c. Ordinary working people do not get their fair share of the nation's wealth	9.9	45.5	26.7	15.1	1.2	1.7
[RichLaw] d. There is one law for the rich and one for the poor	14.3	38.7	24.5	18.6	2.4	1.5
[Indust4] e. Management will always try to get the better of employees if it gets the chance	12.9	40.6	25.0	17.9	1.8	1.7

N=3539

75. And lastly just a few details about yourself.

[RSexChck]
a. Are you …..

	%
Male	46.3
Female	52.7
Not answered	1.0

[RAgeChck]
b. What was your age last birthday?

PLEASE WRITE IN: YEARS

Median   **47 years**
Not answered   1.6%

N=3539

73. Please tick one box for each statement below to show how much you agree or disagree with it.

PLEASE TICK ONE BOX ON EACH LINE		Agree strongly	Agree	Neither agree nor disagree	Disagree	Disagree strongly	Not answered
[TradVals] a. Young people today don't have enough respect for traditional British values.	%	26.2	47.5	16.9	7.2	0.6	1.6
[StiffSent] b. People who break the law should be given stiffer sentences.	%	33.1	47.5	13.8	3.9	0.3	1.4
[DeathApp] c. For some crimes, the death penalty is the most appropriate sentence.	%	28.5	29.9	12.9	16.9	10.6	1.2
[Obey] d. Schools should teach children to obey authority.	%	33.8	50.2	9.9	4.2	0.5	1.4
[WrongLaw] e. The law should always be obeyed, even if a particular law is wrong.	%	8.3	32.4	30.9	24.0	2.8	1.7
[Censor] f. Censorship of films and magazines is necessary to uphold moral standards.	%	19.9	43.9	17.7	12.5	4.5	1.5

[QTimeA]
74a. To help us plan better in future, please tell us about how long it took you to complete this questionnaire.

N=911

PLEASE TICK ONE BOX ONLY

	%
Less than 15 minutes	8.7
Between 15 and 20 minutes	29.0
Between 21 and 30 minutes	30.5
Between 31 and 45 minutes	18.9
Between 46 and 60 minutes	8.0
Over one hour	3.5
Not answered	1.3

[QDate]
b. And on what date did you fill in the questionnaire?

N=3539

PLEASE WRITE IN: DATE   MONTH   2005

BRITISH SOCIAL ATTITUDES 2005 SELF-COMPLETION QUESTIONNAIRE VERSION B

N=842

1. Here is a list of things some people do during elections.
Which, if any, did you do during the most recent general election in May 2005?

Did you:

PLEASE TICK **ONE** BOX
ON EACH LINE

		Yes, frequently	Yes, occasionally	Yes, rarely	No	Not answered
[TalkVote] a. ...talk to other people to persuade them to vote for a particular party or candidate?	%	2.1	6.4	9.3	80.1	2.0
[SuppCand] b. ...show your support for a particular party or candidate by, for example, attending a meeting, putting up a poster, or in some other way?	%	3.4	3.2	6.1	84.2	3.0

N=842

[PtyCont]
2. During the last campaign did a candidate or anyone from a political party contact you to persuade you to vote for them?

PLEASE TICK **ONE** BOX ONLY

	%
Yes	32.8
No	67.0
Not answered	0.3

3. What do you think has been the most important issue facing Britain over the last four years?

N=842

PLEASE WRITE IN:

Note: this open answer was coded to 3 variables in the order that the issues were mentioned.

	[MImpIss1]	[MImpIss2]	[MImpIss3]
	%	%	%
No answer given / Blank / Uncodeable (no further issue mentioned at MImpIss2 or MImpIss3)	9.3	88.1	97.0
Iraq war - War in Iraq/Gulf war/Iraq/War/War in Middle East	17.6	0.1	0.5
Terrorism - Threat from terrorism/International terrorism	23.8	3.1	0.2
Immigration - Immigrants/Influx of foreigners/Emigrants	17.3	2.5	-
Asylum seekers - Letting in too many asylum seekers	1.9	0.9	0.4
NHS - Hospitals/Health	5.1	0.7	0.1
Environment - Climate change/Pollution/Environmental changes	1.3	-	-
Crime - Rising crime/Law and order	2.5	0.9	0.1
Anti-social behaviour - Behaviour/Decline in personal behaviour/Animal behaviour from boys and girls/Yob culture/Poor behaviour of young people/Violence	1.1	0.5	0.1
Civil liberties	0.6	-	-
Europe - Membership of Europe/Membership of EU/EU/The way we are being dragged into the French/German EU federal Europe master plan/European Law	3.1	0.5	-
The Euro - Membership of the Euro/Joining the Euro	0.8	0.1	0.1
Education - Tuition fees	1.9	0.6	0.2
World order - The unsettled situations in other parts of the world/International conflict	0.3	0.1	-
Defence	0.1	-	-
Pensions	0.5	0.1	0.2
The economy - Debt/Unemployment/Cost of living	2.8	0.7	0.2
Transport	0.1	-	0.1
Community relations - Attempting to integrate immigrants and ethnic minorities in the community	0.7	-	-
Poverty - Social injustice/Famine	0.2	0.2	0.1
Other answer	3.1	1.1	0.6
Don't know	2.0	-	-
Not answered	3.7	-	-

[GovtGIss]
4. And thinking about that issue, how good or bad a job do you think the UK government in Westminster has done over the past four years. Has it done...

N=842

*PLEASE TICK **ONE** BOX ONLY*

	%
...a very good job,	2.2
a good job,	34.1
a bad job,	40.3
or a very bad job?	16.8
Don't know	0.5
Not answered	6.0

[GovtGJob]
5. Now thinking about the performance of the UK government in Westminster **in general**, how good or bad a job do you think the UK government in Westminster has done over the past four years. Has it done...

	%
...a very good job,	2.8
a good job,	51.8
a bad job,	38.1
or a very bad job?	3.8
Don't know	0.6
Not answered	2.9

[DemoWork]
6. On the whole, how satisfied are you with the way democracy works in Britain? Are you...

N=842

*PLEASE TICK **ONE** BOX ONLY*

	%
...very satisfied,	9.2
fairly satisfied,	61.9
not very satisfied,	22.7
not at all satisfied?	4.2
Don't know	0.4
Not answered	1.7

[PtyNDiff]
7. Some people say it makes a difference who is in power.
Others say that it doesn't make a difference who is in power.
Using the scale below, (where ONE means that it makes a difference who is in power and FIVE means that it doesn't make a difference who is in power), where would you place yourself?

PLEASE TICK *ONE* BOX ONLY

N=842

It makes a difference who is in power				It doesn't make a difference who is in power	Not answered
% 14.3	22.7	28.3	16.8	17.2	0.7
1	**2**	**3**	**4**	**5**	

[VotNDiff]
8. Some people say that no matter who people vote for, it won't make any difference to what happens. Others say that who people vote for can make a difference to what happens.
Using the scale below, (where ONE means that voting won't make a difference to what happens and FIVE means that voting can make a difference), where would you place yourself?

PLEASE TICK *ONE* BOX ONLY
N=842

Who people vote for won't make a difference				Who people vote for can make a difference	Not answered
% 9.6	13.4	26.3	28.9	21.0	0.8
1	**2**	**3**	**4**	**5**	

[DemoBest]
9. How much do you agree or disagree with the following statement:
"Democracy may have problems but it's better than any other form of government."

PLEASE TICK *ONE* BOX ONLY
N=842

	%
Agree strongly	34.3
Agree	54.3
Disagree	7.4
Disagree strongly	1.1
Don't know	0.6
Not answered	2.3

[Vote01SC]
10. Thinking back to the previous general election in **2001**, do you remember which party you voted for then, or perhaps you didn't vote in that election?

PLEASE TICK *ONE* BOX ONLY
N=842

	%	
Didn't vote/too young/not eligible	27.7	→ *PLEASE GO TO QUESTION 12*
Voted:- Conservative	22.3	
- Labour	33.6	
- Liberal Democrat	11.1	
- Scottish National Party	1.2	
- Plaid Cymru	0.3	
- Other (PLEASE WRITE IN)	0.1	
- UKIP/Veritas	0.1	
- BNP/National Front	0.1	
- Respect/SSP/Socialist party	0.2	
- Green Party	0.7	
Don't know	0.1	→ *PLEASE GO TO QUESTION 11*
Not answered	2.6	

PLEASE ANSWER QUESTION 11 IF YOU VOTED IN THE 2001 GENERAL ELECTION

[VotPtyGd]
11. How well did the party you voted for then perform over the past four years? Has it done...

PLEASE TICK *ONE* BOX ONLY
N=842

	%
...a very good job,	3.7
a good job,	40.2
a bad job,	21.5
or a very bad job?	1.4
Don't know	0.2
Not answered	5.3

EVERYONE PLEASE ANSWER

[ElecRepr]
12. Thinking about how elections in Britain work in practice, how well do elections ensure that the views of voters are represented by MPs?

N=842

PLEASE TICK ONE BOX ONLY

	%
Very well	2.8
Quite well	45.8
Not very well	44.1
Not very well at all	6.0
Don't know	0.1
Not answered	1.1

[PtyRepr]
13. Would you say that any of the parties in Britain represents your views reasonably well?
IF YES: Which party represents your views best?

N=842

PLEASE TICK ONE BOX ONLY

	%
No party represents my views	26.1
Yes – Conservative	21.5
Yes – Labour	31.7
Yes – Liberal Democrat	12.8
Yes – Scottish National Party	1.6
Yes – Plaid Cymru	0.4
Yes – Other party (PLEASE WRITE IN)	–
UKIP/Veritas	0.6
BNP/National Front	0.6
Respect/SSP/Socialist	0.1
Green Party	1.4
Don't know	0.1
Not answered	3.2

[LeadRepr]
14. Regardless of how you feel about the parties, would you say that any of the individual party leaders at the last election represents your views reasonably well?
IF YES: Which party leader represents your views best?

N=842

PLEASE TICK ONE BOX ONLY

	%
No party leader represents my views	32.4
Yes – Tony Blair	29.7
Yes – Michael Howard	17.3
Yes – Charles Kennedy	14.6
Yes – Alex Salmond	1.6
Yes – Dafydd Iwan	0.3
Yes – Other party leader (PLEASE WRITE IN)	–
Roger Knapman	–
Robert Kilroy Silk	–
George Galloway	0.2
Colin Fox	0.2
Caroline Lucas/Keith Taylor	0.1
Don't know	0.1
Not answered	3.5

[PtyClose]
15a. Do you usually think yourself as *close* to any particular political party?

N=842

PLEASE TICK ONE BOX ONLY

	%	
Yes	34.9	*PLEASE GO TO QUESTION 15c*
No	64.1	*PLEASE GO TO QUESTION 15b*
Don't know	0.3	
Not answered	0.7	

PLEASE ANSWER QUESTION 15b IF YOU DO NOT FEEL CLOSE TO ANY PARTICULAR PARTY

[PtyLClsr]
b. Do you feel yourself <u>a little closer</u> to one of the political parties than the others?

*PLEASE TICK **ONE** BOX ONLY*

	%	
Yes	32.8	**→** *PLEASE GO TO QUESTION 15c*
No	30.4	**→** *PLEASE GO TO QUESTION 16 ON PAGE 6*
Don't know	-	
Not answered	1.8	

PLEASE ANSWER QUESTIONS 15c AND 15d IF YOU FEEL <u>CLOSE</u> OR <u>A LITTLE CLOSER</u> TO ANY PARTICULAR PARTY

[PtyIDSC]
c. Which party is that?

*PLEASE TICK **ONE** BOX ONLY*

	%
Conservative	22.7
Labour	32.4
Liberal Democrat	8.6
Scottish National Party	0.9
Plaid Cymru	0.3
Other (PLEASE WRITE IN)	-
UKIP/Veritas	-
BNP/National Front	0.3
Respect/SSP/Socialist Party	0.3
Green Party	1.6
Not answered	2.4

[IDStrSC]
d. How close do you feel to this party…

*PLEASE TICK **ONE** BOX ONLY*

	%
…very close,	6.9
somewhat close,	39.4
not very close?	20.1
Don't know	0.1
Not answered	3.0

N=842

EVERYONE PLEASE ANSWER

16. We would like to know what you think about each of our political parties. Please rate each party on a scale of 0 to 10, where 0 means you strongly dislike that party and 10 means that you strongly like that party. If you come to a party you haven't heard of or you feel you do not know enough about, please tick one of the boxes on the right.

[LikeCon]
a. The Conservative Party

*PLEASE TICK **ONE** BOX ONLY*

Strongly Dislike 0	1	2	3	4	5	6	7	8	9	Strongly Like 10	Haven't heard of	Can't choose	Not answered
% 10.7	7.0	12.0	9.2	9.1	13.9	5.6	8.6	6.0	1.4	4.4	0.2	8.7	3.0

[LikeLab]
b. The Labour Party

Strongly Dislike 0	1	2	3	4	5	6	7	8	9	Strongly Like 10	Haven't heard of	Can't choose	Not answered
% 7.6	3.5	6.8	11.1	7.2	15.4	7.6	9.8	10.9	3.6	6.3	0.2	6.9	3.1

[LikeLib]
c. The Liberal Democrats

*PLEASE TICK **ONE** BOX ONLY*

Strongly Dislike 0	1	2	3	4	5	6	7	8	9	Strongly Like 10	Haven't heard of	Can't choose	Not answered
% 6.1	2.5	5.2	11.2	11.3	20.2	9.3	9.3	6.0	0.9	2.1	0.5	10.6	4.7

[LikeSNP]
d. The Scottish National Party   N=86

PLEASE ANSWER IN SCOTLAND ONLY

	Strongly Dislike 0	1	2	3	4	5	6	7	8	9	Strongly Like 10	Haven't heard of	Can't choose	Not answered
%	10.3	1.0	5.5	8.5	10.9	22.0	8.5	8.8	3.0	2.4	5.6	-	11.1	2.4

[LikePC]
e. Plaid Cymru   N=37

PLEASE ANSWER IN WALES ONLY

	Strongly Dislike 0	1	2	3	4	5	6	7	8	9	Strongly Like 10	Haven't heard of	Can't choose	Not answered
%	10.1	1.1	4.1	11.7	9.9	7.8	6.7	2.9	6.0	1.5	-	6.2	30.5	1.5

17. In politics people sometimes talk of the left and right. Where would you place each party on scale from 0 to 10, where 0 means the left and 10 means the right?   N=842

[LRCON]
a. The Conservative Party

*PLEASE TICK **ONE** BOX ONLY*

	Left 0	1	2	3	4	5	6	7	8	9	Right 10	Haven't heard of	Can't choose	Not answered
%	1.5	1.6	3.6	2.1	2.9	9.0	5.6	15.2	14.8	7.1	8.4	2.7	21.8	3.6

[LRLAB]
b. The Labour Party

*PLEASE TICK **ONE** BOX ONLY*

	Left 0	1	2	3	4	5	6	7	8	9	Right 10	Haven't heard of	Can't choose	Not answered
%	3.9	2.6	5.2	8.6	11.4	19.0	7.8	6.9	4.2	0.8	3.0	2.5	20.1	3.8

[LRLIB]
c. The Liberal Democrats

*PLEASE TICK **ONE** BOX ONLY*

	Left 0	1	2	3	4	5	6	7	8	9	Right 10	Haven't heard of	Can't choose	Not answered
%	2.3	1.5	3.4	9.5	12.2	27.6	6.5	2.3	1.2	0.5	0.2	2.7	25.0	5.1

[LRSNP]
d. The Scottish National Party   N=86

PLEASE ANSWER IN SCOTLAND ONLY

	Left 0	1	2	3	4	5	6	7	8	9	Right 10	Haven't heard of	Can't choose	Not answered
%	2.1	2.5	6.3	12.4	15.3	15.1	5.8	-	4.5	-	1.4	1.3	30.6	2.6

[LRPC]
e. Plaid Cymru   N=37

PLEASE ANSWER IN WALES ONLY

	Left 0	1	2	3	4	5	6	7	8	9	Right 10	Haven't heard of	Can't choose	Not answered
%	6.3	3.9	2.2	6.2	6.5	6.9	4.9	2.9	-	-	-	12.0	48.2	-

18. Over the past five years or so, have you done any of the following things to express your views about something the government should or should not be doing? Have you ...   N=842

*PLEASE TICK **ONE** BOX ON EACH LINE*

		Yes	No	Don't know	Not answered
[ContPol] a.	...contacted a politician or government official either in person, or in writing, or some other way?	18.1	77.0	0.3	4.7
[OnDemo] b.	...taken part in a protest, march or demonstration?	6.4	85.2	-	8.4
[PolGroup] c.	...worked together with people who shared the same concern?	12.5	80.6	-	6.8

(% for each line)

[RespRigh]
19. How much respect is there for individual freedom and human rights nowadays in Britain? Do you feel there is ...   N=842

*PLEASE TICK **ONE** BOX ONLY*

	%
... a lot of respect for individual freedom,	23.7
some respect,	53.8
not much respect,	18.4
or, no respect at all?	2.2
Don't know	0.2
Not answered	1.7

N=842

[Corrupt]
20. How widespread do you think corruption, such as bribe taking, is amongst politicians in Britain? Is it ...

PLEASE TICK ONE BOX ONLY

%

... very widespread, 6.2

quite widespread, 32.7

not very widespread, 48.2

or, it hardly happens at all? 10.1

Don't know 0.5

Not answered 2.3

[LRSR]
21. In politics people sometimes talk of the left and right. Where would you place yourself on a scale from 0 to 10 where 0 means the left and 10 means the right?

N=842

PLEASE TICK ONE BOX ONLY

Left										Right	Can't choose	Not answered
0	1	2	3	4	5	6	7	8	9	10		
%												
2.4	0.8	3.3	6.2	8.8	24.3	10.0	8.4	4.5	1.8	2.6	24.9	1.9

22. For each of these statements, please tick whether you think it is true or false. If you don't know, just choose the box on the right.

N=842

PLEASE TICK ONE BOX ON EACH LINE

		True	False	Don't know	Not answered
[GElec4Yr]					
a.	The longest time allowed between general elections is four years.	% 62.1	24.8	11.5	1.6
[BritPR]					
b.	Britain's electoral system is based on proportional representation.	% 21.4	52.1	23.0	3.5
[WhoPComm]					
c.	MPs from different parties are on parliamentary committees.	% 56.3	5.0	35.5	3.1

23. Are you currently a member of any of the following?

N=842

PLEASE TICK ALL THAT APPLY

%

[MembTU] A trade union 18.2

[MembSA] A staff association 2.3

[MembBusO] A business or employers' organisation (e.g. Chamber of Commerce/Trade, National Federation of Small Businesses, Institute of Directors, Forum of Private Business) 1.9

[MembNFO] National Farmer's Union 0.9

[MembProf] An organisation that organises your profession (e.g. Royal College of General Practitioners, Law Society, Institute of Chartered Accountants) 6.8

[MembNone] None of these 69.9

Not answered 4.0

[LangHome]
24. Which language do you usually speak at home?
If you speak several languages at home, please give the one that you use the most.

*PLEASE TICK **ONE** BOX ONLY*

N=842

	%
English	95.1
Bengali/Bangladeshi/Bangla	-
Gujarati	0.4
Hindi	-
Punjabi	0.6
Scottish Gaelic	0.1
Urdu	0.3
Welsh	0.1
Yoruba	-
Other (PLEASE SAY WHAT)	0.4
Not answered	1.1

NOTE: the following were recoded from the 'Other' category

	%
French	0.1
German, Standard	0.3
Italian	0.3
Kannada	0.1
Polish	0.4
Portuguese	0.3
Tamil	0.2
Chinese/Cantonese	0.4

25. Please tick one box to show how much you agree or disagree with each of these statements.

N=2627

*PLEASE TICK **ONE** BOX ON EACH LINE*

		Agree strongly	Agree	Neither agree nor disagree	Disagree	Disagree strongly	Can't choose	Not answered
[NetTalk] a.	Using the Internet a lot makes people less likely to go out and talk to other people	6.6	37.6	25.8	20.4	3.2	5.2	1.3
[NetCost] b.	Using the Internet is too expensive	3.6	20.4	25.7	34.6	5.0	8.8	1.9
[NetInFd] c.	Most of the information available on the Internet cannot easily be found elsewhere	5.7	39.4	21.8	21.8	2.0	7.4	2.0
[NetShop] d.	It is much safer to use a credit card in a shop than it is to use one over the Internet	9.3	34.3	23.9	20.3	3.3	7.7	1.4
[Net2Comp] e.	The Internet is too complicated for someone like me to use fully	6.7	16.0	11.5	33.0	27.1	4.0	1.6
[NetDnger] f.	Many people exaggerate the dangers children can come across when they use the Internet	4.4	15.7	16.5	39.2	18.1	4.5	1.6
[NetMisso] g.	People miss out on important things by not using the Internet and email	4.2	25.7	29.2	29.8	3.7	5.8	1.7
[NetKpTch] h.	The Internet helps people keep in touch with people who they could not normally talk to very often	15.4	55.0	13.1	9.3	1.1	4.5	1.6

[FrieLv]
26a. Where would you say that most of your **close friends** live?

N=2627

*PLEASE TICK **ONE** BOX ONLY*

	%
...here in your local neighbourhood or area,	34.3
...somewhere else, further away from here,	15.4
or, is it a mixture of both?	46.3
Don't have any close friends	2.9
Can't choose	0.4
Not answered	0.7

[FamLiv]
b. Where would you say that most of your **relatives and family members** live?

PLEASE TICK ONE BOX ONLY

N=2627

	%
...here in your local neighbourhood or area,	25.5
...somewhere else, further away from here,	36.7
or, is it a mixture of both?	35.5
Don't have any relatives or family members	1.0
Can't choose	0.6
Not answered	0.7

27. The following questions are about how much time you spend with various people – **other than those you live with.**

PLEASE TICK ONE BOX ON EACH LINE

N=2627

		Weekly, or nearly every week	Once or twice a month	A few times a year	Very rarely or never	Does not apply	Can't choose	Not answered
[TimeFam] a. Firstly, how often do you spend time with members of your family or other relatives?	%	60.6	17.8	16.3	3.3	1.0	0.7	0.3
[TimeFrie] b. How often do you spend time with friends?	%	59.8	26.1	9.0	2.5	1.0	0.6	1.0
[TimeColl] c. How often do you spend time socialising with people from work?	%	9.3	16.5	24.2	19.8	26.2	2.3	1.8
[TimeOrgs] d. How often do you spend time socialising with people you know through groups or organisations you belong to?	%	15.6	13.6	14.8	19.2	33.1	2.7	1.0

28. How often, if at all, do you use the following to keep in contact with friends and relatives who do **not** live near to you?

PLEASE TICK ONE BOX ON EACH LINE

N=2627

		Often	Sometimes	Rarely	Never	Can't choose	Not answered
[KpTchTel] a. Telephone	%	72.3	21.9	3.8	0.7	0.1	1.1
[KpTchLet] b. Letter	%	4.6	23.5	33.5	25.8	0.5	12.1
[KpTchEma] c. E-mail	%	25.8	21.3	10.0	31.2	0.9	10.8

[PeopAdvt]
29. How often do you think that people would try to take advantage of you if they got the chance and how often would they be fair?

PLEASE TICK ONE BOX ONLY

N=2627

	%
Try to take advantage almost all of the time	4.2
Try to take advantage most of the time	16.3
Try to be fair most of the time	50.5
Try to be fair almost all of the time	15.0
Can't choose	13.0
Not answered	0.9

30. There are many ways people or organisations can protest against a government action they strongly oppose. Please show which you think should be allowed and which should not be allowed by ticking a box on each line.

PLEASE TICK ONE BOX ON EACH LINE

N=842

		Should it be allowed?					
		Definitely	Probably	Probably not	Definitely not	Can't choose	Not answered
[Protest1] a. Organising public meetings to protest against the government	%	50.7	33.5	4.2	3.0	7.3	1.4
[Protest3] b. Organising protest marches and demonstrations	%	39.1	33.6	11.6	5.9	6.7	3.2

31. There are some people whose views are considered extreme by the majority. Consider people who want to overthrow the government by revolution. Do you think such people should be allowed to …

N=842

PLEASE TICK ONE BOX ON EACH LINE

		Definitely	Probably	Probably not	Definitely not	Can't choose	Not answered
[RevMeet]							
a.	… hold public meetings to express their views?	%	15.8	25.9	23.5	28.1	5.8	0.9
[RevPub]							
b.	… publish books expressing their views?	%	14.9	31.7	21.3	22.9	7.2	1.9

[Justice]
32. All systems of justice make mistakes, but which do you think is worse …

N=842

PLEASE TICK ONE BOX ONLY

%

… to convict an innocent person, 52.3

OR

… to let a guilty person go free? 23.4

Can't choose 22.5

Not answered 1.8

33. Please tick one box for each statement below to show how much you agree or disagree with it.

N=842

PLEASE TICK ONE BOX ON EACH LINE

		Agree strongly	Agree	Neither agree nor disagree	Disagree	Disagree strongly	Don't know	Not answered
[PCNoSolc]								
a.	The police should be allowed to question suspects for up to a week without letting them see a solicitor	%	6.2	19.2	15.7	43.9	13.8	-	1.1
[Refugees]								
b.	Refugees who are in danger because of their political beliefs should always be welcome in Britain	%	6.1	22.4	26.5	32.0	11.7	-	1.2
[PCCompln]								
c.	Serious complaints against the police should be investigated by an independent body, not by the police themselves	%	35.7	54.8	5.5	2.0	0.9	-	0.9
[IDCards]								
d.	Every adult in Britain should have to carry an identity card	%	20.7	33.0	22.6	12.7	9.5	0.1	1.4

34. Please tick one box to say how serious a threat to world peace you think each of these countries is likely to be over the next ten years or so?

N=842

PLEASE TICK ONE BOX ON EACH LINE

		A very serious threat	Quite a serious threat	Not a very serious threat	No threat at all	Can't choose	Not answered
[PeaceChi]							
a.	China	%	4.9	23.3	41.1	11.9	13.5	5.3
[PeaceUSA]							
b.	The USA	%	17.8	28.7	20.8	17.6	9.7	5.5
[PeaceIra]							
c.	Iraq	%	21.3	37.2	21.5	5.6	9.2	5.2
[PeaceIsr]							
d.	Israel	%	10.6	37.8	27.2	7.4	11.3	5.7
[PeaceBri]							
e.	Britain	%	4.6	12.7	33.1	33.1	9.7	6.7
[PeaceNKo]							
f.	North Korea	%	12.7	39.0	22.0	4.6	17.2	4.5

[BrPrior1]
35a. Looking at the list below, please tick the box next to the one thing you think should be Britain's highest priority, the most important thing it should do.

N=1732

PLEASE TICK ONE BOX ONLY
Britain should …

%

Maintain order in the nation 51.3

Give people more say in government decisions 19.8

Fight rising prices 8.7

Protect freedom of speech 9.0

Can't choose 9.6

Not answered 1.5

N=1732

[BrPrior2]
b. And which one do you think should be Britain's next highest priority, the second most important thing it should do?

PLEASE TICK **ONE** BOX ONLY
Britain should …

	%
Maintain order in the nation	17.8
Give people more say in government decisions	25.7
Fight rising prices	18.0
Protect freedom of speech	19.0
Can't choose	5.2
Not asnwered	14.3

[Sexualit]
38a. Which of the following **best** describes how you think of yourself?

PLEASE TICK **ONE** BOX ONLY

	%
Heterosexual ('straight')	95.3
Gay	0.4
Lesbian	0.4
Bisexual	0.6
Transexual	0.2
Can't choose	1.7
Not answered	1.4

[PropRep]
36. How much do you agree or disagree with this statement:
Britain should introduce proportional representation, so that the number of MPs in the House of Commons each party gets, matches more closely the number of votes each party gets.

PLEASE TICK **ONE** BOX ONLY

N=842

	%
Agree strongly	14.9
Agree	30.8
Neither agree nor disagree	20.0
Disagree	12.4
Disagree strongly	4.2
Can't choose	16.5
Not answered	1.3

[ComSexu]
b. And how much do you feel that you have in common with people who also think of themselves in this way, compared with other people?

PLEASE TICK **ONE** BOX ONLY

	%
A lot more in common with them than with other people	26.4
A little more in common with them than with other people	18.3
No more in common with them than with other people	47.7
Can't choose	6.4
Not answered	1.2

[VoteDuty]
37. Which of these statements comes closest to your view about general elections?

PLEASE TICK **ONE** BOX ONLY
In a general election …

N=1732

	%
It's not really worth voting	12.2
People should vote only if they care who wins	22.6
It's everyone's duty to vote	64.1
Not answered	1.1

[FEmp3]
39. When you were 14, which of these best describes the job your **father** was doing, or was he not working then?

PLEASE TICK **ONE** BOX

N=1732

	%
He was a **manager** - at a workplace with 25 or more employees	12.3
- at a workplace with less than 25 employees	4.8
He was a **foreman or supervisor** (but not a manager)	15.1
He was an employee without managerial or supervisory duties	37.5
He was **self-employed** - with 25 or more employees	0.5
- with less than 25 employees	7.1
- without employees	6.4
He was not working	2.8
My father had died or I don't know what he was doing when I was 14	8.2
Missed in error, assume working	3.9
Not answered	1.5

PLEASE ANSWER QUESTION 40

PLEASE GO TO QUESTION 41 ON PAGE 16

PLEASE ANSWER QUESTION 40 IF YOUR FATHER WAS WORKING WHEN YOU WERE 14

N=1732

[FType.lb3]
40. Which of these descriptions on this card best describes the sort of work your father did when you were 14?

PLEASE TICK **ONE** BOX

%

Professional occupations
such as: teacher – nurse – physiotherapist – social worker – welfare officer – clergy
artist – journalist – police officer (sergeant or above) – army officer (above NCO)
estate agent – civil service executive officer – accountant – solicitor – doctor – scientist
civil or mechanical engineer – IT professional – software designer   16.4

Clerical and intermediate occupations
such as: secretary – personal assistant – clerical worker – office clerk – wages clerk
call centre agent – building inspector – insurance broker – air traffic controller
civil service or local government administrative or clerical officer – nursing auxiliary
nursery nurse – police officer (below sergeant) – armed forces (NCO & below)
fire-fighter   7.5

Senior managers
such as: finance manager – chief executive – senior public sector manager   3.0

Technical and craft occupations
such as: motor mechanic – fitter – inspector – plumber – printer
tool maker – electrician – gardener – train driver   20.4

Semi-routine manual and service occupations
such as: postal worker – machine operative – security guard – caretaker
farm worker – catering assistant – receptionist – telephonist
sales assistant – care assistant – teaching assistant   10.9

Routine manual and service occupations
such as: HGV driver – van driver – bus driver – taxi driver – cleaner – porter – packer
sewing machinist – messenger –waiter/waitress – bar staff –labourer –building labourer   16.4

Middle or junior managers or proprietors of small businesses
such as: office manager – retail manager – bank manager – restaurant manager
warehouse manager – publican – proprietor of a shop, garage, hairdresser/barber etc   6.8

Don't know   4.4

Not answered   3.3

Note: Questions 41 to 52 are the same as questions 59 to 70 on version A
Questions 53 and 54 are the same as questions 72 and 73 on version A

N=842

EVERYONE PLEASE ANSWER

[qtimeb]
55a. To help us plan better in future, please tell us about
how long it took you to complete this questionnaire.

*PLEASE TICK **ONE** BOX ONLY*

	%
Less than 15 minutes	12.8
Between 15 and 20 minutes	36.7
Between 21 and 30 minutes	27.0
Between 31 and 45 minutes	12.2
Between 46 and 60 minutes	5.6
Over one hour	3.5
Not answered	2.2

Note: The remaining questions are the same as those concluding version A.

BRITISH SOCIAL ATTITUDES 2005 SELF-COMPLETION QUESTIONNAIRE VERSION C

Note: Questions 1 to 10 are the same as questions 37 to 46 on version A
Questions 11 to 15 are the same as questions 25 to 29 on version B
Questions 16 to 20 are the same as questions 54 to 58 on version A
Question 21 is the same as question 35 on version B
Questions 22 to 25 are the same as questions 37 to 40 on version B

N=1786

EVERYONE PLEASE ANSWER

[CompAdv]
26. How much do you agree or disagree with this statement?

"Children with a computer at home have an unfair advantage in their schoolwork over those without a computer."

*PLEASE TICK **ONE** BOX ONLY*

	%
Strongly agree	14.6
Agree	38.0
Neither agree nor disagree	21.5
Disagree	15.7
Strongly disagree	3.8
Can't choose	4.4
Not answered	2.0

27. From what you know or have heard, please tick one box on each line to show how well you think <u>state secondary schools</u> <u>nowadays</u> ...

N=1786

*PLEASE TICK **ONE** BOX ON EACH LINE*		Very well	Quite well	Not very well	Not at all well	Don't know	Not answered
[StatSec1] a. ... prepare young people for work?	%	3.7	39.8	47.5	6.7	0.3	2.1
[StatSec2] b. ... teach young people basic skills such as reading, writing and maths?	%	13.3	58.2	22.9	3.9	0.2	1.5
[StatSec3] c. ... bring out young people's natural abilities?	%	5.2	41.0	44.9	6.8	0.2	1.8

28. And from what you know or have heard, please tick one box for each statement about universities and colleges now compared with 10 years ago.

N=1786

PLEASE TICK ONE BOX ON EACH LINE

	Much better now than 10 years ago	A little better	About the same	A little worse	Much worse now than 10 years ago	Don't know	Not answered
[UniQual] a. On the whole, do you think that students leaving university are better qualified or worse qualified nowadays than they were 10 years ago? %	12.1	21.1	39.0	19.9	5.2	0.5	2.1
[UniTeach] b. And do you think that the standard of teaching in universities is better or worse nowadays than it was 10 years ago? %	9.2	18.4	49.9	15.4	3.6	0.6	2.9
[UniJobs] c. And do you think that students leaving university have better or worse job prospects nowadays than they had 10 years ago? %	7.5	17.2	23.1	35.9	13.7	0.3	2.3

29. Please tick one box on each line to show how much you agree or disagree with each of these statements.

N=1786

PLEASE TICK ONE BOX ON EACH LINE

	Agree strongly	Agree	Neither agree nor disagree	Disagree	Disagree strongly	Can't choose	Not answered
[UniFiBet] a. In the long run people who go to university end up being a lot better off financially than those who don't. %	7.9	42.9	26.3	17.4	1.3	3.1	1.2
[UniDebts] b. The cost of going to university leaves many students with debts that they can't afford to repay. %	19.4	55.7	12.8	9.1	0.4	1.8	0.9
[UniNWort] c. A university education just isn't worth the amount of time and money it usually takes. %	1.6	12.6	29.1	43.1	9.5	2.8	1.3
[DegGdJob] d. Having a degree generally guarantees you a good job. %	3.3	30.8	22.6	34.1	6.5	1.5	1.1
[UniAdv] e. There are more advantages to a university education than simply being paid more. %	14.3	55.7	20.1	5.5	0.7	2.7	0.9

Note: Question 30 is the same as question 70 on version A
Question 31 is the same as question 65 on version A

[Exit1]
32. Suppose a person has a painful incurable disease. Do you think that doctors should be allowed by law to end the patient's life, if the patient requests it?

PLEASE TICK ONE BOX ONLY

N=1786

	%
Yes	80.0
No	18.2
Don't know	0.1
Not answered	1.7

Note: Questions 33 to 35 are the same as questions 71 to 73 on version A

N=891

[qtimec]
36a. To help us plan better in future, please tell us about how long it took you to complete this questionnaire.

PLEASE TICK **ONE** BOX ONLY

%

Less than 15 minutes	21.1
Between 15 and 20 minutes	37.2
Between 21 and 30 minutes	24.1
Between 31 and 45 minutes	7.9
Between 46 and 60 minutes	3.6
Over one hour	2.5
Not answered	1.7

Note: The remaining questions are the same as those concluding version A.

BRITISH SOCIAL ATTITUDES 2005 SELF-COMPLETION QUESTIONNAIRE VERSION D

[SingMum3]
1. Thinking about a <u>single mother</u> with a child <u>under school age</u>.
   Which one of these statements comes closest to your view?

   N=895

   *PLEASE TICK **ONE** BOX ONLY*

	%
She has a special duty to go out to work to support her child	13.7
She has a special duty to stay at home to look after her child	31.1
She should do as she chooses, like everyone else	49.5
Can't choose	5.2
Not answered	0.5

[SMumSch3]
2. And what about a single mother with a child of <u>school age</u>?

   N=895

   *PLEASE TICK **ONE** BOX ONLY*

	%
She has a special duty to go out to work to support her child	41.5
She has a special duty to stay at home to look after her child	7.2
She should do as she chooses, like everyone else	46.8
Can't choose	4.2
Not answered	0.2

[CoupMum3]
3. Now think about a <u>married mother</u> with a child <u>under school age</u>.
   Which one of these statements comes closest to your view?

   N=895

   *PLEASE TICK **ONE** BOX ONLY*

	%
She has a special duty to go out to work to support her child	4.5
She has a special duty to stay at home to look after her child	39.2
She should do as she chooses, like everyone else	52.8
Can't choose	3.3
Not answered	0.1

[CMumSch3]
4.   And what about a married mother with a child of school age?

N=895

*PLEASE TICK **ONE** BOX ONLY*

%

She has a special duty to go out to work to support her child   20.8

She has a special duty to stay at home to look after her child   10.3

She should do as she chooses, like everyone else   64.9

Can't choose   3.8

Not answered   0.2

Note: Questions 5 to 13 are the same as questions 38 to 46 on version A
         Questions 14 to 18 are the same as questions 25 to 29 on version B
         Questions 19 to 23 are the same as questions 54 to 58 on version A
         Questions 24 to 27 are the same as questions 26 to 29 on version C
         Questions 28 to 33 are the same as questions 59 to 64 on version A
         Question 34 is the same as question 70 on version A
         Question 35 is the same as question 32 on version C
         Questions 36 to 38 are the same as questions 71 to 73 on version A

[qtimed]
39a. To help us plan better in future, please tell us about
     how long it took you to complete this questionnaire.

N=895

*PLEASE TICK **ONE** BOX ONLY*

%

Less than 15 minutes   27.7

Between 15 and 20 minutes   37.4

Between 21 and 30 minutes   21.3

Between 31 and 45 minutes   10.3

Between 46 and 60 minutes   2.1

Over one hour   1.2

Not answered   0.1

Note: The remaining questions are the same as those concluding version A.

Subject index

A

Advance directive: *see* Living will
Advance letters 268
Agree to disagree: respect for political opponents 95–118
Analysis techniques: *see* Factor analysis; Regression
Analysis variables 268–273
Are we all working too hard? Women, men, and changing attitudes to employment 55–70
Assisted dying
  arguments for and against 37–38, 50
  and attitudes towards the NHS 45–47
  and disability 44,47
  and the libertarian–authoritarian scale 45–48
  and religion 44, 46–48
  and the sanctity of life 44–48
  see 35–54 *passim*
Assisted suicide 36–37
  assisted by a relative 36, 40–42
  physician–assisted 36–37, 40–42
Attitude scales 271–272

B

British identity 9–13, 16, 28
  as a normative reference group 25–27

C

Care in old age
  and age 74
  and class 74, 79–80, 86
  and equity release 80–82, 86
  family members as providers of 84–85
  free personal care, attitudes to 73–75
  and income 80
  individual responsibility for 73–75
  means-tested, attitudes to 73–75
  policies in England and Scotland 71–72
  and political orientation 82–84
  saving for care, attitudes to 75–78
  see 71–94 *passim*
Civic duty
  trends in 122–123
Civil liberties
  and age 151–152
  and party identification 153–156

and perceptions of the threat of
  terrorism 156–158
trends in attitudes towards 145–151
see 143–182 *passim*
**Civil liberties and the challenge of
  terrorism 143–182**
Class: *see* Social class
Comparative study of Electoral Systems
  xix, 132
Computer Assisted Personal
  Interviewing 268, 279
Conservative Party
  and newspaper endorsement 102–103

D

Death penalty: *see* Civil liberties
DEFT: *see* Sampling errors
Democratic rights 144–145
  see also: Civil liberties
Dependent variables 277
Disability
  and age 218–219, 221–222, 224–225,
    230,233
  attitudes to 222–227
  and education 218, 221–222, 224–225,
    230,233
  future policy 234
  legal definition of 214
  medical model of 213
  perceptions of 216–219, 234
  social model of 214
  see 213–238 *passim*
Disability Discrimination Act 214
**Disabling attitudes? Public
  perspectives on disabled people
  213–238**

E

Electoral competition 95
Electoral reform
  attitudes towards 130
Electoral system
  attitudes towards 128–130
  and electoral participation 131–136

see 119–142 *passim*
Employment
  commitment to 57–58
  see 55–70 *passim*
Euthanasia
  involuntary 37
  Non-voluntary 37, 42–44
  Voluntary 36–37, 38–41, 48–50
  See also: Assisted dying

F

Face-to-face questionnaires 286–381
Factor analysis 278
Fieldwork 267–268
First-past-the-post: *see* Electoral system
Free personal care: *see* Care in old age

G

Goldthorpe class schema 270

I

Imagined community 13–17
Impairments
  attitudes to 230–233
  see also: Disability; Prejudice
Identity cards: *see* Civil liberties
Independent variables 277
Individualisation theory 1–2, 27–29
International human rights law
  attitudes to 166–168
International Social Survey Programme
  xix, 279
Internet use
  and community involvement 246–248
  and face-to-face interaction 240–241
    243–246
  growth of 241–243
  and social bonds 239–240, 254
  and social capital 240–241, 246, 253–
    254
  and social trust 240–241, 251–252
  see 239–260 *passim*

Interviewing: *see* Fieldwork
Isolates or socialites? The social ties of internet users 239–260

J

Job attributes 58–61

L

Labour party: *see* New Labour
Left–right scale 271
  and care, attitudes to 82–84
  and party identity 20–23
Libertarian–authoritarian scale 271–272
Living will 43–44

M

Multiple-Occupancy Indicator 262, 263

N

National Statistics Socio-Economic classification (NS-SEC), definition of 269
New Labour
  and anti-terror legislation 143
  and care in old age 71
  and newspaper endorsement 102–103
  and trade unions 183–185, 201–202
  and the 2005 general election 119, 120
New Labour, New unions? 183–212

P

Party differences, perceptions of 125–126
  across electoral systems 134–135
Pensions
  and income 80
  and political orientation 82–84
  saving for retirement, attitudes to 75–77

and socio-economic class 78–80
Physician–assisted suicide 36–37, 40–42
Political conflict 95
Political identity 6–8, 14–15, 28, 124–125
  as a normative reference group 20–23
Political interest
  and anti-terrorist measures 165
  and electoral participation 126–127
  and perceptions of parties 126, 127
  trends in 121–122
Political respect
  definition of 96
  and interpersonal communication 105–109, 110–111, 113–114
  and the mass media 101–104, 110–111, 113
  measurement of 97–98
  and political disengagement 114
  and political orientation 99–101, 110–111
  and political trust 111–113
  and socio-demographic characteristics 98–99
  see 95–118 *passim*
Political trust
  trends in 123–124
  see also: Political respect
Postcode Address File (PAF) 261–262
Prejudice
  against different impairment types, perceptions of 228–230, 234
  against disabled people, perceptions of 219–222, 234
  see also: Disability
Proportional representation: *see* Electoral system
Proportional representation and the disappearing voter 119–142

Q

Questionnaire plan 285
The questionnaires 283–418

**Quickening death: the euthanasia
debate 35–54**

R

Registrar General's Social Class
definition of 269
Regression
linear 277
logistic 277
measure of variance explained 278
parameter estimates 278
Religious identity 8–9, 15–16, 28
as a normative reference group 23–25
Response rates 267–268

S

Sample design 261–262
Sample size 261–262, 266–267
Sampling
errors 273–276
frames 261–262
points 261–262
Scales: *see* Attitude scales
Scottish Social Attitudes survey xix
Self-completion questionnaires 382–418
Social capital 250–251
see also: Internet use
Social class
definition of 268–269
Social class identity 3–6, 13–14, 28
as a normative reference group 17–20
Social trust 248–250
see also: Internet use
Socio-Economic classification: *see*
National Statistics Socio-Economic
Classification (NS-SEC)
Socio-Economic Group 270
Standard Industrial Classification (SIC)
270
Standard Occupational Classification
(SOC) 268–269
Stratification 261–262
Suicide, assisted: *see* Assisted suicide
System efficacy

and electoral systems 131
trends in 124

T

**Tabulations, Notes on the 281
Technical details of the survey 261–
280**
Terrorism
anti-terrorist measures, attitudes to
159–166
see also: Civil liberties
Trade unions
demand for 198-201
effectiveness of 189–195, 202
effect on wages 197–198, 202
and employment relations 195–196
and free-riders 200–201
membership of 185–189
and New Labour 183–185, 201–202
organisational capacity of 193–194
relationship with management 191–
192, 201
see 183–212 *passim*
Turnout
and party choice 120–121
and political disengagement 120–121
and political knowledge 132–133

W

Weighting
calibration 265–266
non-response 263–265
selection weights 263
Welfarism scale 272
**Who do we think we are? The decline
of traditional social identities 1–34**
**Who should pay for my care – when
I'm 64? 71–94**
Women
and work 56–57, 65–66
see also: Employment; Job attributes;
Work-life balance
Work-life balance 61–65, 66
and social class 64–65